The Hostess

The Hostess

Hospitality, Femininity, and
the Expropriation of Identity

Tracy McNulty

University of Minnesota Press   Minneapolis / London

The University of Minnesota Press gratefully acknowledges the generous assistance provided for the publication of this book by the Hull Memorial Publication Fund of Cornell University.

An earlier version of chapter 1 was published as "Israel as Host(ess): Hospitality in the Bible and Beyond," *Jouvert: A Journal of Post-Colonial Studies* 3, nos. 1 and 2 (1999). Parts of chapter 4 were published as "Klossowski, ce soir," *(a): a journal of culture and the unconscious* 1, no. 1 (Spring 2000): 81–103, and as "Hospitality after the Death of God," *diacritics* (Spring 2006). Chapter 5 was previously published as *"Signed, Dionysus:* Nietzsche's Lost Letter to Freud," *(a): a journal of culture and the unconscious* 2, no. 1 (Fall 2002): 7–24. An earlier version of chapter 6 was published in *Qui Parle* 9, no. 2 (Spring/Summer 1996): 126–59.

Published by the University of Minnesota Press
111 Third Avenue South, Suite 290
Minneapolis, MN 55401-2520
http://www.upress.umn.edu

ISBN-13: 978-0-8166-4740-8 (hc)
ISBN-10: 0-8166-4740-2 (hc)
ISBN-13: 978-0-8166-4741-5 (pb)
ISBN-10: 0-8166-4741-0 (pb)

A Cataloging-in-Publication record for this book is available from the Library of Congress.

Printed in the United States of America on acid-free paper

The University of Minnesota is an equal-opportunity educator and employer.

12 11 10 09 08 07   10 9 8 7 6 5 4 3 2 1

Contents

Introduction

The Uncanny Guest

The soul is itself exiled, errant, an arrival from elsewhere.
Birth is a voyage into a foreign land.
—Plutarch, *On Exile*

The problem of hospitality is coextensive with the development of
Western civilization, occupying an essential place in virtually every
religion and defining the most elementary of social relations: reciprocity, exogamy, potlatch, "brotherly love," nationhood. In almost
every Western religion, hospitality is the attribute or special domain
of the principal divinity (YHWH, Zeus, Jupiter Capitolinus, the
Holy Trinity), who evaluates the character of human hosts by appealing for hospitality disguised as a supplicant. In ancient Greece,
one could even argue that hospitality *is* religion, the defining social
ethics of *Zeus Xénios*, Zeus god of strangers. Similarly, Christian
"eucharistic hospitality" is the medium through which Christians
are invested with a transcendental identity, made "equal" to their
fellows through the love of Christ, the supreme Host. But the capacity of hospitality to effect relation or linkage *(re-ligare)* makes it
a fundamental concern not only of religion but of philosophy. Plato
makes hospitality one of the fundamental duties of the republic,
and Immanuel Kant sees in it the necessary precondition of cosmopolitan law, as the only means to guarantee perpetual peace among
a global society of strangers.

In modern history, the focus on hospitality has largely shifted away from religion and philosophy into two very different areas: the so-called hospitality industry (tourism) and a social and political discourse of parasitism, in which the stranger is construed as a hostile invader of the host nation or group. In this shift, the theological importance of hospitality appears to have been supplanted entirely by something that is mutually exclusive with it: in religious myth, the hospitality act was forbidden to have any economic dimension, and the stranger was held to be divine and to merit the absolute respect of the host. And yet as these increasingly impersonal and formalized means of relating to the stranger displace the ethical importance of a more intimate encounter, the irrational side of our relation to the stranger—fear, anxiety, and hatred—seems to grow ever more virulent.

In some ways hospitality seems to have barely survived its separation from the religious sphere, as witnessed by the disproportion between the enormous significance of hospitality in ancient times and up through the Enlightenment, and its present archaic, or even quaint, signification. In spite of this apparent archaism, however, hospitality has in the last century emerged as an increasingly important *topos* for questions of ethics. What is at stake in this renewed interest is not merely a nostalgic longing for a lost sense of social harmony, but rather a concern with the specific conflicts and contradictions it stages: between unnamable alterity and legal identity, between infinite debt and economics, between ethics and ontology.

I argue that the act of hospitality both embodies, and promises to resolve, a particular tension. On the one hand it is an act that constitutes identity: the identity of the host, but also that of the group, culture, or nation in whose name he acts. It is the act through which the home—and the homeland—constitutes itself in the gesture of turning to address its outside. But as an accidental encounter with what can be neither foreseen nor named, hospitality also insists on the primacy of immanent relations over identity. Hence it both allows for the constitution of identity and challenges it, by suggesting that the home can also become unhomely, *unheimlich*, estranged by the introduction of something foreign that threatens to contaminate or dissolve its identity.

From the Home to the *chez soi*: Hospitality and Ipseity

In his extraordinary study of the Indo-European roots of hospitality, Émile Benveniste demonstrates that the concept of hospitality is linguistically grounded in two very different families of words: one evoking the notion of "reciprocity," the other the seemingly opposed notion of "personal identity." The basic term from which the modern institution is derived, the Latin *hospes,* is an ancient compound made up of the elements *hosti-pet-s,* in which Benveniste identifies two primary roots: *hostis*—meaning "guest" or "host"—and *pet-* or *pot-,* meaning "master."[1] To address the curious interdependence of these apparently mutually exclusive fields of meaning, Benveniste proposes to examine each family of terms separately, through the nouns *hostis* and *potis.*

The Latin *potis* evokes first and foremost the notion of mastery. *Potis* names the master of the home, the one who makes the law in the house—the *casa.* As master of the house, he is also master of all of the subordinates who make up the household (servants, slaves, and dependent women), as well as the livestock or chattel that form his personal property. The Greek *despótes* (lord, despot) and its Latin equivalent, *dominus,* represent the extension of domestic authority into the field of social and symbolic power; both terms designate the "head of the clan," as well as the "lord" or "possessor"—the one who has power over and is able to dispose of his subjects (91–92).

But before he had any subjects, the master was his own subject, a subject properly speaking; the roots *-pet-, -pot-,* and *-pt-,* (Latin *-pte, i-pse*), originally signified "personal identity." Throughout the Indo-European linguistic group, these roots form the basis of a series of adjectives, signifying variously "himself" *[lui-même],* "his own" *[sien propre],* and "of himself" *[de soi-même].* All of these adjectives qualify the "mastery" implied in *potis,* giving it the sense not only of domestic or social power, but of "identity" (89). In Hittite, the enclitic particle *-pet* signifies "precisely" or "itself," establishing the identity of the object it qualifies (90), while the Latin *utpote* identifies an action with its author, the predicate with the one who assumes it (90). The suffix *-pte* designates "its own," or "what is proper to him" *[le sien propre, le sien de celui-là même].* Hence *potis* identifies not only the master, but the master who is "eminently himself" (87), the personification of personal identity. As *despótes,* the master "eminently personifies" not only himself, but the family or clan in whose name he acts (91).

Importantly, though, the notion of mastery is not the source or cause of this "eminent personification of identity," but its

derivative. Benveniste notes that the adjectives marking the identity of the person, signifying "eminently, precisely himself," mark
the original meaning of *pot-*, which only later took on the meaning of "master." In colloquial Latin, *ipsissimus* (from *i-pse*, "personal identity") indicates "the master, the one in charge"; but more
precisely, the man *himself*, the only person who matters (90). The
mastery or power of the *potis* is thus nothing other than ipseity, or
identity as *self*-identity.

The one who offers hospitality must be the master *chez lui*; the
"I am in my place" *[je suis chez moi]* is part of the condition of offering. But as this etymology makes clear, this "place" or *chez soi*
is not just a dwelling place—the house in which the master makes
the law—but the fact of residing within an identity, the *chez soi* of
ipseity in which the master gathers together and disposes of what
is proper to him. The master who is eminently himself offers hospitality from the place where he is "at home," from a position of
ipseity as self-identity.[2]

However, the condition of mastery as self-identity is only one
component of the Indo-European institution of hospitality. The
other primary root of the compound *hosti-pet-s*, the Latin *hostis*,
invokes a family of terms whose connotations are very different
than those of *-pot-* and its derivatives. The primitive idea signified
by the Latin *hostis* is that of reciprocity, or equality by compensation; *hostis* is he who compensates a gift with a counter-gift (94).
Hence *hostis* comes to designate both the host and the guest, who
become identified as reciprocal positions by virtue of the obligation
to counter the initial act of hospitality with gifts or later compensatory deeds. The Greek *xénos* similarly applies to host and guest
alike, and indicates relations of the same type between men who
are bound in a hospitable pact—or *xénia*—concluded under the
watchful eyes of *Zeus Xénios* (Zeus god of strangers), that implies
a precise set of obligations between the two parties, extending even
into subsequent generations (94).

The foundation of the institution of hospitality as a social practice is thus the compensatory relation, the reciprocal bond of obligation linking members of an extended society. Its most faithful
modern example is the institution of potlatch indigenous to the
First Nation tribes of North America, a system of ever-escalating
gifts and counter-gifts that binds parties together in mutual ties

of obligation and is the very foundation of social and religious life (94).[3]

When we put together these two roots—*hostis* and *potis*—we find that the institution of hospitality implies the union of two somewhat contradictory notions: a social or legal relationship defined by reciprocity and exchange, and despotic power, mastery, and personal identity. The history of the institution of hospitality reveals that the relationship between them is far from stable and can develop in at least two fundamentally different directions. One way can result in a feeling of recognition and respect between host and guest, a reciprocal relationship of power and a mutual confirmation of one another's mastery that is guaranteed by relations of debt and obligation (as in the case of potlatch, or the sacred intergenerational pact or *xénia*). The linking of *hostis* and *potis* suggests that hospitality implies not only the power of mastery, but power *over* the guest, by virtue of his debt or obligation to the host. For this very reason, the juxtaposition of the notions of reciprocity or exchange and mastery or power can also have a very different result. It can be a source of anxiety, rivalry, or hostility, in which the host's power over the guest is conceived in a threatening manner, or in which the guest threatens to overtake the host's place as master by usurping his home, personal property, or social position.

In Roman law, *hostis* designates a resident foreigner invested with the same rights as Roman citizens, "equal" under the law (93). But as a consequence, it no longer names the stranger in general, but only the resident alien who has been recognized by and inscribed within the state, identified as having certain rights. This limitation also represents the beginning of a formalization and restriction in Roman law of what was once an unlimited obligation, upheld by sacred rites and protected by the vigilance of potent divinities. In formalizing the host/guest relation, the laws of nationhood also minimize its ethical import, paving the way for a less-favorable treatment of the stranger. Benveniste observes that

> At this historical period, the institution [of hospitality] had lost its power in the Roman world: it presupposed a kind of relation that was no longer compatible with the established regime. When the ancient society became a nation, the relations of man to man, and of clan to clan, were abolished; the only distinction that remained

was between those who were internal to the *ciutas* and those who were outside of it. (95)

From this time forward, *hostis* is applied exclusively to the "enemy," and no longer names the guest (95); similarly, the Greek *xénos* comes increasingly to mean "stranger," to the exclusion of "guest" (96). This transformation in the civic or national attitude toward the stranger explains how *hostis* became the linguistic root of "hostility," an affect that otherwise seems at odds with the institution of hospitality.

The guest's hostility is an immanent possibility within the *hostis* relation, a menacing consequence of his potential interchangeability with the host. In his guise as an enemy, the *hostis* is someone who threatens to overtake the host, who must be excluded by reason of his potential similarity to the host and capacity for usurpation of his power. Western literature and myth are full of legends that cast the relationship between the host and guest as potentially menacing. In classical literature, the figure who best personifies the uneasy position of the host is Odysseus, who returns home to find his wife and his house under siege by unruly suitors, usurping guests who use up their host's property and then deny him the sacred right of hospitality when he appeals to them as a beggar. In the same vein, Aeschylus's Agamemnon and Shakespeare's Gloucester are hosts whose authority is forcibly seized by their guests, who ultimately take their lives. King Lear, on the other hand, meets his demise as a result of having surrendered his rightful authority to become a guest, who is then reviled as an enemy of the state. In each of these cases, hospitality is represented as a threat to the sovereign: the leader, monarch, or lord. But these leaders stand in for the more general target of hospitality, namely, the very possibility of sovereignty as an eminent personification of ipseity: the sovereignty of the state, but more importantly the sovereignty of the subject "itself."

The Ethics of Dwelling

Hence one important tradition maintains that the ultimate aim of hospitality is to uphold and protect this identity, perpetuating the host's "eminent personification" of his own identity as well as that of the family, clan, or state over which he presides. This ideal is perhaps best embodied by Odysseus, whose legend is one of the touchstones of the Western tradition of hospitality. Odysseus is often read as a figure for the dialectical recovery of identity; he is a master who leaves his home only to return to it, victoriously reclaiming the *chez soi*. His involuntary "hospitality"—the opening of his house to the usurping suitors—represents a sinister (but merely temporary) dispossession of his mastery, which is regained when he expels the strangers and retakes possession of what is rightfully his. Odysseus represents the pureness of an ipseity uncontaminated with false pretendants to mastery: the ipseity of the *ipsissimus,* as "the master himself, the only one who matters."

Conceived in this manner, his legend is the index not only of a possible relation to hospitality, but of a certain metaphysical tradition. Gilles Deleuze sees its contours in Plato's thought, which he identifies as the philosophical equivalent of Odysseus's victorious assertion of his identity as the true master:

> Platonism is the philosophical *Odyssey.* The Platonic dialectic is not a dialectic of contradiction or of contraries, but a dialectic of rivalry *(amphisbetesis),* dialectic of rivals or of suitors. The essence of division appears not in breadth—in the determination of the species of a genus—but in depth, in the selection of a lineage. Its function is to sort through the claims, to distinguish the true suitor from the false ones.[4]

Or, in the words of Michel Foucault, Plato's method distinguishes the false from the authentic not by discovering a law of true and false (which opposes truth to error, and not to false appearances), but by looking beyond it to "a model that exists so forcefully that in its presence the sham vanity of the false copy is immediately reduced to nonexistence. With the abrupt appearance of Ulysses, the eternal husband, the false suitors disappear."[5]

Odysseus's struggle to reclaim his home from the suitors is an attempt to distinguish between *xénos* and *xénos,* host and guest, the rightful possessor of the home and the usurping impostor. But even in its victoriousness, this quest is marked by an anxiety or uncertainty concerning his designation as the "true" master, the rightful possessor of the *chez soi* of ipseity. It attests to the unstable or contested position of the master, as someone who is continually menaced with dispossession at the hands of false pretendants to his power, and whose rightful proprietorship must be constantly defended.

The possibility of homelessness is thus contained within the gesture of homecoming as an ever-present menace. Precisely because the home or *chez soi* is a figure for identity or ipseity, the point of departure to which the subject must return in a dialectical recovery of identity, the failure to repossess this home or clear it of strangers can also result in a loss of identity. The home or dwelling can also become unhomely, *unheimlich,* estranged by the introduction of something foreign that threatens to dispossess it of its self-identity; whence the continuum between hospitality and hostility.

However, hostility is not the only potential consequence of this second possibility. In the sacred tradition of hospitality, the opening of the home to the stranger or the foreign is precisely what the hospitality act seeks to effect, the very basis of its ethics. Being a host implies more than just mastery over the home; it means not only residing within the familiarity of the *chez soi,* but opening the *chez soi* of identity to what is unfamiliar to it. As an ethics, the aim of hospitality is not to maintain the ipseity of the host, but rather to open it to the unforeseen stranger: a stranger who is not simply the counterpart, inversion, or negation of the host, but an alterity whose admission into the intimacy of the master's home alters it irreparably. Ethics implies not only identity, but relation: the possibility of a relationship between a "me" and a "you" who are not just pluralities of the "I," a host and a guest who are not merely reciprocal—and therefore potentially hostile—positions.

Jacques Derrida underscores the impossible, aporetical nature of the obligation both to integrate the foreigner and at the same time to respect him, her, or it *as* foreign: two competing notions that today divide European consciousness and whose antinomy marks every act of hospitality.[6] This impossible limit between the maintenance of identity and its opening to what is different from or nonidentical to it identifies a fundamental tension within the hospitality relationship: between identity and relation, or between ontology and ethics. As we have seen, the host "eminently personifies" identity: not only his own identity, but that of the group in whose name he acts. But as an accidental encounter with what can be neither foreseen nor legislated, hospitality also insists on the primacy of immanent relations over identity or law.

The ethics of hospitality is thus in conflict with the "laws of hospitality" that for so long dominated the mores of Western civilization, a heritage I will identify in subsequent chapters with a trajectory extending from Pauline Christianity to Augustine's *City of God* to secular and political incarnations of hospitality, especially after the Enlightenment. While these laws presuppose a positive representation of identity (personal, political, or communal) and a formalizable law regulating interpersonal relations (laws of exchange, laws of citizenship, or even the divine *logos* as guarantor of a transcendent equality), the ethics of hospitality represents the challenge of sustaining relation as "impossible," without any sign or principle to regulate its immanence. It presents a double bind, since the host must both take in the stranger and respect its foreignness, name the stranger and acknowledge its unnameability, welcome the stranger there where he is at home and risk homelessness or dispossession at his hands.

This double bind has implications that extend beyond the social practice of hospitality, informing more general problems of ethics. One might even argue that every ethics is fundamentally an ethics of hospitality, since the original meaning of *ēthos* is "abode" or "dwelling place." In one of his many extended reflections on the genealogy of *ēthos*,[7] Martin Heidegger explores its meaning by commenting on a fragment from Heraclitus, *ēthos anthrōpōi daimōn* (Fragment 119). Although it is usually translated as "a man's character is his daimon," Heidegger stresses that its true sense is something else entirely:

> *ēthos* means abode, dwelling place. The word names the open region in which man dwells. The open region of his abode allows what pertains to man's essence, and what in thus arriving resides in nearness to him, to appear. The abode of man contains and preserves the advent of what belongs to man in his essence. According to Heraclitus' phrase this is *daimōn*, the god. The fragment says: Man dwells, insofar as he is man, in the nearness of god.[8]

To further elucidate the meaning of the expression, Heidegger reproduces a story reported by Aristotle in *De parte animalium*, which agrees with and contextualizes Heraclitus's initial fragment:

> The story is told of something Heraclitus said to some strangers who wanted to come to visit him. Having arrived, they saw him warming himself at a stove. Surprised, they stood there in consternation—above all because he encouraged them, the astounded ones, and

called for them to come in with the words, "For here too the gods are present."[9]

Commenting on the passage, Heidegger notes that the group of visitors are disappointed by their first glimpse of the thinker's abode; there where they hoped to catch sight of him sunk in profound meditation, displaying for them the very essence of a thinker engaged in weighty thoughts, they find instead a thoroughly ordinary spectacle:

> They believe they should meet the thinker in circumstances which, contrary to the ordinary round of human life, everywhere bear traces of the exceptional and rare and so of the exciting. . . . Instead of this the sightseers find Heraclitus by a stove. That is surely a common and insignificant place. True enough, bread is baked there. But Heraclitus is not even busy baking at the stove. He stands there merely to warm himself. In this altogether everyday place he betrays the whole poverty of his life. (233–34)

Disappointed by this all-too-familiar sight, the visitors lose whatever desire brought them to the thinker's dwelling and are on the point of going away.

But seeing their frustration, Heraclitus encourages them to stay with words that address their disappointment in his simple dwelling, revaluing its humble familiarity:

> He invites them explicitly to come in with the words *Einai gar kai entautha theous,* "Here too the gods are present." This phrase places the abode *(ēthos)* of the thinker and his deed in another light. . . . *Kai entautha,* "even here," at the stove, in that ordinary place where every thing and every condition, each deed and thought is intimate and commonplace, that is, familiar *[geheuer],* "even there" in the sphere of the familiar, *einai theous,* it is the case that "the gods are present." (234)

The familiarity of the everyday, he suggests, can play host even to the gods themselves. Hence Heidegger concludes that the full sense of Heraclitus's original fragment, *ēthos anthrōpōi daimōn,* should be rendered as follows: "The (familiar) abode is for man the open region for the presencing of god (the unfamiliar one)" (234). Or, if I might further paraphrase, *ethics is the opening of what is familiar to man to the unfamiliar.*

On the basis of this definition, one might even argue—as Jacques Derrida has—that hospitality is not merely one ethics among others, but the ethics par excellence.[10] In the gesture of the host opening his home to the stranger, what is familiar to man is at the same time made to open itself to what is unfamiliar.

The Uncanny Homecoming of Metaphysics

Because it concerns the unstable and indeterminate limit between the proper and the improper, the hospitality relation presents a special challenge to philosophy, and in particular to the way in which the metaphysical tradition has tended to privilege the notion of identity in its understanding of the subject. Emmanuel Lévinas acknowledges this challenge when he calls for a new understanding of the subject as "welcoming the other, as hospitality."[11] In so doing, he questions the privileging of ontology over ethics in the metaphysical tradition, which has tended to reduce the relation to the Other to being no more than the limit or horizon of the "I's" possibilities, bringing its alterity under the dominion of the identical, the same.

But his critique does not oppose itself to the historical and linguistic genealogy of hospitality, but rather elucidates and affirms the fundamental contradiction at its core. Lévinas concurs with Benveniste's etymological analysis in insisting that the precondition of any act of hospitality is the ipseity of the host, the self-identity of the "I." What defines the "I" is that it has identity for a content; it is the being "whose existing consists in identifying itself, in recovering its identity throughout all that happens to it. It is the primal identity, the primordial work of identification" (36). The "I" lives in a world where it is *chez soi,* eminently itself. But Lévinas stresses that the *chez soi* is "not a container, but a site where *I can*" (37). This characterization has important implications for the hospitality relationship as well. Benveniste notes that the Latin *potis,* the root word meaning "master," is in the same linguistic family as the verb *potere,* which connotes power and ability: *possum* means "I can, I am able to," while *potest* means "I have the power."[12] The "I" is thus derived from the "I can," the ability to exercise power.

Of course, the understanding of the "at-homeness" of the I as a place where "I can" is not original to Lévinas's work, but invokes a long philosophical tradition. To cite only the two thinkers who figure most prominently in Lévinas's account, Kant's theory of the faculties is founded upon the *vermögen,* the "I can," while Heidegger's *Dasein* is defined above all else as "being able to be," *sein können.*[13] But Lévinas's work also offers an important critique of this tradition, insofar as it tends to involve a certain phenomenological reduction. All too often, he argues, the "I can" is the first step in a movement that seeks to bring the other under the power of the same. Hence Kant's "I can" implies the ability to put the whole world in parentheses, while Heidegger's *Dasein* extends the ability to be even to the possibility of being in totality.

In contrast, Lévinas specifies that although the "I" necessarily lives in a world where it is *chez soi,* where it *can,* ethics demands that identity not depend upon or necessitate power over another. Indeed, ethics is an unforeseen encounter with a "stranger" who calls this *chez soi* into question. The stranger, the *other,* is someone who exceeds my mastery, someone over whom I "can't *can*" [*sur lui je ne peux pouvoir*] (39), a being who necessarily "overflows" the concept I have of him.

Lévinas argues that the metaphysical tradition must reconsider its timeworn privileging of ontology over ethics by acknowledging that metaphysics necessarily proceeds toward an other. The fundamental movement of metaphysics is thus the movement from a *chez soi* to a foreign elsewhere:

> [Metaphysics] is turned toward the "elsewhere" and the "otherwise" and the "other." For in the most general form it has assumed in the history of thought it appears as a movement going forth from a world that is familiar to us, whatever be the yet unknown lands that bound it or that it hides from view, from an "at home" [*"chez soi"*] which we inhabit, toward an alien outside-of-oneself [*hors-de-soi*], toward a yonder. (33)

Although his treatment of ethics is in many ways related to Heidegger's analysis of *ethos,* it also involves a critique of the conclusions he draws from it. For what Heidegger values in ethics is above all the "being at home"—man's ability to open himself to or be with the gods there where he is at home—and not its disruption or quitting. In fact, *Dasein* is defined in opposition to what Heidegger calls "homelessness," which consists in the abandonment of Being: "Homelessness is the symptom of oblivion of Being. Because of it the truth of Being remains unthought."[14] In contrast,

Lévinas embraces homelessness, characterizing it not just as an alienated state, but as an ethical one.

To the trajectory of Odysseus, Lévinas opposes the trajectory of Abraham. If Odysseus represents the return of the self to its point of origin,[15] Abraham models an ethics of subjectivity in which the self leaves home never to return:

> The heteronomous experience we are seeking is an attitude that cannot be converted into a category, whose movement toward the Other is not recuperated through identification, and does not return to its point of departure. . . .
>
> But this would require us to think of the Work [penser l'Oeuvre] not as the apparent agitation of a content or ground [fond] that afterward remains identical to itself, in the manner of an energy that remains equal to itself through all of its transformations. Neither could we think of it as the technique whose famous negativity reduces a foreign world [un monde étranger] to a world whose alterity has been converted to my idea. Both of these conceptions continue to affirm being as identical to itself, and reduce its fundamental event to the thought that is—and here we see the ineffaceable lesson of idealism—thought of itself, thought of thought. *The Work radically thought is in essence a movement of the Same toward the Other that never returns to the Same.* To the myth of Ulysses returning to Ithaca, we would oppose the history of Abraham leaving his country forever for an unknown land, and forbidding his servant to lead even his son back to this point of departure.[16]

In Abraham's wake, the biblical injunction to "make the stranger native among you" (Leviticus 19:35 [NRSV]) inaugurates a relation to subjectivity defined by nomadism and dispossession, figuring strangeness as something "native" or uncannily intimate to subjectivity.[17]

The hospitality relation concerns the crisis of what is properly "mine," the limits of the "at home-ness" of identity. To call for an understanding of the *subject* as hospitality is thus to oppose to the notion of identity—with all that it implies of the self-identical, the total, and the integral—an understanding of subjectivity as foreign to itself, as nonidentical. The act of introducing a foreigner into the home thus recalls the dispossession of identity that is uncannily internal to identity itself, to the *chez soi* of having and possessing.

Identity Dispossessed?

The ethics of hospitality, therefore, involves not only welcoming the familiar *into* the home, but calling the home into question: experiencing the dispossession of the *chez soi,* and through it the identity of the host. In fact, one could argue that the ethics of hospitality *requires* this dispossession in order for the act to be fully realized. Pierre Klossowski, whose work I will examine in detail in chapters 3 and 4, even maintains that the master can be realized *as host* only in being dispossessed of everything that defines him as master of the home. Although his articulation of hospitality is particularly extreme, its logic is common to many conceptions of the hospitality act, especially in the sacred or religious contexts. It is evident in the traditional wisdom that the best host is the one who has given the most, even to the point of giving away that which defines him as master and host. This tension identifies an aporetic limit at which identity is established at the very moment of its dissolution, through contact with the nonidentical, the other.

But these formulations clearly beg a question. How can identity—by definition so eminently proper, so thoroughly "mine"—be "dispossessed"? One cannot help but be struck by the ideal quality of what Lévinas describes, which Derrida might characterize as an "absolute" (and therefore impracticable) ethics.[18] How could an encounter with a stranger actually divide me from what constitutes my personhood as an inalienable ipseity? And assuming that this were possible, what would incite the host to submit to this dispossession, to realize his identity as host at the cost of risking everything that defines him as master?

It is probably no accident that the privileged representative of this absolute hospitality—the patriarch Abraham—is drawn from the religious sphere, or that the modern philosophers who have been most concerned with the question of hospitality—Heidegger, Lévinas, and Derrida—have all been accused of privileging religious experience, if not themselves having religious inclinations. Historically, hospitality is not only an institution that derives its ethical force from religion, but the religious relation par excellence. As the absolute, unknowable Other, God represents the possibility of a negativity that is affirmatively construed, as well as the prospect of a dispossession of the subject that can be not only successfully endured, but even valorized. In almost every religious tradition, the unknown stranger or guest is understood as a manifestation of the divine. In the ancient Greek, Jewish, and Christian traditions, the principal deity (Zeus, YHWH, Christ) incarnates hospitality and evaluates the character of human hosts by appealing for hospitality disguised as a supplicant. But this also means that the offer of hospitality is motivated by the potentially sacred nature of the guest. Were the guest not potentially divine, or at least an occasion to gain recognition by the divine, the dispossession of the host by the stranger would simply imply the annihilation—and not the realization—of identity.

This sacred heritage raises a number of questions. First, is there any "stranger" other than God capable of effecting this dissolution? Can such an experience be thought outside of religious experience? And second, if the offer of hospitality is motivated by the rewards that potentially attend it—no matter how intangible—is it ever as selfless as it appears? Or is this "absolute ethics" no more than an unapproachable limit, an inaccessible ideal?

In the monotheist religious context, the dispossession of identity that is mandated by the ethics of hospitality is arguably precluded by its spiritual valorization, which inevitably results in a dialectical recuperation of identity on another plane (where earthly poverty translates into spiritual wealth, the meek inherit the kingdom of God, and immortality redeems the death of the faithful servant). One could even argue that Christianity in particular entails the gradual domestication or even neutralization of divine alterity, since the godhead not only becomes less and less of an unknown (as in the exhortation to "know Jesus"), but functions increasingly to secure the faithful subject's "true" identity even as it contests the claims of his or her "worldly" persona. We see something similar in the Native American ritual of potlatch, whose extreme version of hospitality is facilitated by an elaborate economy in which the giver gains in social prestige what he loses in material goods. The more the master gives, the more he has: because his prestations will eventually be reciprocated by others, but more importantly because his prestige accrues in the act of giving.[19] In this respect, potlatch never effects the pure "expenditure"[20] it seems to mandate, since the precipitous surrender of goods secures the chief's mastery in the very act of jeopardizing it. Both examples confirm the historical and etymological interdependence of "host" and "master," since the master's identity is not so much surrendered as recuperated in another form.

Is it possible for the autonomy of the "I" to be dispossessed without any accompanying recuperation of identity? It is clear that an external challenge to identity is not in and of itself sufficient to contest the autonomy of the *chez soi*. If the breaching of identity in the act of hospitality is not to be immediately recuperated, then something must support this challenge to identity *from within*.

In his commentary of Gilles Deleuze's anti-Platonism, Michel Foucault suggests how the hospitality relation might effect the dissolution of metaphysics as an ontology of purity, by "welcoming" the immanence of an event that would break in on the true model or "inaccessible idea," challenging its ability to gather its appearance to itself in a gesture of pure adequation. The message of Deleuze's critique, he writes, is that

> [we should not] attempt to rediscover the supreme and solemn gesture which established, in a single stroke, the inaccessible Idea. Rather, we should welcome the cunning assembly that simulates and clamors at the door. And what will enter, submerging appearance and breaking its engagement to essence, will be the event; the incorporeal will dissipate the density of matter; a timeless insistence will destroy the circle that imitates eternity; an impenetrable singularity will divest itself of its contamination by purity; the actual semblance of the simulacrum will support the falseness of false appearances. The sophist springs up, and challenges Socrates to prove that he is not the illegitimate usurper.[21]

To the hegemony of Odysseus, the master victoriously repossessing his home and banishing the false suitors, Foucault opposes Plato's sophist. Although he is part of the "cunning assembly that simulates and clamors at the door," the sophist is no longer the "false" usurper, but the one who questions the integrity—and truth—of the master. In a complementary reading of *The Sophist,* Jacques Derrida writes that the stranger is the one who poses the "parricidal" question of being and nonbeing, the question that challenges not only the paternal *logos* or the thesis of the master ("our father Parmenides"), but the ontological doctrine expressed in Parmenides' thesis that "being *is,* and non-being *is not.*"[22] The stranger represents a challenge not only to the master, therefore, but to being "itself," or to the very notion of ipseity as self-adequation.

These readings contest the initial autonomy that Heidegger and Lévinas alike attribute to the "I" or self, for whom alterity can be experienced only as an encounter with a foreign "outside." In Foucault's account, the simulacrum that knocks at the door of being is not an external menace, but something uncannily internal to being to which it involuntarily plays "host." The stranger outside models a stranger *inside,* a negativity internal to being that disrupts it from within.

The Subject of the Unconscious, or the Stranger Within

None of these authors, however, has tried to sort out the implications of the hospitality relation for the *psychical* constitution of the human subject: that is, for the subject of the unconscious. In contrast, I follow Sigmund Freud and Jacques Lacan in questioning the coherence and identity of the self from the outset, seeing in hospitality not only an occasion to confront the self with its outside or other, but to explore those dimensions of the subject that cannot be reduced to "mastery" or "ego," even as a point of departure or as a transcendental illusion. Lacan argues that "Freud addresses himself to the subject to say this, which is new: Here, in the domain of the dream, you are at home *[chez toi]. Wo es war, soll Ich werden.*"[23] Freud's formula, translated in the *Standard Edition* as "there where id was, there ego shall be," had been interpreted by the proponents of ego psychology to mean that the ego must come to dominate or subsume the id, to bring it within its parameters. But Lacan understands his comment very differently. Instead of implying the colonization of the id by the ego, it points to the necessary *expropriation* of the ego *by the id:* there where "it" was— the *es* or id—the subject shall come into being *as a subject of the unconscious,* and not as a self-possessed ego.[24]

In defining the subject's relation to the unconscious as one of cohabitation under the same roof, Lacan reverses the phenomenological interpretation of the *chez soi* as the "at-homeness" of identity, a principle of self-adequation. If the subject is at home in the dream, it is first of all because it cannot be at home in the ego and the homeostatic ideal it upholds.[25] But Lacan makes clear that the unconscious is not simply an uncanny guest in the domain of the ego, an unwelcome force of exile and estrangement. This is because the dispossession it effects not only dislodges the ego but creates a dwelling space for the subject: a space defined not by the proprietary dominion of the *chez soi* but by a singular hospitality. It is only from the vantage point of this "home" that the subject can play host to something else, something the ego cannot entertain.

This is because, says Lacan, the interrogation of its desire causes the subject to run up against something "that it feels within like a stranger,"[26] something foreign or strange that challenges the consistency of the ego, and whose insistence is behind the analysand's demand for analysis. In "The Mirror Stage," Lacan identifies one avatar of this "stranger" in the *corps morcelé,* the fragmented body of the drives that is the legacy of the subject's encounter with the Other.[27] We are "hosts" to the erotic body, which dwells within "us" (the organism, the self) like a virus, overwriting the natural logic of the living being and undermining the integrity of the Self. The question is, how will the subject respond to this dispossession? Will it play host to the body, or will it choose instead to identify with something outside of or beyond its experience, the heterogeneous image of consistency that it wears like a mask in order to repress the body? Freud's *Wo es war* implies the transition from a mode of hospitality dominated by the master/host, who shores up the *chez soi* by identifying with the imaginary principle of identity the ego embodies, to an ethics of hospitality dominated by the internal stranger, who forces the *chez soi* to open on to the Other.

If it seems idealistic to say that an encounter with a stranger can divest me of my identity, this is because any such event inevitably owes its force to an encounter that takes place within the psyche itself. To overlook this psychic dimension is to fail to appreciate fully the stakes of the hospitality relation and its fundamental link to the problem of identity. In Heidegger's and Lévinas's accounts of hospitality, the sacred or religious dimension of the act almost invariably serves as a model for the "sacred" alterity attributed to the stranger or other, because without it there would be no challenging—and above all no relinquishing—of this primordial identity. In contrast, Freud suggests that the subject is engaged in "hosting" the Other from the outset, whether it likes it or not. His focus on the *subject* (of the unconscious) as distinct from the *self* stresses that the alleged ipseity of the "I" is not a fundamental given, but a mask constructed and assumed by the split subject so as to repress the heteronomy of the Other of the drives and the dispossession to which it condemns the human being.

This development begs several questions. How can we reconcile the long history of hospitality, and its many different incarnations, with the thesis that the stranger or other is really "reactivating" what is fundamentally a psychic encounter by modeling the "stranger inside"? In other words, if hospitality is not just one metaphor among others for the divided subject, then how precisely does it allow us to frame the question of subjectivity? Earlier I suggested that if the challenge to identity in the act of hospitality is not to be immediately recuperated, then something must support this challenge to identity from within. What is this uncanny element, and what allows it to assume agency within the host-as-master?

Hospitality in the Feminine

To address these questions, I want to examine an aspect of the hospitality relation that is present from its earliest recorded manifestations, but that has been eclipsed in its most dominant institutional forms and largely ignored by philosophical commentators: the importance of sexual difference, and in particular the role of the hostess. Her function reveals a specifically "feminine" component of the masterful self, one that is rarely acknowledged openly, but whose hidden presence is crucial to the destiny of the masterful self and of the people he represents. My thesis is that the feminine contests the autonomy of the host by giving voice to the alterity within personhood, functioning as the internal marking of the Other.

This focus on the feminine is not in and of itself novel. Emmanuel Lévinas, for example, describes Woman as "the Other whose presence is discreetly an absence, with which is accomplished the primary hospitable welcome that describes the field of intimacy."[28] If woman is innately more "hospitable" than man, he argues, it is because her receptivity to the Other and its alterity is less circumscribed by the "virile" closure of identity. Writing of the role of woman in Jewish theology, he asserts that her function is to question the "virility of being," converting it into "the gentleness of a being that is for the Other."[29]

However, Lévinas tends to link this "feminine hospitality" to qualities supposedly innate in women, like maternal love, empathy, or care. He describes the maternal body, for example, as "pure renunciation, suffering for the Other."[30] The result is an often reductive understanding of femininity, supported by a gender ideology that makes woman no more than a welcoming vessel or a synecdoche of home. For Lévinas, woman is "habitation itself," and thus the inheritor of everything that Heidegger lauds under the name of "Home": "The wife, the betrothed, is not the coming together in a human being of all the perfections of tenderness and goodness which could have subsisted without her; everything indicates that woman is the original manifestation of these perfections, kindness itself, the origin of all kindness on earth."[31]

In her elaboration of Lévinas's account, Catherine Chalier proposes a second, more expansive gloss of femininity, as a modality of relation rather than a description of the qualities of one sex:

> to welcome someone in one's dwelling is a feminine characteristic even if there is in fact no human being of the feminine sex. Without this ontological characteristic of the feminine it would be impossible for the *conatus,* for its virile persistence in being, for its permanent self-satisfaction, for its self-conceit, and for its claims to be reasonable, to turn into this being for the Other where ethics begins. The feminine . . . puts into question the easy conscience of this rationality of self-conceit.[32]

For Chalier, femininity denotes an ontological characteristic within the subject, whatever its sex, that allows the subject to be "for the Other" by questioning the permanence and closure of the self. But if Lévinas insists on attaching "femininity" to traditionally female traits, Chalier arguably makes it a pure figure that no longer bears any reference to the particular stakes of female subjectivity or to the cultural function of femininity.[33] In suggesting that the subject is shaped through the tension between "virile" closure and "feminine" openness, she potentially reduces the differences between them to a simple binary that, if it is not completely arbitrary, ends up presupposing the same kinds of behavioral traits that underlie Lévinas's account. I want to propose an alternative by looking at the role of feminine agency as something irreducible to, but nonetheless not entirely distinct from, female subjectivity.

In my reading, the feminine does not just model an alternate approach to hospitality, one that is more open to and inviting of the other. Instead, it marks the insistence of the Other *within* the self. Although I question some of the assumptions implicit in Lévinas's and Chalier's accounts of feminine hospitality, they do bring our attention to the function of femininity in disrupting an identity to which it is strangely internal. This possibility is hinted at by Lévinas's characterization of woman as "the Other," and not simply as the one who welcomes or attends to the Other. Put another way, she is not only the Other inside who welcomes the Other outside, but the internal marking of alterity, the index of the Other's implication in the self. The close ties in almost every culture between femininity and the divine attest to the feminine function of representing a "beyond" of privative identity, the introduction or intrusion of the Other into the interiority of the home. Indeed, the feminine has long embodied the alterity internal to the *chez soi* of identity, the insistence of the Other within and against the autonomy of the self. In this respect it recalls the "godliness" Heraclitus locates in the humble hearth that gives voice to the sacred within the mundane, the unfamiliar within the intimacy of home, the *unheimlich* within the *Heim*.

I want to take this analysis further by thinking the notion of femininity apart from such allegedly "feminine" attributes as maternal protectiveness, selfless love, and homemaking. I will argue that femininity has no qualitative or ontological features but is instead a structural function that is morally and ethically neutral, although it may be celebrated or reviled depending on the context. My focus is not the feminine as a generous or selfless mode of welcome or "way of being," or the female subject who inhabits the symbolic arena differently than man, but the extralegal status of the feminine, its "thingly" quality, its status as a possession or property "internal" to man. For if woman functions as the internal marking of the Other, what she is internal *to* is an identity figured not only as "virile," but male.

In each of the early religious traditions I examine, as well as in archaic practice, the host is almost invariably male,[34] and even the many terms designating the host have no female equivalent. In these contexts, "feminine hospitality" is almost an oxymoron, since women are rarely hostesses in their own right. In biblical and classical antiquity, as well as in many traditional societies, women are precluded from entering into the reciprocal relation between *hostis* and *hostis,* since they are neither invested with a legal identity or symbolic status nor able to dispose of their own possessions. As a result, their hospitality is always closely related to that of men, whether by "softening" it, commenting upon or questioning it, or aiding or undercutting it in ambiguous ways.

In devoting this book to the hostess, my aim is not to look for exceptional examples that would qualify this general rule, but rather to identify and describe the structural role of "femininity" in even the most canonical acts of hospitality, those in which feminine agency appears to play a minor role at best. I believe that the marginalized or devalued position of the hostess offers a unique lens through which to examine the stakes of identity and ethics in these models. Following Sigmund Freud and Jacques Lacan, I ground my own analysis of the construction and dispossession of identity in hospitality in readings of the logic of sexual difference. Many of these narratives contest the apparent reversibility of an "equal" relation to the other—and even the adequation of subjectivity to the signifier of personal identity itself—with evidence of the fundamental inequality with regard to the phallic signifier that defines the sexual relation. In chapter 6, I draw on Lacan's characterization of the feminine as "not-wholly inscribed within the phallic function" to account for the peculiar agency of the hostess, who tends to undercut the symbolic or mythical determination of the hospitality act by giving voice to a "real" that exceeds or resists inscription within it.

In spite of this inadequation—or indeed because of it—the feminine occupies an essential position in each example of what I call the hospitality relation. It is excluded from many versions of hospitality ("brotherly love," reciprocity, reversibility), and crucial to others, although not necessarily as a subject. In archaic practice, as well as in many biblical narratives, feminine participation in the hospitality act is often limited to the exchange or offering of women between men. In both contexts, the host's wife and daughters are considered not as subjects, but as his chattel: dependent "things" that make up the host's personal property as master of the home. In insisting upon the "thingly" status of woman within the hospitality relationship, however, my intention is not so much to denounce the objectification of women in a male economy as to examine the agency and ethical status of this positioning. The hostess attests to the presence of something improper within the host's personal property, a foreign presence internal to the host's "eminent personification" of identity.

To understand the role and agency of the feminine, we need to examine the status of property within the notion of personhood, or the understanding of ipseity as the "personal property" of the master, the self proper. In the following pages, I will first outline this relationship, and then suggest how feminine property might work to expropriate the "personal property" of the master-as-host through the ethical exigencies of the act of hospitality.

Property and Personhood

If I have chosen the term "personal property" to describe the master's "eminent personification" of personal identity, and not ipseity, it is because I wish to draw attention to the crucial role played by *property* in any account of personal identity, a function as infrequently analyzed as it is widespread. The tradition of potlatch offers a clue to its importance, by demonstrating that the master-as-host accrues prestige by parting with his most treasured possessions, confirming his proper personhood as "the master himself" by disposing of his personal property. And yet once he has surrendered this substance, he is a master only in the sense of possessing the prestige of the host, since he has relinquished (however momentarily) the possessions that define him as master or lord.

As I noted earlier, the abstract notion of personal property—the ipseity or properness of the person—is originally tied to the notion of property ownership. Benveniste demonstrates that the root term *poti-* is the basis not only of *potis*, the master, but of a group of verbs (Sanskrit *pátyate,* Latin *potior*) meaning "to have power over" or "to dispose of" something. Similarly, the Latin *possidere,* "to possess," is formed from the composite *pot-sedere,* which designates the "possessor" as the one who is imprinted upon a thing.[35]

In this semantic genealogy, self-mastery and personal identity extend into social and symbolic authority through the possession and disposal not only of inert property or chattel, but of dependents bereft of symbolic personhood: in particular the household dependents who are defined as the property of the master of the home. The connotations of "lord," "master," and "possessor" are intimately bound up in one another, since the master is *self-possessed* only insofar as he is also possessed *of* material and human property. What is significant about this definition is that these possessions are heterogeneous with the master—owned by or subjected to him—and at the same time constitutive of his "personal property," his personification of identity as what is "eminently, precisely" proper to him.

In its particular staging of the stakes of personal identity, the hospitality relation offers a unique lens through which to consider a more general philosophical—and sociological—debate, concerning the relationship between property and properness, the capacity to possess or dispose of possessions and the self-identity of the *potis*.

Marcel Mauss, in his remarkable study of the notion of the "person," observes that in many North American tribes, personhood inheres in the ownership of certain ritual objects (coins, stamped copper objects, and other paraphernalia), which mark the bearer's responsibility for his whole clan. But at the same time,

> it suffices to kill the one possessing them, or to seize from him one of the trappings of ritual, robes or masks, so as to inherit his names, his goods, his obligations, his ancestors, his "person" *[personne]*, in the fullest sense of the word. In this way ranks, goods, personal rights, and things, as well as their particular spirit, are acquired.[36]

Since personhood inheres in the possession of personal property, it can also be transferred or lost through the acquisition or theft of that property.

This conception of personhood as guaranteed by property is not unique to the Native American context but informs even the Roman system of law on which the legal principles of the modern liberal state are based. In Roman law, the notion of the person—or *persona*—was derived from that of the mask, the image of the dead ancestor kept within the family house. Hence the political concept of the person designated the one who represented the "image" of the ancestor, who possessed his death mask:

> All freemen of Rome were Roman citizens, all had a civil *persona;* some became religious *personae;* some masks, names and rituals remained attached to some privileged families of the religious *collegia.*
>
> Yet another custom arrived at the same final state: that of forenames, surnames and pseudonyms (nicknames). The Roman citizen had a right to the *nomen,* the *praenomen* and the *cognomen* that his *gens* assigned to him. . . . The *cognomen* followed a different historical course: it ended by confusing *cognomen,* the pseudonym that one might bear, with *imago,* the wax mask molded on the face, the   of the dead ancestor kept in the wings of the *aula* of the family house. . . .

> To the very end the Roman Senate thought of itself as being
> made up of a determinate number of *patres* representing the "per-
> sons" *[personnes]*, the "images" of their ancestors. (16–17)

At the same time, the derivation of personhood from the notion
of the mask gives rise to another conception of the *persona,* as a
simulated, artificial, or even duplicitous "mask" of the self:

> It is to the *persona* that is attributed the property of the *simula-*
> *cra* and the *imagines.* Along with them the word *persona,* an ar-
> tificial "character" *[personnage],* the mask and role of comedy
> and tragedy, of trickery and hypocrisy—a stranger to the "self"
> *[moi]*—continued on its way. (17)

In the language of Foucault's critique of Plato, we might say that
the *persona* applies to the "semblance of the simulacrum" just as
much as to the "true" identity it simulates, introducing the possibility that personhood is not an inalienable property of the self, but
something it assumes, appropriates, or disposes of.

In spite of this significant—and still very current—set of connotations, the concept of the *persona* in Roman law came increasingly
to designate not the artificial self or semblance, but its opposite:
"the personal nature of the law had been established, and *persona*
had become synonymous with the true nature of the individual";
hence in time the general "right to the *persona*" was recognized
(17). From a purely contingent attribute, guaranteed solely through
possessions subject to theft, loss, or legation, personhood evolved
into an ontological quality, innate to the individual as a natural
unity. However, this new understanding of personhood did not entirely efface the more contingent conception from which it derived.
Mauss notes that even after being made synonymous with the "true
nature" of the individual, personhood continued to be withheld
from those who were not possessed of the property that guaranteed
it: "Only the slave is excluded from it. *Servus non habet personam.*
He has no 'personality' *[personnalité].* He does not own his body,
nor has he ancestors, name, *cognomen,* or personal belongings"
(17). As in the Native American example cited above, personhood
still inheres in the possession of personal property, and is annulled
in the act of being made the property of another.

These accounts of the relationship between personhood and
property accord with the archaic notion of the master-as-host

described by Benveniste, according to which the personal possessions of the master constitute his personal identity. In other words, the master "eminently personifies" personal identity insofar as he disposes of his possessions, just as the thief in archaic tradition acquires the personhood of a family lineage by usurping the possessions of the household, or the Roman Senator disposes of a *persona* through possession of the mask of his ancestor.

But these examples probably seem far removed from our modern notion of the person, in which the ontological view of personhood—refined and sanctioned by the philosophical and legal thinkers of the Enlightenment—seems to have gained ascendency over these "archaic" ideas, supplanting them with a new way of thinking about the relationship between property and personhood. The eighteenth-century *idéologue* Antoine Destutt de Tracy, one of the founding fathers of modern political economics, maintained that property ownership was not the condition of possibility of personhood, but rather its extension and tangible manifestation. In his *Treatise on Political Economy,* he claims that the property of personhood is the first, inalienable property a man possesses, the basis of all future acquisition: "nature has endowed man with an inevitable and *inalienable property,* property in the form of his own individuality."[37] De Tracy argues that will or *volonté* (which he equates with desire) conditions the personal property of the "I," which in turn conditions the possibility of property ownership.[38] In other words, *because I will, because I am capable of desiring, I am able to possess things*. Possession of things is thus the proof of the properness of the person, but not its foundation.

De Tracy even uses this argument to criticize attempts to limit personal property, on the grounds that property ownership is merely the reflection of the properness of the "I," its extension into the material world. In an implicit critique of Jean-Jacques Rousseau's celebrated thesis,[39] he suggests that it is not property that establishes divisions between people, but the discreteness of personhood that allows for and manifests itself in discrete ownership of property: "Now this idea of *property* can only be founded on the idea of personality. For if an individual had not a consciousness of his own existence, distinct and separate from every other, he could possess nothing, he could have nothing peculiar to himself."[40]

In *The German Ideology,* Friedrich Engels and Karl Marx take issue with de Tracy's account of personhood, declaring that his apparent reversal of the property/personhood argument is actually no more than a naturalization of it. They argue that in equating personality with the ability to possess property, he merely reifies the equation of personhood with property ownership, masking the unfair reality of bourgeois property ownership with the imprint of the *persona:*

> M. Destutt de Tracy undertakes to prove that *propriété, individualité* and *personalité* are identical, that the "Ego" *(moi)* also includes "mine" *[mein],* and he finds as a natural basis for property that "nature has endowed man with an inevitable and inalienable property, property in the form of his own individuality." Having thus made private property and personality identical, Destutt de Tracy, with a play on the words *propriété* and *propre,* like Stirner with his play on the words *Mein* and *Meinung, Eigentum* and *Eigenheit,* arrives at the following conclusion: "It is therefore, quite futile to argue about whether it would be better for none of us to have anything of our own . . ." If, therefore, the bourgeois explains to the communists: by abolishing my existence as a bourgeois, you abolish my existence as an individual; if, therefore, he identifies himself as a bourgeois with himself as an individual, one must, at least, recognize his frankness and shamelessness. For the bourgeois it is actually the case, he believes himself to be an individual only insofar as he is a bourgeois. . . . [But] in reality I possess private property only insofar as I have something vendible, whereas what is peculiar to me *[meine Eigenheit]* may not be vendible at all.[41]

Their critique suggests that de Tracy's use of *property* and *proper* as nearly interchangeable terms—a use that is still very current today—does not so much divorce the notion of personhood from dependence on property ownership as obscure the relationship between them.

It is this relationship—and its potential obfuscation or repression—that this book seeks to analyze, through examples taken from the hospitality tradition. As we have seen, the ubiquitous and often problematic interdependence of property and personhood is one of the key features of the hospitality relationship, apparent both in the etymology of *potis* ("I can, I am able"; the power of ipseity as a power to dispose over things), and in the paradoxical logic of the hospitality relation itself, where the host's mastery is defined by his ability to offer up or dispose of his personal property in furtherance of his hospitality. In the hospitality relation, as in the contexts of philosophy and law, can one speak of personhood in the absence of personal property?

The Divine Foundations of the Persona

We find an indispensable clue to this question in a context that seems far removed from these concerns: Christian theology. Mauss notes that our own notion of the human person "is still basically the Christian one"; it "marks the transition from the notion of *persona*, of 'a man clad in a condition', to the notion of man, quite simply, that of the human 'person'" (20). The Christian notion of the person no longer seems to imply a relationship between personhood and property, but reconceives personhood as a universal attribute. Mauss cites the famous passage from Paul's Epistle to the Galatians, which extends the reach of personhood by grounding it not in property ownership, but in "baptism into Christ":

> Now before faith came, we were confined under the law, kept under restraint until faith should be revealed. So that the law was our custodian until Christ came, that we might be justified by faith. But now that faith has come, we are no longer under a custodian; for in Christ Jesus you are all sons of God, through faith. For as many of you as were baptized into Christ have put on Christ. There is neither Jew nor Greek, there is neither slave nor free, there is neither male nor female; for you are all one person [εἰς] in Christ Jesus. (Galatians 3:23–29)

Although Paul posits man as a human person, this personhood nonetheless inheres in his being possessed by Christ. In other words, he is "one person" to the extent that he plays host to the oneness of Christ's person, which in dwelling within his heart bequeaths to him his "own" personhood. In this respect Paul's reasoning remains indebted to the archaic view of personal identity as a possession or property, since it is only insofar as an individual is the "possession of" (or is possessed by, permeated by, or subordinate to) the nature of Christ that he or she can be characterized as a person. The only difference is that in this instance, personhood is said to inhere both in the supreme person of Christ and in the persons of the human beings who are given personhood through him. As such, the distinctness of this personhood is somewhat paradoxically qualified by its universality, its equal application to all who, through Christ, become "one person"—that is, at one and the same time a singular, discrete person and a conglomerate person, a universal brotherhood who are of "one heart."

In Augustine's conception of hospitality, which I will revisit in later chapters, the identity or personhood of the host is also sustained by the personhood of Christ, guaranteed by the transcendent unity of the supreme Host. It is representative of the enormous historical shift in the conception of personhood effected by Christianity, which results in an understanding of the person as a unified essence. Mauss notes that the notion of the "person" is created out of the notion of the "one," which is in turn conditioned by the unity of the divine persons:

> It is the quarrel concerning the Trinity, the Monophysite dispute, which continued for a long while to exercise men's minds and which the Church resolved by taking refuge in the divine mystery, although however with decisive firmness and clarity: *Unitas in tres personas, una persona in duas naturas,* the Council of Nicea pronounced definitively. Unity of the three persons—of the Trinity— unity of the two natures of Christ. It is from the notion of the "one" that the notion of the "person" *(personne)* was created—I believe that it will long remain so—for the divine persons, but at the same time for the human person, substance and mode, body and soul, consciousness and act. (19–20)

The understanding of the integrity of the person as conditioned by the "unity of the two natures of Christ" has a special significance in Christian hospitality, where the "two natures" refer not only to Christ's status as both man and God, but to his determination as both a host and a guest. Moreover, the reversible relationship of host and guest is guaranteed by their determination as "values" of the one Christ, the divine *hostia*[42] in whose image *hostis* and *hostis* are made one: not only made whole, but rendered equivalent with one another.

The understanding of privative personhood as divinely guaranteed is not unique to the religious context, however, but informs some of the most important philosophical accounts of the subject. In Descartes' Third Meditation, for example, the being that infinitely surpasses its idea in us—or what Descartes calls God—is offered as support for the evidence of the *cogito*.[43] But Descartes is no more inclined than Paul to read in this support the evidence of the subject's dependence upon or possession by an other; the *cogito* is presumed to be free, the thinking agency of the emancipated subject. Its properness inheres entirely in itself.

Jean-François Lyotard offers a critique of both views of emancipation, relating Descartes' conception of a self-possessing subject to the Pauline verse cited above, which links the notion of emancipated personhood to the Christian's liberation from the custodianship of the law:

> Born children, we would have to become owners of ourselves. Masters and *possessors,* Descartes clarified, insisting on the gesture of mastery *[mainmise]* that he hoped to extend over the totality of what is—designated by the name of nature. But master and possessor of what *within* us, if we are fully emancipated? Does something of childhood remain even after childhood? Something unappropriated that remains even after appropriation has made its gesture, and we have become rightful owners *[propriétaires en propre]*?[44]

The very notion of self-proprietorship as a mastery over and possession of the self suggests that there is something improper within us, something alien within the self-mastery of ipseity that requires to be brought under its dominion. What is at stake in the notion of personhood as a personal property, therefore, is not only the possibility of asserting mastery by exercising power over things, but the possibility that there is something improper within the properness of identity, something heterogeneous to its self-adequation that is nonetheless indispensable to the possibility of mastery.

Feminine Property

In the hospitality relation, this "foreignness" internal to identity is often embodied by female property, as a discrete "thing" that is nonetheless integral to the identity of the host who disposes of it. The word *potis* names first of all the master of the house, the one who makes the law in the home. The series of terms that derives from it is thus rooted in a specific interpretation of the sexual relation: the Greek *pósis,* like many other derivatives of the *-pot-* family, is also the word for "husband." Moreover, the master's identity as a subject is defined by his possession of personal property: including (and, and I will argue, most importantly) the dependent women who make up his household. If the master/host is defined by his property, what is the status of that property with respect to his "own" subjectivity?

The first important consequence of woman's designation as the personal property of the host is that she is able to act as an extension of the host's personhood. The host's offer of hospitality often depends upon his ability to dispose of the female dependents who make up his personal property, who he offers to the guest as though giving some part of "himself." Of course, such an ability also calls into question the host's status as a master "equal to himself," by emphasizing that the host's identity is distilled in potentially detachable possessions. Although woman as property contributes to the master's "eminent personification" of personal identity, she also undermines the illusion of self-sufficiency and ipseity that the master is supposed to embody by drawing attention to its dependence on an im-proper attachment or addition, one that remains foreign even in being subordinated and internalized, and whose agency is not entirely under his control.

But the second major consequence of female property being both identified with and in excess of the male master and host is that it is able to facilitate reciprocal relations between men, such as the relationship of mutual obligation that often binds the host and guest following an initial act of hospitality. Structuralist anthropology elucidates the importance of such institutions as hospitality and gift-giving to the social link, which is mediated by "things" that cannot be reduced to personhood traditionally understood. In his analysis of what he calls "elementary" exogamous kinship structures,[45] Claude Lévi-Strauss shows that the exchange of marital partners between rival tribes inaugurates the "mechanisms of reciprocity" that are the basis of social relations.[46] In this context, the marital contract concludes an exchange not between husband and wife (the consolidation of skills or resources or the exchange of sexual services), but between two groups of men. Accordingly, Lévi-Strauss notes that the woman is always the object and occasion of this exchange, not its subject.[47] However, the stakes of exogamous exchange concern not only the consolidation of family or tribal alliances through marital relationships, or the accumulation of wealth and human resources, but a more intimate intermingling. The woman exchanged or offered is a gift, a given Thing possessed of a powerful agency as a result of being part of the offering tribe, but at the same time sufficiently detachable to be given away.

This means that the reciprocal relationship between men—the equal and reversible relation of *hostis* to *hostis*—is guaranteed by the exchange of a third term who exceeds it, a heterogeneous element who sustains this reciprocal relation while remaining external to it. The woman exchanged in this way belongs to both tribes and to neither; she establishes equivalencies between those who exchange her, to whom she herself is not equivalent or equal. Where the individual host is concerned, the inclusion of female chattel within his personal property means that the "one" of personhood is always *more than one,* already playing host to a plurality that undermines its oneness and integrity. In the case of the reciprocal relations between the male host and guest, the role of feminine property in cementing the exchange means that the "two" of the relation is always *more than two,* its reversibility interrupted or destabilized by the intervention of a third term that simultaneously guarantees this reciprocity and contests it.

In this respect, woman occupies the same position as Christ in the Christian conception of hospitality. Both found the social bond by exceeding it, acting as the "third term" that facilitates reciprocal relations between men. And both are presented as offerings, gifts that simultaneously impart personhood and contest its innate or ontological quality. Woman is "part" of man, both his personal property and the support for the properness of his own person. This fact also suggests an important structural affinity between woman and the divine. Each is both "beyond" or in excess of the social link and at the same time its condition of possibility. But it is not just the case that woman "also" fills this function. Long before identity was stabilized and consolidated through Christ, it was concretized in feminine property. In this respect, sexual difference is the paradigmatic example of difference-in-relation, anticipating—or perhaps even underlying—all theological postulations of the insurmountable inadequation between man and God.

In his landmark book *The Gift: The Form and Reason for Exchange in Archaic Societies,* Marcel Mauss argues that the ancient practice of gift-giving serves to effect an "intermingling" of essences, in which "souls are mixed with things, and things with souls."[48] This has several implications. First, "to make a gift of something to someone is to make a present of some part of oneself" (12). Second, the gift itself is not inert. Because it is "of the soul" of the giver, the gift exerts a powerful hold over whoever takes possession of it. Through it the recipient is marked by the giver, inhabited by him, and even in some sense "haunted" by his spirit or essence. According to Mauss,

> What imposes obligation in the present received and exchanged, is the fact that the thing received is not inactive. Even when it has been abandoned by the giver, it still possesses something of him. Through it the giver has a hold over the beneficiary just as, being its owner, through it he has a hold over the thief. (11–12)

Third, it follows that the imperative to return the gift, and to participate in rituals of prestation and counter-prestation, is not simply a moral obligation imposed from without by law or custom. Rather, the gift is possessed of a spiritual agency that obliges the recipient to fulfill his responsibilities toward it on pain of death. This agency is what the Maori people describe as the *hau* or spirit of the gift:

> all goods termed strictly personal possess a *hau*, a spiritual power. You give me one of them, and I pass it on to a third party; he gives another to me in turn, because he is impelled to do so by the *hau* my present possesses. I, for my part, am obliged to give you that thing because I must return to you what is in reality the effect of the *hau* of your [gift]. (11)

If the spirit of the thing is not returned (directly or indirectly) through the medium of a subsequent gift, it may even jeopardize the life of its recipient by placing him under the power of the original owner:

> In this system of ideas one clearly and logically realizes that one must give back to another person what is really part and parcel of his nature and substance, because to accept something from somebody is to accept some part of his spiritual essence, of his soul. To retain that thing would be dangerous and mortal, not only because it would be against law and morality, but also because that thing coming from the person not only morally, but physically and spiritually, that essence, that food, those goods, whether movable or immovable, those women or those descendants, those rituals or those acts of communion—all exert a magical or religious hold over you. (12)

This is why potlatch can "crush" the recipient unable to return a gift. He is not only socially disgraced, but forever indebted to the giver: literally held under his power as if under a magic spell, by virtue of the fact that this giver has left a deposit with him that continues to exert control over his person. More than any other gift-giving ritual, the potlatch lays bare the etymological contiguity between "gift" and "poison" (German *Gift*) implicit in every act of prestation.

But this cultural practice also provides insight into a fundamental feature of human psychological life, which Sigmund Freud glimpsed in the discourse of the psychotic.[49] The delusion describes how the psychotic became subjected to the capricious whims of an all-powerful Other, by means of an "internal object" implanted in him without his knowledge or consent (a transmitter implanted by the CIA to track his movements, internal organs that have been inserted or removed, the "solar rays" by which God takes possession of Schreber's body).[50] The psychotic "knows" what most people have simply managed to repress, that the subject is infiltrated by the Other at the very core of its being. The "internal object" of the delusion gives imaginary expression to the object-cause of desire, a fantasy object "deposited" in the subject by the Other that dictates its every action, prescribing the subject's "own" desires. These associations suggest a profound link between the gift and what Jacques Lacan calls *das Ding,* the fantasy object whose unbearable insistence within the psyche threatens the ego's integrity.[51]

What then is the relation of the gift in general to female property, and to the role of the feminine more broadly speaking in the hospitality act? On the one hand, Mauss notes that women are themselves the archetypal "gifts," the quintessential property. Most obviously, this is because the women and girls offered as brides allow the family or tribe of origin to exert control over the recipients, expanding its reach (since the children will grow up speaking the maternal tongue as well as the host family's language) and its social prestige.

But Mauss also suggests that the gift as such, in its spiritual power, has a "feminine" character. Citing the Samoan distinction between "maternal goods" *[tonga, taonga]* and "masculine goods" *[oloa],* he notes that the feminine *taonga* are the gifts most intimately linked to personhood and clan identity, so potent as to prove fatal to those who fail to fulfill the obligations they impart:

the *taonga* are strongly linked to the person, the clan, and the earth, at least in the theory of Maori law and religion. They are the vehicle for its *mana,* its magical, religious, and spiritual force. In a proverb that happily has been recorded by Sir George Grey and C. O. Davis, the *taonga* are implored to destroy the individual who has accepted them. Thus they contain within them that force, in cases where the law, particularly the obligation to reciprocate, may fail to be observed. (10)

The *taonga* are "native" or "fixed" property, as opposed to movable "masculine" goods like tools (9). Yet, this "nativeness" is defined in a very particular way. It designates property that comes into the family through the wife, that is native *as a consequence of being foreign,* since it comes from elsewhere to take up residence within the family. What is most native to the family's property is also what is most foreign, uncannily "extimate" to the possessor. Moreover, the "nativeness" of feminine property inheres not only in its link to the clan, but in its powerful inclination to return to its place of origin: "Invested with life, often possessing individuality, it seeks to return to what Hertz called its 'place of origin' or to produce, on behalf of the clan and the native soil from which it sprang, an equivalent to replace it" (13).

In the logic of the gift, and of feminine property more generally, we see the insistence of the object that must be passed on, because to keep it would be deadly. Lévi-Strauss appreciated this dimension of Mauss's argument, finding in its logic the source for the incest taboo that founds the mechanisms of exogamous kinship. In a move whose implications have never been fully appreciated, he actually explains the prohibition pertaining to a certain category of woman as a corollary of the logic of gift-giving, which holds that it is unacceptable to consume or keep for oneself certain sacred objects, commodities, and foodstuffs traditionally classed as gifts, which must be passed on to others: "the woman . . . whom one may not take is, for that very reason, offered up."[52] The designation of women as "that most precious category of goods," the "supreme gift,"[53] is thus both the corollary and support of the incest prohibition, since the gift is defined first and foremost as what may not be kept for oneself.

In his psychoanalytic reformulation of Lévi-Strauss's thesis, Lacan suggests a further motivation behind the circulation of feminine property. Following Freud, he argues that the principal target of the incest taboo is the Oedipal relation between mother and son, and not (as Lévi-Strauss implies) between father and daughter or brother and sister. According to Lacan, what the incest prohibition tells us is that "the Sovereign Good, which is *das Ding*, which is the mother, is also the object of incest, is a forbidden good, and that there is no other Good."[54] But if there is no other Good, there are still *goods:* gifts, commodities, and objects of exchange whose allure is derived from this interdicted Good, but that only approximate it in distanced form. More specifically, the traffic in feminine goods represents the metaphoric diffusion and circulation of the supreme Good, since the feminine object both recalls the interdicted object of desire and keeps it at a distance by providing a safe substitute.[55] In this way, the incest prohibition not only allows for exogamy and the reciprocal social relations it supports, but "protects" the subject from the power of the Thing *[das Ding]* that must be kept at a certain distance if it is not to destroy him.[56] Or, to use the language of Mauss's gift thesis, the subject participates in the circulation of goods so that the Thing of the gift will not take possession of him, causing misfortune or death.

The figure of the hostess offers a unique lens through which to examine woman's identification with *das Ding* in the structure of kinship and the social link, which historically has resulted in her being cast not as a human subject, but as an inhuman agency uncannily internal to the personhood of the one who possesses her.

While the host is determined as the perfect embodiment of identity, the one who is "eminently identical" to himself, the hostess is often cast as bereft of individual identity and lacking in ipseity, an indeterminate "thing" rather than an integral moral person. If she is frequently portrayed as capable of dissimulation, or of acting without regard for civic or moral law, it is in part because she is generally not considered to be a full subject in the eyes of the law and is rarely a recognized or public participant in the societal pact. In the Judeo-Christian tradition, the hostess is the excess of the host, the one who is not made in the image of God.

This excessive relation to identity is often negatively inflected, and even occasions some very misogynistic treatments of the hostess.[57] If Western literature is full of tragic hosts, it is equally replete with nefarious or conniving hostesses: Shakespeare's evil Lady MacBeth and ungrateful Regan and Goneril, Aeschylus's

Clytemnestra, Milton's wanton Eve, and the murderous biblical heroines Jael and Judith are but a few examples of the many hostesses charged with duplicitously receiving guests under the cover of an offer of hospitality, only to slaughter them or bring about their ruin. (Suggestively, the modern word "hostess" is not a feminine form of the Latin *hostis,* but a corrupted form of "hostility.") Even in the rare cases where this action is applauded—as in the noteworthy examples of Jael and Judith[58]—the hostess is still cast as a figure of dissimulation or cunning, one capable of saying the opposite of what she means and even of declaring her identification with a sacred law while fully intending to violate it.

Frequently the hostess is cast as someone who, in being deprived of status as a social agent, acts covertly through her husband or some other male figure: often as an inciter of violence or a repository of irrational or unlawful desires. An interesting contemporary example is the widespread vilification of former First Lady Hilary Rodham Clinton. What is the First Lady if not the nation's hostess? And yet she is not paid for this service, and is not really even recognized as an individual entity or "person." Rather, she is offered to the nation by her husband, as a part of "himself." Remember the Clinton campaign slogan promising "two for the price of one"? The ire that this proposal inspired in so many Americans is telling. In dubbing her a "Lady MacBeth," were Clinton's enemies not reacting to the obscene agency of this "thing," who has no active or official role in the symbolic, and yet exerts tremendous influence from within?

In these treatments of the hostess, we see the vicissitudes of woman's excessive relation to the signifier of personal identity, which is alternately celebrated or greeted with alarm. Often, the distinction between the two hinges upon whether she is adequately contained or mastered by the host, subordinated to his personhood. Saint Paul, for example, figures woman's rightful relation to man as that of a "body" to a "head," the last in a series of hierarchical relationships according to which Christ is the "head" of the church and God the "head" of man.[59] But at the same time, the prosthetic structure of this hierarchy also allows for the possibility that once detached from its "head," the "body" might assume its own agency, or even switch its allegiance to other "heads."[60]

In this respect, the hostess's excessive relation to personal identity points to a fundamental tension at the heart of the hospitality relation: between identity as whole or one and identity as split. Although Eve is "part" of Adam, his "other half," her agency undercuts this fantasy of unity by underscoring the split between them. Similarly, the woman who is defined as property within the gift logic of exogamous marriage both contributes to the master's "eminent personification" of personal identity and at the same time undermines the illusion of ipseity, by drawing attention to its dependence on a heterogeneous attachment that remains foreign despite its appendage and subordination to the master, assuming an independent agency that eludes his control.

If the "integral" quality of mastery consists in its claim to embody personal identity, then woman's inadequation to mastery appears in her lack of unified personhood, her exclusion from legal rights or symbolic status. But in its extralegal or nonsymbolic status, her position also highlights the fact that any subject who takes it upon himself to incarnate the master signifier always has an excess or residue—"something extra"—which does not allow itself to be subsumed under the symbolic function. In the following chapters, I will argue that the role of the hostess within the hospitality relation attests to what Lacan calls "extimacy," the nonsubjective agency of that part of the subject that is unequal or inadequate to his symbolic designation.[61] This line of reasoning is relevant even for thinking about hostesses who are no longer "things" in the sense of chattel divested of legal personhood, but who nonetheless have a "thingly" agency as a result of being not wholly inscribed within the symbolic function.

In her "extimate" relation to the host's identity, the hostess recalls not only the strangely animate gift or possession, but the uncanny *Nebenmensch* Freud saw as contesting the narcissistic sovereignty of the ego.[62] Developing the insights of Freud, Lacan sees in the figure of the neighbor the representation of *das Ding,* what is nigh but inaccessible, proximate but inviolable. In his gloss of the Decalogue, he reads the prohibition against coveting the neighbor's wife and goods as an allegory of castration, or the structural impossibility of the ego's quest to integrate the object that would make it whole.[63] Similarly, Lévi-Strauss's account of the incest prohibition suggests that my "Thing" is destined to become the neighbor's thing, distanced from me in being bequeathed to someone else. I will argue that this function is animated not only by the neighbor's wife, the coveted thing interdicted by the law, but by the wife or hostess *as neighbor,* an adjoining property that cannot be annexed by the host's identity.

Outline of the Book

The remainder of this book will explore these questions through three main lines of argumentation, distributed across different chapters: feminine property and divided personhood, hospitality after the death of God, and hospitality and the ethics of subjectivity.

Chapter 1, "Israel, Divine Hostess," is an analysis of hospitality in the Hebrew Bible, beginning with the story of the patriarch Abraham and his wife Sarah. The act of hospitality that immediately follows God's covenant with Abraham (Genesis 18) establishes a pattern in which God or his emissaries appear to human beings in the guise of unknown strangers, challenging the host to prove his worthiness by offering the wanderer food and shelter. In the act of hospitality, I argue that the patriarch compensates for the sins of Eden and Babel, or the attempt to "know" God, precisely by failing to recognize the guest, and thereby honoring his sublime alterity. As such, there is a fundamental tension between the demands of the patriarch's covenantal identity and the fact that Genesis hospitality constructs a subject divided by its inability to incorporate or be equal to the guest it receives, whose alterity resists recognition. I show that this subjective division is both sustained and obscured by the function of the hostess (Sarah, Lot's wife) whose incredulous attitude in relation to the divine guest underscores the incommensurability of God and man. She participates in the host's subjectivity as excluded from or foreign to it, in such a way as to simultaneously affirm the patriarch's covenantal identity and insist upon his inadequation to the divine law he upholds.

When Sarah erupts in laughter on being told by her divine guests that she will bear a child late in life, her laughter is ethical insofar as it insists upon her incommensurability with God. But with the institution of monotheism, and the formalization of Israel's exclusive relation to God, I argue that the Decalogue gradually introduces an antinomy between hospitality and monotheism. For the prophets, hospitality is increasingly bound up in the problem of idolatry, or what the metaphor of Israel's "marriage" to God figures as the wife's adulterous "welcoming" of strangers in the place of her husband. I argue that this figural move involves systematically negating the positive features of the Sarah story in Genesis. As the feminized wife of God, Israel is—like Sarah—"not all" made in the image of God, structurally inadequate or unequal to the exigencies of his law. As a result, the hostess's "receptivity" to strangers is refigured not as an advantage, but as a menace to the unified identity that monotheism inaugurates. This is true not only of the negative figuration of Israel as the too-good-hostess who thereby becomes a bad wife, but also in the murderous hostess Jael and the murderous guest Judith: new, post-Sarah heroines for an embattled nation.

Chapter 2, "Cosmopolitan Hospitality and Secular Ethics," is a reading of Immanuel Kant's *Project for Perpetual Peace*, which casts hospitality as the only viable foundation for cosmopolitan law, and the implicit critique of some of its core assumptions in the work of Friedrich Nietzsche. Kant's essay addresses the question of how to regulate relations between strangers in the increasingly global climate of modern life, where the impersonal economic relations of commerce and travel have supplanted more intimate forms of contact between individuals and groups. But Kant's appeal to "hospitality" is explicitly critical of the religious and social practices that have traditionally gone by that name. He argues that the ravages of colonialism point to the limitations of many sacred hospitality practices, which in mandating that every visitor be received as a god potentially result in the host nation's surrender of its entire civilization to its "guests." Kant's solution is to impute a "right of visit" *(Besuchrecht)* to the guest, which casts his hospitable reception as a legislatable, universal right, no longer dependent upon the goodwill of the host. But the corollary of this "right of visit" is an insistence upon the inviolability of national sovereignty, the fixity of borders that must be respected as the precondition of travel for the purposes of tourism, commerce, or trade. In upholding the sovereignty of the host's identity over the ethics of hospitality, Kant rejects the challenge to personal and group identity that hospitality has traditionally implied, which is now revalued as a menace to be avoided at all costs.

The first consequence of Kant's proposal is to remove hospitality from the status of an obligation, relocating it within the field of rights as a regulated mode of visitation that happens under the sign of a principle or rule. The host country doesn't have to do anything *for* the visitor, it only has to allow him the right of temporary visit. In its "empty," nonprescriptive form, I argue that Kant's imperative involves the displacement or even the elimination of hospitality as such, in favor of what he calls an "unsocial sociability," an impersonal relation that dispenses with the immediate—and therefore potentially uncomfortable or menacing—penetration of the stranger into the intimacy of the home. Despite its intended secularism, I argue that Kant's treatise is not so far removed from the religious models it attempts to displace, since its "economic" treatment of the other both draws upon and resonates with Christian theology (most notably Paul's discourse of cosmopolitanism). Both presuppose a positive representation of identity (personal, political, or communal) and a formalizable law regulating interpersonal relations (laws of exchange, laws of citizenship, or even the divine *logos* as guarantor of a transcendent equality). At the same time, I show that Kant's "right of visit" is not as universal as it purports to be, since it extends only to the foreign national entering the host country for purposes of travel or commerce. In its reliance on impersonal laws and the presumption of national sovereignty, Kant's treatise not only leaves no place for the nomad, displaced person, or asylum seeker, but implicitly allows them to be viewed as parasites or aggressors, hostile threats to the host's sovereignty. As such, I argue that it establishes a paradigm of state hospitality that is ripe for appropriation by the National Socialist discourse that treats the Jews as parasites undermining the health of their "host" country.

Like Kant, Nietzsche understands the crisis of modernity as a crisis of hospitality. But his understanding of post-religious hospitality suggests that it is not the sacred determination of the hospitality act that is outdated, but the way in which the person of the stranger has increasingly been inscribed within categorical determinations. Whereas Kant's proposal substitutes secular "principles" for religious values, the Nietzschean "death of God" entails the annihilation of all principles, the "transvaluation of all values," including the value of personal identity itself. Nietzsche argues that the privative quality of the monotheistic God reifies not only subjective boundaries, but also the unknown itself. With the death of God, then, the unknown is free to manifest itself in other forms. The corollary is that "true" hospitality is once again possible. In place of the biblical injunction to "love thy neighbor as thyself," Nietzsche embraces a love of the "most distant": the foreign, the dissimilar, the unknown. But although Nietzsche sees the "murder" of God as absolutely necessary to this revaluation of the foreign, he also warns that even "after" God we run the risk of preserving or instituting principles that are not a transvaluation of nihilistic Christian values, but simply new and equally insidious ones. For the transvaluation of all values to be complete, he argues, we must overcome not only the monotheist understanding of God, but also the positive idea of personal identity that depends upon it.

In contrast to Kant, Nietzsche affirms the uncanny encounter with the foreign over the privative boundaries instituted by cosmopolitan law or "unsocial sociability." And whereas Kant's formulation of hospitality, like Augustine's, tends increasingly to displace the sacred, "divinity" and "godliness" reemerge as key terms in Nietzsche's philosophy and are given new meaning as the expression of an irreducible excess. Nietzsche calls for a modernity that would dispense with the principles upheld by Kant's cosmopolitan project, liberating the other's alterity and by extension releasing "godliness" into the world. In Nietzsche's wake, the hospitality relation once again becomes the focus of an attempt to maintain an aporetic relation to the unknown in other than compensatory, salvational modes. In its immanence, hospitality sketches the horizon of a modernity that can no longer appeal to a transcendental representation of identity; its dominant figure is the eternal return of the same *as different,* as dispossessed of its identity to itself.

Chapters 3 and 4 deal with the interpretation and elaboration of Nietzsche's "death of God" in the work of French philosopher and novelist Pierre Klossowski, and in particular his fictional trilogy *Les lois de l'hospitalité.* An implicit question informs the entire trilogy: how is it possible to have a relation of hospitality, or even relation at all, after God? In the absence of God, how can we experience the simultaneous dispossession and actualization of identity promised by sacred hospitality? Klossowski's protagonist, Octave, a retired professor of theology, thirsts for an experience of the divine in a post-divine world. Toward this end, he welcomes chance strangers into his home in the hope of realizing his "inactual essence" as host through contact with an unknown other who is called upon to "liberate" him of his privative identity (and thereby assume the role traditionally played by the divine visitor).

But this operation supposes a third term. The "laws of hospitality" names a practice wherein Klossowski's protagonist, Octave, "gives" his wife, Roberte, to chance strangers, fortuitous "guests" who take possession of her in a way that contradicts her symbolic role by revealing the hostess (the stranger-lover) within the wife (the faithful mistress of the home). The hostess is necessary if there is to be some relation between the host and guest that is not reducible to a simple economy of exchange in which identity is left intact. In its exclusion from the reciprocal economy of hospitality between "equals," and its irreducibility to any common measure, the feminine approximates the function of the divine, the third term who allows for relation. But although the feminine shares with the divine its "excessive" quality, it is also ambivalently related to the positive principle of personal identity that the monotheist God, in its particularly Christian interpretation, imparts. This marginal position appears as a singular force in Klossowski's work and suggests how the identity of the post-Nietzschean host might be understood as other than a principle of self-adequation.

Octave suggests that the rupturing of the "privative" designations of master and mistress of the home can be achieved only through the loss of the "incommunicability of souls," the theological principle according to which an individual's being remains attributable only to itself and that constitutes identity as such. In the case of his wife, Roberte, he argues that this incommunicability has been suspended due to her lack of belief, which means that the integrity of her person can no longer be guaranteed. Although Roberte scorns religious doctrine, her disbelief is not reducible to her contempt for Octave's Christianity. When Klossowski writes that all women are "natural atheists," he implies that women are structurally devoid of any belief in—or adequation to—the transcendental integrity of personhood that the monotheist conception of the soul is supposed to impart. But this loss of incommunicability is precisely what allows for hospitality, since only the hostess can "let the stranger in," establishing a "substantial" communication with an alterity beyond the limits of the self.

In her disbelief, Roberte recalls Abraham's wife Sarah, whose incredulous laughter at the words of her divine guests actually facilitates her function as hostess, giving expression to the surplus by which she and Abraham exceed their identities as the faithful followers of God. The host or hostess can execute the laws of hospitality only to the extent that each can be dispossessed of a privative identity, precisely by being untrue to their symbolic designations. While in the Christian logic of hospitality the underlying coherence of the *logos* facilitates the hospitality relation by rendering exchangeable the roles of host and guest, here it is the *infidelity* of each participant to his or her symbolic designation that facilitates this relation, allowing them to "escape" their privative identities.

But if Roberte's loss of incommunicability is due to her femininity, her structural inadequation to the signifier of personal identity, then how can Octave in turn expect to be "liberated" of his identity? Klossowski's answer is that Octave can only experience this dispossession indirectly, through his wife. His solution recalls the paradox I set forth earlier to encapsulate the aporetic logic of the hospitality act: although the host as master is "eminently himself," his identity as host is paradoxically established through the dispossession and surrendering of his substance, evident in the traditional wisdom that the best host is the one who gives the most, even to the point of giving away that which defines him as master. Or, in Klossowski's terms, the husband who offers his wife as a gift is "expropriated" of his identity as master when his "inactual essence" as host is actualized by the guest. When his wife is "surprised" by the guest in her quality as mistress of the home and actualized as hostess, the husband's determination as master (that is, as one who is "eminently equal" to himself and capable of symbolically personifying the household) is rendered improper, alienated. He is realized as host precisely through the loss of his identity as master.

Chapter 5, "Welcoming Dionysus, or the Subject as *Corps Morcelé*," departs from Klossowski's take on femininity to explore an underappreciated aspect of Nietzsche's thought: his intuition that man must undergo "feminization"—that is, lose his privative identity—if he is to shed what Nietzsche calls the "grammatical fiction of the 'I'," the imaginary consistency imparted by the signifier of personal identity. Although for Nietzsche it is the Greek god Dionysus who represents the possibility of a dissolution of the ego that is affirmatively revalued as "divine," and that opposes itself to the redeeming of self represented by Christ, he also asserts that "after" God, man must assume an authentically "feminine" attitude in welcoming Dionysus. He associates with the figure of Ariadne, the one who embraces the dissolution of identity in welcoming the transfiguring advent of the god.

One of the stakes of this chapter is to develop the affinities between Nietzsche's work and the psychoanalytic contestation of the ego's discourse in the work of Freud and Lacan. Nietzsche's

Ariadne anticipates the historical legacy of the hysteric, who invents psychoanalysis by guiding Freud to the errant jouissance inscribed in the somatic body. Ariadne's love for Dionysus recalls the "love for savoir" that guides the transference, the love for the signifiers of the Other that makes it possible for the subject to embrace the erosion of the narcissistic ego to which they lead. I suggest that Nietzsche's Dionysus figures what Lacan calls the "jouissance of the Other," which takes possession of the human being and leaves in its wake a fragmented body *[corps morcelé]* that can no longer appeal to a coherent self or unified body image. Both authors suggest that this divided, fragmented, or objectified body is the true site of the subject. Just as Nietzsche affirms the "multiplicity" of the body over the unified self, Lacan suggests that the aim of analysis is to tear down the edifice of the ego and compel the analysand to assume speech from the position of the *corps morcelé* that the ego works to efface.

Chapter 6, "The Other Jouissance, a Gay *Sçavoir*," reexamines these questions through an analysis of Jacques Lacan's writings on femininity. Lacan follows Freud in noting that the illusion of the unified body image is less stable in women than in men. But he sees this instability as an advantage rather than a handicap in that it allows her to access more readily than man a "jouissance beyond the phallus," a jouissance that is experienced not merely as a menace to the subject, but as the source of a pleasure linked to the experience of the lack or inconsistency of the Other. In Lacan's work, the ethical import of femininity inheres in the specific *savoir*—or knowledge—it accesses: a knowledge about the unfoundedness of the signifier and the unified body image it sustains. He calls it a "gay *sçavoir*," highlighting the importance of the *ça*—the "Thing" or *es* of Freud's theory of the unconscious—in its elaboration. But not incidentally, its name is also a reference to Nietzsche's *Gay Science,* the text in which he announces the death of God and that Klossowski translated into French as *Le gai savoir.* For both Nietzsche and Lacan—albeit in different ways—the gay savoir is the knowledge that results from a relation to the signifier—and to identity—that is no longer sustained by a transcendental guarantee. But for Lacan, as for Klossowski, it is also intimately related to the specific jouissance experienced by a woman, as the one whose relation to the signifier is "not-all inscribed within the phallic function." I draw on this definition to account for the peculiar agency of the hostess, who tends to undercut the symbolic or mythical determination of the hospitality act by giving voice to a "real" that exceeds or resists inscription within it. I argue that her function attests to the agency of what Lacan calls "the object raised to the dignity of the Thing."

Lacan's formulation is central to his work on ethics, especially as it relates to his reading of Sigmund Freud's articulation of the ego's relation to the id: *Wo es war, soll Ich werden.* Lacan sees in Freud's *es* the primacy of the extra-subjective object or "Thing" for the nascence of subjectivity, the "extimate" agency of what Freud calls *das Ding* in the intersubjective topology of the ego. For both figures, this agency is closely linked to femininity. Noting that Freud discovered the "other scene" in the hysteric's discourse, Lacan sees in the experience of feminine jouissance the unconscious knowledge—or *savoir*—of the one who is inhabited by, or plays host to, the *es*. I take Lacan's analysis as the foundation for my own thesis concerning the ethics of hospitality: namely, that the hostess effects the uncanny dispossession of the host-"I" (the master eminently equal to himself) by the host-*es,* the Thing irreducible to the identity of the host that nonetheless executes the act of hospitality.

Acknowledgments

Jean-François Lyotard and Jacques Derrida advised this project from its inception and encouraged me at every stage of the writing process; their generosity and wisdom are much missed. Juliet Flower MacCannell is my guide and inspiration: her work is the gold standard for everything I want to accomplish as a writer, and her unfailing friendship and generosity as a collaborator are without peer. Julia Lupton and Ken Reinhard continue to amaze me with their teaching, their work, their friendship, and their example: if I know anything about hospitality, I learned it from them. My conversations with Peter Canning exerted a profound influence on this project in its formative stages, and Steven Miller, Janet Sarbanes, Eleanor Kaufman, and Wendy Hester shaped it with their comments and discussions. Willy Apollon, Lucie Cantin, and Danielle Bergeron are my teachers in all things psychoanalytic; I thank them for their inspiration and friendship, and for animating a life outside the university. Thanks to Mitchell Greenberg for his generous mentorship and for prodding me to finally put this manuscript in the mail, and to my colleagues in the Department of Romance Studies at Cornell for their support and stimulating exchanges. The semester I spent as a fellow at Cornell's Society for the Humanities provided needed time to revise the manuscript, and the comments of Dominick LaCapra, Michael Steinberg, and Robert Ziomkowski helped me think about how to address my project to a wider audience. The graduate students in my seminars Anthropology and Genealogy, Biblical Diasporas, and Femininity spurred the process of revision with their questions and insights, especially Camille Robcis, Parvis Ghassem-Fachandi, Wyatt Bonikowski, Audrey Wasser, Josh Corey, Hilary Emmett, Nathan Guss, and Carissa Sims. I couldn't ask for a better editor than Doug Armato; his generosity and warmth gave a human face to the otherwise daunting process of publication. Finally I would like to thank my husband, Brad Zukovic, for seeing me through the highs and the lows with his patience and love and for proving that intellectuals don't have to be academics. This book is dedicated to my mother and stepfather, Rose McNulty and Dan Gill; I couldn't have done it without you.

1. Israel, Divine Hostess

In the Introduction I argued that hospitality concerns a fundamental tension between the shoring up of identity and its opening to the other, or between the host's "eminent personification of identity" and the heteronomous nature of the hospitality obligation. Emmanuel Lévinas famously associates the first pole with the Greek hero Odysseus, and the second with the Hebrew patriarch Abraham. But one cannot help but be struck by the apparent strangeness of Lévinas's identifying this second possibility with a patriarch, who is responsible not only for upholding the heteronomous authority of God but for consolidating the symbolic identity of the group (and, through it, the sacred nation of Israel). To understand how this opening to the Other is possible within patriarchy, it is not enough to appeal to the special nature of Abraham's faith. We must also consider the function of femininity and, in particular, the role of the hostess.

In the Hebrew Bible, we first encounter the hostess as someone who is not a subject of the covenant but who nonetheless plays an indispensable role in cementing the ethical pact between man and God. If patriarchy tends toward the consolidation of identity, through the symbolic constitution of the group, femininity represents a surplus that cannot be integrated into that mythico-symbolic trajectory. As an internal excess that opens to the other, it both cements the symbolic relations of group identity and exceeds them. As such, femininity identifies a receptivity to the other that is alternately celebrated by the Hebrews as an ethical ideal

1

and repudiated as a sinful scandal. Through the feminine, we encounter the conflict—or even antinomy—between two different understandings of religion: on the one hand the sacred function of excess, and on the other the "political" contours of monotheism as a discourse of identity and identification.

This tension is internal to Hebraic hospitality, as an act of devotion and prostration that lies at the origin of the Yahwist religious practices later formalized as Judaic monotheism. It opens up a space for the Other beyond the reciprocal relations of identification and incorporation that define the social link. The ethics of hospitality marks the transition from the "political" to the "religious," in the particular sense in which Lévinas understands these terms. He defines politics as "the realization of the struggle for recognition," which tends toward equality and reciprocity and culminates in the production of an identity. Conversely, religion is "the possible surplus in a society of equals."[1] Understood in this way, religion represents the excess of identity, whether personal or cultural. It presents a challenge not only to metaphysical conceptions of selfhood, but to cultural particularism. It supposes a nonpositive understanding not only of the guest, but of the identity of the host, which is revalued as a heterogeneous subjectivity. In its affirmation of negativity, religion points to the way in which the sign of identity fails to preside over the relation between host and guest, affirming the irreducibility of this relationship either to cultural integration or to the reified opposition between the native and the foreigner.

But insofar as it names not only an ethics, but a doctrine and a cultural practice, any particular religion necessarily oscillates between the "political" and the "religious" as such, in the terms of Lévinas's opposition. As a religion is institutionalized, it inevitably—indeed necessarily—becomes wary of the very "surplus" or excess it initially sustained and increasingly works to limit its place. Where the hospitality act is concerned, this limitation takes the form of a codification of hospitality practice and limits on the reception of the stranger, which work to consolidate and protect the identity of the host. The Jewish religion is one of the exemplary instances of this tension in Western civilization, since its tradition repeatedly confronts the problem of how to translate a "negative" ethics into a formalizable cultural practice. On the one hand it proposes a highly creative response to this tension that does not simply resolve its impossibility, while on the other the mandate of Jewish "chosenness" and its Zionist manifestations tend to consolidate and defend Jewish identity in a highly politicized way.

The first part of this chapter examines how the hospitality of the Hebrew patriarchs challenges the notion of identity by introducing a vision of subjectivity as dependent upon an other: a dependence that characterizes the subjectivity not only of the host but also of the Israelites who are constituted as a culture through their reception of the divine. The second part of the chapter considers how, in its problematic passage from the desert to the city, the tent to the tabernacle, and the unspecified faith to the formalized religion, the sacred nation of Israel comes to embrace a national and religious identity that is defined in opposition to foreign nations and the worship of foreign gods. In the process, the Israelites become increasingly suspicious not only of the hospitality act itself but of the divided subjectivity implied by its ethics of openness to and prostration before the unknown other. The turning point between these two moments is the institution of monotheism, through the naming of the Jealous God to Moses. Whereas Abraham's hospitality is an "absolute ethics," supposing an infinite obligation toward the stranger, post-Exodus hospitality is increasingly codified, proscribed by the demands of monotheist adherence. The Decalogue introduces an antinomial relation between monotheism and hospitality, an antinomy not present in the Genesis stories. The tension between the two ethics turns upon the problem of nomadism, the erring in the desert that is both the source of Israel's commitment to hospitality and at the same time the scene of her straying from God.

Finally, I consider the condemnation of hospitality in the books of the Hebrew prophets as an attempt to resolve its antinomial relation to monotheism. Generally writing from a position of exile and national disaster (an enforced, second-order, catastrophic "nomadism"), the prophets are increasingly wary of Israel's relations with strangers in the form of foreign alliances, intermarriage, idolatry, and temple prostitution. The act of hospitality is thus increasingly bound up in the problem of idolatry, or what the metaphor of Israel's "marriage" to God figures as the wife's adulterous "welcoming" of strangers in the place of her husband. The alignment of idolatry and adultery reflects the changing meaning of "feminine receptivity" pre- and post-Decalogue, since it casts the antinomy as a conflict between an ethics of unlimited receptivity to the Other, coded "feminine," and the formalized laws (of hospitality, of monotheism, of identity) that are erected as a barrier against this feminization. Israel is the too-good-hostess who thereby becomes a bad wife. This figural move not only identifies the "errant subjectivity" of Israel as a specifically "feminine" problem but leads to a systematic negation of the positive features of the Sarah story in Genesis. As the feminized wife of God, Israel is—like Sarah and Eve—"not all" made in the image of God, structurally inadequate, or unequal to the exigencies of his law. But in this case, the hostess's "receptivity" to strangers is figured not as an advantage but as a menace to the Jewish religion and state.

The Hospitality of the Hebrew Patriarchs

As the first of the Hebrew patriarchs, Abraham inaugurates a tradition of wandering that marks the departure of monotheism from its polytheist rivals: God tells Abraham to leave the land of his birth and follow him into the desert (Genesis 12:1), uprooting his first follower from the worship of local gods and place deities that defined the religion of his ancestors. This spatial dislocation is tied to the singularity of YHWH himself as the only god who is not part of his creation. In his analysis of YHWH's early manifestations as a nomadic "god of way," whose primary function was to guard over travel, Martin Buber notes that the Israelite God differs from all other "gods of way" in that he is not regularly visible in nature:

> It is assuredly something more than a mere coincidence that the name of the city of Harran, which together with Ur was the chief city of the moon cult and in which Abraham separated from his clan, meant "way" or "caravan," and would appear to have designated the spot where the caravans met and from which they started out. The God by whom Abraham, after "straying away" from Harran, is led in his wanderings, differs from all solar, lunar and stellar divinities, apart from the fact that He guides only Abraham and His own group, by the further fact that He is not regularly visible in the heavens, but only occasionally permits Himself to be seen by His chosen; whenever and wherever it is His will to do so. This necessarily implies that various natural things and processes are on occasion regarded as manifestations of the God, and that

it is impossible to know for certain where or wherein He will next appear.[2]

YHWH cannot himself be located in nature. But more important-ly, the human beings who follow him are forbidden the means to locate *themselves* in nature, to orient themselves in relation to the caravan routes and natural landmarks by which man masters na-ture only at the cost of prostrating himself to it. For Abraham, to follow God's itinerary is not only to "stray away" from his clan but to lose his bearings: to wander blindly, only occasionally and at unpredictable moments receiving some indication from God about where he is to go.

In this sense, YHWH is not so much a god of way as a god who *waylays,* who forces his adherents off the beaten paths of the known world to err in the desert. In Genesis 12, Abraham's ad-herence to God's commands is described in language associated with the procedures of nomadic life,[3] suggesting an intimate link between the fact of nomadic uprootedness and the special nature of YHWH's covenant with Abraham and his descendants. He in-stitutes an ethics of exile and displacement that will come to de-fine the Israelites, as a wandering people whose privileged relation to God is defined by an estrangement that both conditions God's offer of the promised land (Genesis 12:7) and complicates it with indefinite deferral and the daily reality of exile: "Know this for cer-tain, that your offspring shall be aliens in a land that is not theirs" (Genesis 15:16). Abraham himself will live as a "stranger and a sojourner" (Genesis 23:4), wandering the earth for one hundred years only to die in a foreign land.

The ambivalent character of estrangement is partly due to its roots in sin, the dispersion over the face of the earth mandated by expulsion from Eden and the scattering of the languages after Babel. We first encounter the future patriarch as Abram, a child of the generation scattered—geographically as well as in speech—by the destruction of Babel (Genesis 11). Up to this point, wandering has a punitive connotation in the Bible. Adam and Eve are made to roam "east of Eden" as penance for original sin, and the word "wanderer" is first used to describe the murderous Cain, made a "fugitive and a wanderer" by his fratricide (4:19). Cain settles in the land of Nod, which in Hebrew means "wandering." This most paradoxical of place-names suggests that for the generations born of original sin, even the land itself will not provide a stable "ground": a premonition confirmed by the great flood, in which God reminds his surviving remnant that the land itself is revocable, and so ruptures the autochthonous fantasy of a primordial link between the human being *('adam)* and the soil *('adamah)* or earth. But at the same time, God's covenant with Abraham suggests that the chosen people will redeem its fallen condition not by overcoming this estrangement but by assuming it as the defining characteristic of its relationship with God. In this sense, Abraham's pulling of his tent stakes to follow YHWH echoes Noah's "pulling up anchor," breaking his bond with the earth in order to drift over its surface. The patriarch will redeem estrangement by repeating and reliving it, but with a difference.

Entertaining Strangers: The Estranged Host of the Covenant

Hospitality emerges as the act through which the patriarch will paradoxically come to "eminently personify," and bind together in a cultural identity, a multitude of strangers. The Hebrew patriarchs are exemplary among hosts, since they are perhaps the ultimate embodiment of the contradictory relation to personal identity that the act of hospitality implies. Their personification of group identity extends not only to the family unit but to the twelve Hebrew tribes who constitute the chosen people of Israel. But the biblical paradigm of hospitality introduces a further complication: even when the host is human, it is clear that the description of the host as the "eminent personification" of personal identity applies best—and even exclusively—to God himself. If the divine host represents the imaginary promise of identity, it is precisely because this possibility is structurally inaccessible to humans. Relative to the absolute Other, the Guest, the host's own identity can never attain complete mastery. Hence the patriarch's "identity" must involve something other than self-adequation. The task of the host as patriarch is all the more complex in that the group he is called upon to represent is none other than the sacred nation of Israel. He is asked to personify the chosen people of God, but presumably to personify them differently than God himself does. As patriarch his task must be to uphold the equation "Abraham's people = God's people," but without ever pretending to the syllogistic corollary "Abraham = God."

Abraham's hospitality immediately follows his covenant with

God, grounded in the ultimate symbolic act: "You shall circumcise the flesh of your foreskins, and it shall be a sign of the covenant between me and you" (Genesis 17:11). The cutting of the flesh results in Abram's elevation to the status of patriarch and his renaming as Abraham, "father of nations." In this way, the covenant of circumcision bestows a transcendent identity on the "chosen people," by simultaneously marking the elect and "cutting off" those who do not accept the law: "Any uncircumcised male who is not circumcised in flesh of his foreskin shall be cut off from his people; he has broken my covenant" (17:14). If God's command to leave the land of his ancestors marks Abraham's break with the natural world and its polytheist encodings, the covenant of circumcision "reterritorializes" the disoriented, nomadic subject with the mapping of a new spiritual terrain. Despite God's guarantees concerning the promised land, however, the form of the covenant works to deepen—rather than reverse—the turn away from nature begun in chapter 12, since the mark of divine election causes the organ of natural sexuality to fall under the dominion of the Other.[4]

Although the covenant of circumcision imparts the identity of chosenness, it also makes clear that this identity will be something other than ipseity. Any man who remains uncut, and thus "whole" from a natural point of view, is "cut off" from his people. Conversely, Abraham "eminently personifies" the group only insofar as he, and they, are cut. The patriarch is thus charged with embodying the lack or split within the Israelites as much as their election.

This split identity becomes increasingly evident as the narrative unfolds. God assures Abraham that if he keeps the covenant (performs circumcision upon himself and his male dependents), he will have a son named Isaac. But the manner in which Abraham greets the tidings of this miraculous event hardly seems in keeping with his new status as a subject of the covenant: "Abraham fell upon his face and laughed, and said to himself, 'Can a child be born to a man who is a hundred years old?'" (17:17). Although he accepts and submits to the covenant, his response underscores his inadequation to it, in the form of his ignorance or misrecognition of the divine nature underwriting the promise.

As the first gesture he makes as a subject of God's covenant, Abraham's act of hospitality will confirm his status as patriarch by upholding two apparently contradictory positions: that of the host/

master eminently personifying identity and that of the remainder unequal to this designation, that part that laughs. As the act that both seals and puts to the test the patriarch's status as a subject of the covenant, hospitality will demonstrate that the subject is not wholly engaged in this new symbolic identity. The law is "visited" upon Abraham first as a cutting of the flesh, and second through his hospitable reception of the divine. What then is the relationship between them, and how does the second realize the first?

Abraham initiates the first act of hospitality recorded in the Bible when he welcomes as guests three disguised angels of God under the oak trees of Mamre. But while the gesture of hospitality is extended by a host who is also a master, a recognized patriarch, the act is marked by the absence of symbolic recognition:

> The LORD appeared to Abraham by the oaks of Mamre, as he sat at the entrance of his tent in the heat of the day. He looked up and saw three men standing near him. When he saw them, he ran from the tent entrance to meet them, and bowed down to the ground. He said, "My lord [Adonai], if I find favor with you, do not pass by your servant. Let a little water be brought, and wash your feet, and rest yourselves under the tree. Let me bring a little bread, that you may refresh yourselves, and after that you may pass on—since you have come to your servant." So they said, "Do as you have said." And Abraham hastened into the tent to Sarah, and said, "Make ready quickly three measures of choice flour, knead it, and make cakes." Abraham ran to the herd, and took a calf, tender and good, and gave it to the servant, who hastened to prepare it. Then he took curds and milk and the calf that he had prepared, and set it before them; and he stood by them under the tree while they ate.
>
> They said to him, "Where is your wife Sarah?" And he said, "There, in the tent." Then one said, "I will surely return to you in due season, and your wife Sarah shall have a son." And Sarah was listening at the tent entrance behind him. (18:1–10)

Abraham's guests are unnamed, unknown.[5] The narrative retains all the features of a classic hospitality legend, common to most Mediterranean religions, in which a deity or its emissaries appear to human beings in the guise of an unknown strangers, challenging the host to prove his character by offering food and shelter. In this context, the host necessarily both *knows* and *does not know* the identity of his divine guest: hospitality is motivated by the potentially sacred nature of the guest, whose true identity must nonetheless remain unknown for authentic hospitality to take place.

But although this paradigm is familiar in legend, it casts a perplexing light on the narrative that precedes it. If Abraham has just entered into a covenant with God, why would he not recognize his emissaries? One could easily imagine a different outcome (one common in fairy tales), where the point of the test would be to see whether Abraham would be *able to recognize* the divine guest, and thus prove the closeness of his bond with God. Here, though, the act of hospitality happens in such a way as to insist upon the host's ignorance or misrecognition of the divine nature, rather than his identification of or with it. What is important is not just that he welcomes God, but that he welcomes God *as a stranger,* as an unknown. The host has to "receive" the word of God, but to receive it in a way that acknowledges his inadequation to it. In spite of his unquestioning adherence, Abraham is necessarily estranged from God, a stranger to his true nature.

In this sense Abraham is very much an heir to the heritage of Eden, where Adam and Eve are forced to grow up and become strangers: to God, to one another, and even to themselves. But in the act of hospitality, the patriarch compensates for the sins of Eden and Babel, or the attempt to "know" God, precisely by failing to recognize the guest, and thereby honoring his sublime alterity. His narrative tells us that human hospitality will redeem the loss of divine hospitality—or paradise—by relinquishing the prideful fantasy of knowing and coming to accept the discontinuity between them. It is a separation of man from God in which man becomes worthy of divine favor by assuming his lack of knowledge, inaugurating a relation to subjectivity not based on the presumption of wholeness.

The Hostess

Although Abraham's fulfillment of the covenant establishes him as a patriarch, making him the knowing inheritor of God's promise, his knowledge is far from complete. For while Abraham takes his place in the symbolic trajectory of the covenant, his former unknowing is not lost but merely transferred. Here, as in Eden, the critical limit of the hospitality relation is approached not by one character, but by two: a hospitality couple (Abraham and Sarah) that both recalls and revises the coupling in "one flesh" of Adam and Eve. At first glance, Sarah's role in the hospitality act is a minor one. Without even meeting the visitors, to whom her husband alone speaks, she busies herself with preparing their meal. But on hearing the declaration that she will have a child, Sarah "laughed to herself, saying, 'After I have grown old, and my husband is old, shall I have pleasure *['ednah]?*'" (18:12). Her mirth echoes and revives Abraham's own burst of laughter upon hearing the same promise in the preceding chapter, sustaining the incredulity that has been displaced—but not eliminated—by his knowing participation in the covenant. Importantly, Sarah doubts not only her own ability to bear a child late in life but also her husband's. Unknowing (in the form of Sarah's *disbelief*) passes from one half of the hospitality couple into the other, and it is this portion of unknowing that makes hospitality as such possible.

In relation to the myth of Eden, Sarah redeems what Jean-François Lyotard calls Eve's "wicked emancipation."[6] While Eve incites Adam to strive for complete knowledge, to succumb to the serpent's invitation to "be as gods, knowing good and evil" (3:5), Sarah maintains Abraham's doubt in the miraculous prophecy rather than bolstering his sense of knowing. Significantly, Sarah's incredulous laughter concerns the possibility of knowing "pleasure," *'ednah,* in the twilight of her life. Since the word is cognate with Eden (meaning "delight") Sarah's doubt suggests a healthy skepticism about a mere mortal reclaiming something of the "delight" lost to original sin.

But she also offers a sober reflection on the fantasy of marriage as a union in "one flesh" by underscoring the divisions internal to that union. In his reading of the Eden story, Robert Alter suggests that man's incompleteness is "mitigated but not entirely removed by the creation of woman, for that creation takes place through the infliction of a kind of wound on him, and afterward, in historical time, he will pursue her, strain to become 'one flesh' with her, as though to regain a lost part of himself."[7] Like the lovers invoked by Aristophanes in Plato's *Symposium,* they are "bifurcated halves of a primal self who are trying to recapture that impossible primal unity."[8]

Woman, in this fable, is the name for a split within man, a "lost part of himself." But importantly, Adam and Eve do not themselves perceive this split, even as it leaves them open to temptation.

Alter observes that "after being invoked as the timeless model of conjugal oneness, they are immediately seen as two *[and the two of them were naked, the man and his woman]*, . . .vulnerable in their twoness to the temptation of the serpent, who will be able to seduce first one, and through the one, the other."[9] Despite their union in "one flesh," Adam and Eve are not of one mind, and this division has catastrophic implications. The story underscores the tension between an imaginary "one" and a more fundamental two, a twoness born of the alienating effects of language.

This split within "the" subject is both repeated and redeemed in the case of Abraham and Sarah. By assuming Abraham's laughter, Sarah bolsters her husband's status as a subject of the covenant by externalizing—and thus appearing to remove—that part of his character that remains inconsistent with its demands.[10] In the humorous conclusion to this episode, God chides Sarah for her laughter, saying to Abraham,

> Why did Sarah laugh, and say, "Shall I indeed bear a child, now that I am old? Is anything too wonderful for the LORD? At the set time I will return to you, in due season, and Sarah shall have a son." But Sarah denied, saying, "I did not laugh"; for she was afraid. But he said, "Oh yes, you did laugh." (18:13–15)

God's rebuke is more comical than truly stern, since in her own doubt Sarah both assumes and deflects attention from that of her husband, who is now expected to share in God's confidence in his own miraculous abilities.[11] As long as some part of the composite host is ignorant of the truth of the visitor's declaration—ignorant of the divine essence underlying his words—authentic hospitality is still possible.

Pretexts

In my view Sarah and Abraham must be understood not as two distinct subjects who voluntarily join together to complete the act of hospitality but as representatives in displaced form of the conflicting tendencies of a single—albeit divided—subject of hospitality. My reading of Genesis 17–18 is thus completely at odds with Paul's New Testament interpretation, which maintains that Abraham's and Sarah's righteousness consists solely in their "unquestioning faith" in God's promise. Strikingly, Paul's sober synopsis of

Genesis 17 not only makes no mention of Abraham's laughter but maintains that the patriarch felt no doubt or distrust whatsoever concerning the divine promise:

> He *did not weaken in faith* when he considered his own body, which was already as good as dead (for he was about a hundred years old), or when he considered the barrenness of Sarah's womb. *No distrust made him waver* concerning the promise of God, but he grew strong in his faith as he gave glory to God, being *fully convinced that God was able to do what he had promised*. (Romans 4:19–21, my emphases)

In the same way, the brief summation of the hospitality narrative in Hebrews (an anonymous treatise generally attributed to the Pauline school) suggests that "through faith also Sarah received strength to conceive seed, and was delivered of a child when she was past age, because she judged him faithful who had promised" (Hebrews 11:11). This revision effaces both the unknown character of the divine guests and the "unknowing" preserved by Sarah's disbelief, converting the hospitable encounter into a scene of symbolic recognition where Sarah "receives the word" without any estrangement from it. In contrast, I would suggest that both symbolic and extra-symbolic characteristics, faith *and* disbelief, are visible within the composite "host," passed between the two partners by a laughter become infectious.

This imputation of faith is worth analyzing in more detail, however, since it is central to what is probably the best-known interpretation of Abraham's and Sarah's hospitality. In Paul's interpretation of Genesis, developed and expanded by Augustine, Sarah marks another kind of passage altogether. As a prefiguration of the annunciation, her reception of the promise anticipates a "free Israel" made whole in the spirit of Christ, the emancipated Christianity born of the promise of the New Covenant, and so liberated from enslavement under the law. But it also supposes a very different understanding of the subject, as identified with the divine will and therefore consistent in itself.

In *City of God*, Augustine argues that participation in the covenant makes possible a community of grace in which many are bound together in "one heart."[12] But while the community of shared love may be "whole-hearted," the precondition of its wholeness is a necessary exclusion, in this case of "private will" or personal interest:

> Isaac, who was born as a result of a promise, is rightly interpreted as symbolizing the children of grace, the citizens of the free city, the sharers of eternal peace, who form a community where there is no love of a will that is personal and, as we may say, private, but a love that rejoices in a good that is at once shared by all and unchanging—a love that makes "one heart" out of many, a love that is the whole-hearted and harmonious obedience of mutual affection (XV:3).[13]

The participants in Abraham's act of hospitality, whose relation was predicated upon unknowing, are at once recalled and radically homogenized by Augustine's "free city." Any notion of alterity is necessarily excised from the community of grace, where all members renounce private will in order to "make 'one heart' out of many."

The neutralization of the guest's difference under this generalized affection, which integrates and dissipates the stranger's strangeness, is also at work in many doctrinal interpretations of hospitality. In the words of one theologian,

> The practice of hospitality, the sharing of the goods of the earth with another fellow creature, the unconditional acceptance of the stranger and his integration into our life, constitute the very essentials of a eucharistic relationship with the Creator of all. By giving generously of what has been bestowed on us to the stranger, by sharing the fruits of the earth, we render to God our thanksgiving for what has been generously offered to us. The stranger becomes the pretext, the means through which we enter into eucharistic communion with the Creator. Thus, the stranger acquires a sacred character.[14]

The stranger or guest as "pretext" is an anticipation or prefiguration of another text or *logos,* the Word that must both enter into the exchange and be reproduced by it if the hospitality relation is to have any symbolic significance or value. This interpretation of the hospitality event has a long history in Christianity, infusing the iconography of hospitality in particular.

Philoxenia, "the love of strangers," is the ancient Greek word for hospitality. In Christian iconography, *philoxenia* is the name given to icons celebrating the hospitality of Abraham—but with a strangely retroactive revision, whereby the configuration of this primal hospitality scene becomes the mystical prototype of the Holy Trinity. The most famous of the *philoxenia* icons, Andrei Roublev's fifteenth-century "Hospitality of Abraham" (or "Old Testament Trinity"), establishes the iconographic model for Christian hospitality, in which the three guests, understood as the Trinity, both subsume and displace the three distinct entities of host, hostess, and guest. The three angels are shown in a typical "Mystical Supper" arrangement, which figures the eucharistic relationship binding the Trinity: "the circular outline of the three angels clearly suggests the form of a chalice, and repeats the form of the chalice on the table, the receptacle through which they both contain and are contained by the feast."[15]

In the reading of the stranger as "pretext," as in these iconographic interpretations, the guest is cast as a mediator between God and man, as an occasion for widening the inclusive circle of "affection" by integrating one more stranger, divesting him of his unknown quality. In Abraham's narrative, on the other hand, the stranger gives meaning to the hospitality act precisely by reason of his unknowability, his absolute foreignness. The angels Abraham receives are radically heterogeneous with him, emissaries of the absolute Other with whom he could enjoy no identificatory bond. But in these accounts, the mediation provided by the guest reinscribes him into the totality, the circle; the stranger, the other, becomes a means of reappropriating the holy family. The guest is also a "pretext" in the more pejorative sense of the term, since the hospitality encounter that attempts to integrate him into the oneness of the Christian community "recognizes"—and so fails to appreciate—his alterity.

As the most *recognizable* interpretation of the Abraham narrative, the trinitarian reading is also—within the logic of the hospitality act itself—the one most at odds with its meaning and function as a *hospitality* narrative. In Augustine's articulation of the hospitality bond, as in this doctrinal interpretation of the stranger, the host welcomes the unknown in the hopes that it might not be so unknown after all, that behind the unknown name of the stranger there might lie hidden an essence (the "whole-hearted" substance of the divine), which he does "know," or rather knows how to *name*, to resume under the inclusive *logos* of the divine signifier.[16] But within the logic of Genesis, the significance of Abraham's hospitality is that the divine is only "recognized" in the guest to the extent that God's *unknowability* finds expression in the stranger's radical otherness. This unknowing is further in evidence in the child produced in recognition of the hospitality event. For although Isaac's miraculous birth attests to the divine identity of Abraham's guests, his name—meaning "he laughs"—is the echo of Abraham's and Sarah's laughter and disbelief at the divine promise.[17] Abraham's name "father of nations"—and with it his identity as a patriarch—are fulfilled when Isaac is produced: but produced as both the reminder and the *remainder* of this covenantal identity, the part that "laughs," that deforms the signifier, that disbelieves or feels unequal to the divine promise upholding the covenant.[18]

As Jean-François Lyotard suggests, Sarah's incredulous laughter serves as a reminder that the subject's link with the divine signifier can never be guaranteed—as Paul would have it—"once and for all." YHWH's unknowability is manifest in the possibility for misrecognition that always presides over the transmission of the divine signifier: "the pure signifier, the tetragram . . . can always turn out to be lacking, to signify something other than what the chosen one believed it to say. It is this failure, this breakdown, that provokes laughter."[19]

The importance of the slippage between covenantal and extracovenantal properties at work in Abraham's and Sarah's hospitality becomes even more obvious in the second hospitality narrative in Genesis, the story of Lot. While residing in the evil city of Sodom, slated for divine destruction, Lot offers protection to two disguised angels of God, who are menaced with rape by the men of Sodom. In recognition of his hospitality he is preserved from destruction and allowed to flee Sodom with his family. Like Abraham, though, he must "pass into" a subordinate hospitality partner in order to successfully complete the hospitality act. This ability comes into play most powerfully when Lot, reluctant to leave Sodom, is able to "dispose" of this reluctance in the form of his doomed wife:

> When morning dawned, the angels urged Lot, saying, "Get up, take your wife and your two daughters who are here, or else you will be consumed in the punishment of the city." But he lingered; so the men seized him and his wife and his two daughters by the

hand, the LORD being merciful to him, and they brought him out
and left him outside the city. When they had brought them outside,
they said, "Flee for your life, do not look back or stop anywhere
in the Plain; flee to the hills, or else you will be consumed." And
Lot said to them, "Oh no, my lords; your servant has found favor
with you, and you have shown me great kindness in saving my life;
but I cannot flee to the hills, for fear the disaster will overtake me
and I die. Look, that city is near enough to flee to, and it is a little
one. Let me escape there—is it not a little one?—and my life will
be saved!" He said to him, "Very well, I grant you this favor too,
and will not overthrow the city of which you have spoken. Hurry,
escape there, for I can do nothing until you arrive there." Therefore
the city was called Zoar. The sun had risen on the earth when Lot
came to Zoar.

   Then the LORD rained on Sodom and Gomorrah sulfur and
fire from the LORD out of heaven; and he overthrew those cities,
and all the Plain, and all the inhabitants of the cities, and what
grew on the ground. But Lot's wife, behind him, looked back, and
she became a pillar of salt. (19:15–26)

Lot's wife is not so much a character in her own right as she is a
figurative representation of a part of her husband: the part that
lingers, that cannot separate itself from the iniquity of Sodom but
must be "seized by the hand" and forcefully compelled to go. This
interpretation is supported not only by the wording of the passage, but by a philological fact: the verses evoking Lot's wife and
her salty fate are known to be secondary additions, inserted by an
early redactor of the "J" manuscript.[20]

   The figurative transfer of Lot's reluctance into the figure of his
wife allows for the symbolic recuperation of the hospitality deed,
which according to other references in Genesis might not otherwise
have been realized. Why, after all, would Lot—who is revealed
in other chapters to be of unremarkable character—be preserved
from the fate of Sodom? The biblical answer is unambiguous: "it
came to pass, when God destroyed the cities of the plain, that *God
remembered Abraham,* and sent Lot out of the midst of the overthrow" (19:29). Lot is spared because he is Abraham's relative.
Hence, the female half of this composite "host" is first invented
and then decisively disposed of so that symbolic movement can take
place, so that Lot can take his place in tradition, in the genealogy

of the book of the patriarchs. In Eden, the fact that Adam and Eve are "not of one mind" leads to catastrophe. Here Lot himself is "not of one mind," but the narrator uses his wife to distance the potentially unsavory connotations of this divided mentality from Abraham's relative.

Through a process of displacement, the narrative makes use of a second figure to represent a characteristic that it is for some reason unable or unwilling to attribute to the hospitable subject of the covenant. Here, as in the Abraham story, this displacement is facilitated by the fact that the wife is not herself a subject of the covenant, but is instead bound to it through her husband's allegiance. Legally, the ancient Hebrews considered a wife to be the chattel of her husband, just as an unmarried daughter was the property of her father.[21] But this legal dependence assumes a special importance within the hospitality act, where the principle of personal property the host embodies is intimately tied to a certain interpretation of the domestic economy and the sexual relation. As the master of the house, the host is also master of all of the subordinates (servants, slaves, and dependent women) who make up the household, as well as of the livestock or chattel that form his personal property;[22] whence the etymological link between the host-as-master and the husband. The host is the "eminent personification" not only of his own identity, but of all of the household subordinates who are equated with him precisely because they do not have distinct legal identities. Interestingly, the first other of the hospitality relation is not the guest, but rather the multiplicity of the host "himself," to the extent that his "identity" is already the expression of a collection of heterogeneous elements.

However, when I say that conflicting attributes are "displaced" onto the figure of the wife, I do not mean that one integral host is simply "disguised" in another representative, but rather that this seemingly integral subject is himself split, imperfectly related to the signifier that represents him as a partaker of the covenant. What is at stake in the wives' function is the possibility of being unequal to the name, of being more or less than the signifier that represents the host as a subject of the covenant. The hospitable coupling of husband and wife is not an imaginarily integrated unity (as for example in the fantasy of marriage set forth in prelapsarian Eden), but a dis-integration of the identities of husband and wife under the signifier of the "one" host, divided by that signifier into two positions: the subject named by the covenant and the extra-covenantal object or "thing" that allows for the execution of the hospitality act.

To use Jacques Lacan's term, the wives' relation to their husbands' hospitality is one of "extimacy": they participate in the host's subjectivity precisely *as* excluded from or foreign to it.[23] This "extimacy" grows out of the historic determination of the husband-wife relationship but also has implications that extend beyond it. As her husband's rightful possession, the wife is one of the series of "things" or chattel constituting the host's property, and through it his identity as the host proper. But in another sense she is also the "Thing" that insists within his "own" agency as improper to it, irreducible to the signifier of identity the host incarnates. She is that part of the host that is not named by the covenant, the excess of the signifier which thereby animates the function of what Lacan calls the *objet a*,[24] that spot of pseudo-consistency that appears to fill in or make up for the splitting of the subject at the same time that it serves as a persistent reminder of that split. Within the logic of personal property, the wife's function marks the point of convergence of two contradictory but interdependent dimensions of the fantasy of identity: imaginary and real. As an object or possession, the wife as "property" asserts the identity of the host, the proof of what Benveniste calls the "eminent personification" of group identity (and of the "property" of the I as a self-possessed master and subject). But as a "Thing" possessed of a singular agency within the host who both possesses and is possessed *by* her, the wife animates the extra-covenantal excess of the host, that part of the host proper that had to be "cut off" to allow for inscription in the covenant.

In both the Abraham and Lot narratives, the "passive," objectified wife ultimately functions as the motivating force behind the successful completion of the hospitality act. The wives represent the discontinuity inherent in the relationship between the human host and the divine guest (Sarah with her disbelief, Lot's wife with her reluctance and disobedience), the unintegrated residue of the signifier that paradoxically works to fulfill the hospitality imperative. Sarah's incredulous laughter at the guests' promise refutes the capacity of the enunciation to approximate God's substance, challenging the word's equation with the unknowable essence of the divine, and so manages not to compromise the unknowing upon which hospitality depends.

At the most basic level, the wives' actions serve as reminders of the impossibility of sustaining a reversible hospitality relation with God. The host's relation to his divine guest is characterized by a fundamental dissymmetry, introduced by the fact that the patriarch is called upon to uphold a law to which God alone is equal. The subject of hospitality is thus divided by the very law it enunciates: in other words, by the signifier, which always indicates a fundamental lack of reciprocity or symmetrical reversibility.

In both narratives, what is put in question in the hospitable relation between husband, wife, and guest is the position of enunciation, whose importance is inherent in the relation between the human and the divine. The hospitality couple's "extimate" execution of the hospitality deed insists upon a fundamental disproportion between the one who gives the law (YHWH), its subject (Abraham), and its executor (Sarah), bearing witness to the division incurred by the apparently autonomous, self-possessed subject of hospitality by virtue of his naming in the covenant. But it is also manifest in the uncertainty concerning God's position of enunciation, itself uncannily "extimate" to the human host. Although God speaks to Abraham and Lot directly, delivering imperatives and commands, it is always on the condition of not revealing from where he speaks. As Erich Auerbach has noted, Abraham's God is a disembodied voice; "it is always only 'something' of him that appears."[25] Put another way, some *thing* always mediates the hospitable relation between God and man. Whether that Thing is God's disembodied voice, the angels who appear in his place, or the wife who serves as the reservoir of the host's extra-covenantal properties, it works to fulfill the act of hospitality relating the human to the divine at the same time that it serves as a traumatic reminder of the discontinuity of that relation, of the impossibility of encircling host and guest in an inclusive totality or full symbolic from which nothing would be lacking.

Paternity and Privation

The fact that the host's identity is necessarily established through the dispossession and surrendering of his substance presents a particular challenge to the patriarch's role as the symbolic origin of group identity. What does it mean for the host/master who speaks in his own name that his enunciation is fundamentally divided? To what extent is the legacy of his hospitality act ever truly his "own"? The question is particularly problematic when considered in terms of the other, more personal dimension of patriarchy: paternity. How do the exigencies of the hospitality act impinge upon the patriarch's fulfillment of his function when he is also a progenitor and when the legacy of his act is his posterity, the race he is supposed to eminently personify? The host's ambivalent relation to his "legacy" is implicit in the original sense of the term: a giving up, a surrendering. How much of himself must be other than himself if the host is to be master of himself and of others? How much of himself must the host give up in order to eminently personify all that he has?

The master's surrender of his "own" substance is at work in Lot's narrative not only in the "disposal" of reluctance in the figure of the wife, but also in the extraordinary offer he extends as part of his hospitality. When the men of Sodom surround his home and threaten his guests with rape, Lot declares: "Look, I have two daughters who have not known a man; let me bring them out to you, and do to them as you please; only do nothing to these men, for they have come under the shelter of my roof" (Genesis 19:8). That Lot's decision to hand over his virgin daughters should count as a sacrifice of "himself" is not especially astounding in a biblical context, for historically an unmarried daughter was considered to be the property of her father, just as a wife was the chattel of her husband.[26] But the father's ability to "dispose" of his female dependents is due not only to historical factors, but to the structural requirements of the hospitality act in Genesis. Like his wife, Lot's daughters are not merely property, but instrumental "things" mediating the host's relation to the divine.

The second part of Lot's extraordinary tale begins with his escape to Zoar. Fearing life in the city, Lot goes to dwell in a cave with his daughters. What follows is one of the most contested and most extensively revised passages in Genesis, with decisive consequences both for the Abraham narrative and for the Israelites in general:

> And the firstborn said to the younger, "Our father is old, and there is not a man on earth to come in to us after the manner of all the world. Come, let us make our father drink wine, and we will lie with him, so that we may preserve offspring through our father." So they made their father drink wine that night; and the firstborn

went in, and lay with her father; he did not know when she lay
down, nor when she rose (19:31–33).

The second daughter follows suit, and both become pregnant and
bear sons. What is striking in this passage is that filiation is only
able to happen without the father's knowledge, recognition, or
memory: "he *did not know* when she lay down, nor when she rose."
Here too, active and passive roles were most likely exchanged in
the revision process to enhance the symbolic value of the narrative: "the fact that the two daughters are unnamed suggests that in
the original tale their named father had played the more important
part and that the initiative had been with him."[27]

Why must memory be blotted out in order for the father's seed
to be preserved, especially since his progeny, as the sole survivors
of Sodom, have the potential to act as a memorial to his act of
hospitality and of the righteousness that made it possible? Lot's
story proposes a model of filiation that is confused or lost even as
it is produced. His sons are not recognized by him as such; they are
named not by him but by his daughters, and they go on to found
lineages of their own. The first son's name, Mo-ab, is generally
taken to be the equivalent of the Hebrew *me'abh,* meaning "from
a father."[28] The child recalls not so much his *own* father as he does
paternity in general, the heritage of a father imperfectly remembered. The name as rem(a)inder of the hospitality event is both its
signifier and its traumatic, real residue.

Like a *symbolon,* the token gift traditionally given in memory
of the hospitality deed, each son acts as a reminder of the hospitality act only insofar as he is also a partially repressed or excised
remainder of it; the mythic chain (history, patriarchy) is necessarily
resumed in a leftover that can recall it only as expulsed from it. It
is interesting to remember that etymologically, the *symbolon* is a
token broken into two parts and retained by a brother and sister
so that if they should ever meet as strangers, they will be prevented
from committing incest; the bond that generates the *symbolon* is
simultaneously remembered and repressed by it.

Incest is similarly memorialized in Christian doctrine by the
symbolic structure of "affection," which only partially succeeds at
re-encoding and thereby neutralizing the scandalous prevalence of
incest among the earliest Israelite hosts. Augustine's reflections on
the importance of affection appear in the context of a discussion of

incest, whose value for the first patriarchs he acknowledges while at the same time arguing for its suppression:

> affection was given its right importance so that men, for whom so-
> cial harmony would be advantageous and honourable, should be
> bound together by ties of various relationships. The aim was that
> one man should not combine many relationships in his one self,
> but that those connections should be separated and spread among
> individuals, and that in this way they should help to bind social
> life more effectively by involving in their plurality a plurality of
> persons.[29]

The goal of "affection" is to sustain both the subjective integrity of the individual and the wholeness of the community. The proliferation of sexual roles is repudiated in the individual ("one man should not combine many relationships in his one self") in order to guarantee the proliferation of a desexualized "one-heartedness" constitutive of group identity. And yet incest, which scrambles the symbolic ordering of the family and of the community by undermining the signifier's capacity to fix the subject's place in the symbolic order (Lot's daughters are at once the mothers and the sisters of their children, he is their father and grandfather and yet retains no patriarchal relation to them), is nonetheless the material support without which the symbolic community could not survive, although it defines itself in opposition to it (recall Augustine's relegation of incest to the heathens excluded from the City of God).

In contrast to Augustine's reading, the evidence of the Genesis text suggests that the multiplicity of roles within the host—or what I have described as the host's "excess" with regard to the signifier—is absolutely fundamental to the successful completion of the hospitality act. Attempts to inscribe the hospitality participants within the circle of "affection" or the redemptive transubstantiation of the Word acknowledge only the imaginary component of the hospitality fantasy—the harmonious relation between host and guest, human and divine—and not its equally important "real" dimension: the essential discontinuity and lack of reciprocity interrupting the relation between host and guest, a (non)relation predicated upon a fundamental loss or renunciation. As the embodiments of that surplus or discontinuity, the female participants in the preceding hospitality narratives attest to the "extimate" agency of the extra-symbolic within the subject of hospitality, challenging the fantasy of unity inherent in Augustine's "one heart" community.

In Abraham's and Lot's hospitalities, religion names the intersection of two somewhat contradictory notions: the construction and continuation of a cultural articulation or linkage, and what Emmanuel Lévinas calls the "possible surplus in a society of equals," the excess or residue of that relation that always attests to its impossibility. As the one who exceeds the link as a symbolic continuity even while perpetuating it, woman allows for the coexistence of these seemingly divergent determinations.

In this sense it is the wives, more than their patriarch husbands, who will offer the most compelling model for Israel's relation to God. They prepare the way for one of the dominant metaphors of the prophetic books, the characterization of Israel's relation to God as that of a wife to a husband. If Israel is God's wife, is she also a hostess? As a wife and hostess, what relation would she have to the letter of the covenant? Following Sarah's example, Israel's task will be to embody the excess of the divine and not to pretend to approximate or know the divine will. But at the same time, she will also receive the word of God with disbelief, incredulity, and skepticism.

The scene of Israel's naming—Jacob's struggle with the angel in Genesis 32—gives an idea of just how far Israel has to go from any simple idea of "faith" in order to fulfill her covenantal status. Jacob's story is not a hospitality narrative in any strict sense of the term: it retains none of the ancient practices and conventions (the washing of feet, the ceremonial offer of food) still in evidence in Abraham's and Lot's hospitalities. But it has close structural affinities with their narratives in that in each case the patriarch confronts a disguised angel who, in the place of telling his name, issues a new name and a blessing concerning the "host's" status as a personification of the chosen people. The manner in which Jacob "receives" the divine emissary and his blessing is very much the inheritor of the scene of Sarah's blessing and also foretells the relation that Israel will have to the divine word:

> The same night he got up and took his two wives, his two maids, and his eleven children, and crossed the ford of the Jabbock. He took them and sent them across the stream, and likewise everything that he had. Jacob was left alone; and a man wrestled with

him until daybreak. When the man saw that he did not prevail against Jacob, he struck him on the hip socket; and Jacob's hip was put out of joint as he wrestled with him. Then he said, "Let me go, for the day is breaking." But Jacob said, "I will not let you go, unless you bless me." So he said to him, "What is your name?" And he said, "Jacob." Then the man said, "You shall no longer be called Jacob, but *Israel*, for you have striven with God and with humans, and have prevailed." Then Jacob asked him, "Please tell me your name." But he said, "Why is it that you ask my name?" And there he blessed him. So Jacob called the place Peniel, saying, "For I have seen God face to face, and yet my life is preserved." The sun rose upon him as he passed Penuel, limping because of his hip. Therefore to this day the Israelites do not eat the thigh muscle that is on the hip socket, because he struck Jacob on the hip socket at the thigh muscle. (Genesis 32:22–32)

The divided subjectivity implied in the hospitality act has been internalized as a fundamental tenet of the patriarchs' relation to God: and, through it, Israel's. The subject emerges "limping"—one foot in each world—from his encounter with the divine. He is damaged, but this flaw is also the token of his strength. The dual determination of his wounding at the hands of the angel is reflected in the dual meaning of *Israel*: "the one who strives with God" or "God strives." Jacob's narrative suggests that God's benevolent relation to his chosen people must also be an adversarial one, a struggle in which disbelief, challenge, and skeptical scrutiny play a greater role than faith. It is as though God and man must both struggle for the representation of Israel, which can only be personified in this tension. Israel is the "striving" between man and God, the discontinuity in their relation.

Welcoming Temptation: Hospitality and Sin in the Prophetic Books

Abraham's and Sarah's estrangement is actually essential to their relation with God, a sign of respect. Abraham's nomadism indexes his ability to pick up and follow God at a moment's notice, to present himself as ready and willing for an as yet unspecified ethical commitment. This episode shapes the articulation of the Israelites' duties in relation to the stranger in Leviticus: "When a stranger sojourns with you in your land, you shall not do him wrong. The stranger who sojourns with you shall be to you as the native among you, and you shall love him as yourself; for you were strangers in the land of Egypt" (19:35). The Israelites are enjoined not only to welcome the stranger among them, but even more importantly to welcome strangeness, to let strangeness be "native" to them.

The stranger is not simply "someone" who can be identified and then evaluated as good or bad, a difference that introduces itself into the same and so becomes defined in relation or in opposition to it. Rather, the stranger is something "native" to identity itself, the foreignness internal to the self-possessed subject. The stranger is a modality of being, or more properly of *being dispossessed:* being alienated from itself, estranged, unhoused, in transit, deprived of group and personal identity. The stranger identifies the Israelites themselves as the people of the covenant. It is the "roving" side of identity, its uprootedness.

In this sense the problematic of the stranger is also very closely bound up in the origins of hospitality in Genesis, since the first man to be named as a stranger in the Bible is also its first host: Abraham presents himself to the Hittites among whom he dwells as "a stranger *[ger]* and a sojourner among you" (Genesis 23:4). As God's elect servant, Abraham is perceptible within the Levitical injunction as its implied object, the "stranger" whom God loves above all others. Being a stranger is thus intimately related to the fact of chosenness, the privilege of being the object of God's steadfast love. But it is a bittersweet election, in which the bountiful possessions God promises his people will be obtained only through their complete dispossession and oppression: "The LORD said to Abram, 'Know this for certain, that your offspring shall be strangers *[gerim]* in a land that is not theirs, and shall be slaves there, and they shall be oppressed for four hundred years; but I will bring judgment on the nation that they serve, and afterward they shall come out with great possessions'" (Genesis 15:13–14).

Although they will be rescued from slavery, the Israelites will never *not* be strangers in the land in which they dwell. They will simply transfer their tenancy from one master or landlord to another, absolute and irreplaceable one, YHWH himself: "The land shall not be sold in perpetuity, for the land is mine; with me you are but strangers *[gerim]* and tenants" (Leviticus 25:23). In reference to this passage, Franz Rosenzweig writes:

In contrast to the history of other peoples, the earliest legends
about the tribe of the eternal people are not based on indigenous-
ness. Only the father of mankind sprang from the earth itself, and
even he only in a physical sense. But the father of Israel came from
the outside. His story, as it is told in the holy books, begins with
God's command to leave the land of his birth and go to a land God
will point out to him. Thus in the dawn of its earliest beginnings, as
well as later in the bright light of history, this people is a people in
exile, in the Egyptian exile and subsequently in that of Babylonia.
To the eternal people, home is never home in the sense of land, as
it is to the peoples of the world who plough the land and live and
thrive on it, until they have all but forgotten that being a people
means something besides being rooted in a land. The eternal people
has not been permitted to while away time in any home. It never
loses the untrammeled freedom of a wanderer who is more faithful
a knight to his country when he roams abroad, craving adventure
and yearning for the land he has left behind, than when he lives in
that land. In the most profound sense possible, this people has a
land of its own only in that it has a land it yearns for—a holy land.
And so even when it has a home, this people, in recurrent contrast
to all other peoples on earth, is not allowed full possession of that
home. It is only "a stranger and a sojourner." God tells it: "The
land is mine." The holiness of the land removed it from the people's
spontaneous reach while it could still reach out for it. This holiness
increases the longing for what is lost, to infinity, and so the people
can never be entirely at home in any other land.[30]

Exile is not just a historical moment but a state of being in which
one is never "at home." Whenever hospitality takes place, therefore, it necessarily serves as a reminder of its own impossibility. The Israelites are never truly "hosts"—that is, self-possessed
masters and proprietors—because they are always and above all
"strangers" enjoying the hospitality of God.

Abraham is a stranger who receives strangers, that is, a divided
subject who receives the divine presence or law as a stranger to it.
But although this estrangement and the aporetic relation to identity it implies is essential to this originary act of hospitality, after
Genesis it becomes problematic, and even treacherous. Although
the Israelites are enjoined to love the stranger, the price for doing
so is potentially invoking God's jealous rage and so becoming further estranged from him.

In subsequent books, the Bible attempts for the first time to define the stranger and to establish its place in Israel's faith. The demands of the Israelites' concrete political and historical situation call for a limitation of the infinite obligation to the stranger implied by the mythical narratives of Genesis. Israel is now a nation, defending itself against those who would want to destroy it. Honoring God now involves not only respecting his alterity and unknowability, but also maintaining the purity and inviolability of his chosen people. As a result, the boundaries between host and stranger, which in Genesis are fluid or even nonexistent, also become increasingly reified. In the books of the prophets, the host/stranger relationship of the Torah, whose terms were dictated not by nationality or faith but by a structural relation (between the sedentary and the transient, the housed and the homeless), is increasingly displaced by the oppositional pairing of Israelite and non-Israelite, which recasts the stranger specifically as a "stranger" to the Jewish faith.

Hospitality now marks a limit for religion as a cultural practice, at once essential to it and potentially menacing to its integrity or self-identity. The cultural imperative of self-preservation, and the increasingly ontological conception of Israel's identity that it mandates, gradually introduces an antinomial relationship between hospitality and monotheism. In the process, it also supplants the ethical value of a divided subject who openly "welcomes" the other, by supposing a subject who would be equal to the law. The formalization of the Israelite faith inaugurates an increasingly "political" conception of the Hebrews' religion, which runs counter to the articulation of religion in its "real" dimension, as the celebration of an irreducible excess or surplus.

What has changed between Genesis and later imperatives concerning the stranger is the advent of the formal law, in the form of the ten commandments of the covenant. The attempt to formalize the relation to the stranger coincides with the declaration of a new obligation, the demand for monotheist allegiance. In the Jewish count, the first commandment of the Decalogue reads: "I am the LORD your God, who brought you out of the land of Egypt, out of the house of slavery; you shall have no other Gods before me" (Exodus 20:2–3). That the declaration of monotheism includes a reference to the Egyptian exodus suggests that it is already complexly—if obscurely—related to hospitality. The liberation from Egypt is, among other things, a liberation from bad hospitality: the avenging of strangers held not as guests, but as slaves. God's rescue of the Israelites displaces or relocates the question of hospitality within the problematic of monotheism, his supremacy over the rival gods who reign in the homes of the Egyptian slave lords.

The Israelites' fealty is now due to a new master, who takes the strangers under his protection. But what then is their relation to hospitality? Are they now "guests" of God? Voluntary or involuntary "servants" in God's house? Strangers alien to his house, but residing in it? And to what extent are they themselves able to receive strangers? The second commandment further complicates the Israelites' relationship to the possibility of hospitality by demanding that their relation to "strangers" respect the boundaries established by monotheistic adherence:

> You shall not make for yourself an idol, whether in the form of anything that is in heaven above, or that is on the earth beneath, or that is in the water under the earth. You shall not bow down to them or worship them; for I the LORD your God am a jealous God, punishing children for the iniquity of the parents, to the third and fourth generation of those who reject me, but showing steadfast love to the thousandth generation of those who love me and keep my commandments. (20:4–6)

The qualification of God's steadfast love for his people as a "jealous" love lays the groundwork for one of the key metaphors of the Hebrew Bible, the extended conceit of Israel as the "wife" of God, bound in a monogamous marriage. But the trope of jealous love implies not only the sanctity of the marriage, but the threat of its violation: the possibility of alternate objects of desire with which God's bride might practice infidelity. When she makes idols or worships other gods, Israel not only violates the commandment against idolatry, she also contaminates the sanctity of their marriage with "adultery." As a result, a new avatar of the stranger emerges: the extramarital lover, a potential rival for God's love.

The two principal words for the stranger in Hebrew—*ger* and *zar*—access a rich semantic field that attests to the complexity and ambivalence of the stranger's position within the Israelite community. In the Torah, the word used almost exclusively to designate the stranger is *ger,* which denotes the alien, sojourner, or one passing through; in a more restricted sense it can name the resident alien living among the Israelites, or the convert to their faith.[31] But in the historical and prophetic books, the word *zar* almost entirely replaces *ger* as the dominant word for the stranger. *Zar* is a primary root meaning "to turn aside," especially for lodging; hence by implication the "stranger," "foreigner," or "alien." *Zar* is the stranger stranger, the more foreign or alien of the two. It also designates the more general category of foreignness, signifying "strange," "profane," or even "strange god." As an active participle it can mean "to commit adultery," "to go astray," or "to estrange," or may designate an "estranged thing or woman."[32]

After Genesis, the act of receiving strangers is increasingly bound up in the problem of idolatry. Any act of welcoming the stranger runs the risk that the "divine" visitor may turn out to be one of God's rivals, that the *zar* might be not only a "stranger," but a "strange god." The Deuteronomist draws upon this expanded sense of *zar* in his indictment of the Israelites, who betrayed YHWH's jealous love by consorting with idols: "They stirred him to jealousy with strange gods *[zarim];* with abominable practices they provoked him to anger. They sacrificed to demons which were no gods, to gods *[elohim]* they had never known" (32:16–17).

But the characterization of the Israelites' attitude toward the *zarim* as a prostration before "gods they had never known" could apply equally well to Abraham's hospitality, in spite of the different symbolic values of each act. The word *elohim* refers to the category of "gods" or "divinities" in general, but is especially used in reference to YHWH or his agents; in the plural, it often designates the angels God sends in his stead. What is celebrated in Abraham's case—he welcomes *elohim* he had never known, and never would know—is repudiated in the case of the wayward Israelites as a transgression of the commandment of monotheistic allegiance. Hence although the sinful tenor of Israel's adultery would seem to oppose it to the exalted holiness of Abraham's hospitality, they are structurally very similar.

In fact, the Babylonian Talmud infers from the story of Abraham that hospitality to strangers must take precedence even over an interview with God. When Abraham runs out to meet his guests, saying "My lord, if I find favor with you, do not pass by your servant," the rabbinic analysis holds that these words are addressed not to the leader of the three men, but to God himself. The

Midrash interprets this passage as if Abraham had been in conversation with God when the strangers arrived, and asked him to wait until he had welcomed the three visitors into his tent:

> Rab Judah said in Rab's name: Hospitality to wayfarers is greater than welcoming the presence of the *Shechinah* [the glory of God], for it is written, *And he said, My Lord, if now I have found favour in thy sight, pass not away,* etc. [Genesis 18:3; he thus left God, as it were, to attend to the wants of the three wayfarers. On this interpretation he was speaking to God, and begged Him to remain whilst he saw to his guests v. Shebu. 35b]. R. Eleazar said: Come and observe how the conduct of the Holy One, blessed be He, is not like that of mortals. The conduct of mortals [is such that] an inferior person cannot say to a greater man, Wait for me until I come to you; whereas in the case of the Holy One, blessed be He, it is written, *and he said, My Lord, if now I have found favor,* etc.[33]

The rabbis interpret the episode to mean not only that the guests are not God, but that YHWH himself must stand aside and wait for them to be served *before* him. In this sense, the perversion of the welcoming of strangers into idolatrous adultery is already implicit in the ethics of hospitality, in the divinity or sacredness that is imputed to the chance guest, whose identity must nonetheless remain unknown and unrecognized.

The many contradictory connotations of the word *zar* testify to the transgressive potential inherent in the act of welcoming, the "turning aside" from God that is introduced as a possibility whenever one turns the stranger away from his route to offer hospitality. For the adherent to monotheism, the ethics of hospitality now presents a double bind. The host must "know" that the guest he worships is (of) YHWH if he is to be absolutely free of this risk, and yet according to the aporetic logic of hospitality his act is compromised if he does. Idolatrous stranger-worship is not merely a blasphemous departure from the holy act of hospitality, therefore, but the logical limit with which it necessarily flirts.

Accordingly, Israel's "adultery" marks the problematic intersection of two competing discourses: the obligations of a "jealous" monotheism and the pluralist exigencies of the hospitality act itself, which presuppose the unknowability of the guest and a celebration of his alterity. But the figuration of Israel as an adulterous wife also suggests that her wayward relation to God's jealousy is uniquely "feminine." In this respect it is modeled on the femininity of the hostess, as the embodiment of an "unknowing" relation to guest and God alike. As the feminized "wife" of God, Israel is—like Sarah and Eve—"not all" made in the image of God, structurally inadequate or unequal to the exigencies of his law. But whereas the wife's misrecognition or disbelief of the law was an asset to Abraham's hospitality, it is revalued within the marriage metaphor as a crime against the husband.[34]

In each case, femininity is both internal to and in excess of the marriage bond. In the Genesis narratives, the host and hostess together constitute "one" (divided) subject of hospitality, who both embodies and is fundamentally heterogeneous with the covenant. The marriage bond allows this inadequation to the host's symbolic role to be acknowledged as a dimension of the subject that is not only accepted by the exigencies of the covenant, but even required by them. In contrast, the prophets' indictment of Israel's adulterous idolatry insists upon the incompatibility of Israel's femininity with her role as God's wife. Her femininity serves as a reminder that she is never fully adequate to the signifier that represents her as a subject of the covenant, and is therefore always in excess of or unequal to the integral identity summoned by the Decalogue's command for exclusive allegiance to God's jealous love. Within the relation of "jealous marriage," Israel is herself a stranger, a foreign presence uncannily internal—or "extimate"—to the holy union. The destructive potential of this revalued strangeness is implicit in the word *zar,* which designates not only the stranger or strange god, but the "adulteress" or "estranged woman"—in other words, the one who contaminates the jealous marriage with strangeness by welcoming strangers into it.

The fraught relationship between hospitality and monotheism exemplifies the tension between what Gilles Deleuze and Félix Guattari call "deterritorialization" and "reterritorialization."[35] They identify deterritorialization with the stateless nomad, whose uncontained dispersion and constant movement defy the territorial logic of the state, which seeks not only to circumscribe the subject's movements, but to map its identity within a closed system of signification. In contrast, the state apparatus is a force of reterritorialization, "striating" or mapping the smooth space of nomadism with signifying inscriptions. Religion represents one such reterritorialization, exemplified in their argument by monotheism as a "state" organization hostile to nomads. In the preceding development, we saw that hospitality is a force of deterritorialization operating within the territorialized space of religious practice, threatening to contaminate monotheist exclusivity with its polytheist "outside," just as the more codified practices of post-Exodus hospitality work to reterritorialize this "outside" by defining and delimiting the stranger, mapping value-laden significations (estranged, sinful, idolatrous) onto the "smooth" alterity of the stranger of Genesis, who defied recognition or naming. In this dialectic, "femininity" emerges as a site of de- and re-territorialization that is appropriated by many signifying systems, but has no ontological reality. The hostess as *zar* is the point of slippage between the logics of monotheist marriage and adulterous idolatry, a "nomadic operator" underscoring the permeability of the boundary between them.

Nomadism and Nationhood

YHWH's oft-repeated reminder that "you were strangers in Egypt" establishes Israel's fundamental estrangement as the source of her commitment to hospitality. But she also retains a problematic relationship to it, since this estrangement is something that is supposed to be—at least partially—put to rest. As the pre-history of the Israelite people, hospitality represents the "nomadism" at the core of covenantal subjectivity, an estranged wandering that is never fully contained in being subordinated to the laws of the covenant.

Deleuze and Guattari's argument offers insight into why the law itself is both hostile to, and haunted by, the specter of the nomadic. They point to the linguistic and genealogical interdependence of the Greek *nomos* (law) and *nomas* (nomad), both of which derive from the root *nemein*, "to distribute or divide."[36] Whereas the *nomos* entails distribution or division into categories (the function of the law as "categorical imperative"), the *nomas* implies distribution in space, a horizontal or metonymic dispersion without any ordering principle or organizing metaphor. But since the *nomos* as open space or dispersion is latent within the law as categorical imperative, the law of the *polis* or state, it always threatens to undo the divisions or "striations" that mark its dominion over the spaces and bodies it maps—and vice versa.

In the prophetic books, the nomadic lifestyle that is closely tied to the emergence of hospitality is treated in increasingly negative

terms, tainted by association with Israel's straying from God and
her many exiles. The seventh-century prophet Jeremiah evokes the
trappings of nomadic life in his condemnation of Israel's adulterous
lust, suggesting a close structural affinity between the two modes
of "errancy":

> How can you say, "I am not defiled, I have not gone after the
> Baals"? Look at your way in the valley; know what you have
> done—a restive young camel interlacing her tracks, a wild ass at
> home in the wilderness, in her heat sniffing the wind! Who can
> restrain her lust? None who seek her need weary themselves; in her
> month they will find her.
>   Keep your feet from going unshod and your throat from thirst.
>   But you said, "It is hopeless, for I have loved strangers [zarim],
> and after them I will go." (Jeremiah 2:20–25).

The erring in the desert that the Torah portrays as a scene of testing and judgment is now identified with straying away from God,
reliving the exile from which marriage was supposed to offer some
reprieve, that is recalled by every instance of receiving the stranger.[37] The stranger is not only a reminder of the exile, therefore,
but a potential cause of exile and alienation. In her wanderings,
is Israel like the "knight errant" of Rosenzweig's passage, who is
never more faithful to his home than when he roams abroad? Or,
in its "untrammeled freedom," does Israel's errantry risk lapsing
into errancy, a sinful straying away from God?

Abraham's hospitality comes before the articulation of the
Decalogue, at a time when the nomadic mores that shape his act
are not yet colored with the possibility of idolatry, precisely because they precede the imperative of monotheism. In this sense
hospitality also represents an "earlier" stage of the subject, which
comes both historically and logically before the law: the part of the
subject that is unequal to the law, that cannot be made consistent
with its designation. As a relic of the prehistory of the Israelites'
formalized faith, hospitality is at once its cause and its repressed remainder, the residue of an extralegal—or even illegal—subjectivity
that insists uncannily within the legal articulation of Israel's identity. The hospitality of the patriarchs, like all archaic hospitality,
involves an openness to and worshipping of the foreign that is only
partially negated by the advent of the Decalogue. In the logic of
Genesis, this divided attitude confirms not only the authenticity of

hospitality, but the faith in the name of which the host acts. But it also conflicts with the version of subjective identity proposed by the Decalogue, modeled on God's "jealous" integrity.

It is significant that the imperative to offer hospitality is not included in the Decalogue—either in the duties to God or in the duties to the neighbor—in spite of being the supreme embodiment of human holiness in Genesis. One way to explain this exclusion is that the purpose of the Decalogue is to demarcate, to draw boundaries between people, possessions, and lives. In the fullest sense of the term, it aims at a definition of the *property* of the subject, an articulation of personal identity as distinct from and limited by the property of the other. The delimitation of the personal property of God's subjects could even be seen as deriving directly from the commandment of monotheistic allegiance, insofar as the "jealous" integrity of God conditions the property and proper-ness of the human subjects made in his image. For God's "jealousy" is also the index of his oneness, as expressed by the Deuteronomical articulation of the key tenet of the Jewish faith: "Hear, Israel, the Lord our God, the Lord is one" (6:4). The Decalogue's postulation of God's jealous love demands an integral oneness of his subjects, as well: their undivided allegiance to him, but also the differentiation and untransferability of their personal property. The thrust of the Decalogue is to prevent the intermingling of distinct properties, the contamination of oneness with heterogeneity: on the one hand the violation of God's jealous love through idolatry, and on the other the contamination of distinct identities through the appropriation or intermingling of properties: goods, houses, and wives.

In this sense, hospitality is directly opposed to the tenor of the Decalogue: where the Decalogue forbids having other gods before YHWH, hospitality calls for the host's prostration before unknown divine guests; where the Decalogue forbids the appropriation of the neighbor's house and goods, the ethics of hospitality require the host to surrender his home, his household stores, and even his virgin daughters (Genesis 19:8) on his guest's behalf; where the Decalogue forbids adultery, the laws of hospitality dictate that the host offer up his female companion for sexual violation sooner than allow the same fate to befall his guest (Judges 19:21).

Adherence to the laws of hospitality thus risks inciting transgression of the covenant. In fact, the defining quality of the ethics of hospitality is its ability to suspend all other laws, to take prece-

dence over every other ethical obligation. This priority is all the
more menacing to the tenor of the Decalogue in that it takes the
form not of a direct blasphemy, but of a passive blurring of boundaries, a subtle dissolution of jurisdictions and properties.

Jacques Derrida identifies in the act of receiving a stranger a
necessary tension between the absolute and unconditional "Law"
of hospitality—an infinite hospitality that by definition cannot be
limited or subject to selection—and the conditional "laws" of hospitality, the particular imperatives, rules, or guidelines that act to
regulate, codify, or prescribe the manner of receiving the stranger
within any given culture.[38] The laws of hospitality serve to draw
boundaries and mark limits; but in so doing, they also transgress
the Law of hospitality. There is an antinomy inherent in their relation, because the two antagonistic terms are not symmetrical; the
absolute Law is above the laws. But it is therefore also *illegal,* in
the strictest sense of the term.

Hospitality marks the contested and uncertain boundary between nomadism and monotheist identity, the tension between
the hospitable tent and the exclusive temple: an opposition that is
complicated—as we will see—by the fact that the tent persists and
insists within the temple. The following pages will be devoted to
the examination of selected passages from the book of the sixth-
century prophet Ezekiel, who is writing in the period between the
establishment of the Jerusalem temple and its destruction in the
sixth century. In the temple period, which follows immediately
upon the Egyptian exodus, the wilderness exile is now "behind"
Israel, as well as immediately ahead of her as a troubled future.
I will argue that the prophets need to suppress certain aspects of
the Hebrew patriarchs' unconditional hospitality—to eliminate
the "worshipping" of foreignness and the fundamental unknowing that characterize it—in order to reconcile hospitality with the
duties of the Decalogue, and through it the demands of Israel's cultural identity as a monotheist nation.

As if to neutralize the "lawless" quality of absolute hospitality,
the prophets argue increasingly for the need to exclude categori-
cally all reception of strangers. Ezekiel is one of a number of prophetic authors who accuse Israel of adulterously receiving strangers
instead of her husband. But in this case, the charge of stranger-
worship extends not only to idolatry, but to the act of hospitality as
a reception of *human* strangers:

> You played the whore with the Egyptians, your lustful neighbors,
> multiplying your whoring, to provoke me to anger. Therefore I
> stretched out my hand against you, reduced your rations, and gave
> you up to the will of your enemies, the daughters of the Philistines,
> who were ashamed of your lewd behavior. You played the whore
> with the Assyrians, because you were insatiable; you played the
> whore with them, and still you were not satisfied. You multiplied
> your whoring with Chaldea, the land of merchants; and even with
> this you were not satisfied. . . . Adulterous wife, who receives
> strangers [zarim] instead of her husband! (Ezekiel 16:26–32)

"Receiving strangers" is now an act of adulterous sin in and of
itself and not just a subset or implied ancestry of the worship of
foreign idols. The reception of strangers is now a recognizable sin
and not simply an ambivalently coded but fundamentally sacred
act. The inclusion of "neighbors" and "foreigners" in the catalogue
of adulterous lovers translates the specific condemnation of the
worship of foreign gods into a more general denunciation of all
instances of consorting with or paying tribute to strangers. Any receptivity to the foreign, as such, now risks being determined as an
infidelity to Israel's divine husband. Ezekiel's text identifies three
possible connotations of "stranger love," all of which are closely
related: the welcoming of strangers (hospitality as such), the idolatrous worship of foreign gods, and engaging in acts of prostitution
(allowing strangers to "enter").

In her adulterous errancy, Israel surpasses even the crimes of
those sinners of legend, the Sodomites and the Samarians, whose
wickedness has already incurred God's wrath and led to their destruction. Ezekiel characterizes Israel and her traditional enemies
as feminized "sister cities," whose different sins are encapsulat-
ed in their manner of receiving strangers. Samaria's crime is the
idolatrous worship of foreign idols, in the form of the golden calf;
Sodom's is the mistreatment of guests. But Jerusalem's adulterous
reception of strangers makes the iniquity of her sinning "sisters"
pale in comparison:

> Your elder sister is Samaria, who lived with her daughters to the
> north of you; and your younger sister, who lived to the south of you,
> is Sodom with her daughters. You not only followed their ways,
> and acted according to their abominations; within a very little time
> you were more corrupt than they in all your ways. As I live, says

the Lord GOD, your sister Sodom and her daughters have not done as you and your daughters have done. This was the guilt of your sister Sodom: she and her daughters had pride, excess of food, and prosperous ease, but did not aid the poor and needy. They were haughty, and did abominable things before me; therefore I removed them when I saw it. Samaria has not committed half your sins; you have committed more abominations than they, and have made your sisters appear righteous by all the abominations that you have committed. Bear your disgrace, you also, for you have brought about for your sisters a more favorable judgment; because of your sins in which you acted more abominably than they, they are more in the right than you. (Ezekiel 16:46–52)

In singling out Jerusalem's sin, Ezekiel's analogy forces a reconsideration of the gesture of hospitality. For whereas Sodom's fault is withholding hospitality from needy strangers, Jerusalem's far more heinous crime is surrendering herself entirely to strangers in forgetfulness of God. The revaluation of their respective sins overturns the premium placed on hospitality in Genesis, submitting that it is worse to overzealously receive the stranger than to refuse to receive him at all.[39] Implicitly, the "turning aside" of the stranger from his route, and the gesture of turning aside from one's usual obligations to welcome him, leads to the perversion (literally, the "turning away") of Israel's faith, her straying from God.

The Tent and the Tabernacle

The ambivalent relation of the Israelite faith to its nomadic origins appears most powerfully in Ezekiel 23, where the prophet develops an extended conceit of the sister cities Samaria and Jerusalem as two adulterous "wives" of God. YHWH's relationship with Jerusalem proceeds in two stages, beginning when he discovers her as a young girl wandering the countryside, naked and abandoned. When she grows to puberty, he clothes her in finery, causes her beauty to be known and admired, and then joins with her in marriage. Jerusalem's adultery then violates this marriage to such a degree that God has no choice but to destroy her, surrendering her to the violence of her "lovers." Chapter 23 stages the ultimate affront to God's marriage by Jerusalem and her "sister," who violate the sanctity of God's house by wantonly receiving strangers there in an outrageous act of "hospitality."

YHWH gives the two sisters symbolic names: Oholah ("she has a tent") for Samaria, and Oholibah ("my tent is in her") for Jerusalem. Oholibah's name refers first of all to the fact that Jerusalem is supposed to be YHWH's sanctuary; the Hebrew word *ohel*—meaning "tent"—also names the tabernacle, the sanctuary within the temple building. Ezekiel's identification of the woman Jerusalem with the tabernacle is confirmed by his description of her garments, which are depicted throughout the book with words normally reserved exclusively for the furnishings of the tabernacle.[40]

But the tent as "tabernacle" names not only God's sanctuary, but also its idolatrous alternatives; the sisters have dedicated "tents" to idols, worshipping and sacrificing at foreign altars (Oholah's name, "she has a tent," is interpreted as a reference to the idolatrous sanctuary). The sisters' errant inclination to "pitch their tents" elsewhere than with God also attests to the nomadic heritage of the tent, its transience and openness to passersby. The word *ohel* is pitched at the contested border between monotheistic nationhood and nomadic dispersion, between the inviolate temple and the permeable tent. The tension between the two manifests itself as a crisis of hospitality: for whereas the tabernacle is off limits to strangers, the nomadic tent stands open in hospitable welcome of them. But when the temple tent inclines to hospitality, Ezekiel suggests, the results are disastrous:

> The Lord said to me: Mortal, will you judge Oholah and Oholibah? Then declare to them their abominable deeds. For they have committed adultery, and blood is on their hands; with their idols they have committed adultery; and they have even offered up to them for food the children whom they had borne to me. Moreover this they have done to me: they have defiled my sanctuary on the same day and profaned my sabbaths. For when they had slaughtered their children for their idols, on the same day they came into my sanctuary to profane it. This is what they did in my house.
>
> They even sent for men to come from far away, to whom a messenger was sent, and they came. For them you bathed yourself, painted your eyes, and decked yourself with ornaments; you sat on a stately couch, with a table spread before it on which you had placed my incense and my oil. The sound of a raucous multitude was around her, with many of the rabble brought in drunken from the wilderness; and they put bracelets on the arms of the women, and beautiful crowns upon their heads.

> Then I said, Ah, she is worn out with adulteries, but they carry
> on their sexual acts with her. For they have gone in to her, as one
> goes in to a whore. Thus they went in to Oholah and to Oholibah,
> wanton women. (Ezekiel 23:36–44)

The sisters' perversity manifests itself first of all as a monstrous act
of hospitality, a grotesque caricature of the host's prostration before the stranger: the food they offer to their "guests" is their own
sacrificed children. But the wayward women also embody the hospitable tent within the monotheist temple, whose openness invites
penetration and violation by strangers. Ezekiel's conceit establishes
an analogy between the women's "tents" and their sexual organs:[41]
he notes that the wanton sisters have been "entered" by strangers,
in the way that one "goes in to a whore." Jerusalem is both the
"tent" of God—his most intimate sanctuary—and at the same time
an uncannily "extimate" site within it, the foreignness camped at
the very heart—or, more accurately, the womb—of the temple.

The *ohel* as "tabernacle" is supposed to maintain the strict separation between native and foreign, pure and impure, and so prevent
the defiling and profanation of YHWH's sanctuary. But the fugitive, unfixed, nomadic quality of the *ohel* as "tent" dissolves this
rigidly demarcated topology, contaminating the sacred interior of
the temple with its polluted outside. As permeable "tents," God's
wanton brides invert the distinction between the proximate and the
distant, the proper and the improper: men who "come from afar"
are allowed to penetrate their "tents" and so enter the innermost
sanctum of the temple, at the same time that what is most near
and dear to God—his inviolable sanctuary—is rendered improper,
estranged, uncannily foreign. Jerusalem's "hospitable tent"—her
stranger-loving womb—is a repository of adulterous idolatry within the intimacy of the exclusive marriage.

But the conceit of Oholibah's contaminated womb as a hospitable tent is also a kind of inverted reference to Sarah, who stands
"there, in the tent *[ohel]*," barren, and whom God miraculously
provides with a child.[42] Sarah is in many respects the antithesis of
Oholibah, the inviolate woman bound in wedlock whose fertility
is dependent upon God's grace. But her blessing is due precisely
to having received strangers, a fact that links her to Oholibah as a
possible role model or predecessor. Because Sarah's tent serves to
welcome strangers, her "tent"—her inviolate but barren womb—is
blessed. And out of it springs "God's house," the nation of Israel.

The parallels between Sarah's and Oholibah's hospitable tents once again reveal hospitality to be ambivalently related to the demands of marital fidelity, since it is both the condition of possibility of the divine marriage—the source of the nation of Israel—and its repudiated prehistory. Sarah's and Abraham's tent is the original *ohel* of the Israelite faith, the model for the temple and the purity at its origins. But at the same time, the nomadic tent at the center of the established faith has to be repressed—or at least contained, anchored in place, walled in, and made inviolate to strangeness[43]— in order to preserve the sanctity it both makes possible and risks contaminating.

We have seen how Abraham's absolute hospitality could acquire an "illegal" or transgressive quality in relation to the terms of divine marriage, since as an ethics of limitless receptivity to strangers it would seem to justify the sinful "hospitalities" of the wayward Israelites. In the same way, the impregnation of Sarah's barren "tent" could be interpreted as a symbol both of the sanctity of the marriage and of its ultimate violation. The hospitality of Sarah and Abraham is the proof text for the *chuppah* or marriage canopy of the Jewish wedding, which is supposed to recall the nomadic tent that stood open on all sides in welcome of passersby.[44] But the tent's status as an emblem of marriage implies that it can be a prooftext for adultery as well, when the "tent" is entered by someone else. The "hospitable" disposition of the tent/woman represents the hinge between one signification and the other, the turning point between marriage and adultery, monotheism and its idolatrous subversion. In this sense, Sarah's miraculous impregnation through hospitality could be seen as paving the way for the adulterous debauchery depicted by Ezekiel, the sacred scene "giving birth" to its transgressive opposite.

One of the most interesting biblical responses to the potential dangers of this feminine receptivity to strangers is to dispense with the ethics of hospitality altogether, sacrificing the traditional obligation toward the stranger in favor of an absolute commitment to the purity of YHWH's temple that may even call for the stranger's annihilation. Most often these offensives are initiated by women— including some of the most famous heroines in the Hebrew Bible— who manipulate the conventions of hospitality to bring about the demise of foreign enemies. In the process, they act to redeem the potential evils of femininity by altering the meaning and effect of their reception of strangers, which now becomes an instrument in the service of YHWH's demand for exclusive allegiance.

The narrative that presents the most radical contrast to Sarah's and Oholibah's openness to strangers is the story of Jael in the Book of Judges, who kills the enemy leader Sisera in her tent (4:17–5:27). On the eve of Sisera's almost certain destruction of the poorly armed Israelite troops, the prophetess Deborah assures the Israelite commander that "the LORD will sell Sisera into the hand of a woman" (4:9). When all of Sisera's men are slain in battle, he escapes to the nearby tent of Jael and her husband—which, like Abraham's tent, is camped in the shade of an oak tree (4:11)— where Jael warmly greets him with the standard hospitality formula: "Turn aside, my lord, turn aside to me; have no fear" (4:18). What is most extraordinary about Jael's conduct—and most scandalous, from a Genesis perspective—is that she nurtures her guest's confidence and trust only to betray it, explicitly violating the laws and protocol of hospitality in order to advance the political cause favored by YHWH. After offering her guest milk and a covering of clothes, she goes to him while he is sleeping and drives a tent peg through his temple and into the ground. In recognition of her cold-blooded murder of her guest, Jael is celebrated by Deborah as the "most blessed of tent-dwelling women" (5:24), an homage that both recalls and displaces Sarah's status as the hitherto most blessed of tent-dwellers. Where Sarah is blessed for her nomadic hospitality, Jael is blessed for having anchored the nomadism and openness of stranger reception to the foundation of Yahwist fidelity. Significantly, Jael pins the warrior to the ground with exactly the same gesture used to pin a nomadic tent to its foundation: the fatal tent peg is made to anchor—and thereby transform and redeem—the potential for errancy inherent in hospitality.

A related episode of hospitable conversion is the story of the Jewish heroine Judith, who kills the enemy captain Holofernes in his tent; this time it is the host who is killed, but at the hands of a guest whose actions are vindicated by her chaste allegiance to YHWH (Judith 10–15). In both narratives, the heroine's sex plays an important role in the motivation and justification of her act. Since Jael is a married woman, the preservation of her "tent" from strangers has a dual significance. And Judith's widowed status confirms her reputation for chastity and reinforces her zealous love for YHWH and undivided dedication to his cause. Like Sarah,

Oholah, and Oholibah, Jael and Judith are not only "tent-dwelling women," but themselves sacred "tents," the sanctuaries of God. As such, the stranger-slaying heroines point to a tension within the ethics of hospitality: maintaining the inviolability of God's temple means violating the laws of hospitality in one's own tent, precisely because their tents are not properly speaking their "own," but rather YHWH's.

In each of these cases the antinomy between exclusive allegiance to God and the absolute obligation toward the stranger manifests itself as a tension between two hospitalities, two homes—that of the mortal host and that of God. For implicit in Ezekiel's text is a questioning of the limits of God's love of strangers. Does God owe consideration or protection to the "strangers" who enter his tent, the inviolable sanctuary of the monotheist faith? For Ezekiel at least, he does not. The hospitality of Oholah and Oholibah is all the more grotesque to the prophet in that it takes place in God's house: YHWH complains that "they have defiled *my* sanctuary . . . *my* house." "Their" hospitality is thus also uncannily "his"; the property they surrender is not their own, but that of a higher host. It is an expropriation of YHWH's most intimate property. Although the adulteress Jerusalem is the host (or rather hostess) who "receives" strangers, allowing them to enter her tent, God is the host whose sanctuary is violated by strangers: not only the foreign gods and "men from afar," but the one who is already a "stranger," the impure adulteress (adulteress, we will recall, being one of the possible meanings of *zar*).

Ezekiel's text stages the antinomy between the conditional laws of hospitality (the particular rules or interdictions pertaining to Israel's manner of receiving strangers) and the unconditional Law of hospitality, the infinite ethical obligation toward the stranger that characterizes the patriarchal hospitality of Genesis. But his portrayal of Jerusalem's ultimate sacrilege as an act of limitless hospitality also goes much further than other prophetic condemnations of hospitality. Beyond merely attacking the sinful consequences of stranger-worship, Ezekiel's text works to uproot entirely the ethical justification for an unconditional Law of hospitality.

By shifting the scene of hospitality to God's house, Ezekiel's conceit identifies for the first time an absolute limit beyond which hospitality must not go. The iniquity of the sisters' hospitality consists in having introduced strangers into the innermost sanctuary of YHWH's temple, the place that should be *beyond* hospitality. Ezekiel's YHWH expresses horror and outrage at what the host Abraham welcomes, the prospect of "men from afar" entering his house. Within an ethics of absolute hospitality, God is a bad host. But precisely because he is "God of Gods, Lord of lords," the supreme embodiment of a self-identity uncontaminated by estrangement, YHWH's absolute ipseity must be inhospitable to difference.

Taken to its logical conclusion, Ezekiel's text suggests that not offering hospitality—although it is technically a violation of the Levitical injunction to love the stranger—is actually synonymous with obeying a "higher" law, that of the sanctity of God's temple and the inviolability of his person. It poses monotheism and hospitality as two ethics that are not only at odds with one another, but even mutually exclusive: the ethics of hospitality demand a transgression of monotheism, just as the ethics of monotheism demand a transgression of hospitality.

Ezekiel's logic effects a double exclusion of hospitality. The ban on hospitality applies not only to God and his temple, but more importantly to the human host who acts in his name. The divided host cannot offer hospitality, precisely because "his" hospitality is never his own to offer. Taken to its logical conclusion, the argument of the passage suggests that the Israelite could never justify an offer of hospitality even in his "own" home because he is himself only a temple of God, a domicile into which strangers have been denied access, and not a subject capable of extending hospitality in his own name. Paradoxically, ipseity is thus both the precondition of an offer of hospitality and at the same time structurally inhospitable, intolerant of and incapable of hosting difference.

Ezekiel pushes this double bind to the limit in his foretelling of the destruction of the proud at the hands of strangers:

> Because your heart is proud and you have said, "I am a god; I sit in the seat of the gods, in the heart of the seas," yet you are but a mortal, and no god, though you compare your mind with the mind of a god. . . . I will bring strangers *[zarim]* against you, the most terrible of the nations; they shall draw their swords against the beauty of your wisdom and defile your splendor. They shall thrust you down to the Pit, and you shall die a violent death in the heart of the seas. Will you still say, "I am a god," in the presence of those who kill

you, though you are but mortal, and no god, in the hands of those who wound you? You shall die the death of the uncircumcised by the hand of foreigners [zarim]; for I have spoken, says the Lord GOD. (Ezekiel 28:2–10)

A vulnerability to strangers belies the prideful mortal's godlike pretensions, since it is wholly antithetical to the impervious ipseity of the divine. The degree of the stranger's penetration is thus directly proportional to the ungodliness of the Israelite "host" it infiltrates. Either one actually is a god—and thus inviolate to strangers, in the logic of chapter 23—or one is not a god, and thus so vulnerable to strangers as to suffer complete annihilation at their hands. Hence the stranger is both a motivating cause behind the violation of monotheistic allegiance and—indirectly—the means by which the crime is avenged, insofar as strangers end up annihilating those who are open to their advances. In threatening that the Israelites who welcome foreigners will now "die the death of the uncircumcised," Ezekiel both alludes to and revalues the original meaning of circumcision, as the act that marks the subject's inscription in YHWH's covenant. Receptiveness to strangers cancels the benefits of circumcision, since it suggests that the Israelites have come to embody the "excess" of God's covenant, the part "cut off."

These examples make the hospitality paradigm the frame for the covenant, both in the sense that it introduces it as an ethical parable (Genesis) and that it signals its ultimate dissolution, the breaking of the covenant by God. Hospitality is liminally related to the covenant, but precisely as its outer limit or moment of dismantling. The event of hospitality, as such, signals that the people are "outside" the law, *outlawed*. At the same time, it testifies to the existence of an "outside" of monotheism, an outside that is also a timeless exteriority of ethical obligation "before the law." Hence hospitality also puts the lie to a totalizing account of monotheism. As a self-equivalent "oneness" from which estrangement has been banished, monotheism is haunted by its uncanny remainder, the estrangement that belies its self-identity.

In conclusion, I would argue that hospitality is the place in monotheism where the idea of subjectivity as *identity*, and as modeled upon the integrity of the one God, is called into question and defined instead as a necessarily divided attitude. As we have seen, hospitality really demands a double infidelity. First, Israel's infidelity to her exclusive symbolic designation as the chosen people of

YHWH, implied in her receptive worship of the unknown stranger; but second, and more generally, the host's infidelity or inadequation to his symbolic status as master and patriarch, the "eminent personification" of identity. In both cases, the infidelity required by hospitality insists upon the impossibility of being adequately represented by the signifier that designates the patriarch—and the people he personifies—as the subject of YHWH's covenant. Both infidelities, moreover, are signaled by and modeled upon the hostess's infidelity, in the form of her excessive relation both to the host and to God and her incredulity concerning the divine promise. As the excess of the host's symbolic designation, the hostess insists upon the discontinuity inherent in the relation between the human and the divine, the unknowing or misrecognition that always characterizes the transmission of the divine signifier.

2. Cosmopolitan Hospitality and Secular Ethics: Kant Today

The last chapter developed an account of hospitality as an ethical act, an encounter with an unknown that dissolves subjective integrity. The hospitality relation embodies a specific tension, which I characterized as having the structure of an aporia or impossible limit. Etymologically, the host is the "master," the one who "eminently personifies" identity: not only his own identity, but that of the group in whose name he acts. But as an accidental encounter with what can be neither foreseen nor legislated, the act of hospitality privileges immanent relations over identity. In my analysis of Genesis hospitality, I argued that the ethics of hospitality embodied the challenge of sustaining relation as "impossible," without any sign or principle to regulate its immanence. It thus presents a double bind, since the host must both take in the stranger and respect its foreignness, name the stranger and acknowledge its illegibility.

The ethics of hospitality is thus in conflict with the "laws of hospitality" that have for so long dominated the mores of Western civilization, since these laws necessarily presuppose a positive representation of identity (personal, political, or communal) and a formalizable law regulating interpersonal relations (laws of exchange, laws of citizenship, or even the divine *logos* as guarantor of a transcendent equality). As Jacques Derrida suggests, there is an antinomial relation between the unconditional ethics of hospitality and the particular laws by which this ethics is rendered practicable.[1] In the last chapter, we saw how this antinomy played out in the conflict between the ethics of hospitality and the law of monotheism. Now I would like to consider how it shapes the secular domain of political life through an analysis of Immanuel Kant's 1795 essay "To Perpetual Peace: A Philosophical Sketch" *(Zum ewigen Frieden. Ein philosophischer Entwurf)*.

Although Kant's treatment of hospitality is limited to the domain of secular public life, the problem he confronts is really the counterpart or underside of the dilemma confronting the Hebrew prophets. In Kant's day, the reception of the stranger is no longer tinged with the possibility of idolatry, but instead is marked by an evacuation of the potentially sacred character of ancient hospitality, which makes the intermingling of host and guest increasingly susceptible to hostility or warfare. But like the prophets—and, later, Saint Augustine—Kant proposes to mitigate this potential for hostility by subordinating the hospitality relation to formalizable principles, submitting the stranger's fundamental illegibility to legislation so as to endure a universal and perpetual peace.

Hospitality as an "Unsocial Sociability"

Kant turns to the practice of hospitality as a way to put an end to the state of hostility and warfare that prevails among the reigning powers of Europe, and that threatens to dominate the emerging world scene over which they preside. Hospitality affords the possibility of securing a "perpetual peace" that is not dependent upon the particularities and contingencies of a political treaty, but is instead grounded in a universalizable moral maxim. But why hospitality? What is unusual about this choice is that the problem Kant is addressing is political hostility and warfare, generally motivated by the desire for territorial gains. As an archaic, intimately personal, and fundamentally religious relation, what can hospitality contribute to the solution of a problem whose parameters are modern, global, and secular?

In his appeal to hospitality, Kant is not advocating—as others have before him—a "Christian brotherhood" or other spiritual community that would unite a fundamentally hostile world. And yet the "perpetual peace" of Kant's title is not without religious overtones, especially given its allusion to the essay's most immediate source, l'Abbé de Saint-Pierre's *Vers la paix perpétuelle (Toward Perpetual Peace)*. Kant borrows from the world of religion not only the hospitality relation as such, but the particular formulation of it on which his own essay is based. But while Saint-Pierre's argument for hospitality draws explicitly upon Christian theological sources, Kant's is secular in form. His aim is to transpose the moral and ethical import of the hospitality relation into the language of everyday world citizenship, universalized to account for all peoples.

By emphasizing the importance of territorial disputes to the ongoing hostilities that define worldwide political relations, Kant stresses that the impediments to perpetual peace are not limited to the lack of brotherhood or charity among the peoples of the earth. The contemporary cosmopolitan stage, as Kant sees it, is defined by a tension between the inevitable dispersion and displacement of populations and the need for some kind of territorial sovereignty or national integrity. He thus translates into global terms the kind of aporia or impossible limit that the hospitality relation has traditionally been called upon to address: how can one integrate the foreigner and at the same time respect it as foreign? How can one behave ethically toward the stranger without risking the dispossession or destruction of one's own identity? These familiar aporias hover in the background of Kant's essay, with the difference that the stakes of identity are now considered in national terms. The situation he confronts is not unlike that faced by the newly formed nation of Israel, for whom the demands of nationhood stood in an antinomial relation to the demands of absolute or unconditional hospitality.[2]

But the purview of Kant's treatise introduces a further complication, because the context he considers is "cosmopolitan" [weltbürgerlich] rather than people-specific. As a result, the hospitality paradigm required to address its ills needs to be grounded in principles that are valid for all peoples, and not specific to a single cultural or religious context.

According to Kant, the goal of perpetual peace requires dual action where the ethics of hospitality are concerned. On the one hand, guests or visitors seeking entry into foreign territory must not abuse or violate the sovereignty of the "host" nations they visit. But on the other, host nations must not impede the movement of visitors across their territory. This is because national sovereignty must respect the limitations imposed by the finite surface of the globe, which prevents the infinite dispersion of populations and thus necessitates a peaceable sharing and cohabitation of the earth.[3] These two fundamental tenets both acknowledge and maintain a tension between the open and the closed, the sovereign and the common, what is allowed the individual and what is allowed the nation-state.

Nonetheless, the argument that ultimately leads to Kant's formulation of a universal hospitality imperative is grounded in the premise that the sovereignty of nations must be respected and guaranteed in order for world peace to reign perpetual. Kant posits that "No independent nation, be it large or small, may be acquired by another nation by inheritance, exchange, purchase or gift" (108). However, it is not immediately obvious what this premise would have to offer an ethics of hospitality, since it seems to depart from, or even run counter to, everything that the practice traditionally implies: the blurring of borders, the circulation of property through exchange or gift-giving, and the surrender of the host's home, personal effects, or even his dependents to the guest.

In a dense and highly suggestive passage, Kant translates his quintessentially Enlightenment view of sovereignty into the archaic language of hospitable practice:

> A nation is not (like the ground on which it is located) a *possession (patrimonium)*. It is a society of men whom no one other than the nation itself can command or dispose of. Since, *like a tree, each nation has its own roots,* to incorporate it into another nation as a graft, *denies its existence as a moral person, turns it into a thing,* and thus contradicts the concept of the original contract, without which a people *[Volk]* has no rights. Everyone is aware of the danger that this purported right of acquisition by the *marriage of nations* to one another—a custom unknown in other parts of the world—has brought to Europe, even in the most recent times. It is a new form of industry, in which influence is increased without expending energy, and territorial possessions are extended merely by establishing *family alliances.* (108, my emphases)

Whether intentionally or not, this citation revisits all of the major *topoi* of archaic hospitality tradition. The image of the nation as a living "tree" recalls the most ancient and widely recognized symbol of hospitality, the oak tree, which welcomes and offers protection to guests on the condition that it not be cut down or otherwise violated by them. But here the image of the tree is also a figure for the sovereignty of the nation, in relation to which many of the other essential components of the traditional hospitality relation will now be construed as potentially menacing. While the paradigm of nationhood appeals to the underpinnings of hospitality, it also revises them in view of a new context, which requires a reconsideration of the archaic relation and its key terms.

From Marriage to Common Law

For Kant, the moral right of the nation not to be acquired by or "married" to other nations is founded on the premise that the nation is not a *patrimonium* or possession, but a "moral person." But although the illegitimate proprietor in this case is presumably the hostile force seeking to annex the nation to its territory, Kant's language suggests that the nation's resistance to appropriation by a new master is itself grounded in or reflective of the nation's emancipation with regard even to its "own" master. One of the most tenacious obstacles to perpetual peace, in Kant's view, is the presumed ability of the monarch or autocratic head of state to enlist the nation in war, as though it were "his" possession to dispose of at whim (113). If the *patrimonium* names the possession of a "father" or patriarch, Kant's argument is deeply critical of paternity or patriarchy as legitimate bases for political authority. He accuses the monarch who engages his populace in hostilities of falsely acting on behalf of a nation that he cannot pretend either to embody or to rightfully dispose of as his "own."

Kant's imagery, therefore, both recalls and rejects the origins of nationhood in archaic, clan-based practices of social exchange, including and in particular the hospitality relation. The leader of the nation is no longer the host-patriarch who embodies the group identity of the people in whose name he acts (Abraham), whose role both authorizes and requires him to dispose of his possessions—his *patrimonium*—in the name of hospitality. As a "moral person," the nation is itself possessed of an innate *right* to self-determination and self-proprietorship, and thereby exempt from the powers of disposal traditionally imputed to the host-patriarch as the embodiment of group identity. Indeed, to presume such a right of disposal over the nation now would be construed as a violation of hospitality rather than an extension of it, an uprooting of the hospitable "tree" of the nation that would endanger its moral integrity.

Two consequences result where hospitality is concerned. First, the position of the "host" as such is downplayed or even eliminated. "The nation" receives visitors, but not through the intermediary of a designated host, either private or public. Second, in relation to the monarch, the nation's status is no longer that of a dependent child or wife answering to a patriarchal "father," but rather that of an "emancipated woman" whose rights cannot be compromised or altered through forced "marriage" to a master. The nation is liberated from the chattelhood that marriage traditionally imposed upon it, becoming a "moral person" and not a "thing."

In dismissing the figural "marriage" of nations as an archaic form of ownership incompatible with republican rights, Kant thus reverses a long tradition that holds marriage—both the sexual union and its political counterpart—to be essential to the growth and preservation of the social group. Exogamous marriage is traditionally the basis for reciprocal and mutually beneficial intersocietal relations, since it both allows for the extension and consolidation of the group and at the same time preserves its vitality through the incorporation of new members. And as we saw in the introduction and chapter 1, marriage is also a major mode of receiving the stranger, a key avatar of the hospitality relation.

Kant's account of national autonomy attempts to dispense with its repudiated past, the origins of nationhood in "marital" alliances. Nations are now distinct, separate entities; there is no intermixing, no "marriage," and no possibility for intimate liaisons between them. The rationale for this argument is that Kant associates hostility with the intermingling of nations, insofar as hostility is natural to living in close proximity:

> The state of peace among men living in close proximity is not the natural state *(status naturalis)*; instead, the natural state is one of war, which does not just consist in open hostilities, but also in the constant and enduring threat of them. The state of peace must therefore be *established,* for the suspension of hostilities does not provide the security of peace, and unless this security is pledged by one neighbor to another (which can happen only in a state of *lawfulness*), the latter, from whom such security has been requested, can treat the former as an enemy. (111, emphases in original)

In the place of "marriages" between nations, what is needed is a relationship between "neighbors" recognizing a common law. Within the logic of Kant's argument, lawlessness is synonymous with hostility, since it means the absence of any convention, formula, or other common measure to regulate the relation of one stranger *(hostis)* to another. The identification of proximate nations as "neighbors," on the other hand, implies that each must have a legal status, a legal personhood that allows it to act as a partner in a pledge.

The first premise of Kant's argument is thus the sovereignty of the nation in relation to hostile "guests" or invaders. The second concerns the treatment due the nonhostile guest, the alien who seeks to enter or pass through a foreign territory.

In this second instance Kant defines hospitality as "the right of an alien [eines Fremdlings] not to be treated as an enemy [nicht feindelig behandelt zu werden] upon his arrival in another's country" (118). In linking hospitality to rights and to legal status, Kant is drawing upon a Roman legal tradition that expands the meaning of hostis—the stranger or guest—to include the legal representation of the person as a subject of rights. The primitive idea signified by the Latin hostis is that of equality by compensation; hostis is the one who compensates a gift with a countergift. But in Roman law, hostis comes to designate the resident foreigner who is invested with the same rights as Roman citizens, "equal" under the law.[4]

Kant mandates that the stranger be received as a guest (a legal alien or visitor possessed of rights, a hostis) and not as an enemy. However, the two notions are inseparable both historically and logically. The Latin hostis means "enemy" as well as "guest," and is also the linguistic root of "hostility," which developed when relations between individuals or clans were supplanted by a general distinction between those internal and external to the city-state.[5] Hostility is thus contained within the notion of the guest as an implicit possibility. Indeed, the tendency of one meaning to bleed into the other is precisely what Kant identifies as a problem: hosts are hostile to their guests, or guests abuse their status to exploit their hosts. In essence, Kant's solution is to eliminate one meaning of hostis, to prohibit that the alien be considered as an enemy. But while laudable, this solution is also highly problematic, for reasons inherent to the fundamental structure of the hospitality relation.

Hospitality after Religion

Traditionally, the only thing that keeps the hospitality relation from mutating into hostility is the presence of some potent symbolic structure to account for and valorize the risk the host assumes in welcoming a stranger. In the absence of such a structure, the unregulated and indeterminate coexistence that is so fundamental to the hospitality relationship becomes particularly precarious and menacing. As we saw in the introduction, this problem is most commonly resolved through recourse to religion. In most religious traditions, the guest is invested with a sacred quality and is often considered to be a god in disguise. Were the guest not potentially divine, or at least an occasion to gain recognition by the divine, the dispossession of the host by the stranger would simply imply the annihilation—and not the realization—of his identity. But such a paradigm is clearly inadequate to regulate relations between strangers in the international climate to which Kant addresses himself, where the immediate and intimate contact with an unknown stranger that traditionally qualifies hospitality has increasingly been supplanted by the more impersonal relationships involved in trade, travel, and warfare.

"Cosmopolitan" life introduces a further complication, one that affects the security and well-being of hosts and guests alike. The finite quality of the globe and the need for world trade necessitates increased exploration and travel, with all of its attendant risks. For example, Kant laments the "barbarian" tribes who attack commercial ships, thereby endangering the safety of travelers and impeding their access to distant parts of the earth (119). But the thirst of nations—and developed nations in particular—for resources and objects of trade has also changed the face of hospitable relations. "Host" countries are now more than ever susceptible to plundering by "guests" who may be interested not merely in traversing their territory but in stripping it of its natural resources. Thus although the explicit aim of Kant's essay is to show how hospitality can contribute to the creation of a perpetual peace, its argument is nonetheless driven by an implicit recognition of a crisis of ancient hospitality, which has enormous implications for resource management, the relationship between local and global economies, and the displacement of populations.

The changing face of foreign travel, Kant suggests, exerts very particular pressures upon relations between hosts and strangers. And these pressures are no longer adequately addressed by the old paradigm of hospitality, which valorizes the stranger's difference by construing him as potentially divine. In his study of cosmopolitan hospitality, René Schérer notes that Columbus and Cortez were also taken to be gods by the native hosts who received them.[6] In these cases, as in so many others, the sacred laws of hospitality were insufficient to protect indigenous hosts from the complete dispossession and annihilation of their cultures. The ravages of colonialism point to the limitations of the archaic system of hospitality, which in mandating that every visitor be received as a god potentially results in the host nation's surrender of its entire civilization. Implicitly, the paradigm that views the stranger as a god is no longer viable. The world's dominant economic powers for the most part no longer subscribe to this view, and those who do suffer from it at the hands of "modern" men whose visits are no more than opportunities for abuse and plundering.[7]

This crisis of hospitality is thus implicitly a problem of secularization. In the global arena, religion has become too fragmented and idiosyncratic to function as a legitimate guide for human relations. How then can the modern nation, state, or people assure the favorable treatment of the stranger-guest while at the same time guarding against its potential for hostile appropriation or pillaging? The crisis Kant confronts is that the increasing secularization of human relations has simultaneously left no place for the other to be considered as divine and at the same time provided no compelling new reason for the host to accept the dispossession of his identity that hospitality implies.

Underwriting Kant's treatise, therefore, is the premise that the emerging cosmopolitan nature of human relations requires a cosmopolitan approach to hospitality, grounded in universalizable maxims rather than in local mores or indigenous religious practices. But what new paradigm can replace the old one? And how can the potential for hostility the guest implies be welcomed into the intimacy of the home?

Kant's solution is twofold. First, he imputes a "right of visit" *(Besuchrecht)* to the guest, which casts his hospitable reception as a legislatable, universal right rather than as an appeal to the goodwill of the host. The "right of visit," says Kant, intuitively belongs to all men as inhabitants of a finite globe. But it is distinct from the right to inhabit a country on a temporary or permanent basis, which is not covered by the moral imperative and remains subject to the laws and mores of individual nations:

> He [the foreigner] may request the *right* to be a *permanent visitor* (which would require a special, charitable agreement to make him a fellow inhabitant for a certain period), but the right to visit, to associate, belongs to all men by virtue of their common ownership of the earth's surface; for since the earth is a globe, they cannot scat-

ter themselves infinitely, but must, finally, tolerate living in close proximity, because originally no one had a greater right to any region of the earth than anyone else. (118, emphasis in original)

In relation to archaic practice, the first consequence of Kant's proposal is to remove the hospitality relation from the status of an obligation, relocating it within the field of rights. The host country does not have to do anything *for* the visitor, it only has to allow him the right of visit and contract not to view him as an enemy.

The form of Kant's imperative is thus negative or empty, rather than a positive prescription. In this sense "Perpetual Peace" draws directly upon the analysis of the moral law in the *Critique of Practical Reason* and its guidelines for formulating maxims. In Kant's reasoning, one cannot actually mandate that states, or for that matter even individuals, be compelled to keep and maintain guests; to do so would be antithetical to the design of the categorical imperative. As a result, proximate cohabitation is now conceived as a matter to be taken up within the framework of religious or civic benevolence—what Kant calls "charitable agreements"—and not the domain of the moral imperative. In fact, as Schérer observes, Kant's treatise could even be interpreted as explicitly allowing for the turning out or turning away of guests.[8] He notes that the wording of Kant's hospitality imperative borrows from Latin and French the neologism *Hospitalität,* rather than the German *Gastlichkeit,* which is derived from the root word *Gast* ("guest"). In Kant's particular use of the term, *Hospitalität* designates a right of visit *(Besuchrecht),* but not of welcoming or receiving *(Gastrecht).*[9]

The second major consequence of Kant's proposal is thus the displacement or even elimination of hospitality as such in favor of an impersonal relation that does not involve the penetration of the guest into the intimacy of the dwelling. In fact, he treats with some disdain the notion that hospitality should involve *actually* taking strangers into one's home and proposes instead that it consist in an affirmation of world commerce *(Verkehr),* as a "non-pathological relation among men."

Commerce and the Devaluation of Nomadic Life

Before exploring in detail Kant's notion of "commerce," we should situate it within the broader context of his understanding of cosmopolitanism. When Kant characterizes his hospitality imperative as "cosmopolitan," he means that it must be valid for all peoples and not limited to a single cultural or religious context. His formulation of hospitality is thus driven by the attempt to replace such "pathological" spurs for social interaction as religion or ethnicity with bases for action that are moral, and therefore universalizable. In his 1784 essay "Idea for a Universal History with a Cosmopolitan Intent," which precedes "To Perpetual Peace" by eleven years, Kant invents the notion of "unsocial sociability" *(ungesellige Geselligkeit)* to describe how a "pathologically enforced agreement" among men could be transformed into a society and, eventually, into a "moral whole":

> *The means that nature uses to bring about the development of all of man's capacities is the* **antagonism** *among them in society, as far as in the end this antagonism is the cause of law-governed order in society.* In this context, I understand antagonism to mean men's *unsocial sociability,* i.e., their tendency to enter into society, combined, however, with a thoroughgoing resistance that constantly threatens to sunder this society. This capacity for social existence is clearly embedded in human nature. Man has a propensity for *living in society,* for in that state he feels himself to be more than man, i.e., feels himself to be more than the development of his natural capacities. He also has, however, a great tendency to isolate himself, for he finds in himself the unsociable characteristic of wanting everything to go according to his own desires, and he therefore anticipates resistance everywhere, just as he knows about himself that for his part he tends to resist others. Now this resistance awakens all of man's powers, brings him to overcome his tendency towards laziness, and, driven by his desire for honor, power, or property, to secure status among his fellows, whom he neither *suffers,* nor *withdraws from.* In this way, the first true steps from barbarism to culture, in which the unique social worth of man consists, now occur, all man's talents are gradually developed, his taste is cultured, and through progressive enlightenment he begins to establish a way of thinking that can in time transform the crude natural capacity for moral discrimination into definite practical principles and thus transform the *pathologically* enforced agreement into a society and, finally, into a *moral* whole.[10]

Man's propensity for "living in society" is a merely pathological basis for social organization because it feeds on his innate hunger for social contact and for participating in a whole that is larger than himself. It becomes a moral construct only when it is based on the rational cultivation of culture by men of discernment and taste, who do not "need" social life, but rather choose it rationally as an improvement upon a barbarous state. Although "unsocial sociability" derives from the antagonism between the egoism within every individual and the propensity to be among others, it is nonetheless the very condition of fruitful society.

Schérer rightly suggests that the same principle is at the core of Kant's formulation of hospitality, insofar as the particular society in which man lives—in other words, the communities he adheres to voluntarily or participates in by virtue of his religion, ethnicity, or regional provenance—is itself superseded by a universal cosmopolitanism sustained by moral maxims rather than by pathological affinities between men living in proximity to one another.[11]

But another important parallel between the two different essays is that in each case, the movement from "barbarism" to cosmopolitan society entails a gradual repression of what has traditionally come under the purview of hospitality. Both of Kant's "cosmopolitan" projects eschew not only the intimate interpersonal contact that is so crucial to ancient hospitality, but also the nomadic lifestyle that first gave it meaning and relevance as an ethical practice. In the continuation of the passage just cited from "Idea for a Universal History," Kant makes clear that

> without those characteristics of unsociability—which are in themselves quite unworthy of being loved and from which arises the resistance that every man must necessarily encounter in pursuing his self-seeking pretensions—man would live as an Arcadian shepherd, in perfect concord, contentment, and mutual love, and all talents would lie eternally dormant in their seed; men docile as the sheep they tend would hardly invest their existence with any worth greater than that of cattle; and as to the purpose behind man's creation, his rational nature, there would remain a void. Thus, thanks be to nature for the incompatibility, for the distasteful, competitive vanity, for the insatiable desire to possess and also to rule. (32)

When contrasted with the ideal of "unsocial sociability," the pastoral image of the nomadic shepherd living in "mutual love" with his fellow man is transformed into an emblem of rude existence, severed from the rational purpose behind man's creation.

If Kant sees in the distasteful proclivity of man for property ownership, vain competition, and incompatibility with his fellow men the ultimate redemption of human society as a moral undertaking, it is because of the value he places on the separation of peoples from one another, in contrast with the tendency of nomadic society to constitute itself as an amorphous, undifferentiated "flock" in which the talents of individual men are no more developed than those of the animals they tend. While the borders between people were fluid or even unidentifiable in nomadic life, Kant's vision of cosmopolitan society is concerned less with maintaining this fluidity than with establishing the need for clearer divisions between men. This need appears most obviously in the premium placed on "unsocial sociability" and its attendant propensity for isolation, but also in the more general call for rationally constructed societies in which the unity of the social body or state is predicated upon this fundamental separation between individuals.

As we return to "Perpetual Peace," we can now see how Kant's championing of "unsocial sociability" both shapes the articulation of his hospitality imperative and at the same time hints at some of the underlying assumptions on which it is predicated: a rejection of nomadic life and close interpersonal relations in favor of a society based on formal, moral maxims, in which the social link is regulated through impersonal means. Earlier we saw that respect for the sovereignty and autonomy of individual nations is the first tenet of Kant's proposal for perpetual peace. But as the essay unfolds, this fundamental tenet is paradoxically combined with the right to roam the world unimpeded, which appears at first glance to be the very essence of the nomadic lifestyle that the "Idea for a Universal History" frowns upon. For Kant, however, there is an implicit distinction between the two models, since modern hospitality must respond to the fact that communities are situated within a global economy, which requires men to leave the security of their homes in pursuit of resources and opportunities. Kant's vision of cosmopolitan hospitality is thus underwritten by the notion of commerce.

Curiously, though, the importance of commerce is in turn rooted in the premise of common ownership of the surface of the earth:

> Uninhabitable parts of this surface—the sea and deserts—separate these communities, and yet ships and camels (the *ship* of the desert) make it possible to approach one another across these unowned regions, and the right to the earth's surface that belongs in common to the totality of men makes commerce possible. (118)

Commerce very literally follows in the tracks (the camel tracks, in this case) of nomadic travel, the privileged scene of hospitality in the ancient world. But although the notion of common ownership of the earth's surface would seem to take nomadism as its model, the reverse turns out to be true. Ultimately, the notion of commerce evokes the nomadic heritage of hospitality only in order to repress and supplant it.

Although the hospitality imperative is rooted in the idea that men must disperse themselves across the globe, Kant is suspicious of such dispersal in its nomadic form. His solution is to supplant nomadism as such with commerce, a regulated mode of visitation that happens under the sign of a principle or rule. Commerce spans the "uninhabitable" parts of the earth, the places that were former-ly the domain of nomads with no developed system of commercial relations: and thus, for Kant, no true society. What distinguishes this civilized, cosmopolitan hospitality from its "barbarous" pre-decessor is that commerce guarantees peaceable interpersonal re-lations by making way for the formulation of laws, which are the indispensable precondition of a moral society. But because it tran-scends the jurisdiction of national laws, commerce also represents the promise of a moral society that is global in scope, held together by its adherence to a "cosmopolitan constitution": "In this way distant parts of the world can establish with one another peaceful relations that will eventually become matters of public law, and the human race can gradually be brought closer and closer to a cosmo-politan constitution *(weltbürgerliche Verfassung)*" (118).

Paradoxically, though, the expanding horizon of lawfulness—which is moving humanity "closer and closer to a cosmopolitan constitution"—corresponds to a reduction of actual closeness, the uncomfortable proximity that Kant associates with hostility. As the most recognizable manifestation of this proximate intermingling, nomadism is now associated with some of the most egregious vio-lations of the cosmopolitan hospitality imperative and is even seen as promoting a climate of unpredictable and irrational violence. Kant criticizes the most legendarily hospitable of peoples, the Arab Bedouins, of using their knowledge of the desert to plunder travel-ing merchants (118), and even argues that the nomadic lifestyle of the hunter almost inevitably inclines to warfare:

> Of all forms of life, the *life of the hunter* is without doubt most contrary to a civilized constitution, for, having to live separately, families soon become estranged and, dispersed as they become in immense forests, also soon become enemies, for each requires

a great deal of room in order to provide for its nourishment and clothing. (122n, emphasis in original)

Like the "Arcadian shepherd" considered earlier, the roving hunter represents a premoral form of social existence. But whereas the shepherd lives in a slothful state of contentment in which "mutual love" is assured through the sacrifice of man's rational development, the hunter illustrates the Kantian thesis that the natural state of strangers living in close proximity is war (111).

Nomadic hunting is viable as a lifestyle only when there is enough space for men not to come into contact with one another, since when they do they have no rational means to assure the acquisition of food and resources without warfare. In contrast, commerce makes the most of a finite globe, in which men necessarily live near to one another. It maintains a certain distance or separation within the reality of proximate cohabitation, allowing for the "unsocial sociability" that is the precondition both of rational human development and of any possible moral society. Kant's indictment of nomadic life is thus based on the underlying premise that hostility—and, more generally, "inhospitableness"—results from inappropriate modes of intermingling: in other words, those that are not consistent with or regulated by the rational principles of commerce.

Kant identifies two kinds of inhospitableness [Unwirtbarkeit], both of which concern relations of commerce. Unwirtbarkeit is derived from the root word Wirt, meaning "host"—in particular, the innkeeper or master of the home. The first class of offenders against hospitality is thus made up of hosts who abuse their guests. In particular, Kant condemns the Unwirtbarkeit of the "savage" peoples who endanger visitors to their lands, or who impede the safe passage of commercial ships. Beyond merely perpetrating violence and hostility, the seriousness of their action for Kant is that it stands in the way of a general opening-up of the world.

Of course, a potential drawback to Kant's call for greater hospitableness on the part of "savage" hosts in particular is that it exposes indigenous peoples to the menaces of imperialism, and to dispossession at the hands of guests whose motives may be less than friendly. The potential menace to indigenous hosts extends beyond the hostile subjugation dramatized by colonialism, to the more subtle ideological imperialism of economic progress, and in particular the move toward a market-based economy in which trade is mediated through the impersonal and abstract medium of money. Commerce is not as neutral or impersonal as it appears, since it necessarily takes place in relation to some standard of exchange and thus favors those peoples who deal in an abstract unit of trade like money, and whose social relations are submitted to some kind of legal standard. Kant certainly does not seem to view the "barbarous" peoples mentioned earlier as agents of commercial exchange. They are represented more as an extension of their flocks than as true proprietors, having renounced rational development to live "like the sheep they tend." Schérer even argues that Kant's imperative unequivocally privileges a Eurocentric model, since it reserves for Europeans the ability to initiate commercial ties with indigenous peoples, opening the way to a "cosmopolitan constitution."

Sovereignty and Ownership

Of course, Kant himself is not unaware of this potential problem. His vision of cosmopolitan hospitality does not naively extol the virtues of commerce, but it does recognize that a certain responsibility comes with the capacity to initiate commercial relations; a society cannot call itself morally founded if it merely exploits this capacity with no view to its potential consequences. Hence the second kind of inhospitableness applies to guests who abuse their hosts, which Kant identifies with the Europeans who pillage overseas countries. Their violation of hospitality consists not only in plundering their hosts, but in overstaying their visit, and thereby violating the premises of the *Besuchrecht*:

> the injustice that they display towards foreign lands and peoples (which is the same as *conquering* them), is terrifying. When discovered, America, the lands occupied by the blacks, the Spice Islands, the Cape, etc., were regarded as lands belonging to no one because their inhabitants were counted for nothing. Foreign soldiers were imported into East India under the pretext of merely establishing economic relations, and with them came subjection of the natives, incitement of various nations to widespread wars among themselves, famine, rebellion, treachery, and the entire litany of evils that can afflict the human race.
>
> China and Japan, which have had experience with such guests,

have therefore wisely restricted contact with them. China only per-
mits contact with a single European people, the Dutch, whom they
nonetheless exclude as if they were prisoners from associating with
the natives. (119)

These "guests" violate the principle of hospitableness by choosing
not to recognize the sovereignty of the nations they visit, which
they deem to have no rightful owners simply because they do not
credit their inhabitants as people. But Kant suggests that this violation of hospitality might also be a direct or indirect consequence
of the foreign guests' dedication to commerce when he admits that
this is "the inhospitable conduct of civilized nations in our part of
the world, especially commercial ones" (119). Although commerce
is the cornerstone of Kant's proposal for perpetual peace, it also
brings with it the potential for a new kind of hostility: namely, the
dismissal or devaluation of indigenous peoples who, because they
do not engage in commerce, are counted as worthless.

Although he acknowledges this discrediting as a potential problem, Kant is nonetheless guilty of the same attitude where nomadic
peoples are concerned. When he calls the desert regions traversed
by commercial trade "uninhabitable," he suggests that the nomads
who dwell there are not real inhabitants. How then does this gesture differ from the "inhospitable" dismissal of indigenous peoples
by foreign discoverers? Implicitly, the difference for Kant is that
these nomadic desert dwellers have not constituted themselves as
an independent nation, or even as a defined people—they resist or
are unable to assume an identity as a sovereign nation. And if they
are not a sovereign nation, then they are not truly hosts, either.
By implication, therefore, their dispossession by foreign "guests"
is not a real violation of hospitality. And if the desert—as an "uninhabitable" region—is further characterized as "unowned," it is
because the men who dwell there are not sufficiently developed as
creatures of reason to assume ownership or claim property as the
expression of their individual talents and capacities. Since nomads
do not even conceive of themselves as the owners or proprietors of
the region in which they live, they have no "moral society," and
therefore cannot be parties either to commercial transactions or to
a legal constitution. And since the "unsocial" cultivation of man's
talents is what gives human life its worth, we can infer that within
the terms of Kant's argument these nomadic peoples are not only
ignorant of commerce, but themselves without value.

This is why the impulse to own property—or what Kant described earlier as "the insatiable desire to possess and also to rule"—is so important to his argument. The notion that the earth is commonly owned does not imply for Kant, as it does for Proudhon, that "property is theft."[12] In fact, common ownership of the surface of the earth is paradoxically the *corollary* of property ownership, as one of the defining features of rational human life. As we have seen, Kant's "moral society" is predicated upon the rational participation of men whose "unsocial sociability" expresses itself through the desire to possess. The fact that we live in a world that is both finite and global makes commerce inevitable, because men can survive only by buying and selling goods. As a result, natural right dictates that commercially motivated passage through foreign terrains cannot be prevented.

However, the fact that the "right of visit" is predicated on commerce also works to restrict certain kinds of mobility. Kant makes clear that the *Besuchrecht* does not allow for a generalized or unconditional visitation of foreign lands, since natural right "extends the right to hospitality—i.e., the privilege of aliens to enter—only so far as makes attempts at commerce with native inhabitants possible" (118). Since they have not yet acceded to commercial relations, "barbaric" and nomadic peoples would presumably get no protection of the free mobility that has traditionally been the basis of their lifestyles.

These limits or contradictions within the positing of the right to hospitality point to an interesting tension within Kant's argument. In the long citation quoted above, Kant suggests that the offense of the second kind of inhospitableness is that "guests" use the promise of establishing economic relations merely as a pretext for generalized plundering; in other words, they seem to violate the intent or purpose of economic relations, and to exploit it for other ends. However, the relationship between impersonal commerce and the possibility of unjust treatment or plunder is not as contingent as Kant seems to suppose. The fact that the relationship between two peoples is regulated by economics means that the potential for one party to be "counted for nothing" is already in place. If everything has a price, then everything can be bought and sold: and also devalued or discounted. Moreover, economy or commerce as a measure of human development already entails a devaluation of human life, since a life has value or worth only to the extent that it conforms to principles and laws, common measures that allow its currency to be evaluated and traded upon. The German word translated as "commerce," *Verkehr,* designates relations between men, in addition to the circulation of goods and services. But in the societal economy Kant envisions, the two connotations are virtually indistinguishable; relations between men are reduced to the regulated circulation of goods and services that becomes their ordering principle.

Freedom as Dependence on Law

Kant's "cure" for inhospitableness not only reformulates the question of ethics, therefore, but arguably displaces ethics as such as the framework for hospitable interaction. In submitting the hospitality relationship to impersonal transactions of commerce, Kant attempts to eliminate not only the exploitation of hosts and guests, but the ethics he charges with having made that exploitation possible in the first place. René Schérer notes that in the popular eighteenth-century stories of noble savages who welcome discoverers with open arms, Kant is interested not so much in the generosity of the hosts, but in the greed of the guests so willing to take advantage of it.[13] Although Kant's hospitality paradigm may reduce the visitor or guest to a "common measure," he would probably argue that this is better than crediting him with a divinity he then abuses, only to colonize, plunder, and submit to his dominion another population. But at the same time, we can see all too well from our postcolonial perspective that commerce has not offered any real solution to this dilemma: not only in the sense that it participates in colonization, but in the sense that the traffic in persons and goods does little to foster a cosmopolitan sensibility and everything to submit cosmopolitan relations to the reign of exchange value.

Although relations of commerce may diminish the dissymmetry between host and guest, they arguably erase hospitality in the same gesture, by devalorizing the contingent, unforeseeable, or irreducible nature of the encounter between strangers. Kant's proposal potentially limits the exploitation of hosts, but at the same time devalues the real interpersonal risk and potential for personal loss that generosity—and the sacred debt economy in which it takes part—embraces as a necessary part of hospitality.

Earlier I argued that Kant's reformulation of the ethics of hospitality as a legislatable "right of visit" results in the elimination of the uncanny dimension of the stranger's penetration into the master's "own" home, and thus a reduction of the personal risk traditionally assumed by the participants in the hospitality act. Hospitality is no longer an obligation, and neither the host nor the guest are any longer indebted to one another. The separation of the host from his most intimate property that qualifies archaic hospitality is here dispensed with altogether in favor of an impersonal relation from which even the "relationality" has been eliminated. Hospitality no longer implies a risk on my part, but neither is it "mine" to give: it is an impersonal *right* of the guest, requiring him to be treated according to principles and maxims that departicularize the host/guest relation by replacing it with law. The hospitality relation is the object of an abstract, legal contract between cosmopolitan citizens of the world, rather than an immanent, accidental encounter with what can be neither foreseen nor legislated.

Kant's attempt to delimit the intermingling and interpenetration of host and guest is thus inseparable from the question of sovereignty: not only the national sovereignty protected by the first article of the treatise, but the sovereignty of the person as a free, autonomous agent. In fact, the sovereignty of the nation is actually modeled on the privative quality of the individual moral person. Kant notes that the idea of international right presupposes the existence of many separate, independent, adjoining nations that resist "melding into a universal monarchy" (124); but that resistance inheres in each nation's status as a "moral person." In the preceding section, Kant's remarks suggest that the condition of making the ground commonly accessible to all is not only respecting the personhood of the nation, but reifying the sovereignty of the individual as one whose property and space are no longer subject to expropriation by the guest. Although the stranger is entitled to traverse the "commonly owned surface of the earth," he must do so without disrupting or violating the demarcated personal spaces of autonomous individuals.

Kant's view of law is predicated upon the distinctions between discrete persons, whose rights are to be protected with discretionary divisions that uphold their proprietorship of their own persons. But what is at stake in this formulation is not only an elimination of personal risk, but a refusal to risk the person: in other words, to challenge the ideal of privative personhood on which this notion of sovereignty is based. Kant's conception of hospitality privileges ontology over ethics, identity over relation. It is precisely what Emmanuel Lévinas challenges when he critiques the premium placed on ontology in the metaphysical tradition, which reduces the relation to the Other to being no more than the limit or horizon of the "I's" possibilities, bringing its alterity under the dominion of the same. For Lévinas, the "I" necessarily lives in a world where it is "chez soi," but ethics is an unforeseen encounter with a "stranger" who calls this *chez soi* into question. The conflict between Kant's and Lévinas's different views of hospitality hinges upon the role of law, which takes the place of ethics as a penetration of the other into the *chez soi* of identity and therefore allows the autonomy of personhood to be remain unchallenged.

In his linking of sovereignty, property ownership, and the inviolability of the person as the three indispensable axes of the hospitality imperative, Kant is one of the founding fathers of the modern notion of the "emancipated" subject, which Jean-François Lyotard defines as the ideal of a subject who would be his "own proprietor," or what Descartes describes as the "master and possessor" of his own person.[14] Lyotard argues that since the writing of Paul and Augustine, emancipation implies leaving behind an alienated condition—subservience to a master, to God, or to the Law—and moving toward the horizon of a *jouissance du propre,* or a state of self-enfranchisement.[15] But this movement really reaches its apex in the Enlightenment, which embodies what Lyotard calls the "modern occidental ideal of emancipation": namely, to "bring about an emancipation without an other" (F15/E9). The autonomous, emancipated view of the subject disavows the ethical implication of the other in one's "own" subjectivity: its aim is to give *oneself* the law, and thereby cancel any debt to the other:

> the modern Western ideal of emancipation confuses all the orders. Its aim is to attain a full possession of knowledge, will, and feeling. *To give oneself* the rule of knowledge, the law of willing and the control of affections. To be emancipated is to owe nothing to anyone but oneself: to be absolved of any debt to the other. (F7/E3–4, translation modified)

The same logic is at work in Kant's account of hospitality as an "insociable sociability," which in precluding the interpenetration of host and guest denies the involvement of the other in "my" moral subjectivity. What it supposes is precisely an "emancipation without other," one that justifies itself in relation to legal rights as the guarantor of subjective sovereignty. And since the sovereign nations whose citizens visit one another are the impersonal, abstract corollaries of the autonomous persons who make up their citizenry, Lyotard's formulation invites a further question: how can this sovereignty have an "other"?

As the "right of visit" replaces more intimate dealings between strangers, and the impersonal domain of public commerce supplants the private home as the favored arena of hospitality, the preeminent avatar of the guest is now the businessman or tourist, the world traveler whose commerce with foreign lands is based on monetary transactions. In the commercially mediated relationship between host and guest, all debts are paid in full: one side offers enjoyment of its resources, attractions, or space, while the other side compensates this offering with a payment set in accordance with an impersonal standard of exchange. But at the same time, this new avatar of the guest is defined in opposition to other potential modalities of the stranger/guest, including the supplicant, the nomad, and the alien seeking asylum. As we saw earlier, Kant extends hospitable protection only to visits for the purpose of initiating commerce with the inhabitants, and not, for example, to the need for protection, or to flight from deplorable living conditions in one's own country.

In its reification of the self-other dichotomy, this "emancipation without other" rejects not only the other, but the irreducibility within identity itself. The supposition of the individual's integrity or unity ultimately results in a reduction of this individuality to a common measure. As a result, Kant's insistence on the emancipation or autonomy of the individual is both in tension with and dependent upon the "commerce" in identity that hospitality implies, which is based on the legal conception of the subject as "equal" in the eyes of the law. Paradoxically, then, the freedom and autonomy of all parties to the cosmopolitan constitution consists in their shared dependence on a common source of legislation:

> The sole established constitution that follows from the idea *[Idee]* of an original contract, the one on which all of a nation's just *[rechtliche]* legislation must be based, is republican. For, first, it accords with the principles of the *freedom* of the members of a society (as men), second, it accords with the principles of the *dependence* of

everyone on a single, common [source of] legislation (as subjects), and third, it accords with the law of the equality of them all (as citizens). (112, emphases in original)

The subject's adequation to his legislative identity is what allows for the "commerce" between equals, who put themselves into circulation as exchangeable counterparts.

Juliet Flower MacCannell has argued that Kant's projection of a rationally legislated moral society is predicated upon the supposition that the ego is identical in all men. Kant's rational self, or what she calls the "Kantian ego," is "supposed to be the final base on which the 'general self' of humanity [is] formed," the only possible basis for a synthetic unity:

> For Kant, the ego is itself the producer of all objectivity: the bewildering variety of sense impressions reduces their heterogeneity to formal unity only because the ego is a unit that makes synthesis possible. As Georg Simmel put it, the Kantian ego is "the ultimate legislator of the cognizing mind" because it is the only unshakable basis on which the world could be known. The world is thus a production of the ego, which is identical in all men, and it is the basis of their homogeneity.[16]

If what Kant calls the "dependence of everyone on a common legislation" is able to be conceived as a source of freedom, it is because this "neutral" legislation is articulated not as an external law or demand, but as a moral maxim that is coextensive with the moral subject, a projection of the unified ego as a rational agent. However, this means that "cosmopolitan society" is conceivable only as a multiplication of the ego, a homogeneous multitude whose "common law" is a product of narcissistic projection. According to MacCannell,

> civil, urban society . . . resembles Freud's 'artificial' group, crowded with egos and their individual projections . . . Its imaginary, which permits identification with the other (the ideal of sympathy, pity) and the exchange of places with the other (the ideal of democracy), results in "freedom"—but of a limited or special sort: the freedom to set an exchange value on oneself. With brotherly love and industrial capitalism, he/she/it—all free to sell their labor-power—are technically commodities. (32)

In its reciprocal exchangeability with all others, the ego assumes the status of a universal "value," which loses nothing in its exchange or duplication. But as MacCannell observes, this "odd form of potential self-determination" goes hand in hand with the "betrayal of personhood," as something in excess of or irreducible to economy (32).

The sovereign nations who are parties to the universal "cosmopolitan constitution" are the corollaries of these homogenous, identical egos. Kant notes that three levels of rights must be addressed by any cosmopolitan constitution: the civil rights of men in a nation; the rights of nations in relation to one another; and the rights of world citizenship, "insofar as men and nations stand in mutually influential relations as citizens of a universal nation of men" (112n). These three levels of rights are completely interdependent, insofar as the rights pertaining to man as an individual model the other levels of rights. But this interdependence of national and personal rights is both the strength and the weakness of Kant's formulation of hospitality. If the sovereignty of the nation is guaranteed by the sovereignty of the person, then a threat to the unity or homogeneity of the nation is implicitly a threat to the person. In other words, when the foreigner does not simply "visit" (with) the nation, but takes up residence there, he represents a risk not only to the nation's sovereignty, but to the integrity or unity of the host's personhood.

Hostility

Earlier we saw how Kant's account of hospitality as a means to perpetual peace acknowledges and takes as its point of departure the fundamental hostility that characterizes relations between men. Kant proposes that this hostility should be neutralized through a moral maxim that would effectively erase one aspect of the guest's determination as *hostis*—his potential to be regarded as an enemy. His treatise represents a historical shift in the social and philosophical conception of the hospitality relationship, which since the Enlightenment has tended increasingly to diminish or erase the fundamental inequality between host and guest, "resolving" its conflictual nature by neutralizing the undecidable limit between proper and improper. In Kant's case, this resolution takes the form of an absorption of the stranger's foreignness under a common measure: a legal designation or principle of economic exchange.

Beyond its obvious idealism, why has this model failed to gain prominence as a viable means of legislating relations and assuring peace between strangers? I would argue that the potential for hostility that Kant identifies must be understood not simply as the "natural" state among men, but as a direct consequence of the very principle of impersonal equality on which Kant's conception of hospitality is predicated. As I noted earlier, *hostis*—the word that signals the formal reversibility of host and guest—is also the linguistic root of "hostility." Because it leaves no place for an understanding of the other as different, the reversible model of hospitality can never acknowledge the stranger's alterity as anything other than a menace, a traumatic resurgence of difference within an equality that is always only apparent. Paradoxically, then, hostility results not so much from the *refusal* to grant equality to the stranger, but from the failure to appreciate the uncanny difference internal to a supposedly reversible relation. Because it leaves no place for this excess, a relation of "equality" can only receive alterity as something monstrous, an uncanny aberration at the heart of the same.

From a psychological point of view, Sigmund Freud suggests that the relation between self and other is anything but hospitable. In his essay "Thoughts for the Times on War and Death," Freud suggests that the unconscious is "murderously inclined toward the stranger" and if not adequately checked by a strong symbolic order will try to annihilate the other in its difference.[17] While Kant represents hostility as a symptom of the "pre-social," as something prior to the cultivation of rational principles, Freud suggests that the development and autonomy of the individual ego is the impetus for hostility. This characterization goes to the heart of what is at stake in hospitality. As I noted earlier, the undecidability concerning the "property" of the host that is so fundamental to the hospitality relationship becomes particularly precarious and menacing in the absence of a potent symbolic structure to account for and valorize the dispossession of the host's "identity" through contact with a stranger.

Of course, Kant's solution to this dilemma is to eliminate opportunities for this potentially menacing dispossession to take place, and thus maintain the host's sovereignty as inviolable. But although his aim in so doing is to eliminate the potential for hostility, the reification of the boundaries between the host and the stranger risks having the opposite effect. For whether or not it is literally welcomed into the home, the stranger's alterity presents a challenge to the "sameness" of the ego. In the face of this uncanny threat, Kant's "empty" legislation of the host/guest relationship provides no strong safeguards, since it does not constitute a symbolic order in any real sense. Because the societal relation is conceived as a reflection of the ego's unity, it can never be more than imaginary. And as MacCannell suggests, its imaginary quality inclines to—rather than mitigates—hostility toward the unfamiliar:

> Freud has noted, in his "Group Psychology," that the "artificial" group of today is fundamentally structured by the inherent appeal in a mirroring of the "same." If *die Masse* is not formed by a set of relations to others (a kinship network at whose purely provisional center stands an ego defined solely on the basis of those relations— "I am wife, son, nephew," etc.) it can only be formed by an extension or expansion of the ego, multiplied and endlessly reflected. Indeed, Freud tells us, the group demands uniformity, conformity, so that the ego at its root finds no opposition. So it is that a major feature of this group is, not surprisingly, an aversion to sexual difference (the root paradigm for difference-in-relation). . . . The positive quality in this is evident: not only is one freed from irrational ties (sexual, familial) but one is apparently freed from divisiveness. But this seeming liberation is only for the few: in fact, Freud reports (and our contemporary experience corroborates), such groups have an unlimited aggressive narcissism: though they brook no internal difference, they also know only aggression and hostility against those who are not fully incorporated into it—outsiders, non-believers, other groups, and, of course, the other sex. (34)

This "imaginary" societal pact implies a narcissistic reduction of the other to a reflection of myself, a reflection that is called "reasonable" by virtue of its homogeneity. But should it cease to accord with this image, it risks being determined as unreasonable, irrational, or—in Kant's language—barbaric. Hence the hated outsider is menacing not only for the potential hostility it represents, but because it gives form to something within the host: his own inadequation to the "eminent personification" of identity that autonomous subjectivity is supposed to imply.

In theorizing the intersubjective topology of the unconscious, Freud refutes the Enlightenment ideal of a free, autonomous self with evidence of the other's structural implication in the subject's "own" identity. Freud's work suggests that what Lyotard called the modern ideal of an "emancipation without other" is the embodiment not only of a historical shift in the philosophical treatment of ethics, but of a subjective stance predicated upon a disavowal of the other. Hence the reification of the self-other dichotomy implied in autonomous "emancipation" corresponds to—and even arises from—a rejection of that part of the other that is in me. Its unconscious effects may be extremely volatile, since the disavowal of what is foreign or alien within identity can easily lead to a rejection of the alien other.

The recent treatment of the "guest workers" *(Gastarbeiter)* in Germany offers a vivid dramatization of this dilemma, one that illustrates the potentially negative fallout of the "cosmopolitan" hospitality paradigm. The reception of foreigners for purposes of commerce is exactly the kind of situation that Kant's hospitality imperative was designed to address, and in this case the legal designation of the foreigner as a "guest" worker even appears to allude to this heritage, by casting his relation to the host country in terms of hospitality. But as the tragic persecution of these legal workers by German nationalists made clear, hosts are not always eager to accept the challenge to their identity that such a welcoming necessarily implies, whether or not it happens under the impersonal auspices of commerce and labor law. The characterization of these strangers as "guests" did not prevent them from being subjected to hostility, and even death.

While we can assume that the torture and murder of guest workers is not at all in the spirit of Kant's treatise, the "indifferent," impersonal, and commerce-based reception of the foreigner certainly is. And although this mode of reception is supposed to eliminate potentially "pathological" relationships between individuals, by replacing them with a formal, universally applicable code of behavior, the treatment of the guest workers suggests how this code might actually give rise to hostility in its very impersonality. For within a commerce-based model, the stranger is not welcomed in its alterity, but in view of economies of relation. In this sense, the Kantian heritage is more ubiquitous in modern hospitality than the quaint utopianism of its purely philosophical presentation would seem to suggest.

Although the "cosmopolitan constitution" may have failed to

materialize in the form that Kant envisioned, its underlying tenets are fully in evidence in the most dominant modern avatar of the hospitality relation, the so-called hospitality industry of tourism. In the Kantian paradigm, the hotel replaces the home as the privileged site of hospitality, since it corresponds to the reduction of hospitality to the impersonal, economic logic of the "right of visit." Ultimately, the hospitality-as-hotel relation is not as benevolent or as respectful of the stranger as it pretends to be, since the welcoming is always only provisional and contingent upon the "guest" having something to offer in exchange.

As we saw earlier, the corollary of Kant's "right of visit" as a right of tourism or visitation is the rejection of the stranger's right to asylum or permanent residence. The hospitality imperative specifies that the integration of the foreigner into the community remains the province of religious or civic benevolence and has nothing to do with the moral imperative. The foreigner's ability to pass through or do commerce within the country is therefore obtained only at the cost of losing his ability to settle there or be integrated into the nation as an equal citizen. If Germany has an abundance of "guest" workers, it is in part because German law prohibits the extension of citizenship to those of non-German blood; hence the prevalence of "hospitality" as a political or commercial relation actually betrays a fundamental unease with and exclusion of the stranger.

This is why the situation of the nomad or displaced person, as someone who is not covered by the "right of visit" as a right merely to pass through or conduct commerce on sovereign ground, is so crucial to understanding the logic of Kant's hospitality imperative. In European history, the ugly underside of this formally neutral logic has surfaced time and again in the treatment of the Jews, a displaced people whose repeated attempts to gain asylum in foreign lands read like a material history of the hospitality relation and its vicissitudes, and attest to the ethical limitations of some of its many permutations. Since they have historically been errant and without a homeland, the Jewish people are in a sense the archetypal guests of European history, alternately viewed as welcome additions to their host countries' social and economic life and as hostile strangers. Although they were almost always "welcomed" into their host countries for economic reasons, Jews were made into objects of persecution and hatred when conditions changed, and even blamed for the degeneration or erosion of the host culture that received them.

In an essay on fascist discourse, Mladen Dolar cites a passage from Hitler's autobiography, *Mein Kampf,* which recounts a chance meeting with a stranger that played a critical role in the development of the future Führer's anti-Semitic "philosophy":

> As I was walking one day in the city center of Vienna, I stumbled upon an apparition *(eine Erscheinung)* dressed in a huge kaftan, with long black curls. My first thought was, "is it a Jew?"... In secret, I observed this man very attentively; but the longer I stared at this foreign visage and the more carefully I examined its every trait, the more this first question transformed itself in my mind into another: "is it a German?"[18]

In his analysis of this episode, Dolar notes that the nefarious quality of the Jew consists for Hitler in his ability to monstrously conjoin the same and the different, to be at once "German" and "Jew":

> Looking at this apparition, Hitler asks himself "is it a Jew," as if he were asking whether the man were an Englishman, a Frenchman, or a Slovene. His question doesn't differ in the least from these other questions, but it differs in its result: there is no interest in asking whether an Englishman is a German. The Jew alone is this strange being who allows for the transformation of the first question into the second.[19]

The resident alien is the most uncanny of foreigners, since it represents the introduction of something foreign not only into the homeland, but into identity itself. His reception betrays the most anxious dimension of the hospitality relationship, the crisis of what is properly "mine," the limits of what Lévinas calls the "at homeness" of identity.

Hitler's nascent hatred toward the resident Jew would seem to be squarely addressed by the second premise of Kant's proposal for perpetual peace, which holds that the guest must not be treated as an enemy. However, the nature of Hitler's awakening of hostility in this scene allows us to see the potential limitations of this formula. The Jew is not an enemy in the way that an Englishman or a Russian is an enemy, since the menace he embodies is that of an alien element *within* German identity, rather than the alien outside in opposition to which Germany defines itself on the global stage, and that is mutually exclusive with its national identity. If only Hitler's initial question had been "is it an Israeli?" and not "is it a Jew?" the impact of the scene would have been very different. Here, though, the fact that the Jew is potentially less identifiable as an enemy than a foreign national paradoxically makes him more susceptible to hostility, since the menace he represents is not the prospect of foreign domination or warfare, but a more insidious and uncanny threat that strikes at the heart of German identity itself. As a guest who is truly displaced, without any sovereign homeland to reference or return to, the Jew represents an elusive insinuation of the foreign into the most intimate recesses of the German national identity.

Of course, Kant's proposed hospitality imperative both anticipates and circumvents this potential for uncanny hostility by eliminating the possibility of proximate cohabitation altogether. As we will recall, Kant makes clear that the "right of visit" in no way entails a right of asylum, or even allows foreigners to take up residence in the host country. But although this caveat potentially preempts the possibility for hostility latent in the intermingling of hosts and guests, its broader implications are unsettling. Must the nomad "convert" to the host culture to gain entrance to the city?

European Nihilism: From Kant to Nietzsche

The treatment of European Jewry is an exemplary case where the overlap of cosmopolitanism and hospitality is concerned, since the tension between cosmopolitanism and nomadic life is in many ways analogous to the tension between Christian universalism and Judaism. Kant even suggests a possible parallel between them when, in his indictment of the hostility inherent in nomadic life, he notes approvingly that the early Church made the conversion of heathens to Christianity contingent upon their renunciation of the nomadic lifestyle (122n). In order not to be perceived as potentially hostile, the nomadic must be defined, named, and fixed in place: either resolutely constituted as foreign, or converted to and inscribed within the same. The historic conflict between Jews and the Christian nations in which they have taken up residence is particularly illustrative of this dilemma, since it turns in part on the antinomy between two visions of hospitality. Judaism has always had a different relationship to hospitality than Christianity, since for most of its history the relationship of the host to the stranger has not been bound up in the defense of city or national borders. Conversely, Christianity has in many ways served as a model for national or state hospitality, anticipating the legislative treatment of the stranger with its emphasis on the conversion or incorporation of the guest—its inscription within the parameters of Christian identity—over its alterity or strangeness.

Augustine's *City of God,* especially when read as a theological apology for the political authority of the Holy Roman Empire, marks an important break with the Hebraic hospitality considered in chapter 1 because it makes possible what Judaic law forbids: the incarnation of divine law within a human institution. Augustine's formulation of hospitality marks a transition from the "religious" to the "political," in the particular sense in which Emmanuel Lévinas understands these terms. He defines politics as "the realization of the struggle for recognition," which tends toward equality and reciprocity; religion, on the other hand, is "the possible surplus in a society of equals."[20] Augustine's notion of hospitality eliminates the fundamental inadequation of the human host to the law in favor of a reversible relation between a host and a guest made equal in the spirit of the law as "values" of Christ.

Christian "eucharistic hospitality"—the doctrinal name for the practice of communion—is the transubstantive equivalent of this secular reciprocity, since it allows for the faithful to be made equal as "values" of the one Christ by their consumption of the host. (Even the word "host" as a name for Christ is borrowed from the secular context of Roman law, in which *hostis* designates the victim whose offering "compensates" the anger of the gods.) In Christian doctrine, the biblical injunction to "love thy neighbor" gradually absorbs and supersedes the particular ethical significance of the hospitality act, even though the notion of the neighbor is radically different from the unknown stranger of the nomadic, Hebrew tradition. As in the secular, legal context, a reciprocal relation of "equality" replaces the fundamental disproportion and incommensurability that defines archaic hospitality. Nonetheless, the possibility of a hostile relation to the stranger is implied in any hospitality relation that reduces the guest's alterity to a common measure, no matter how apparently generous its formulation. Sigmund Freud's work has drawn attention to the narcissism and aggressivity inherent in the biblical injunction to "love thy neighbor as thyself," which can only acknowledge the other by reducing him to a modality of "myself."[21]

The failure of early Christian hospitality to address the encounter with real difference goes hand in hand with its increasingly exclusive and even nationalistic self-determination. In medieval times, the Hospitallers of the Order of St. John, the so-called Knights of Malta, abandoned their practice of performing hospitable acts to become violent warriors in the Christian crusades, killing "strangers" to the faith.[22] Even Augustine, who conceived of the hospitality act as the foundation of the City of God, narrowed its definition to encompass only the relation of one Christian to another, mediated by love of God. The stranger had an important place in Augustine's scheme, but not necessarily as worthy of love and respect; in fact, the City was defined in opposition to "heathenous" strangers, in this case the Israelites precluded from entering the state of grace by their nonparticipation in Christian hospitality, their refusal to "welcome" Christ. In a sense the holocaust could even be characterized as a grotesque literalization of Augustine's allegorical call to defend the City of God against the "heathenous" Israelites, an extreme example of the drive to annihilate the stranger in his difference.

In this sense the "economic" treatment of the other that we tend to associate more narrowly with the secularizing tendencies of Enlightenment humanism actually draws upon and finds resonances within Christian theology itself, insofar as the irreducible alterity of the godhead is converted into a universal "value." In relation both to Judaism and to pagan life, Christianity already represented the loss of alterity rather than its preservation: it was already "cosmopolitan," despite its positive and "pathological" form. In both the Christian and Kantian models, we see an erasure of the "religious" as such, in the particular sense in which Lévinas defines it: the irreducible excess within an apparent equality. According to this definition, what is at stake in the receding of "religion" is not only the loss of what Freud called the "opiate of the masses," the superegoic suppresser of violence, but the receding of ethics as the possibility of a relation to the other that does not take place under the sign of a positive principle of identity. Although Kant's moral maxims propose to take the place of religion as a nonpathological guide to ethics, and as a means of suppressing hostile behavior, they are no more successful than the "political" articulations of Christian theology at welcoming the other as an alterity.

Fundamentally, the problem with a reversible model of hospitality is that it assigns a positive content to what is essentially unknowable, to whatever of the other necessarily exceeds the concept I have of him. The aporetical nature of the hospitality relation is compromised whenever the negative form of the aporia—the impossible, the unknown—is replaced by a positive content or form, a generalizable *principle* of identity. Although Kant dismisses religion as a "pathological" motive for ethical action, the notion of reciprocity that underwrites his formulation of the hospitality maxim is not unlike the Christian one. Both the Kantian emancipatory model of hospitality and the Christian transcendental view ultimately function according to the principle of "commerce" or "value," as a common measure allowing for exchange or conversion.

And as in Christianity, Kant's commerce in economic values is conceived as a means to obtain a unified, peaceful "whole." The ultimate aim of cosmopolitan hospitality, like Christian eucharistic hospitality, is "universal peace." And where Christian hospitality is supposed to inaugurate a universal "brotherhood," Kant's cosmopolitan model is supposed to result in the creation of "a universal nation of men" (112n). Like the Church Fathers, and Augustine in particular, Kant strives for some notion of a united human community, based on the dependence of all men on some common measure:

> Because a (narrower or wider) community widely prevails among the Earth's peoples, a transgression of rights in one place in the world is felt everywhere; consequently, the idea of a cosmopolitan right is not fantastic and exaggerated, but rather an amendment to the unwritten code of national and international rights, necessary to the public rights of men in general. Only such amendment allows us to flatter ourselves with the thought that we are making continual progress towards perpetual peace. (119)

The world community united by a cosmopolitan constitution is the nonpathological equivalent of Augustine's "one heart" community discussed in chapter 1. But although Kant's community is not defined by ethnic or religious adherence, it nonetheless encounters the same problems as Christian hospitality: a reduction to a common measure that is the necessary by-product of a universal oneness.

In both models, the unconverted alterity latent in any relation of "equality" is given no place or value. In the "one hearted" community of Christian love, what place is left for those of a different heart? And in a cosmopolitan hospitality regulated by commerce, what value is assigned to those who fail to accede to commercial relations? Precisely because they fail to appreciate the stranger's alterity, both models also fail to subsume or erase entirely its potentially menacing quality. The fact that the frictions between hosts and guests have persisted even after the secularization of the modern European state acts as a reminder that the uncertain and ambivalent status of hospitality in the modern world results from the tension not only between different religious views of hospitality, or between religious and nonreligious hospitalities, but between the nomadic and the fixed, the disenfranchised and the sovereign, the nameless wanderer and the formally constituted nation or state.

By emphasizing the parallels between Kantian hospitality and its early Christian counterpart, therefore, I do not mean to claim that there is a disguised or disavowed Christianity hiding under Kant's critical project. Rather, I would suggest that both models are guided by similar principles, especially as concerns their understanding of the subject. Friedrich Nietzsche has perhaps articulated more forcefully than anyone else the dependence of Kant's moral philosophy on a theological understanding of personal identity. In *The Antichrist* he writes: "Among Germans one will understand immediately when I say that philosophy has been corrupted by theologian blood. The Protestant pastor is the grandfather of German philosophy, Protestantism itself is its original sin . . . Kant's success is merely a theologian's success."[23]

In protesting the "Protestant" flavor of Kant's philosophy, Nietzsche is indicting not only the values it implicitly upholds, but the understanding of the subject on which it is based: namely, a subject that is consistent with and identical to the moral law it upholds. In his analysis of Nietzsche's statement, Gilles Deleuze articulates the problem in the following terms:

> What is concealed in the famous Kantian unity of legislator and subject? Nothing but a renovated theology, theology with a Protestant flavour: we are burdened with the double task of priest and believer,

legislator and subject. Kant's dream was not to abolish the distinction between two worlds (sensible and super-sensible) but to secure *the unity of the personal* in the two worlds. The same person
as legislator and subject, as subject and object, as noumenon and
phenomenon, as priest and believer. This arrangement succeeds as
theology: "Kant's success is only a theologian's success." Can we
really believe that by installing the priest and the legislator in us
we stop being primarily believers and subjects? The legislators and
the priest practice the ministry, the legislation and the representation of established values; all they do is internalize current values. Kant's "proper usage of the faculties" mysteriously coincides
with these established values: true knowledge, true morality, true
religion . . .[24]

In arguing that Kant's dream was to "secure the unity of the personal in two worlds," Nietzsche suggests that what MacCannell
calls the homogeneous "Kantian ego"—the synthetic agent that
produces the objective world as a unified whole—has a theological support as well as a psychological one. The subject's ability
to synthesize the heterogeneity of the sensible world as a formal
unity is upheld by a super-sensible unity, a transcendent subjectivity. Nietzsche suggests that while Kant may dismiss religion as
a pathological basis for ethical action, he nonetheless retains what
is most crucial to its status as an institutor of positive, prescriptive values: the transcendental unity of the subject, understood as a
consistent ego equal to the moral principles it upholds.

Nihilism, the Uncanniest of Guests

Although they approach it from very different angles, both Kant
and Nietzsche are concerned with the same fundamental question:
what is the status of hospitality "after" God? In some ways hospitality seems to have barely survived its separation from the religious sphere, as witnessed by the disproportion between the enormous significance of hospitality in ancient times and up through
the Enlightenment, and its present archaic, or even quaint, signification. What relation does modern hospitality name? What would
it mean to practice hospitality—as a means of establishing relation
with the other—"after" God? In what sense should this "after" be
understood? One "after" might name the extrareligious quality of
hospitality, the displacement of its sacred status by secular "princi-

ples." A second and very different "after" is implied by the *murder* of God proclaimed by Nietzsche. In both "afters," the hospitality act plays a crucial role in determining the subject's identity in relation to the other.

With the first "after," we confront the prospect of having no other means to relate to the other as different. This possibility is inherent in what Jean-François Lyotard calls the modern ideal of an "emancipation without other." He contrasts this ideal with the Judaic tradition, where man is the subject of an infinite debt toward God that cannot be "bought" back with any common measure.[25] But his argument also suggests that the death of God as "other" is not only a postreligious phenomenon, but appears even where the principle of divinity would appear to be most present. Lyotard sees this call already at work in Paul's New Covenant, where faith in the "spirit" of the law serves to emancipate Christians from the "yoke" of its prescriptive content. Christ might even be considered as the first figure of hospitality "after" God; New Testament understandings of the hospitality act are already a departure from the Hebrew Bible, and not only participate in but also shape the contours of modern hospitality.

The conversion of sacred hospitality into measurable "principles" annuls the alterity of the guest, and in this sense could be understood as a kind of "death of God," insofar as God in his unknown quality is the ultimate guest, the stranger unassimilable in its difference. But the focus of my investigation in the next two chapters is another understanding of the death of God, informed by the philosophy of Nietzsche, with profound implications for hospitality and subjective identity. In a sense God died twice: the first time by not being taken seriously in his unknowability, being neutralized as principle or value (trinitarian doctrine, Enlightenment humanism); the second time by being *murdered*. Whereas the first death results in the institution of secular "principles" in the place of religious values, the Nietzschean murder of God entails the annihilation of all principles, the "transvaluation of all values"— including, and perhaps most importantly, the value of personal identity itself.

In his philosophical writings, Pierre Klossowski stresses that the logical conclusion we must draw from Nietzsche's argument is that for the transvaluation of all values to be complete, identity itself must disappear with God. Since God is the sole guarantor of the identity and integrity of the ego, the "death of God" also effects the radical dissolution of the "I."[26] Hence Nietzsche's "transvaluation of all values" really entails the end of the positive idea of personal identity that the monotheistic understanding of God both allows and perpetuates. The privative quality of the monotheistic God not only reifies subjective boundaries, but also the unknown itself; with the death of God, the unknown is free to manifest itself in other forms. And with this liberation, Nietzsche suggests, "true" (i.e., impossible, aporetic, and expropriative) hospitality is possible once again.

In the place of the biblical injunction to "love thy neighbor as thyself," Nietzsche embraces a love of the *Fremd:* the foreign, the dissimilar, the unknown. But in order for the *Fremd* to be appreciated as such, he argues, it is necessary first to effect a "transvaluation of all values," including the reduction of host and guest to "values" of Christ. However, while Nietzsche sees the "murder" of God as absolutely necessary to this transvaluation, he also warns that even after God we run the risk of preserving or instituting "principles" that are not a transvaluation of nihilistic Christian values, but simply new and equally insidious ones. For the transvaluation of all values to be complete, we must overcome not only the monotheistic understanding of God, but also the positive idea of personal identity that depends upon it. Identity itself must disappear with God.

If Nietzsche indicts Kant's critical project as "corrupted by theologian blood," it is because his critique simply puts man—the homogenous "Kantian ego"—in the place of God as a principle of underlying unity or coherence. But this shift from the sphere of the divine to the sphere of autonomous legislation does nothing but relocate the idea of a conditioning unity, which still remains fully intact. According to Gilles Deleuze,

> When the little man reappropriates little things, when the reactive man reappropriates reactive determinations, is it thought that critique has made great progress, that it has thereby proved its activity? Does the recuperation of religion stop us being religious? By turning theology into anthropology, by putting man in God's place, do we abolish the essential, that is to say, the place? All these ambiguities begin with the Kantian critique. In Kant, critique was not able to discover the truly active instance which would have been capable of carrying it through. It is exhausted by compromise:

it never makes us overcome the reactive forces which are expressed in man, self-consciousness, reason, morality and religion. It even has the opposite effect—it turns these forces into something a little more "our own."[27]

The consequences for the hospitality relation are enormous, since the more we make these "reactive forces"—conventional values— "our own," the less we are able to welcome the other into the properness of our autonomous, self-contained identity.

The death of God—and the philosophy of the Eternal Return that results from it—has important consequences for the hospitality relationship, since it accomplishes a dissolution of the host's identity as integral and "equal" to itself. But while Nietzsche is critical of the notion of identity upon which a certain understanding of hospitality is predicated, he does not dismiss the importance of hospitality altogether. In fact, he emphasizes that the hospitality relation is where the "transvaluation of all values" will take place, making way for the possibility of a nonidentical, "dissolved" subjectivity. In the opening lines of *The Will to Power,* Nietzsche writes: "Nihilism stands at the door; whence comes this uncanniest of all guests?"[28]

As a figure of the guest, nihilism lends itself to at least two possible interpretations where hospitality is concerned. First, nihilism is uncannily internal to Christian hospitality, in the form of the hostility toward the stranger that Nietzsche sees as latent in its relation to the guest; in the words of his Zarathustra, "It is the distant man who pays for your love of your neighbor; and when there are five of you together, a sixth always has to die."[29] But while Christianity is for Nietzsche the dominant expression of European nihilism, he also envisions its abolition through the "ultimate nihilism," the logic of the Eternal Return. As the ultimate nihilism, the Eternal Return is also, presumably, the most uncanny of guests: uncanny first of all to Christian nihilism itself, whose cult of monotheism and the positive principle of identity that depends on it preclude any sense of the other as unknown, and therefore can only experience the difference implied in the Eternal Return as hostile, foreign, and destructive. But the uncanniness of the Eternal Return also opens the way for a new understanding of subjectivity, as divided, multiple, dissolute, and irresponsible.

Like Kant, then, Nietzsche understands the crisis of modernity as a crisis of hospitality. But his solution to this crisis is different, since he affirms the uncanny encounter with the foreign over the privative boundaries instituted by cosmopolitan law or "insociable sociability." And whereas Kant's formulation of hospitality, like Augustine's, tends increasingly to banish the "religious" as such, "divinity" and "godliness" reemerge as key terms in Nietzsche's philosophy and are given new meaning as the expression of an irreducible excess. Nietzsche calls for a modernity that would do away with the principles upheld by Kant's cosmopolitan project, liberating the other's alterity and by extension releasing "godliness" into the world.

In Nietzsche's wake, the hospitality relation once again becomes the focus of an attempt to maintain an aporetic relation to the unknown in other than compensatory, salvational modes. In its immanence, hospitality sketches the horizon of a modernity that can no longer appeal to a transcendental representation of identity; its dominant figure is the eternal return of the same *as different,* as dispossessed of its identity to itself.

Although Nietzsche's "death of God" is a privileged figure of this possibility—both in my own argument and in the work of the many contemporary philosophers who have recently turned to hospitality as a model for an ethical relationship not based on economies of identity—I do not mean to oppose the philosophical stakes of the hospitality relation to its many theological interpretations. In fact, what is striking about Nietzsche's celebration of the unknown liberated by the death of God is that it actually aligns itself with the concerns of ancient, "divine" hospitality. Similarly, one of the most interesting features of post-Nietzschean attempts to rethink hospitality is that they actually allow for a new appreciation of "divinity" or "religion," in an other than positive or transcendental mode.

In fact, I would argue there are numerous and important parallels between contemporary philosophical treatments of hospitality and those theologies that are negative in structure, not supposing an integral, positive representation either of the divine or of identity itself. Jacques Derrida, for example, appeals to the language of Negative Theology, and in particular the work of Meister Eckhart and Angelus Silesius, to justify the choice of a negative form (the aporia) to designate a duty to practice hospitality that, through the impossible or the impracticable, nonetheless announces itself in an affirmative fashion.[30] In my own analysis, Judaism maintains a particular privilege in the elaboration of an aporetic relation to hospitality, and in this sense is allied with Nietzsche's philosophy in its opposition to the logic of Pauline Christianity.

As a means of establishing relation, moreover, hospitality could be understood as inherently "theological," without necessarily depending upon a positive understanding of God. Deleuze suggests that while "God" may be dead, in another sense our era is only just discovering theology: "We no longer have any need to believe in God. What we look for instead is 'structure,' a form that may be filled by beliefs, but that in no way needs to be in order to be called theological."[31] Hospitality is one such privileged structure, whose capacity for establishing relation makes it uniquely "theological" in form. When Emmanuel Lévinas, in *Totality and Infinity,* calls for a new understanding of the subject as "a welcoming of the other, as hospitality," he specifies that although subjectivity as hospitality is "religion"—what he defines as the possibility of a relation to exteriority—it nonetheless rests upon the fundamental "atheism" of the "I," an absolute separation from the Other that is anterior to any affirmation or negation of belief.

But as "relation," hospitality has to do not only with theology, but also with the sexual relation. The next two chapters will be devoted to the fiction of Pierre Klossowski, who has outlined very suggestively the possible consequences for hospitality of Nietzsche's "death of God." Like Deleuze and Lévinas, Klossowski makes the "atheism" of the subject the basis of a new kind of theology or "divinity." But his work also goes one step further, by associating this nonreligious divinity with *woman,* as the one who exceeds or is unequal to the legal designation of privative personhood. His work offers an affirmative revaluation of what has traditionally led to the exclusion of women from societal pacts, including those—like Augustine's "brotherly love" and Kant's reciprocal equality—that are predicated upon hospitality. As the embodiment of difference-in-relation, woman represents the possibility of an uncanny introduction of difference into the intimacy of the same, which from the vantage point of a hospitality predicated upon homogenous equality can only be construed as potentially hostile.

Klossowski's work both alludes to this tradition and departs from it. His fiction focuses on woman not as a source or as an object of hostility, but as representing the promise of a hospitality based on a "dissolved" subjectivity that is valorized in its own right, rather than a reductive equality. In the introduction, I argued that the role of the hostess within the hospitality relation could be understood through reference to what Jacques Lacan calls "extimacy," the nonsubjective agency of that part of the subject that is unequal or inadequate to its symbolic designation. The "difference-in-relation" that the hostess represents can also serve as a means to discover "difference-in-identity," the difference internal to the host's "eminent personification" of personal identity. In this sense the first "other" of the hospitality relation could be said to be the multiplicity of the host "himself." Beyond simply considering the role of the hostess in the hospitality relation, Klossowski's work allows us to evaluate more generally the privilege of what I will call "femininity" in the construction of a uniquely hospitable subjective identity "after" God. When there is no Host in whose model and in whose image he can constitute himself, can the host continue to "eminently personify" personal identity?

3. Under the Sign of the Hostess: Pierre Klossowski's *Laws of Hospitality*

In the last chapter we saw how, despite its apparent archaism, the hospitality relation emerges as an essential concern for modernity, offering a unique avenue through which to challenge metaphysical notions of identity. The work of Pierre Klossowski represents a particularly interesting point of entry into these questions. Among the work of an impressive group of contemporary thinkers who have recently turned to hospitality as a model for a mode of relation not based on economies of identity, his contribution is perhaps the most original. His singular interpretation of hospitality both engages with and comments upon the entirety of its long cultural and philosophical history, but with a particular view toward the place and meaning of the hospitality act "after" God. In fact, the entirety of Klossowski's novelistic output could be understood as an attempt to realize in fiction the consequences of the "death of God" declared by Nietzsche.

The next two chapters will offer readings of *The Laws of Hospitality*, a trilogy made up of three novels published between 1954 and 1960: *La Révocation de l'Edit de Nantes*, *Roberte, ce soir,* and *Le Souffleur*. Although Klossowski's fiction is perhaps most immediately recognizable for its "perverse" quality and free adaptation of the stock themes of erotic literature, its extreme complexity and philosophical overdetermination prevent it from being easily dismissed as mere erotica. To the extent that it is perverse, it must be taken seriously for everything that this designation implies. For like all great manifestos of perversion, Klossowski's work proceeds implacably toward the demonstration of a thesis about the status of the signifier or law,[1] a demonstration staged here through the meticulous exposition of the erotic awakening of "hospitality" in a woman. What it "demonstrates" is the unfoundedness of the law of identity, by virtue of the death of God.

Klossowski's Archaic Turn

Although Klossowski shares many of Kant's concerns about the perpetuation of hospitality in a modern, secularized world, his articulation of the hospitality relationship represents a radical departure from the fundamental tenets underlying Kant's formulation of cosmopolitan hospitality. For as we saw in the last chapter, Kant's hospitality maxim is grounded in the notion of individual and national sovereignty. Its advocation of "insociable sociability" as the privileged embodiment of cosmopolitan hospitality presupposes a relation of "commerce" between discrete subjects. His task is to guarantee the foreigner's right of passage, while at the same time safeguarding the host country against the threat of contamination or dissolution at its hands by arguing against a more intimate cohabitation or "intermingling."

Klossowski, on the other hand, is interested not so much in the guest as a foreigner, or in the foreignness of the host and guest in relation to one another, but rather in the foreignness *within* the host, the alienation internal to the notion of inalienable rights. In this sense his vision of hospitality is closer to the biblical problematic considered in chapter 1 than to Kant's modern treatment. And like the Bible scenarios we have already examined, it both develops and challenges the host's ethical personhood through a consideration of the role of the hostess, the one traditionally marginal to questions of world citizenship and the discourse of rights.

Klossowski elaborates the problematic of hospitality within the domain of the sexual relation with a particular view to the status of woman within it. *The Laws of Hospitality* departs from the explicitly philosophical orientation of his earlier work to engage the relationship between a husband and wife, and the peculiar "laws of hospitality" that govern their marriage. In this "custom" or practice, the hostess is the key term in a highly sexualized hospitable relationship whose purpose is the "actualization" of the "in-actual essences" of the host, hostess, and guest at the expense of their privative identities. If the ideal of Kant's philosophy is what Lyotard called an "emancipation without other," an emancipation *into* autonomy that allows for the possession of inalienable rights, Klossowski opposes to it an emancipation or liberation *from* an autonomous identity. Moreover, Klossowski suggests that the host's emancipation from his privative identity can happen only with the aid of two others: the guest who "liberates" the host, and the hostess who facilitates this operation by surrendering to the advances of a fortuitous and illegitimate possessor, thereby alienating the master from his personal property.

Although Klossowski's treatment of hospitality is archaic and biblical in feel, it takes as its focus the moral and sexual *Bildungsroman* of a woman who is not a mere objectified possession, but a free subject. In so doing, it poses a challenge to Kant by questioning the place of women in the cosmopolitan scheme. Women would seem to be model subjects for Kant's examination of world hospitality, insofar as they—more than men—have always freely crossed the borders between families, tribes, and nations. But at the same time, they have done so in a way that has tended to subvert—rather than guarantee—the notion of individual sovereignty. For women have historically been unaffiliated parties—nonsubjects—who have crossed borders primarily under the aegis of exogamous marriage. The mode and manner of their exchange thus presents a particular challenge to the notion of cosmopolitan hospitality, which presents itself as an affirmation of certain inalienable and sovereign rights due the nation, figured as a free woman "emancipated" from the mastery of a tyrannical husband and the constraints of forced marriage.

In making the hostess the centerpiece of his conception of hospitality, Klossowski both departs from the familiar contours of the hospitality tradition and, at the same time, recovers something latent within that tradition from its archaic origins that has tended to be suppressed and overlooked in its dominant institutional forms. Although the feminine traditionally occupies an essential position within the hospitality relation, we have seen in previous chapters that it is generally not as a subject.

Klossowski's attention to the hostess challenges these models with evidence of their limitations. But importantly, it does so not simply by giving her "equal" importance, allowing her to take her place alongside the men. Rather, the hostess is essential precisely because she exceeds the economy of exchange, having no place in the reciprocal relation established between the male host and guest. Woman contests the apparent reversibility of an "equal" relation to the other with evidence of the fundamental *inequality* with regard to the signifier that defines the sexual relation. As Renata Salecl has argued, "woman is a symptom of the rights of man";[2] she refutes the capacity of legal rights to be applied "equally" to all subjects. The marginal position accorded to femininity by traditional understandings of the subject gives voice to the *alienation* inherent in the notion of inalienable rights, insofar as the subject can never be adequately designated by the signifier of personal identity that represents her or him to other subjects.

This marginal position appears as a singular force within the hospitality relation as conceived by Klossowski, since it suggests how the identity of the post-Nietzschean host might be understood as other than a principle of self-adequation. The "impossible" quality of the sexual relation—its irreducibility to a signifier or equation—finds its echo in the ethics of hospitality, which similarly sustains relation as "impossible," without any sign or principle to regulate its immanence. In its exclusion from the reciprocal economy of hospitality between "equals," the feminine approximates the divine, insofar as both elude representation or reduction to a common measure.

But at the same time, the feminine embodies a "religiosity" or "divinity" that has no transcendent dimension, but is firmly materialist. For although the feminine approximates the divine in its "excessive" quality, its negativity, it is in part because of its ambivalent relationship to the positive principle of personal identity that the monotheist God, in its particularly Christian interpretation, imparts. The hostess is traditionally the excess of the host, the one not made in the image of God—and, therefore, not equal to the principle of identity he incarnates. Against the unifying image, she embodies the excess of unity, the surplus in opposition to which the "whole" defines itself.

Klossowski delves into the sexual relation in order to stage a deconstruction or critique of economy. Paradoxically enough, however, this critique is played out through the "offering" of a woman between men; the "laws of hospitality" names a practice wherein the master of the home "gives" his wife over to chance strangers, fortuitous "guests" who apprehend the unsuspecting hostess in such a way as to solicit an emotion that escapes the control of her will, a response in contradiction with her symbolic role.

But while Klossowski draws upon archaic tradition, his scenario is also thoroughly modern, proper to the era of legislative freedom in which his characters live. More than almost any woman, his character Roberte lives "in a man's world," asserting the possible equality of a legislative subject under democracy. Roberte is a thoroughly Kantian type, an emancipated woman who embodies the ideals of secular democracy; her husband Octave, on the other hand, is an anachronistic throwback to another world. In his own words, "Madame wages the good fight for brotherhood, for world-wide democracy; I just live and die for the sake of beauty and hence for the cause of the mean sons of bitches in this world."[3] Nonetheless, these two opposed types are joined in the "one flesh" relation of marriage. Roberte is at once the emancipated woman and the exchanged patrimony of the master, embodying in her "hospitality" the contradictory overlap of these two positions.

Additional details of the relationship between Octave and his wife enhance this already inherent tension. Octave is a retired professor of scholastic theology, as well as a writer of perversely erotic fiction. But his young wife belongs to another world altogether. She is a high-ranking official in the French government, a member of the Chamber of Deputies. The most prominent and powerful woman in the radical party (148), she is also a decorated veteran of the French Resistance. Her moral leadership extends to her duties as the president of the commission of censorship, where she is responsible for banning pornographic literature: including, at one point, her husband's own novel, *Roberte, ce soir.*

In many ways Roberte is the supreme achievement of Enlightenment ideals, the very cliché of the "emancipated woman." She's a real Virginia Slims kind of girl, a feminist *avant la lettre.* She is really the last person one would expect to see involved in such an intrigue, which is part of the point. Moreover, she is a secular humanist, an atheist of Protestant origins who affirms her individual freedom both within the legislative domain and in relation to her husband. But Octave suspects that there is more to her than this, an unknown that eludes the conjugal gaze.

The Revocation of the Edict of Nantes, or the Hostess as Good European

The Revocation of the Edict of Nantes, the first novel in the trilogy, is a story of modern times set in Paris in the 1950s. But as the title suggests, its depiction of the easy freedom of postwar republican

France is inflected by numerous elliptical references to another period in French history, the era of the Edict of Nantes—which granted French Protestants religious freedom and civic rights—and its eventual revocation by a repressive Catholic monarchy. In each of the three novels that make up *The Laws of Hospitality,* this historical conflict over religious freedom is reenacted in miniature in the relationship between Roberte and her Catholic husband, who delights in theorizing the significance of her "freedom"—her extramarital and libertine adventures—in grandly theological terms. *The Revocation* adds to this collapsing of two different historical epochs a juxtaposition of two different periods from Roberte's life: her present-day existence as a distinguished legislator, and her experience as a member of the French Resistance living under Nazi occupation in the late months of World War II. But despite the density of this religious and political frame, the action of the novel is made up of a series of intrigues of a very different order, whose relationship to these historical dramas is both important and extremely oblique.

In the present of the novel, we see Roberte going along with or surrendering herself to chance encounters with all manner of strangers, which despite their random and fortuitous character take place with astonishing regularity in the most varied locales. In "giving" herself in this way, Roberte flies in the face not only of marital fidelity, but also of her loyalty to her symbolic persona, her status as a public official and upholder of liberal ideals.

In one present-day scene, Roberte is on her way to the Chamber of Deputies, where "they were awaiting her . . . for an important resolution bearing on the State Education issue" (157). On her way there, she stops in at a women's club to have tea. As she is leaving, she passes through a lounge where she encounters two young schoolboys advertising shoe shine services. Gazing at herself in a mirror, she absentmindedly places a foot on the box that has been thrust under her leg, and the two boys set to work. But as Roberte is applying her lipstick, the lights suddenly go out, and the roles of each of the three participants "are shifted in a trice" (155). Her arms and legs suddenly immobilized, Roberte finds that her efforts to wrest herself free are in vain. But as she struggles under the boys' fumbling caresses, an unexpected sense of pleasure comes over her that "splits her final struggles into two contradictory solicitations" (157): the plea to be set free to attend to her legislative obligations, and the competing—and ultimately victorious—urge to succumb to her pleasure and see where this untoward scene will lead her.

As he recounts what he has been able to piece together of the illicit scene, Octave notes with satisfaction Roberte's abandonment of her legislative responsibilities in the face of this unseemly enjoyment: "her thighs and behind dripping with the impertinence of our two neophytes, Roberte surrendered to the last of her spasms, panting hoarsely and letting all her legislative obligations go straight to the devil, the parliamentary lawmaker turning whore between Condorcet and Lazare" (159). What is at stake in these erotic episodes is not merely a libertine surrender to sexual pleasure, then, but a staging of the straying or negation internal to the personification of a symbolic identity.

These scenes are interspersed with episodes from an earlier period in Roberte's life, before she became the distinguished lawmaker and decorated veteran of the novel's present. The narrative juxtaposes the present day of the "lawmaker becoming whore" against Roberte's first-person recollections of her wartime experiences as a volunteer nurse and as a member of the Resistance, somehow linking this sexual surrender to her role as a patriot and a liberal lawmaker:

> What could a woman be expected to do in such a situation . . . ? Scream, obviously, bring the whole building running—in such a busy section of the city—but we, the women who rode in the Red Cross vans, on "the front lines of charity," we, the women who are now at the helm of the nation, we women who "have been around" and through too much—if ever we be fair, if ever we have retained our beauty—we can do but one thing, and that is say nothing. (139)

Despite its apparent inconsistency with her role as an elected official and guardian of public morality, Roberte justifies her "ethics of saying nothing" in relation to her experience during the war. In this context, "we women who 'have been around'" clearly has a double resonance, describing both the cosmopolitan scope of her legislative and war experiences and the sexual dalliances that pepper her daily life. But this duality also establishes the singularity of Roberte's symbolic identity, which is defined not by its firm identification with one position of enunciation, but by a fluid slippage between apparently incompatible positions marked by a dissolute silence.

The Revocation of the Edict of Nantes opens with a series of diary entries, penned by Roberte, entitled the "Roman Impressions." These fragments recount the scene that precedes and gives birth to Roberte's role as hostess, prior to either her political engagement or her marriage to Octave: they evoke the first fantasy, whose meaning is as yet unknown except that it introduces her into the pursuit of a double life, a complicity with opposed positions. The first full installment of the "Roman Impressions" shows Roberte embarking upon a secret mission whose details and meaning are unclear, but that involves overturning or challenging traditional views of hospitality. We see Roberte penetrate—scantily clad—into the inner sanctum of a church, where she violates a tabernacle and overturns a chalice of hosts in furtherance of a mission whose aim will be revealed only at the end of the novel.

Roberte's journal testifies to the burgeoning of her "hospitable" nature at an ambiguous crossroads, suspended between the claims of neutrality and national allegiance, religion and secular life, fraternal loyalties and sororal collaborations, and, most importantly, the sexualization of all of these scenarios as somehow key to the emergence of the hostess within her. Roberte's sexual surrendering of herself allegorizes a larger political, religious, and philosophical dynamic in which collaboration, sacrilege, and complicity emerge as forms of dual identity irreducible to the symbolic economies of national allegiance, morality, or personal integrity.

Roman Hospitalities

The "Roman Impressions" catalogue Roberte's experiences as a young woman living in occupied Rome in the waning days of World War II, when she served as a volunteer nurse in the days just preceding the city's liberation by the Allied powers. Roberte's first-person accounts offer a condensed presentation of the political questions and thematic issues around which the trilogy will turn, staging the emergence of her hospitable nature against the backdrop of a conflict between competing religious and political views of hospitality. Much like Kant's "Perpetual Peace," *The Revocation* presents an image of hospitality in crisis, its traditional mores succumbing to the pressures of modernity. On more than one level, it is significant that the novel is situated in Rome. For if Rome—as the former capital of the Holy Roman Empire, as well as the enduring host to the papal seat of the Catholic Church—has traditionally represented the triumph of a certain vision of hospitality, Roberte's journal depicts a Rome whose hegemony is in jeopardy, that is no longer able to present itself as the unified, earthly manifestation of the City of God.

Roberte discovers a Rome in which the relationship of host to stranger is uncertain and undecidable, a city struggling with the different claims to power represented by "Mussolini's fall, the setting up of the Badoglio government, the struggle between the Italian administration and the camouflaged residues of the Fascist police and the Gestapo" (194). In this murky political landscape, covert alliances take precedence over national law, and foreign "guests" hold their hosts hostage with occupying armies. As the disputed frontier of the war between Nazi Germany and the Allied forces, Rome is the wager in a battle between different secular powers, each of whom is seeking to define a new standard of hospitality by appropriating or gaining control of the Christian capital. The occupation of Rome by Nazi Germany, for example, could be interpreted at least on one level as the succumbing of the Christian ideal of hospitality to a force whose hostile attitude toward the resident stranger seems to embody the systematic negation of its ethical principles. For what is the Final Solution if not the most significant reversal of hospitality in the Western tradition, the radical rejection of the guest as a hostile parasite?

As a Frenchwoman, and member of the Resistance, Roberte would seem to represent another perspective altogether. By the time she records these war memoirs (February 1954), Roberte has been awarded the Resistance Medal and elected Commander of the Legion of Honor (113–14). She is the archetype of the Allied hero(ine), a dedicated public champion of the Western liberal ideals of freedom and democracy. At the time the war broke out Roberte was a student of law (194), and in the novel's present we know her as a member of the Assemblée Nationale. But this profile is tempered by the fact that she is in Rome in a neutral capacity, with no political affiliation. With the assistance of an uncle, a Swiss medical professor, she was able to gain entry to the "Eternal City," even though she was a French citizen. With his help she joined a convoy of doctors and nurses bound for Rome, which was hastily assembled in Geneva in August 1943.

Through its metonymic association with the Geneva Convention, political fraternity, and international government, Geneva functions as a signifier of neutrality, of the fluidity and openness of borders, and of cosmopolitan law. Roberte's status as a volunteer attached to the Red Cross intensifies these associations, identifying her as a free agent without clear partisan allegiances. Moreover, both Geneva and the Red Cross are intimately associated with hospitality. The Geneva Convention guarantees the hospitable—or at least humane—treatment of enemies as "guests" possessed of minimal rights, even when they are held as political prisoners. And the Red Cross represents the modern continuation of the great hospitality tradition, albeit in the relatively impersonal and institutional form of the hospital.

Further complicating any attempt to distinguish between the different forces battling for control of Rome, Roberte tells us that the "neutral" parties with which she is aligned are quite literally lodged at the center of Christian Rome, having taken up residence in the Vatican palace:

> We [the Red Cross] alone, along with the neutral diplomats, had access to the Vatican, and the most charming Monsignors were always on hand to facilitate our mission. Two famous convents turned over their annexes while we were still waiting for suitable space to be prepared in the hospitals, already jammed with prisoners and serious cases. (195)

As Roberte's description unfolds, Rome begins to read like a Russian doll of hospitable possibilities, one nestled inside the other. The neutral diplomats and Red Cross agents, representing the forces of international law, are ensconced within the Vatican, itself a sovereign state situated within the political limits of Rome; Rome is in turn occupied by the residues of the Gestapo, which are themselves under attack by the approaching Allied army. Moreover, each of these forces is "hospitable" to the others in very curious ways: Mussolini's Rome warmly receives its Nazi occupiers, the secular forces of international law operate within a Christian institution and paradigm, and secret agents pass themselves off as members of the opposing side, strangers masquerading as hosts. In juxtaposing these myriad interpenetrations, both topographical and ideological, Klossowski reminds us that hospitality involves an incorporation of alterity into identity that extends beyond mere physical cohabitation, effecting a dissolution of discrete identities through the act of welcoming.

The obvious heterogeneity of this arrangement, which stresses the national, religious, and ideological differences between host and stranger even while juxtaposing them, presents many of the same problems addressed by Kant in "Perpetual Peace." Although this scene is cosmopolitan in the broadest sense, it is qualified more by the clashes and oppositions brought about by difference than by their peaceful cohabitation. But within this atmosphere of politically charged hostility, Roberte's position in Rome seems instead to affirm this cohabitation and dissolution, serving all sides equally and minimizing questions of partisan allegiance. It should therefore come as no surprise that the way in which Roberte conceives of her neutrality is heavily informed by Kant's treatment of cosmopolitan hospitality:

> I have never had any instinctive sense for what would distinguish an enemy from another man; with its branches spread throughout various countries in Europe, my family has for centuries had no enemy other than the Papacy, no homeland other than Freedom of Conscience. (201)

Roberte's idealistic declaration pays homage to the major tenet of Kant's essay, namely that the stranger may not be treated as an enemy. The "branches" of Roberte's family, which spread throughout Europe, also recall the sovereign nation "tree" of Kant's example. But whereas Kant uses the image to represent the sovereignty of the nation—which, like a tree, has its own roots, and thus cannot be "grafted" onto another nation without denying its existence as a moral person—here the tree is already "cosmopolitan," its branches spread throughout Europe and firmly rooted in the homeland of Freedom of Conscience.

But Roberte's "cosmopolitan" position and its underpinnings are complicated in two ways. First, her staunch support for Western liberalism is inflected by her religious upbringing and her self-identification as "the daughter and great-granddaughter of Calvinist ministers" (200). This fact also gives new resonance to Roberte's association with Geneva, the city Calvin both lived in and presided over as a skilled statesman renowned for his legal judgment. As the passage continues, Roberte qualifies her "Kantianism" by associating this cosmopolitan paradigm with Protestantism, as the embodiment not only of a non-national, cosmopolitan sensibility, but also of a dedication to "freedom of conscience" that associates the right of foreigners not to be treated as enemies with a "freedom to choose" that should be immune to judgment or censorship:

> Ever since the Revocation of the Edict of Nantes, Protestant freedom, so I assumed, was as good as barred from life; Rome had won out on a good many scores, not at all, mind you, that Rome was the Church, but because life defied the condemnation the Evangile hurled at Rome. And, carrying the faculty for free inquiry to the point of absurdity, I had opted for that defiance, not so much from love for life as to assert what I then took to be my freedom. Consequently, all the rest—why these nations were fighting at the moment, in the name of what humane and pleasant ways of life and thinking against other deliberately atrocious ones—everything led back to this freedom to choose for or against life. By what right could you deny it to others, even if their choice might be in favor of the very worst—that's what I wasn't able to understand. But was I only trying to understand? Charity came to my rescue: no more problems! Go join the Red Cross: as if tending to the blind, you'll tend indiscriminately to them who know not what they do, the "guilty" and the "innocent" alike. (201)

Roberte maps Kant's treatment of the nation's innate sovereignty, and its oppression at the hands of an illegitimate authority, onto the question of the conflict between Protestantism and Catholicism: a conflict that in France resulted in the 1685 revocation of the Edict of Nantes, the royal proclamation that had formerly granted French Huguenots freedom of conscience and full civic rights. In this remapping, Protestantism is identified with cosmopolitanism and the permeability of borders, and Catholicism is implicitly identified with the "master" of Kant's treatise, the leader who attempts to imperiously assert its authority over what is by rights an emancipated, sovereign nation. This invocation of the Catholic persecution of Protestants offers the first gloss of the novel's title, one that provisionally aligns the Edict of Nantes with the cosmopolitan opening of borders under the aegis of a "free" hospitality unfettered by doctrinal or national considerations, and its "revocation" with the censure or delimitation of this possibility.

But Roberte's association of the Catholic persecution of the Protestants with the imperialist violation of national sovereignty has another important implication. It suggests that this religious imperialism is not without some analogy to the Nazi occupation of Rome, the very gesture that was initially legible only as a reversal or violation of Catholic ethics. The Nazi forces could be construed as violators of hospitality on two fronts. First, they have violated the (Kantian) laws of hospitality by designating the resident Jewish population as a parasitic enemy. Second, they have themselves become a "bad guest," a parasite that profits from its warm reception into Italy to overtake the country. In another way, though, Roberte's meditation suggests that this second possibility was facilitated by the Church itself, which in designating free thinkers as "enemies" laid the groundwork for its own conversion into an object of hostility, an embattled stronghold under siege by a hegemonic regime. In these multiple allusions and analogies, the Nazi persecution of the Jews, the Nazi occupation of Rome, and the Catholic persecution of the Protestants are all inextricably linked as violations of hospitality.

Charity and the Law

At the same time, this indictment of religious imperialism, in the form of Roman Catholicism, is countered by a rearticulation of cosmopolitan ethics in terms of "charity," a uniquely Christian mode of erasing borders. Roberte's invocation of "charity" refers first of all to the nature of her participation in the war. She is in Rome not only under the auspices of the Red Cross, but as a volunteer nurse attached to a religious order of "Sisters." Moreover, her resolution to "tend indiscriminately to those who know not what they do" is an allusion to the words of Jesus on the cross: "Father, forgive them; for they do not know what they do" (Luke 23:34). But when Roberte associates her mission in Rome with that of none other than Christ, we have to understand this analogy in a particular way. Roberte is presented as a kind of Christ figure, but a universal, apolitical Christ rather than the Christ of Catholic Rome: a Christ who opposes indiscriminate charity to particularist distinctions. In other words, "charity" (and, above and beyond it, Christ) names the potential transcendence of the distinction between "friend" and "enemy," the potential for a relationship of reversibility, equality, or mutual recognition between *hostis* and *hostis*.

But while Roberte's "charity" is related to her work with the Sisters and the Red Cross, it is also defined in opposition to it. As an indiscriminate gesture of openness to the other that undercuts institutional or denominational divisions, Roberte's Christ-like charity distinguishes itself from the way in which the gesture of charity has been institutionalized within the Christian Church, rigidified into a stern and resentful morality. The perfect embodiment of this wan and lifeless code is Roberte's supervisor, Louise: "lean, hollow-eyed from all-night vigils, she was a perfect specimen of the toughened old maid. . . . Austerity, bereavement, courage, and resignation were all incarnated in her single skinny person, the living denial of all joys, permissible as well as forbidden" (202). Through Louise, Roberte paints a portrait of a weakened, cynical Christianity, whose fullest expression is no longer an indiscriminate, universal hospitality, but rather the politicized *hospital:* an institution that reduces charity to the dispensation of standardized care for weak dependents, rather than an encounter with and celebration of the stranger in its difference. Louise, for example, dotes on cowardly, pasty-faced French soldiers, while dispensing only the most minimal cares to those of the other side and making no secret of her contemptuous indifference to them. In this impoverished pseudo-charity, the invalid's right to "charitable" care does not prevent him from being classed and treated as an enemy.

In contrast, Roberte will work to revive a "true" hospitality: but one whose Law will necessarily come into conflict with the laws of national interest, the particular laws governing the relation between the native and the foreign, the ally and the enemy. This is because the indiscriminate "charity" that Roberte serves demands a disruption or superseding of national or partisan allegiances, answering to a "higher" (if at this point largely ambiguous and undefined) law. In this sense Roberte's characterization of "charity" also signals a collapsing or fusion of the Christian and cosmopolitan views, in which the gesture of tending to "the 'guilty' and the 'innocent' alike" is aligned with the gesture of drawing no distinction between friend and enemy.

The implications of this position can be seen in the surprising conclusion to Roberte's complaint against Roman Catholicism, namely that Protestant freedom has been barred from life since the Revocation of the Edict of Nantes:

> Rome had won out on a good many scores, not at all, mind you,
> that Rome was the Church, but because *life defied the condemna-*

tion the Evangile hurled at Rome. And, carrying the faculty for
free inquiry to the point of absurdity, I had opted for that defiance,
not so much from love for life as to assert what I then took to be my
freedom. (201)

Paradoxically, the Calvinist Roberte is unable to support the condemnation of the very entity she blames for barring Protestant
freedom. Her interpretation of freedom leads her to defy any condemnation of a free choice, even the condemnation that, according to her Protestant education, the New Testament hurls at Rome.
Thus although Roberte conceives of her Christ-like role in explicitly Protestant terms, she also critiques or refuses to act upon the
Protestant interpretation of the gospel as a condemnation of Rome.[4]
In other words, she refuses—in the spirit of Christ—to name an
"enemy," a guilty party, even when the result is that her own oppressor goes unaccused.

   In placing "freedom" above even the "love for life," Roberte-
as-Christ takes the Savior's *ethos* one step further, inaugurating
a brand of charity that, far from defending the cosmopolitan or
humanist cause against its monarchic or religious oppressor, extends its charitable consideration to "guilty" and "innocent" alike,
upholding the freedom of each to choose even "the very worst":
"everything led back to this freedom to choose for or against life.
By what right could you deny it to others, even if their choice might
be in favor of the very worst—that's what I wasn't able to understand." Her freedom of conscience goes so far—"to the point of
absurdity"—as to affirm the "freedom to choose" even of those
very doctrines or persons that have contributed to her persecution:
Catholic Rome, but also the Nazi forces that currently occupy not
only Italy, but also her own country—a surprising position for a
future holder of the Resistance Medal to take.

Resistance and Collaboration

The gesture of "tending to guilty and innocent alike" is thus
aligned not only with political neutrality or the openness of borders, but also with the implicit potential for political collaboration. Although Roberte is a member of the French Resistance at
home, she is in the city of charitable hospitality as a neutral party
who "gives" herself to both sides. Her "indiscriminate" offering
of herself to friend and enemy alike allows for a passive slippage

between—and complicity with—opposing positions, which happens under the cover of charity without necessarily being consistent with its aims. Significantly, the preceding reflection occurs in
the context of Roberte's decision whether or not to assist a Nazi in
a mission that is both sacrilegious and potentially treasonous. The
shocking climax of the novel is that Roberte will "give" herself to
a Nazi as the fullest expression of her Christ-like (and Western,
neutral, "liberal") mission to "tend to all alike."

While working as a volunteer in the Red Cross hospital, Roberte
enters into an illicit relation with one von A., a severely wounded
but very handsome German soldier rumored to be a high-ranking
officer of the S.S. (197). He calls upon her in her capacity as a
"Sister" to come to his assistance in a way that conflicts with her
most elementary loyalties. At von A.'s urging, Roberte embarks
upon a secret mission involving the retrieval of some documents he
has hidden in a tabernacle, located in a small chapel in the hospital's basement. For this purpose, he provides her with a small key,
which Roberte accepts in spite of her awareness that participating
in this mission amounts to an act of treason that utterly violates
her "consciousness of duty":

> And here was the war, which as a woman I thought I could foil
> by means of the fortuitous incidents that composed it, such as
> this meeting with von A., forcing its most awful aspect upon me:
> the consciousness of duty! If indeed this key really did belong to
> a tabernacle, and if this tabernacle did contain some secret docu-
> ments, elementary loyalty demanded that I myself reveal the affair
> to the hospital chaplain. And doing that went terribly against the
> grain. (202)

The "grain" that the claims of elementary loyalty goes against is
Roberte's philosophy of indiscriminate care. Her meditation on her
"Christ-like" role presents itself as her solution or response to this
dilemma: she takes the side of taking no side, she refuses to draw a
distinction between friend and enemy in her feminine "charity."

Considered from this vantage point, Roberte's disinterested
charity—tending to the needs of guilty and innocent alike—is the
point of entry into a divided identity, a collaboration with two opposed positions. "Charity" is not a principle of unity, but a bar
of disjunction between two different—and mutually exclusive—
positions. Its mechanism can be understood through reference to

what Gilles Deleuze calls the "disjunctive synthesis," an *either/or* disjunction affirmatively reinterpreted as an *and*.[5] This dissolution of binary oppositions is one of the defining features of Klossowski's work, which always emphasizes the potential for the betrayal or negation of a positive identity that is implicit in the gesture of identifying with it.

Roberte's gesture of charity embodies the potential for what I will call *collaboration within resistance*. In his exquisite homage to Klossowski, "The Prose of Acteon," Michel Foucault suggests that the hallmark of Klossowski's style is the use of what Foucault calls "alternators of experience," aporetic structures that provoke the sudden twists and reversals by which apparent opposites reveal themselves to be simulacra of one another: most notably, hospitality and theater.[6] But in calling the mechanism of Roberte's charity "collaboration within resistance," I mean both to draw upon Deleuze's and Foucault's analyses and to develop them in a particular direction. With its political overtones, "collaboration within resistance" suggests how these philosophical concerns might be articulated to the novel's historical frame. At the same time, it points to how the structure of hospitality, as an "alternator of experience," informs the stakes of cosmopolitan hospitality in particular, and what I have identified as the problematic core of Kant's essay: the impossibility of the legislative subject ever being equal or adequate to her symbolic designation. And since it refers first and foremost to Roberte's charitable "offering" of herself to opposing sides, "collaboration within resistance" identifies femininity as the privileged expression of the disjunctive synthesis of personal identity, where this inadequation is articulated in an affirmative fashion.

Roberte's potential for "collaboration," the effortless way in which she slips between contradictory symbolic positions, is related to her Kantianism and to her Protestantism, but ultimately has to do with neither of these views of hospitality. Her hospitality subverts these possible identifications in a uniquely "feminine" way, which inheres in the mission she undertakes under the cover of her role as a "Sister" of charity.

The uniqueness of Roberte's position comes into play when von A. reveals that the secret documents he has asked her to recover from the tabernacle are the correspondence that chronicles his incestuous love affair with his sister Malwyda, which von A. is anxious to retrieve so as not to heap scandal on his family if they are uncovered by his enemies (199). When Roberte asks why he has selected this particular repository for his illicit treasure, von A. explains that the insinuation of the letters into the company of the Holy Sacrament was intended to sanctify the incest between brother and sister. This detail in turn casts Roberte's Protestantism as essential to the success of von A.'s mission. If he asks Roberte to recover them in his stead, it is because he imagines that as a Protestant who does not believe in the "real presence," she does not risk any transgression by breaking into the tabernacle: a view Roberte confirms when she sneeringly derides the holy habitation as a "pretendedly sacred piece of furniture" that is "in no way inviolable" (200).

Roberte's mission involves violating the Catholic tabernacle: in other words, there where the "host" should be.[7] In the diary entry that describes her illicit fulfillment of von A.'s mission, Roberte's first gesture is to "overturn" the chalice of hosts while giving herself to a guest in her first "hospitable" act: "I knocked over the chalice, scattering Hosts right and left" [*je renversai le calice et toutes les hosties se répandirent*] (E105, F19). The burgeoning of Roberte's hospitable nature indexes the overturning or subversion[8] of traditional hospitality, the dispersion of the old order embodied by the Host. Within the context of the novel, this "overturning of hosts" resonates on a number of different levels: the Nazi overturning or occupation of Rome; Roberte's subversion of the authority of the hospital chaplain, whose building "hosts" both the hospital in which she works and the secret tabernacle; and the overturning of the Host, the eucharistic Christ, as guarantor of the hospitable Christian community. Roberte's hospitality not only draws upon the meaning and power of the Host, therefore, but overturns it, fragments its unity, and feminizes it. In contrast to the "brother" of secular humanism or the Christian community, Roberte inaugurates a "sisterly" hospitality, one grounded in a disruption or overturning of the eucharistic unity.[9]

Beyond Brotherly Love: Sisterhood and Negativity

Roberte's complicity with von A. hinges upon her "sisterhood," developing an aspect of her nature that has important implications for the *The Laws of Hospitality* as a whole. Von A. appeals to Roberte as a nonbeliever and as a "Sister," which in the end amounts to the same thing. Roberte's "sisterhood" signals the fact that she is a free agent on a number of different planes—a nonbeliever, a "neutral" nun with no political allegiances, and a woman able to penetrate into the intimacy of a masculine community without being identified with or legislated by it. In each of its possible connotations, "sister" names the one who, in being outside of or marginal to the "brotherhood," retains a kind of passive slippage between or collaboration with different positions, having only the most elusive relation to the coherence that the signifier of group identity imposes.

The sister is the marginal sibling, the one not quite named by— or under the jurisdiction of—the law. But this marginality can operate in two distinct ways. On the one hand, the sister (in the guise of the Sister of Charity, the nun or nurse) does not have to recognize secular laws; she is "neutral," she "lends herself" (here quite literally) to both sides. On the other, the sister has an undefined relation to the male master, functioning as an uncanny double of fraternity or even as a figure of incest. In her "hospitable" guise, her willing fulfillment of von A.'s mission, Roberte evokes both the extralegal quality of the "sister" and her unseemly, unlawful, or incestuous side. She is called *Schwester* by a man who not only appeals to her for medical attention, but also hallucinates that she is *his* sister, the object of his incestuous passion: "Schwester . . . You resemble Malwyda, oh, you look so much like her!" (198).

By appealing to these two different aspects of Roberte at once, von A.'s objective is to solicit the *Schwester* within the Sister, the "something more" that exceeds Roberte's official role (her charitable neutrality) even while appearing to grow out of it (her refusal to draw any distinction between friend and enemy, innocent or guilty). The name "Schwester," like "charity," is a bar of disjunction between two different orders, which serves not so much to unite them as to stage their mutual opposition and overturning.

The importance of this disjunction is revealed when we learn that von A.'s initial story about the papers hidden in the tabernacle is actually just a cover for another, even more covert one, a treasonous act of "hospitality" that von A. is trying to keep secret to protect himself from his German superiors:

> For several weeks . . . he had been the man in charge of a camp of hostages. . . . he had soon received an order to send some Jewish families to Germany . . . [but] hadn't had the strength, he said, to ship the children out, and by persuading his second in command

that there would be an advantage in hanging on to them, he had managed to spare them from deportation; and a little later he'd been able to confide them to that Italian chaplain, the condition being that the chaplain keep them on tap in case he needed to have them back. (206)

After Roberte has already agreed to offer her assistance, von A. reveals that the papers hidden in the tabernacle are not letters from Malwyda, but rather another kind of document altogether: "Schwester, there have never been any letters from Malwyda . . . There's nothing else there, down there, nothing . . . but the list of Jewish children" (211).

Malwyda's letters were really Hebrew "letters," Jewish names. What von A. wants to efface, then, is not the record of an incestuous relation, but rather the names of the children who were sheltered: in other words, the record of an act of hospitality.

How then should we understand the role of the "sister" in this shift from an insular, incestuous relationship among Germans to a transnational, transreligious hospitality epic? First, it is significant that Roberte's "sisterly" quality is evoked with a German word. For Malwyda is also the name of the "sister" of another convalescent and slightly deranged German, who presides over Roberte's nascent hospitality in a number of ways: Friedrich Nietzsche. Malwyda von Meysenbug was not Nietzsche's biological sibling, but the friend he "venerated like an older sister"[10] and with whom he maintained a long correspondence until the onset of his madness. An intimate of Richard Wagner's circle, von Meysenbug first became acquainted with Nietzsche while reading *The Birth of Tragedy* and served as a sounding board for many of his future books. She often took dictation while he wrote, and—like Roberte—even played the role of amateur nurse, caring for Nietzsche while he recovered from a prolonged illness.[11] A self-described progressive and "emancipated woman," Malwyda hoped to establish a "cloister for free spirits" with Nietzsche, combining his "gift for friendship" and "vocation for cultural reform" with her goal of "groom[ing] female students into the noblest representatives of women's emancipation."[12] In 1882 she formed the so-called Roman Club, an intellectual society made up of idealistic young girls.[13]

But the allusion to Malwyda von Meysenbug also leads to two more "sisters" of Nietzsche, both of whose histories shed some light on the Roberte–von A. relationship. The most noteworthy of Malwyda's Roman Club protegées was Lou Salomé, who eventually met Nietzsche through this connection. Lou was a fearless, attractive, and extremely intelligent young woman whom Nietzsche alternately regarded as an intellectual peer, a student for his teachings, and a potential romantic interest. The encounter between Nietzsche and Lou, like that between von A. and Roberte, took place in Rome, on the grounds of the Vatican, at St. Peter's Cathedral.[14] (Moreover, the immediate link between them was a Jewish friend, just as the relationship between Roberte and von A. ultimately revolves around a Jewish connection.) But the description of von A.'s love for his sister also points to Nietzsche's real sister, Elisabeth Förster-Nietzsche, for whom he had a semi-incestuous love as a child.[15]

All three figures—Malwyda, Lou, and Elisabeth—are linked on at least two levels. Nietzsche briefly established households with each woman, and each was at one time the object of his lifelong—and ultimately fruitless—search for a "sister soul," an interlocutor and collaborator capable of engaging with and furthering his philosophy. Each of these "sisters," then, was the object of Nietzsche's quest both for a housemate and for a soulmate—roles that ultimately hinged upon her qualities as a hostess. Which one of them would best receive, nurture, and welcome not only his person, but his thought? Elisabeth, the one-person fan club of his youth, eventually betrayed her brother's confidence both by renouncing his philosophy as immoral and by marrying the anti-Semite Bernhard Förster. In a letter to Malwyda, Nietzsche said of his sister: "There can be no question of reconciliation with a vengeful anti-Semitic goose."[16] And in one of the letters preceding their break he wrote to Elisabeth: "Souls like yours, my dear sister, I do not like, especially when they are morally bloated."[17] In contrast, Nietzsche was so impressed by Lou Salomé that he was moved to call her his "sister soul,"[18] hoping to find in her companionship and her writing the peer that had eluded him. Ultimately, though, Lou was too young and too fickle to commit herself to the rigorous standard of friendship he demanded.

Of the three women, Malwyda was the most trustworthy friend and companion. But despite her avowed progressiveness, she too was ultimately too attached to the values and morals of Nietzsche's time to prove a true "sister" to his thought. For although Malwyda was a tireless supporter of Nietzsche's work, she was also a reluctant witness to his turn away from the idealized Germanic and Greek themes—and above all the anti-Semitism—that characterized the intellectual circle around Wagner in the late 1870s. At this period Nietzsche was writing *Human, All-Too-Human,* a book greatly influenced by his friendship and intellectual collaboration with the French psychologist Paul Rée, a Jew. Nietzsche's friends (including Malwyda) were distressed by this shift in his work, feeling that Nietzsche had been "seduced" by Judaism.[19] In a letter from this period, Malwyda wrote to him: "Unlike Rée, you were not born for analysis [i.e., Judaism]. Your approach must be artistic [i.e., German]."[20]

The Malwyda reference thus has two different, and even contradictory, connotations. On the one hand she is a collaborator, nurse and "sister," a nurturing accomplice to Nietzsche's work. But on the other she is an anti-Semite who balks at the "seduction" of the Jewish letter, even when it is integral to the development of the very work she is trying to nurture. In this second guise, Malwyda can also be seen as an avatar both of Elisabeth, who resisted Nietzsche's philosophy in its most crucial articulation, and of Lou, who refused to go all the way and embrace the collaboration that was proposed to her. This second side of Malwyda contradicts the meaning and value of her first aspect for Nietzsche, representing her prescriptive, "positive," morality-bound side. It also complicates the meaning and value of her role as a "nurse," which now lends itself to a more ambivalent or even pejorative interpretation: that in trying to nurse Nietzsche back to health she might be trying to "cure" him of his infectious relation to Judaism.[21]

The problematics of the "sister," the intellectual peer, and anti-Semitism are all related through the motif of seduction. Each of Nietzsche's three "sisters" was susceptible to his seduction on some level (intellectual, romantic, incestuous, etc.), but each also resisted it on another. In two of the three cases the breach between Nietzsche and his "sister" concerned an anti-Semitic resistance to the allure of Judaism, and in each case it had to do with Nietzsche's relationship to Paul Rée: Lou Salomé betrayed Nietzsche's confidence with him, and Elisabeth and Malwyda—to varying degrees—were opposed to Nietzsche's friendship with him.

Nietzsche's correspondence with Malwyda is, at least on one level, the record of his "seduction" by Judaism. The fictional von A.'s correspondence with Malwyda also presents itself as the record of a seduction, but this time in the form of incest.[22] Ultimately, though, von A.'s "seduction" is itself no more than a cover for an illicit liaison with Judaism, as his confession of the tabernacle's true contents reveals. And just as Nietzsche's correspondence with Malwyda records his betrayal of anti-Semitic German ideals, von A.'s "correspondence" (i.e., the list of Jewish names) records his betrayal of the Nazi regime.

The theme of betrayal relates back to the "betrayal of elementary loyalties" discussed earlier, wherein Roberte's collaboration, and her "hospitality," were shown to follow a logic that supersedes questions of national and political allegiance. In this exchange, von A./Nietzsche becomes the apologist for this negative relation, extending Roberte's critique of national and political laws to a more general critique of the positive laws of personal identity that condition them: drawing upon a philosophy that, in its negativity, transcended such values as "German," "Christian," and "Nazi." This parallel allows us to understand the fuller meaning of the Malwyda reference and of the ambivalent place of the "sister," as well. For the failure of Nietzsche's search for a "sister soul" was due in part to his thought being assigned a positive or prescriptive content by those—like his sister Elisabeth—who sought to "clarify" its meaning or interpret it as a political program. Implicitly, the true "sister" would be one who collaborates in and contributes to this dissolution of positive identities, who in her marginal relation to the law of personal identity models a negativity that welcomes the contamination internal to identity, rather than moralistically upholding "health" (etymologically, "wholeness") as an ethical and aesthetic ideal.

Welcoming Negativity: Nietzsche as Hostess

Roberte as *Schwester* is thus not only a "sister soul," but a "feminized" Nietzsche whose hospitality will combine the philosopher's critique of morality with a distinctly feminine inadequation to laws of identity: whether national, religious, or personal. In this respect it is significant that Roberte's story contains suggestive parallels not only to the lives of Nietzsche's "sisters," but to that of the philosopher himself. Like Roberte, Nietzsche was a wartime volunteer with connections to Switzerland. In the Franco-Prussian war he served as a volunteer medical orderly under the Swiss flag, having transferred his citizenship from Germany in 1870.[23] Roberte's portrayal of herself as a citizen of Europe recalls Nietzsche's self-identification as a "good European,"[24] and both figures derive their respective political philosophies from idiosyncratic interpretations of Enlightenment ideals. Like Roberte, Nietzsche was descended from a long line of Lutheran ministers. And like her, he had to break with religious morality in order to truly embrace the negativity implied by his "transvaluation of all values."

Earlier we saw that Roberte characterizes her indiscriminate "charity" as one that answers to a higher law, and whose execution sometimes requires the suspension or even flagrant violation of the laws of national or religious allegiance. But von A. will in turn challenge "charity" as the form Roberte's hospitality assumes, questioning its religious underpinnings and finally revealing it to be no more than a possible—but ultimately contingent and unstable—manifestation of a more essential relation. The encounter with von A. effects a transformation in Roberte, releasing the *Schwester* within the Sister of Charity by forcing her to overcome or "transvalue" the residues of Christian morality in the way she conceives of her hospitality. In the process, Roberte discovers that the "higher law" she answers to in her disinterested "charity" is the law of hospitality, which von A. brings into relief by ridding it of all remaining moral sentiment.

Roberte's reaction to the true nature of von A.'s mission shows the "last gasp" of Christian morality in the woman about to become a "hostess," the ultimate break of Roberte-as-Christ from Christian morality. When she hears von A.'s story about the Jewish children, she is indignant about the apparently mercenary quality of his actions (his desire to "keep them on tap" in case he should need them later . . .) and cannot help but scold him; in contrast, she is relieved at hearing about the actions of the chaplain who completed the mission:

> Having found out that the chaplain had hurriedly got the Jewish children out of harm's way by scattering them around in various convents, I sat up, literally relieved at being given something like a serious reason for paying von A. more attention than I ordinarily should have. He was continuing, almost in a tone of recrimination. The S.S. had come to him demanding those children, a thorough investigation had been made. As a disciplinary measure they had

sent him to the front, down at Anzio, and they'd shot the priest. He paused, holding his chin in his hand. He had put me on a track; was I going to follow it? join all the bright-eyed girls in their rut of wanting to do something useful? Were he to be willing to go on talking, von A. would surely give me more clues. "A true martyr, that priest," I insinuated. (207–8)

Roberte's reaction is consistent with our general view of Nazism, which in its calculated disposal of its own "guests" and occupation of its Roman hosts manifests itself as the antithesis of hospitality, the complete opposite of the Christian ethics here embodied by the martyred priest. In fact, though, neither of these postures is as it first appears. As it turns out, *this* Nazi is actually the orchestrator of a covert operation of "hospitality," in which Jewish children designated for treatment as enemies, and destined for the camps, are actually being turned into guests, hidden in non-Jewish homes. At the same time, we learn that the priest, Vittorio, who appears to be the very embodiment of Christian charity, is really acting out of self-interest, exacting payment for this less-than-disinterested act of "hospitality." This "martyr" is actually a double-crossing spy: "the only thing priest about him had been his cassock. . . . it wasn't a question here of the clandestine activity of a brave man or a resistance hero, but of an utter swindler: under the cover of an act of charity he got himself paid a veritable ransom by the threatened families for each one of their children" (208).

Roberte's "rut of wanting to do something useful"—the helpful posture of the good Christian—is associated with a morality-bound tendency to take things at face value, to see "charity" in empty appearances.[25] The interested, economic logic of Vittorio's hospitality—a hospitality already aligned with the hotel—betrays the fact that "charity" is not without a certain hostility toward the stranger, as Nietzsche's argument on Christian nihilism suggests. At the same time, von A.'s duplicitous mission reveals a hospitable reception of the foreign within the apparent will to annihilate it.

The point of this potentially scandalous inversion of the Christian and Nazi positions is to show that the gesture of hospitality effects a reversal of apparent positions, a challenge to and revaluation of positive identities.[26] Hospitality is, to use Foucault's term, the ultimate "alternator of experience," the relation within which Vittorio and von A. simulate one another in their apparent opposition.[27] Hospitality as such resists all moral content and cannot be reduced to "doing good"; it follows a logic of its own, which cannot be reconciled to the aims of the church or of any other institution.

By revealing the Nietzsche within the Nazi, and the latent hostility toward the stranger internal to "charity," Klossowski challenges the capacity of any such symbolic designation to be consistent with or represent fully the subject it names. But at the same time, the implicit grounding of his narrative in the Nietzschean "transvaluation of all values" further nuances this fundamental observation. As we saw in chapter 2, Nietzsche's "transvaluation of all values" aims at the transformative dissolution of all "principles," even the impersonal or disinterested principles that replace Christian morality (for example, the Enlightenment form that Roberte's post-Christian and yet Christ-like hospitality assumes).[28] Following Nietzsche, Klossowski demonstrates that within the act of hospitality, the dissolution of positive ideas of personal identity is not the contrary or negation of identity, but rather its interior axis.[29]

Jewish Letters

In its covert quality—its intimate relation to hiding, disguise, and the dissimulation of one thing under the mask of another—the mission that von A. and Roberte undertake gives shelter to the unknown: not only the unknown guest (in this case, the Jewish children), but also the possibility of receiving something that resists recognition, translation, or interpretation. In this sense the liberation of the *Schwester* within the Sister of Charity corresponds to the surprise disclosure discussed earlier, in which the Christian tabernacle turned out to be a sanctuary of Jewish letters. There where we expected to find the "real presence," the embodied Spirit of Christ, we find instead the inscrutable Hebrew letters. As we saw in chapter 1, the Hebrew *ohel*—the tabernacle as "tent"—is the place of refuge of the divine letters (the covenant or laws) and not the "real presence." This fact sheds new light on the nature of Roberte's involvement in von A.'s secret mission, as well. Initially we are told that her Protestantism is important to the mission because her disbelief in the "real presence" allows her to penetrate unhindered into the tabernacle, which is inviolable to believers. But Roberte's status as a nonbeliever remains important even when it turns out that what the tabernacle really discloses are Hebrew "letters," since it grows out of a negative-theological propensity not to attribute a positive meaning or value to the sacred, but rather to receive it in its inscrutability.

The parallels between sisterhood and Judaism also give new meaning to the "cover" theme of incest, which—like the Jewish "letters"—refers back to the Hebraic origins of hospitality. Earlier we saw how the difference between the two ways that von A. presents his mission to Roberte hinges upon the question of whether what he wants to efface is the record of an incestuous relation or the record of an act of hospitality. Now we would have to qualify this transition further by noting that although the story of incest functions as a cover for a hospitality narrative, it is also true that incest is already coded "hospitality." As we saw in chapter 1, the act of incest is closely linked in the biblical tradition with the obligation to receive the stranger. Even Abraham's wife Sarah was his half-sister (Genesis 12), a fact he uses to mislead the Egyptian Pharaoh into thinking he is only her brother, and not her husband. Klossowski's implicit allusion to this tradition also gives new resonance to the problem of the sister, since Sarah—like Roberte—is both misrecognized as a biological sibling and at the same time later called upon in her capacity as a "sister" to serve as a hospitable accomplice. In both cases, moreover, the "sister" is instrumental in welcoming or safeguarding the Hebraic "letter"—in the first case the inscrutable word of YHWH, and in the second the secret list of Jewish names.

Roberte's alignment with the cause of the Jewish names, and with the "sisterhood" of the great Hebrew hostess, is but one expression of the interest in the link between Protestantism and Judaism that informs much of Klossowski's work, and that centers upon their mutual affirmation of the negativity internal to the sign. Jeffrey Mehlman, in an essay on Klossowski's reading of Hamann, notes that "the Protestantism of Klossowski's Hamann is Judeocentric or better, Judeo-eccentric: it is the Hebrews' way of straying from the divinity they were given to incarnate which is the reality to be affirmed."[30] Moreover, this straying is inseparable from the "constitutive inadequacy of the (Jewish) sign," its inscrutable illegibility. But if this inadequacy is to be celebrated, and not condemned, it is because in its ambivalent relation to referentiality, it "can modulate to an affirmation of the principle of *coincidentia oppositorum*."[31]

This affirmation defines the contours of Roberte's mission, as well. Her "feminine" hospitality, in its complicity with the inscrutable letter, celebrates the inadequacy of the sign by giving refuge to the remainder or excess that resists meaning or translation. It opposes itself to the economies of identity that would seek to identify the unknown, assign it a meaning and value, and put it into circulation.

In his reading of the mission to rescue the Jewish names, Mehlman suggests that the Nazi persecution of the Jews stands in for the Catholic persecution of the Protestants, the overturning of the Edict of Nantes to which the title refers.[32] Although this is certainly true, the preceding analysis shows that the complete picture is in fact even more complex. If the novel's multiple allusions, reversals, and inversions all point to a common logic, it is the one manifest in the tension between the persecution or betrayal of the letter and the act of welcoming it as an unknown. This betrayal appears most centrally in the threatened disclosure of the names of the Jewish children, destined to be sold to the Nazis. This sale allegorizes a number of other important appropriations, foreclosures, or translations of the letter, most immediately that of Nietzsche's sister Elisabeth, who "sold" his name and his work to Hitler as a kind of logo for the Nazi movement.[33] But more generally, the co-opting and persecution of the letter defines not only the fascist appropriation of Nietzsche, but also the Catholic persecution of the Protestants, the Christian translation of Judaism, and, as we shall see in the next section, the Roman Catholic appropriation of pagan Roman hospitality.

In welcoming the letter or sign, the "sister" opposes her hospitality to this reductive economics of signification. Unlike Malwyda or Elisabeth, Roberte as *Schwester* will not deride the Judaic, but rather rescue and resuscitate the Jewish "letters" within the Christian tabernacle. Implicitly, the real "sister soul" is the one who takes collaboration to its very limit, who does not balk at finding the Jewish letters there where she expected to find "spirit": a spirit variously coded within the novel as the "real presence" the Catholic worships against the heretical Protestant, the embodied Christian Word of Paul's dialectic against the Jews, the artistic German *Geist* that Malwyda exalts over Jewish "analysis," or the alleged "essence" of Nietzsche's thought that Elisabeth distills for the benefit of the Nazi party. For Roberte as well as for Nietzsche, to be "seduced" by Judaism is to be seduced by and into negativity, to oppose the inscrutable "letter" or name to the transcendental positivity of spirit.[34]

Von A. draws upon this seduction when he initiates Roberte into the ways of hospitality. In seducing her as a "sister," he appeals to her as someone whose hospitable relation to personal identity will be divided and ambivalent: a sister whose hospitality is now coded not only "Nietzschean," but also "Jewish," insofar as she embodies a covert and undecidable relation both to identity and to the letter. The *mise-en-abîme* quality of these successive encodings, the vertiginous way in which a seemingly infinite number of contradictory possibilities are embedded within one word or gesture, underscores the structural inadequation to the signifier of privative identity that defines Roberte's sisterly hospitality. For if there is a pattern to this chaos, it is simply that in each of these infinite reversals, it is the negative, the unknown or inscrutable, that triumphs over the positive or prescriptive.

Dissolution as Liberation

In the final installment of the "Roman Impressions," the multiple allusions, reversals, and inversions that have structured Roberte's journal entries take on yet another twist, perhaps the most improbable of all. It turns out that von A.'s original mission had another, unrealized component: to kidnap the Pope and take him to Nuremberg[35] in order to "reinstate Jupiter Capitolinus" in Rome (209). Roberte's rescue of the Jewish letters within the tabernacle is thus doubled by von A.'s attempted liberation of the pagan polytheism underlying Christian belief. But despite their many differences, the two projects share a common aim. The code name of von A.'s aborted mission, *Operation Apostata*, references the same logic identified by Foucault in the "alternators of experience," the mechanism through which apparent opposites reveal themselves to be simulacra of one another.[36] The code name draws an analogy between the Nazi von A.'s subversive stance in relation to the cynical Church and the "contrarian" role of Milton's "apostate angel," Satan, who in William Blake's romantic account emerges as the "true" Messiah *(The Marriage of Heaven and Hell)*. This analogy allows us to read Klossowski's contrary setup as a kind of transvaluation of values through the "alternators of experience," a questioning of fixed positions that effects their mutual dissolution in one another.

The same logic informs Roberte's role as a hostess. In her first act of "hospitality," which is not yet even identified as such, Roberte experiences the "dissolution" of her symbolic ties to the world, realizing the full negative potential of "collaboration within resistance." In the closing scene of the novel, Roberte accompanies the ailing von A. onto the balcony of the hospital, commanding a vista of the entirety of Rome. There he proceeds to grip her in a lascivious embrace, which seals Roberte's "hospitable" fate: "My hand soon grew still and, while my palms were seeking his lips, the ties dissolved that bound me to this world in which I had been taught to perform gestures of devotion, of self-sacrifice, of charity" (212). But the scene is interrupted, suspended; at the exact moment of Roberte's "dissolution," a pair of American soldiers bursts onto the balcony, announcing the penetration of the Allied forces into Rome: the liberation has begun (213).

But the coincidence of these two events begs a question. What exactly has been liberated? Rome, the Vatican capital, from its secular occupiers? Or Roberte, the "sister," from the moral code of self-sacrifice and charity with which she once identified herself? These two possibilities coalesce in a third, whose stakes both draw upon and transcend their constituent parts. Namely, that *hospitality itself has been liberated:* from Rome, from religion, from the laws of cosmopolitan Europe. Earlier we saw that the "higher" law Roberte answers to in her disinterested charity is ultimately the law of hospitality itself, "liberated" from all moral systems. At this moment of instability, which stages the confrontation or overturning of religious traditions, we witness the ascendancy of the law of hospitality through the resurgence of the dissolute or the multiple within the One: the figurative overthrowing of a unified, transcendent, Catholic hospitality in favor of one paradoxically coded both Hebraic and polytheist.

The moment of "liberation" gives new weight to von A.'s projected reinstatement of Jupiter Capitolinus, the divinity who is the Roman avatar of Zeus, the pagan god of hospitality. Even though the plot to kidnap the Pope does not go as planned, von A. suggests merrily that "someday it may be pulled off" (209). The groundwork has been laid, and in fact it is the trilogy of the *Laws of Hospitality* itself that will effect this "apostate operation," through the "polytheist" hospitality that Roberte will offer under her husband's eyes. Just as Roberte's "hospitable" nature emerges out of her "charitable" disposition, to which it is nonetheless fundamentally opposed, pagan hospitality does not have to overthrow its Christian counterpart so much as reassert its primacy within it, as a latent tendency that only needs to be given new voice.

The figure of Jupiter Capitolinus not only represents this possibility but also links it in an essential way to the logic of hospitality. As the major iconographic model for Trinitarian art,[37] the Capitoline triad (Jupiter, Juno, Minerva) haunts Christian ontological monotheism as its barely repressed polytheist heritage, periodically reasserting itself within the trinity that has only superficially displaced it, without ever managing to erase it entirely. The projected reascendance of Capitolinus signals the resurfacing of pagan hospitality within the inclusive Christian community, the reemergence of a dissolute disbelief within "one heart." And like Roberte's hospitality, this movement consists in a "feminization" of unity that dissolves its coherence. It involves a reassertion of the feminine (Juno, Minerva) within the trinity, the division or difference—and also the jealousy[38]—internal to the doctrine of ontological similitude.

Roberte's violation of the tabernacle extends this feminine dissolution to the Word itself, in the form of the gospel she desecrates in the course of her mission to extract the list of Jewish names. In the following long citation, which describes the climactic moment of her secret mission, we see how Roberte's hospitality comes into being in opposition to that of the Christian Host; the first two gestures we associate with Roberte are the scattering of Hosts and the violation or effacement of the Word. This is further important in that although the violation of the tabernacle is chronologically the last of the episodes Roberte describes it is nonetheless placed first in her narration of the "Roman Impressions." This ambiguous but sacrilegious act presides over the entirety of the chronicle, which happens under the sign of a Word transgressed by the ambiguous corporal gesture of a woman:

> I don't deny that to penetrate in such a way—my face disguised behind a mask, my hands gloved, but for the rest accoutered about as lightly as one could be—into this high-vaulted and dark place, lit only by the weak glow of the night light, sent a first shiver running down my spine. . . . My presence here and at this hour, in this costume, was known, and I was by no means sure my gestures were not under observation; but if he who was charged to survey them

was actually there, was he sharing my excitement at that very instant, and was he not also on the verge of losing control of himself?
I was near to it, my heart pounding at the thought of the gesture
I was about to execute, already forgetting everything of this gesture's significance apart from the success or failure of my raid. . . .
By a pillar showed the contours of a figure, a figure too huge not
to be the semblance of another world: leaning on the shaft of his
halberd, wearing a Renaissance lansquenet's outfit, his eyes flash-
ing beneath the visor of his helmet, completely unreal, it was as
if he had stepped straight out of a painting by some old master
to watch my own unreality in this situation. Upon coming to the
realization that this was a Pontifical Guardsman, all feeling of seriousness simply drained out of me. . . . Almost put on edge to see
him stand immovable, his legs planted wide, his doublet ending in
a peculiar pouch at his groin, I started to climb the steps leading
to the altar; keeping my eyes on him all the while, I fitted the key
into the lock of the tabernacle, and opened its door; but off there
in the darkness he remained frozen in this position. I reached my
bare arm toward the tabernacle's silk-lined interior and with my
gloved hand touched the base of the sacred vessel: lifting the chalice, I drew it out, and then groping with my other hand found the
secret catch von A. had mentioned. I pressed it and a roll of paper
emerged; I crooked a finger and slid it out of its hiding place, folded
it, and tucked it inside the opening in the palm of my glove. Pausing
there, again I waited and once again scanned the shadows behind
me. Then, losing all patience with this stony indifference or with
this handsome fellow's insufferable standoffishness, I knocked over
the chalice, scattering Hosts left and right. At that same instant
the butt of the halberd came down once, twice, three times on the
floor; opposite me the tabernacle opened at the rear. And then, daz-
zling white in the light streaming through from the other side, two
feminine hands—two slender hands whose similarity to mine was
frightening—advanced, seized my wrists and held them in a grip
positively of iron. Behind me the huge person began to move, and
his slow, almost processional footsteps boomed in cadence with my
beating pulse. . . . I made an effort to get free and when I'd understood that no amount of effort would help, my jitteriness turned
into something agreeable: I saw myself as I had been, walking up to
the altar, masked, gloved, half-naked, and with the mad desire to
taste the consequences of my effrontery. And indeed, these girlish,

viselike hands, holding me by I don't know what power—the one
I attributed to them—started to remove the gloves from my own
slender and flawless hands. Having turned them over, they spread a
salve upon my palms, moistening my fingers to the very tips. Trying
to elude their burning caresses, I wrested myself away. But there
already, towering over me, he pressed himself against my back and
wedged me between his breeches and the holy table. And, having
brought the open missal near, he applied my sticky palms to a page
of the Gospel. Then without letting go of me for an instant, he
sprinkled some charcoal dust over the parchment and blew it away.
My fingerprints were revealed and the lines of my hands stood out,
printed there forever, upon the Word of God. . . .
   "You who have insulted the Word, who are you?"
   Aiming the beam of the flashlight at me, he saw me such as I
was there: laced tight in my corset, shoulders, arms and legs bare.
(E102–6, translation modified; F17–20)

Roberte's hospitality is construed as a violation of the Word,
marked by the application of her hands to the pages of the New
Testament. But in violating the unity of the sacred word, Roberte
also loses access to the semblance of unity that has heretofore presided over her actions. For the strange "punishment" she receives
involves not so much her censure by someone else, but rather a
kind of splitting in two of her own will: she is held in check by two
suspiciously familiar feminine hands, which protrude from within
the tabernacle like the mirror reflection of her own hands reaching
in. It is as though one part of her will has concretized in defense of
the tabernacle's sanctity, even as the other desecrates it in pursuit
of a hospitality enacted in violation of the Word.
   In the following section, we will see how the implications of this
scene are obliquely developed by Roberte's husband, Octave. As
I mentioned earlier, Roberte's first-person accounts are only one
component of The Revocation. Her "Roman Impressions," in the
form of a series of diary entries, are interspersed with pages from
the diary of her husband. The inscrutable or compromised quality
of the letter or sign will be reexamined by Octave in relation to
the corporal gesture as "solecism," an ambiguous movement that
simultaneously expresses two contradictory impulses—thereby
resituating the principle of coincidentia oppositorum as an erotic
tension within the body. Just as Roberte's hand effaces the word

of the gospel, the staging of the solecism will efface and deface the word as the guarantor of a transcendental unity in favor of a dissolute operation of expropriation.

The Visual Solecism, or the Spectator as Guest

Octave's journal entries also concern the oscillation between two different positions, the contradiction between two opposing roles. However, they approach this material from a different vantage point, informed by a reflection on the relationship between body and soul, letter and spirit that is both an esoteric theology and a perverse pornography: what Gilles Deleuze describes as a "superior pornology of forms."[39] Octave's status as a retired professor of scholastic theology is qualified by two further obsessions. First, he is a passionate collector of the works of the (imaginary) Mannerist painter Frédéric Tonnerre, whose large compositions in the *tableau vivant* style eroticize the moment of moral hesitation experienced by women submitting to sexual advances. Second, he is a writer of perverse fiction, whose Latinate syntax strives to approximate the same highly eroticized conflict captured in Tonnerre's visual compositions. The two obsessions unite in Octave's analysis of what he calls the "visual solecism" in the paintings of Tonnerre, which his diary both elegizes and identifies as the inspiration for his own erotic meditations.

Solecism, or "speaking incorrectly," is a rhetorical device coined by ancient Greek writers to describe the corruption of the Attic dialect by the Athenian colonists on the island of Solis. In modern usage, it is generally defined either as an "offence against grammar or idiom" *(Concise Oxford Dictionary)* or as a "faulty concord" *(OED)*. While in its more restricted linguistic sense it connotes a violation of the rules of grammar or syntax, or an impropriety in speech or diction, it may be used more generally to describe any breach of good manners or etiquette *(OED)*.

But although solecism generally has a pejorative connotation, its corruption of the relationship between word and referent—or gesture and signification—can also be positively inflected, insofar as it implies an expanded power of suggestion, the ability to signify contradictory possibilities simultaneously, or poetic wordplay. Hence solecism is sometimes identified with poetic license, or with the detachment of the sign from regimes of signification.[40] Octave's idiosyncratic treatment of solecism plays upon each of these possible connotations. He justifies its adaptation to the visual medium through reference to a remark from Quintilian's *Institutio Oratoria,* which serves as the epigraph for his first journal entry: "Some think there is solecism in gesture too, whenever by a nod of the head or a movement of the hand one utters the opposite of what the voice is saying."[41]

Tonnerre develops this possibility through paintings of rape scenes, often on historical themes, which dramatize the tension between a woman's chaste moral attitude (often linked to her social class, religion, or marital status) and her gradual surrender to an assailant's advances. In these compositions, solecism is present most often in ambiguous gestures of the hand, a movement that simultaneously expresses the defense of modesty and its surrender: for example an inflection of the hand that, while pushing away an assailant, seems at the same time to be drawing him closer. According to Octave,

> What Tonnerre was endeavoring to express was moral repugnance and the irruption of pleasure simultaneously gripping the same soul, the same body; and he rendered this conflict through the position of the hands, one of which is lying and the other avowing a crime which seeps from its fingers. . . . For, in placing the back of a hand in front of an unveiled fleece, in imparting this or that expression to fingers, in modeling the palm of a hand, in stressing index and thumb, he counterpoises a spiritual agitation against the tangible mass of this or that part of the body. *And there, at that point, one can measure the exact degree to which the woman is in possession of herself or finds her charms slipping out from under the control of her will. We are witness to the unending expropriations of the body subjected to an outside gaze, and also to a budding complicity between the woman and an image of herself that she may have spent years combating* . . . (111/112, my emphases, translation modified)

The aim of Octave's analysis is not merely to foster the reader's aesthetic appreciation of Tonnerre's work, however. In the image of an "outside gaze" that is called upon to effect an expropriation of the body, and thereby bring into relief a woman's "complicity" with an unwilled image of herself, Octave articulates the very expropriation that his "laws of hospitality" seek to effect in Roberte. Both here and in *Roberte, ce soir,* he uses this framework to think

about the sexual surrendering of his wife to chance strangers, fortuitous "guests" who apprehend the unsuspecting hostess in such a
way as to solicit an emotion that escapes the control of her will, a
response in contradiction with her symbolic role.[42]

We have already witnessed this split or contradiction in Roberte,
which she even characterizes as the basis of her ethics. In fact, the
moral oscillation within one soul that Tonnerre depicts could even
be understood as the interiorized, spiritual equivalent of the conflict dramatized in Roberte's political complicity with opposing
sides. For "collaboration within resistance"—the name I gave to
the way that Roberte's "indiscriminate charity" supersedes laws of
partisan allegiance—is an almost exact summary of what happens
in Tonnerre's visual solecisms, with the difference that here the oscillation between two contradictory positions is conceived not politically, but morally. In other words, the conflict it dramatizes is
not between different political allegiances or symbolic identities,
but between the moral soul and the carnal soul.

However, this distinction is not as clear-cut as it may appear.
For Octave's analysis suggests that the conflict between different
symbolic identities is at heart *always* a conflict between the moral
soul and the carnal soul, insofar as it concerns the tension between
a moral identification with a symbolic role and the desires or impulses that are inconsistent with it. We see this tension at work in
Roberte's diary as well, in the involuntary ecstasies of the "lawmaker turning whore" (159) at the hands of impudent strangers. In
the burgeoning of pornographic eroticism within the prim gestures
of the Inspectress of Censorship, we are confronted with the solecistic emergence of a contradictory impulse at the very heart of the
gesture to which it is opposed.

In one present-day scene from *The Revocation of the Edict of
Nantes,* Roberte is resting in her bath after a hard day's work at
the National Education Commission, where she has just been instrumental in censoring her husband's latest novel, *Roberte, ce
soir.* But as she recalls some of the book's lewder scenes, and con-
gratulates herself for publicly condemning its obscenity, two of the
characters from Octave's novel—the Giant and the Hunchback—
burst in on her bath, assuming a tangible reality and thereby proving the offensive premise of her husband's book: namely, that they
"are nothing else than the at first vaporous figments of my own
reverie, [which] take on consistency the longer I maintain my si-

lence" (167). The contradiction between Roberte's moral silence and her immoral thoughts is precisely what allows for the corporal manifestation of the figures she has censored, who now proceed to enact upon her the very erotic fantasies she has refused to let be pronounced.

In his reading of this passage, Deleuze describes the conflict in Roberte as that between "pure words" and "impure silence"—a conflict rooted in the body-as-language:

> What is the dilemma? Of what does the disjunctive syllogism that expresses it consist? The body is language. But it may conceal the speech it is made up of, it may cover it over. The body can, and usually does, wish for its works to be left in silence. Rejected by the body, but thereby also projected, delegated, and alienated, speech thus becomes the discourse of a beautiful soul, who speaks of laws and virtues, but who is silent about the body. In this case, it is clear that the speech itself is so-called "pure," but that the silence upon which it rests is impure.[43]

Solecism names the tension between body and speech, or rather between public words and the silent speech of the body. But whereas Roberte casts her ability to keep these two realms separate as the basis of her ethics as a liberal lawmaker, her "ethics of saying nothing," Octave's meditation on the visual solecism develops this notion of compromised silence in a different way, approaching it not as a matter of ethics, charity, or the fulfillment of a public role, but rather as the reflection of an internal subjective division.

The Rape of Lucretia is for Octave the ultimate subject of solecism, since it dramatizes the limit between moral purity and carnal desire, representing the second as the contrary—but also the ultimate expression—of the first. In his description of Tonnerre's treatment of this classical theme, Octave evokes the power of this oscillation in the following terms:

> Contemplating the scene, are we witnesses to the dilemma in which the Roman heroine is struggling? If she yields, she obviously sins; if she doesn't yield, she will be thought to have sinned, since, killed by her aggressor, she will be calumniated as well. Do we see her yield having first decided to destroy herself once she has published her defeat? Or has she first decided to yield, though it be to die afterward, once she has spoken? No question but that if she yields

it is because she has been reflecting; had she not been, she would kill herself or have killed herself there and then. Now from reflecting upon her design for death, she throws herself into Tarquin's arms and—as St. Augustine insinuates—perhaps impelled by her own lust, later punishes herself for this confusion, for this solecism; which comes to succumbing to dread of dishonor, as Ovid puts it. *She succumbs, is the way I would put it, to her own lust which splits in two: the lust of her own chastity separates from chastity and becomes carnal.* (109, translation modified; my emphases)

Lucretia's dilemma is that she has no witness to her moral state, which can convey itself only by means of ambiguous signs. These signs are in turn subject to the interpretation of an observer, who is witness not to her interior state, but to the "dilemma" itself: in other words, witness to the inadequation between the state of her will and the sign by which it conveys itself. In this case, the dilemma concerns the relationship between the gesture of suicide and her internal state: does it express her extreme chastity, or her guilty violation of it?

More generally, her predicament arises out of the tension between moral personhood—the attempt to live in accordance with a principle, code, or dogma—and the excessive impulses that underlie it. For Lucretia is not just any victim of rape, but a woman renowned for her chastity and virtue. Ironically, though, her principled life is itself her downfall. By virtue of trying to live according to a principle or maxim of chastity, she exposes herself to the "confusion" implicit in solecism. Once it is reduced to a sign, the moral will is susceptible to the hesitations and ambivalences internal to the sign, its capacity to signify both the positive gesture and its opposite or negation. Hence her own lust "splits in two," the lust of chastity separating from chastity and becoming carnal. In this account, the dilemma of Lucretia's position is that the moral gesture of resistance so exceeds itself as to mutate into its opposite. As "lust," the very ferventness with which she defends herself lends itself to two different interpretations. Lust of chastity *becomes* carnal lust, resistance *becomes* collaboration.

Like the mechanism of Roberte's "collaboration within resistance," Tonnerre's visual solecism demonstrates the inadequation of the moral subject to a law of identity. But here it is not only the moral integrity of the subject that is challenged, but also the integrity of the body. This means not only that the person is not "whole" or undivided, but also that this duplicity or duality is expressed in the body as an erotic tension, with the body animating the excess of the moral soul. As the passage continues, Octave specifies that the "splitting" of Lucretia's lust for chastity

> happens in a twinkling of an eye, *and it's the twinkle of a painter's eye*. And our painter, what has he done? Only consider the adorable discretion with which Titian represented the scene: Tarquin threatens his prey with a dagger and seizes her by the arm. Lucretia, already bending, still implores. But what reserve in each of their attitudes! Let me be forgiven for mentioning Titian in connection with Tonnerre . . . anyhow, the latter shows us Lucretia lying full length upon a couch, propped upon one elbow, her head, seen in profile, erect, one leg straight, the other thigh lifting in a suspicious manner, as if perhaps repelling the aggressor: *but at the same time, the viewer will think, preparing the way for him*. Already lowered over her, Tarquin brings his face near the lady's cheeks, wrapping an arm around her waist, one hand clutching her breast while she, her other elbow raised, her hand open, tries to fend off the young man's lips as the arm upon which she is leaning reaches down toward her belly where that hand, all its fingers extended, seems less to be covering her too visible shame than to be waiting . . . (translation modified; my emphases)(110)

The visual solecism seeks to apprehend the moment of "reflection" that betrays the splitting of the moral impulse. But if it happens "in the twinkling of an eye," it is because this hesitation can only be rendered by locating the precise moment at which a single corporal gesture is capable of signifying two mutually contradictory possibilities. The transposition to the aesthetic medium of painting is thus key. For "reflection" names both the inaccessible, interior thought process and the mechanism through which this hesitation is reflected outward, framed or staged for the viewer's benefit through the capturing of an ambiguous sign.

Affection

The story of Lucretia is one of the key early passages in *The City of God,* Augustine's major treatment of hospitality, in which "affection" is characterized as a sentiment capable of binding a plurality of men in "one heart."[44] But in marked distinction to Octave's torrid meditation on Tonnerre's painting, Augustine uses Lucretia's dilemma to introduce the idea of the purity of the Christian soul and its transparency before God. His discussion of the episode occurs within the context of a broader argument, devoted to the defense of Christian women who—unlike Lucretia—did not kill themselves after they were raped: "We maintain that when a woman is violated while her soul admits no consent to the iniquity, but remains inviolably chaste, the sin is not hers, but his who violates her."[45] Although Augustine here implicitly suggests that Lucretia may have lusted, and then killed herself to expiate her guilt, he also goes on to resolve the double bind of implied culpability by arguing that God—and God alone—is capable of seeing into a woman's soul and judging whether she has committed adultery. Hence the innocent woman need not kill herself to establish her innocence, because she has a "witness" to her moral state. How then is this argument related to the larger thesis of Augustine's work, namely that "affection" is a community sentiment that binds many together in "one heart"? Implicitly, the fact of being of "one heart" with God is what allows the good Christian woman to be undivided in *her* heart, "admitting no consent" and remaining unwavering in her sinlessness.

Octave's discussion of Lucretia's dilemma follows the steps of Augustine's argument almost to the letter, but with a key substitution that completely alters the conclusion he draws from them. In the passage cited above, the "outside gaze" who is called upon to evaluate the "exact degree to which the woman is in possession of herself" is the viewer of the work of art. In relation to Augustine's text, the spectator thus assumes the place traditionally occupied by God. But whereas God possesses an unambiguous knowledge of a woman's soul by virtue of being of "one heart" with her, the viewer of the artwork is able to gaze into her soul only insofar as it is not undivided, but rather betrays itself by ambiguous signs. Moreover, he is himself an implicated party who gazes at an object that is exposed and expropriated by his gaze, and who actualizes the "sin" of pleasure precisely by witnessing it. The viewer of the artwork must decide among the "multitude of possible significations to a crease in the hand" (F24), deducing from the "spiritual agitation" of the ambivalent gesture a moment of moral hesitation, and thereby apprehending the woman in contradiction with herself. What he discovers in the woman submitted to his gaze is not simply her "guilt" or "innocence," of course, but rather an illicit enjoyment erupting within the attitude of moral repugnance itself, which betrays her momentary detachment from her moral will rather than confirming her pure "one-heartedness."

Octave's reappropriation of the Lucretia story is not so much a departure from Augustine, however, as an illumination of a division internal to the doctrine of affection itself. In his first journal entry, Octave cites Augustine in a way that subtly perverts the intention of the Church Father's theology, identifying the moment where "affection" divides from itself and mutates into something recognizable not only as its opposite or contradiction, but as its implied underside. In other words, "affection" is itself revealed to be a solecism. Octave first introduces Augustine not through his theological writings, but through his metonymic association with the beauty of Roman women: "In we Westerners, the incurable heirs of Augustinian Manicheism, attractiveness resides in the austere appearance of the face, dissimulating—it's this that counts—all the more exuberant charms" (99). Augustine as the figure for Christian unity is thus doubled and partly contradicted by Augustine as a figure for the dissimulating physiognomy of the Roman woman, an austerity simultaneously hiding and belying an erotic exuberance.

In his elegy to Tonnerre, Octave indirectly alludes to Augustine in his invocation of "affection," marking the place where this "community sentiment" splits—like Lucretia's "lust for chastity"—into two contradictory impulses: " 'Affection' would here designate the feeling in the sole lover of his work, myself—though a man in his sixties—moved at seeing survive, thanks to his indiscreet brush, that race of Second Empire beauties . . ." (98). In this instance, "affection" names not the experience of participating in a divine community through the mediation of Christ, but rather the feeling inspired in the viewer by looking at Tonnerre's canvases. Nonetheless, this feeling of "affection" is also the expression of a community sentiment. But here this sense of community—which the spectator of the work is instrumental in maintaining—is predicated upon solecistic discord, rather than unifying one-heartedness.

Confession and Community

The difference between the two positions inheres in their different interpretations of the relationship between community and "putting in common." For Octave, affection names not a sentiment shared in common by a disparate group of individuals, but the putting in common of a woman that effects the expropriation and the dissolution of her moral integrity. However, both brands of "affection" depend upon the production and putting in common of a sign:

> At the outset one is rather hard put to make out the relationship established between gesture and speech; certain gestures are being made by the various figures represented, and that seems to be all. To what words do these gestures relate? Probably to those the painter supposes said by his personages, no less than to those the viewer may be saying as he contemplates the scene. But if solecism there be, if it is something *opposite* which the figures *utter* through this or that gesture, they must say something in order that this opposition be palpable; but painted, they are silent; does the spectator speak in their behalf, in such a way as to sense the opposite of the gesture he sees them performing? There still remains the question of whether, having painted such gestures, the artist wished to avoid our solecism; or whether, from painting the kind of scene he chose, he was, to the contrary, trying to demonstrate the positiveness of the solecism which could be expressed only through means of an image. (97)

The third party observer is instrumental in enunciating or bringing forth a silenced word, producing a kind of "confession." This dimension of the spectator's role also alludes to another key component of Augustine's theology. For Augustine is the source not only for the Roman story underlying Tonnerre's painting, but also for the confessional genre and its relation to hospitality. In his *Confessions,* Augustine maintains that the relation of "sharing" inaugurated between the three terms of the hospitality act (host, guest, and God) is reproduced in the practice of confession, where a third party is called upon to act as a mediator between man and God. The point of inviting a third party (who may be a priest, a fellow man, or even the reader of a confessional text) to participate in the confession is to spread "affection" among brothers, sharing and thereby increasing their love for God.[46]

In contrast, the "third party" in Octave's scenario—the spectator or viewer of the artwork—does not complete the circle or inscribe the individual experience within a meaningful whole, but rather articulates the contradiction or ambivalence positivized by the image. But precisely insofar as he is not of "one heart" with the unwilling confessant he observes, the spectator nonetheless participates in something like a circle of affection: with the important difference that he stands *outside* of the circle, rather than being included within it. The spectator's relation to the painting will model the position of the guest in Octave's formulation of the "laws of hospitality," the chance "divinity" who allows for the production of a communal relation through the putting in common of an ambivalent sign.[47] But the position of the spectator before the work of art is also analogous to the experience of the reader of *The Revocation,* who is invited to experience Roberte in her expropriation.

While the diary genre of *The Revocation* clearly alludes to the Augustinian confessional, it has a different purpose and effect. A diary is personal, private—a confession of what is *not* avowed publicly, much like the moral ambivalence expressed as a solecism. The religious confession, conversely, is an autobiographical narrative retroactively considered from the vantage point of a conversion, which imposes meaning upon a series of acts that were previously illegible. It distills what is structural or universal from what appeared to be a discreetly personal experience in order to transmit it for the benefit of others. Whereas Augustine's confession departs from the personal to address what is universal, Roberte's "confession" parts from a position of enunciation identified with charity and brotherhood, only to split this point of departure into a number of conflicting positions of enunciation that no longer articulate a universal, and that have the effect of sundering—rather than edifying—the one-hearted "City of God."

One mark of this is the fact that Roberte's and Octave's separate diary entries not only are not read by one another, but even offer radically contradictory views of the "same" events, founding discrepancies rather than a harmonious single interpretation or sense of community project. Each has a different take on the "laws of hospitality" and what they mean, and how their different ideals of community ethics are related to them. As a result, the reader has to reckon with both of these positions and must forge a link between these radically different "confessions" by some means other than simple reconciliation or amalgamation. The novel is composed entirely of Roberte's and Octave's diaries, which are juxtaposed without any attempt to reconcile or mediate between them. Their separate "confessionals" serve not to bind the two spouses in "one heart," but to insist upon the contradictions and disjunctions internal to this "union."

Klossowski evokes the confessional genre only to pervert it, taking as his model subject and protagonist not the faithful Augustine, but the ambivalent Lucretia. As a result, the "confession" maps the trajectory not of faith discovered, but of faith compromised or betrayed—dissolved in the unexpected "welcoming" of an unknown. It highlights the moment of hesitation or ambivalence, rather than the retroactive recovery and inscription of this moment within a logic of unified faith. We see the same mechanism at work in Roberte's journal entries, which combine elements of both the diary and the confessional genres. They recount events that happened in the past, but in a way that insists upon the solecismic tension of a momentary encounter, rather than its eventual resolution or recognition from the vantage of a "conversion."

In the climactic episode of the "Roman Impressions," Roberte's "confession" leads directly to the solecismic violation of the word. As Roberte enters the chapel on her way to complete von A.'s secret mission, she ducks into a confessional booth where she meets up with the "priest" Vittorio, to whom she addresses the conventional words "Father, may I confess?" (103). This detail is significant on another level as well, since Roberte's violation of the tabernacle is the first episode to be narrated in the novel. Her first words imply that her autobiographical accounts are to be understood as a kind of confession, an impression intensified by the *Bildungsroman* quality of her wartime experiences. But in this scene—as in the novel as a whole—the confession never takes place: Roberte's formula, we learn, is part of a code that the coconspirators have agreed upon in advance, for the purpose of avoiding detection. The intention of her "confession" is thus to hide, not to divulge. The form of the confession is there merely to dissimulate the "hospitable" action, which has another intention altogether: to violate the tabernacle and in the process profane the very gospel whose words she appears to be looking to for guidance.

Roberte is someone who has violated the rules of the Word, one definition of solecism that here combines with Octave's: someone whose moral gestures belie an immoral motive. But on another level, her "confession" is itself a solecism: she grounds her actions in the

words of the gospel, even as her actions serve to violate and profane those words.[48] Her words and her acts are at odds, "bespeak-
ing" different impulses. Moreover, this contradiction is marked by
a very solecism-like gesture: the laying on of two hands "whose
resemblance to [her] own is frightening." As she withdraws from
the tabernacle, Roberte notes that her wrists were seized by two
"girlish, viselike hands, holding me by I don't know what power:
the one I attributed to them" (105). Her own hands are simultaneously violating the tabernacle and punishing this violation, the corporal equivalent of the contradiction, dissimulation, and speaking
at cross purposes that defines her "confession." Roberte's violation
of the gospel is thus a solecism on three different levels: a breach of
manners or etiquette, an offense against the language of the New
Testament, and the expression of an ambivalent gesture marked by
suspended hands.

Voicing Opposition

The notion of two gestures that contradict one another or speak at
cross purposes brings us back to the theological framework underlying Octave's meditations and Roberte's "Roman Impressions,"
both of which are concerned with uncovering the different "voices"
within what appears to be a single theological tradition, thereby
bringing to light the fissures within the community that the confessional genre is supposed to unite.

These possibilities are represented in condensed form in the
name of Octave's imaginary idol, Tonnerre, whose compositions offer condensed enactments of these same contradictions.
Tonnerre's name, meaning "thunder," resonates on at least three
different levels. First, it evokes one of the attributes of Jupiter,
the reinstated hospitality divinity of von A.'s *Operation Apostata*
in the "Roman Impressions." Second, it recalls a line from
Augustine's *Confessions*, which applies equally well to the subjects
of Tonnerre's compositions and to the vagaries of Roberte's own
life as a hostess. In a curious apostrophe to the lascivious fables so
ubiquitous in Roman paganism, Augustine writes: "Do I not read
in thee of Jupiter sometimes thundering, and sometimes adulter-
ating? But verily both these could not one person do: but this is
feigned, that there might be authority to imitate true-acted adultery; false thunder the mean while playing the bawd to him."[49] In

The Revocation, and especially in *Roberte, ce soir,* Roberte will be revealed as that "one person" who contains both of these possibilities, against Augustine's idea of a consistent deity.

The possibility of one person accomplishing two incompatible things at once leads to the third reference behind the painter's name. It appears to be an allusion to an important tract of Gnostic scripture, entitled "The Thunder—Perfect Intellect." This Greek language tract is written in the genre of a "wisdom monologue," in which an unidentified speaker offers clues to its identity in the form of a series of paradoxes or riddles. "The Thunder—Perfect Intellect" is a monologue in the feminine voice, pronounced by a speaker who calls herself "afterthought."[50] The mode in which she identifies herself is solecismic in structure: she is a voice of innumerable sounds, but at the same time incomprehensible silence; hers is a discourse made up not of words, but of images. But these images nonetheless "speak" a name:

> It is I who am incomprehensible silence:
> And afterthought, whose memory is so great.
> It is I who am the voice whose sounds are so numerous:
> And the discourse whose images are so numerous.
> It is I who am the speaking: of my (own) name.[51]

The Gnostic passion for resonant contradictions infuses not only Octave's characterization of Tonnerre's paintings, but the trilogy of the *Laws* as a whole. In *Le Souffleur,* the character Valentine K—Roberte's simulacrum or "sister"—is named for Valentinus, the great Gnostic theologian who competed with Tertullian for the leadership of the church of Carthage, and whose school presented the most serious challenge to the development of the early Christian church.[52]

Gnosticism thus represents a suppressed—or even repressed—trajectory: the course that Christianity did not take, what got lost in the Roman consolidation. It is an alternate "voice," one that expresses a hesitation within the Christian doctrine of belief—in part by giving a central place to the question of the sexual relation. This allusion also relates to Octave's earlier mention of "Augustinian Manicheism," whose intention is in part to evoke the Gnostic underpinnings of the Church Father's faith. It hints at how Augustine himself remains unassimilable to the "true" Christian faith with which he later identifies himself "whole-heartedly," and from whose perspective he retroactively evaluates his whole life. Even for Augustine, Octave implies, "affection" has a dual—and potentially contradictory—resonance.

The inversion or rewriting of fundamental Christian tenets is one of the great legacies of Gnosticism, whose scriptures include numerous apocryphal "gospels" that are either significantly altered versions of the recognized New Testament text, or original meditations—like "The Thunder—Perfect Intellect"—that lead in entirely different directions and are frequently penned in a female voice. Roberte's and Octave's separate journal entries could be understood as avatars of these apocryphal "gospels," each providing different renditions or interpretations of the meaning of Roberte's "Christ-like" hospitality. In the next chapter, we will see how this theological polyvocity informs Roberte's and Octave's separate elaborations of the "laws of hospitality."

4. Hospitality after
the Death of God

In *The Revocation of the Edict of Nantes,* the problematics of hospitality and the "collaboration" that makes it possible were situated within the quasi-historical framework of secular politics and cosmopolitan ethics. But in the second novel in Klossowski's trilogy, *Roberte, ce soir,* the problem of hospitality is brought home, played out within the domestic space occupied by a husband and wife and articulated within their marriage as an expression of the contradictions internal to the notion of monogamous property. Roberte's articulation of the conflict between Catholic imperialism and Protestant freedom in the "Roman Impressions" doubles a conflict within her marriage. In *The Revocation,* we encounter Roberte as an emancipated woman and a Protestant "world citizen," a liberated figure who asserts her freedom from mastery by denying her Catholic husband's claims to exclusive ownership. But in *Roberte, ce soir,* her husband, Octave, will play upon the indifferent "charity" that is the cornerstone of Roberte's ethics of hospitality—the impossibility of "distinguishing an enemy from another man"—in order to confront her with a hospitable "custom" of his own design that exploits the presence of chance strangers in order to challenge the ideal of personal freedom by which she lives.

Octave will transpose Roberte's earlier articulation of the terms of hospitality in two ways: first, he will seek to surround her with indifferent, aimless men, who will make equal appeal to her hospitality; second, he will use his collection of paintings as a springboard for the elaboration of a relation wherein the cherished person of his wife is both made "common property"—offered up to chance passersby—and at the same time withheld from circulation, in much the same way that the painted subject is both proffered to the viewer and beyond his grasp. In the process, his own "laws of hospitality" will paradoxically assert the truth of property even as they undermine it, by insisting upon something irreducible within the hostess that eludes cosmopolitan equality and exposes it as a vulgar logic of exchange.

Whereas *The Revocation* dealt with the subjective hesitations experienced by *a* woman, a modern legislative subject, *Roberte, ce soir* will deal with the "objective hesitation" implicit in *Woman,* as the one who is ambivalently related to the signifier of personal identity. Even more than in *The Revocation,* the sexual relation becomes the arena through which a larger linguistic and philosophical point is made. Klossowski's meditation on the sexual relation is the occasion for a unique reflection on syntax and signs: the constitutive inadequacy of the sign, but also the multiplicity of possible significations implicit in solecism.

It is certainly not insignificant that Octave's—and Klossowski's—beloved Latin is the source of the solecism called *hostis,* that place where multiple possibilities coalesce in one ambivalent gesture of naming. Klossowski exploits this ambivalence by playing upon the fundamental contradiction at its core. For although the host-guest relationship allows for a kind of reciprocity or reversibility between the two terms, Klossowski demonstrates that the radical irreversibility of their different relationships to the hostess—the fact that they both possess her differently—attests to the structural impossibility of ever truly trading places or occupying the same place as equal or indifferent variables. Octave's "laws of hospitality"—and the singular "custom" to which they give rise—offer a highly developed critique of the logic of exchange. But in the process, they also allow us to critique the nature of the reversibility the sign guarantees, or what it means to "make no distinction between friend and enemy," between host and guest, between *hostis* and *hostis.*

The Moment of the Open Door

Octave hopes to discover in his wife something that eludes the conjugal gaze. He believes it can be discovered through the intermediary of a chance stranger who, in surprising his wife, will reveal to him a part of his wife's nature to which he has no access within the proprietary relation of monogamous marriage.

In *The Revocation,* we saw how this covert nature was developed in opposition to Roberte's public personality, her status as an arbiter of public morality through her position as the president of the commission of censorship. Beneath her "pure speech," Octave suspected the presence of an "impure silence," which he hoped to see revealed through fortuitous encounters with chance strangers (including, at one point, the characters Roberte had censored from her husband's own novel, *Roberte, ce soir*). In that scene, as in Tonnerre's visual compositions, Octave sought to elicit evidence of a moral hesitation, a conflict between the public manifestation of a woman's virtue and chastity and the impulses that were at odds with it. But in *Roberte, ce soir,* what interests him is not the conflict between propriety and impropriety, but the tension between two identities, two roles: those of the wife and the hostess. Within the context of the marriage relationship, Octave hopes to solicit in Roberte something that exceeds the part of her nature claimed by marital fidelity, something at odds with her status as "mistress of the home." Here the actualization of what Octave calls the "inactual essence" of his wife becomes the focus of a ritualized custom, which he christens the "laws of hospitality."

As described by his nephew, the "laws of hospitality" names a practice in which the guest is invited to usurp the master's position in relation to his wife, thereby allowing the master to become a guest in his own home:

> When my Uncle Octave took my Aunt Roberte in his arms, one must not suppose that in taking her he was alone. An invited guest would enter while Roberte, entirely given over to my uncle's presence, was not expecting him. And while she was in fear lest the guest arrive—for with irresistible resolution Roberte awaited the arrival of some guest—the guest would already be looming up behind her as my uncle made his entry, just in time to surprise my aunt's satisfied fright at being surprised by the guest. But in my uncle's mind it was all over and done with in the blink of an eye, and once again my uncle would be on the point of taking my aunt in his arms. It would be over in the blink of an eye . . . for, after all,

one cannot at the same time take and not take, be there and not be there, enter a room when one is already in it. My Uncle Octave would have been asking too much had he wished to prolong the instant of the opened door; he was already doing exceedingly well in getting the guest to appear in the doorway at the precise moment he did, getting the guest to loom up behind Roberte so that he, Octave, might be able to sense that he himself was the guest as, borrowing from the guest his door-opening gesture, he could behold them from the threshold and have the impression that it was he, Octave, who was taking my aunt by surprise.[1]

The reader will immediately recognize this scene as having the same structure as the "visual solecisms" considered in the last chapter, with the difference that the spectator or "third party" is now part of the tableau, which is enacted in the master's own home under the aegis of the hospitality extended to an unknown stranger.

Through the custom initiated by the "laws of hospitality," Octave hopes to realize something that will approximate the solecism staged within Tonnerre's compositions: the capture of an ambivalent gesture, an "objective hesitation" in the body that betrays a "splitting in two" of the moral person. But here, the solecism is staged within the marital relationship, where it solicits and animates something in excess of marital fidelity. Whereas the "splitting in two" depicted by Tonnerre's visual solecisms was inspired by compromising public scenes, Octave relocates this operation within the hospitality extended by a husband and wife within the privacy of their home. Here the ambivalent gesture of the solecism finds its corollary in the aporetic quality of the "laws of hospitality," the "blink of an eye" in which the host both loses and regains his status as the master of the home, surrendering his wife to a chance stranger and almost in the same instant taking her back into his arms, reclaiming her as his own once again.

This last detail introduces a new qualification, an extension of the logic of solecism to the undecidable limit between ownership and offering up that Octave's "laws" seek to locate. The solecism-like quality of the act of hospitality identifies a contradiction not only within the moral character of the woman, but also within the property of the master of the home. The key to this operation is the "blink of an eye" in which the guest looms up in such a way as to loosen the husband's hold over his wife, making him "sense that he himself was the guest" by providing for the voyeuristic appraisal of something not intended for his eyes.

The "Laws of Hospitality," or the Expropriation of the Proper

The "laws of hospitality" that Octave has conceived, and in which his wife participates, are elaborated in an extremely dense and cryptic argument, whose handwritten pages are framed under glass and hung, appropriately enough, in the couple's guest bedroom:

> THE LAWS OF HOSPITALITY
>
> The master of this house [maître de céans], having no greater nor more pressing concern than to shed the warmth of his joy at evening upon whomever comes to dine at his table and rest under his roof from a day's wearying travel, waits anxiously at the gate for the stranger he will see appear like a liberator upon the horizon. And catching a first glimpse of him, though he be still far off, the master will call out to him, "Come in quickly, for I am afraid of my happiness.". . . For with the stranger he welcomes, the master of the house seeks a relationship that is no longer accidental, but essential. At the start the two are but isolated substances, between them there is none but accidental communication: you who believe yourself far from home in the home of someone you believe to be at home, you bring merely the accidents of your substance, such accidents as conspire to make a stranger of you, to him who bids you avail yourself of all that makes a merely accidental host of him. But because the master of this house herewith invites the stranger to penetrate to the source of all substances beyond the realm of all accident, he inaugurates a substantial relationship between himself and the stranger, which will be not a relative relationship but an absolute one, as though, the master becoming one with the stranger, his relationship with you who have just set foot here were now but a relationship of one with oneself.
>
> To this end the host actualizes himself in the guest; or, if you prefer, he actualizes a possibility of the guest, just as you, the guest, actualize a possibility of the host. The host's most eminent gratification has for its object the actualization in the mistress of the house [maîtresse de céans] of the inactual essence of the hostess. Now, upon whom is this duty incumbent if not the guest? Does this mean that the master of the house expects betrayal at the hands

of the mistress of the house? Now it seems that the essence of the hostess, such as the host visualizes it, would in this sense be undetermined and contradictory. For either the essence of the hostess is constituted by her fidelity to the host, and in this case she eludes him the more he wishes to know her in the opposite state of betrayal, for she would be unable to betray him in order to be faithful to him; or else the essence of the hostess is really constituted by infidelity, in which case the host would cease to have any part in the essence of the hostess who would be susceptible to belonging accidentally, as mistress of the home, to some one or other of the guests. The notion of the mistress of the house reposes upon an essential basis: this essence is therefore subjected to restraint by her actual existence as mistress of the house. And here the sole function of betrayal, we see, is to lift this restraint. If the essence of the hostess lies in fidelity to the host, this authorizes the host to cause the hostess, essential in the existent mistress of the house, to manifest herself before the eyes of the guest; for the host in playing host must accept the risks—and these include the consequences of his wife's strict application of the laws of hospitality and of the fact that she dare not be unmindful of her essence, composed of fidelity to the host, for fear that in the arms of the inactual guest come here to actualize her *qua* hostess, the mistress of the household exist only traitorously.

If the essence of the hostess lay in infidelity, the outcome of the game would be a foregone conclusion and the host the loser before it starts. But the host wishes to experience the risk of losing, and feels that, losing rather than winning in advance, he will, at whatever the cost, grasp the essence of the hostess in the infidelity of the mistress of the house. For to possess the faithless one *qua* hostess faithfully fulfilling her duties, that is what he is after. Hence by means of the guest he wishes to actualize something potential in the mistress of the house: an actual hostess in relation to this guest, an inactual mistress of the house in relation to the host.

If the hostess's essence remains thus indeterminate, because to the host it seems that something of the hostess might escape him in the event this essence were nothing but pure fidelity on the part of the mistress of the house, the essence of the host is proposed as an homage of the host's curiosity to the essence of the hostess. Now this curiosity, as a potentiality of the hospitable soul, can have no proper existence except in that which would look to the hostess,

were she naive, like suspicion or jealousy. The host however is neither suspicious nor jealous, because he is essentially curious about
that very thing which, in everyday life, would make a master of the
house suspicious, jealous, unbearable.

Let the guest not be the least uneasy; above all let him not suppose he could ever be cause for jealousy or suspicion when there is
not even anyone to feel these sentiments. . . . Let the guest understand his role well: let him then fearlessly excite the host's curiosity
by that jealousy and that suspicion, worthy in the master of the
house but unworthy of a host; the latter enjoins the guest loyally
to do his utmost; in this competition let them surpass each other
in subtlety: let the host put the guest's discretion to the test, and
the guest make proof of the host's curiosity: the term generosity
has no place in this discussion, since everything is generosity, and
everything is also greed; but let the guest take all due care lest this
jealousy or this suspicion grow to such proportions that no room
is left in the host for his curiosity; for it is upon this curiosity that
the guest depends for his prestige. If the host's curiosity aspires to
actualize itself in the absent cause, how does he hope to convert
this absence into presence unless it be that he awaits the visitation
of an angel? Solicited by the host's piety, the angel is capable of
concealing himself in the guise of a guest—is it you?—whom the
host believes fortuitous. . . .

In order that the host's curiosity not degenerate into jealousy or
suspicion, it is for you, the guest, to discern the hostess's essence in
the mistress of the house, for you to cast her forth from potentiality
into existence: either the hostess remains sheer phantasm and you
a stranger in this house if you leave to the host the inactualized essence of the hostess, or else you are indeed that angel, and by your
presence you give an actuality to the hostess: you shall have full
power over her as well as over the host. And so, cherished guest,
you cannot help but see that it is in your best interest to fan the
host's curiosity to the point where the mistress of the house, driven
out of herself, will be completely actualized in an existence which
shall be determined by you alone, by you, the guest, and not by
the host's curiosity. Whereupon the host shall be the master in his
house no more: he shall have carried out his mission. In his turn
he shall have become the guest. (E12–16, translation modified;
F110–13)

The "actualization" that the laws of hospitality effect assumes an "essential," almost spiritual form, obvious in the heavily theological tone of the "laws." (We must remember that they are composed by a Catholic theologian, albeit one who has been banned from his post for his predilection for writing perversely erotic fiction.) The allegory that frames Octave's elaboration of the "laws" is an obvious allusion to what is perhaps the most famous religious narrative of hospitality, Abraham's reception of the angels in Genesis 18. In the Jewish and Christian traditions, the legacy of this act is the celebration of the unknown guest as an occasion for godliness. Any guest is potentially a messenger of God, and any host his potential willing servant. The relation between them is "essential" to the extent that the host is "actualized" through his reception of the divine host, the "absent cause" of his own identity. In this instance, the angels come to announce the transformation of Abraham's merely mortal state into a holy one through the miraculous birth of his only son, Isaac. The act of hospitality is thus the vehicle for an "essential actualization" of the host's nature, and, through it, of a holy community. But in Genesis, as in Klossowski's scenario, the host's transformation can only be achieved through the actualization of an inactual possibility of his wife, the hostess. In this case, the angels promise to realize the "inactual essence" of the hostess Sarah by giving the barren woman a child. She is the medium through which the identities of host and guest are joined in an essential relation, and for this reason is often read by Christians as prefiguring the annunciation.

However, when Octave describes the affect of curiosity as the "potentiality of the hospitable soul," and calls for it to eclipse the master's jealousy, he seems to be alluding to another important hospitality paradigm, Augustine's understanding of Christ's hospitality as the basis of a transcendent community that effects an essential relation between host and guest by neutralizing their "private wills" within a "whole-hearted affection."[2] In Christian theology, Abraham's hospitality becomes a figure for the Holy Trinity and represents the possibility of "actualizing" a higher identity by seeking "communion" with the "absent cause." In the words of one doctrinal interpretation, "The stranger becomes the *pretext*, the means through which we enter into eucharistic communion with the Creator. Thus, the stranger acquires a sacred character."[3] But the result is that individual strangers become less strange, reduced to the status of "pretexts" for some already-familiar manifestation. In many Christian interpretations of hospitality, Christ is present in the host and guest alike, and allows for a possible equality by mediating between the different participants, who become "values" of the one Christ through the act of communion. In other words, they enter into relation with one another only to the extent that they "actualize" the inactual essence of Christ.

When Octave writes that what he seeks with the stranger is a "relationship of one with oneself," upheld by "laws," he seems to advocate a similar reduction to a common measure. However, Klossowski's vision of hospitality both alludes to the Christian tradition and departs from it. To begin with, both the hostess and the guest appear to have "Christ-like" roles. The hostess, as an "offering," is the medium through which two distinct entities enter into a substantial relation, akin to Christ's eucharistic status as a "gift" who is both handed over to strangers and offered in sacrifice.[4] But the guest also serves a similar function, since he enters into the intimacy of the marriage in order to realize something latent within it, and in so doing acquires a quasi-divine status.

But against the notion of either personal or communal identity as "whole" or "one," Klossowski makes hospitality synonymous with a conflict or division internal to identity. His three-term relation is not so much a trinity as a sexualized *threesome,* where the third term is important not so much as an agent of unification, but as an intruder who introduces a fissure into a reciprocal relation between two people. As a third term heterogeneous to the reversible dyad of host and guest, the hostess both facilitates the relation between them and insists upon its fundamental impossibility. Her function as a divine gift is qualified by her status as an object of rivalry or even theft: he does not so much mediate between the host and the guest as *come* between them, in two ways. She is suspended between them, stuck in the middle, caught between the arms of the host and the stranger who, "in the blink of an eye," looms up in such a way as to loosen her husband's hold over her. But she also "comes between them" in the sense that she incites a kind of rivalry, a contest in which the host and guest meet as opponents in a struggle for prestige. As a result, her role in "actualizing" the hospitable relation between host and guest depends not on her status as a universal "value" or constant, as in the example of Christ, but on her *inconstancy,* in the fullest sense of the word.[5]

In the same way, the guest's role involves not sharing or unity, but "competition," "prestige," and the threat of loss. In marked distinction to Augustine's appeal for a hospitable community united in "one heart," Klossowski's host invites the guest to do his utmost to incite an emotion resembling jealousy: a very un-Christian turn of events. He is called upon to undertake the very delicate operation of introducing a specific division into the bond between husband and wife. If he pulls it off he will be heralded as an "angel," and if not the essences of the different participants will remain unrealized. Later on in the novel, Klossowski sums up the guiding principle of the "laws of hospitality" when he writes: "In the beginning was betrayal . . ." (91). An originary "betrayal" is called upon to realize hospitality as a principle of incoherence or dissolution, displacing the Word, the Christian *logos,* as source of communal coherence.

Gift and Theft

But the notion that the host's identity can only be "actualized" through this splitting or division points to yet another field of associations evoked by Octave's laws: the logic of potlatch, a highly ritualized form of hospitality that also promises to realize or "actualize" the giver's sacred status through loss or expropriation. The partial surrender of his substance ultimately confirms the mastery and prestige of the host, which grows in direct proportion to the loss or destruction of goods. The more the master gives, the more he has: because his prestations will eventually be reciprocated by others, but also—and most importantly—because his prestige accrues in the act of giving. In the same way, Octave-as-host augments his prestige by offering his most cherished good up to others.

But while his hospitality relation approximates the logic of potlatch, it is also subtly different. Although Octave proposes to offer up his wife to chance strangers, he neither expects, nor gets, anything in return. He receives neither monetary compensation nor honor from his "guests" (who in fact dismiss him as a lecherous old pervert with a libertine wife), nor does he enjoy other wives in exchange for his own. To understand the nuances of Octave's conception of the gift, we have to appreciate its continuity with theft, or what might even be called a logic of "sacred expenditure." The aim of this prestation is not merely to accrue symbolic prestige by generously bestowing goods, but to effect the forcible erosion or dissolution of the master's personal property. Roberte as hostess is a gift who must be *stolen* from the host, who in turn must recognize and accept her theft by a worthy guest. The guest's status as an "angel" is thus qualified by his role as *thief*, a possessor as "illegitimate" as he is "fortuitous."

The joining of these two apparently antithetical qualities in the person of the unknown stranger has a long cultural history and harkens back to a context in which the "offering" of women is celebrated as the foundation of a prestige economy whose stakes cannot be reduced to mere commodification or exchange. Claude Lévi-Strauss argues that the aim of exogamy—above and beyond the cultural objectives of prohibiting incest or guaranteeing the spread of language—is to establish and maintain an economy of prestige, in which a family attains its status through the matches it arranges for its daughters, who function as a kind of "social currency."[6] The daughters must always marry up, and in principle will always do so as long as the family is on the ascent. If, on the other hand, the family has fallen from favor, the daughters will be unable to marry up and the family's downward mobility will be sealed. But the paradox is that as a family accrues prestige and advances up the social hierarchy, it becomes harder and harder for it to find suitable matches for its daughters. This, according to Lévi-Strauss, is what explains the phenomenon so common in legend, in which the most prized virgin in the realm, for example the princess or daughter of the ranking chieftain, is unable to be married at all.

This is where the function of the guest or outsider as "thief" comes in, and acquires its prestigious or even sacred dimension.[7] For if this prize virgin is barricaded in a tower or consigned to God, it isn't just because there are no worthy suitors in the realm; rather it is because *no* suitor is good enough for her, according to the laws of social prestige. Hence she is "given to God": either literally removed from the sexual economy, by taking religious vows or assuming a sacred function (including sacrifice), or given to the one who presents himself either as a god, or under the sign of godliness—in other words, the guest. In the guise of the "knight errant" or "stranger from afar," he wanders the countryside like the gods of old, seeking out chance encounters through which prestige can be established. By solving a riddle, winning a joust, or otherwise establishing his worth, the guest wins the hand of the elite virgin or princess. The function of the interloping stranger is thus to "steal" as his wife or Lady the woman who is too good simply to be given away through available avenues of exchange. Paradoxically, the stranger "proves" the value of the woman he takes by removing her from circulation, establishing her transcendence of all economies of exchange by introducing a gap into the reciprocity-based economy of social relations.

Of course, Klossowski adds a significant twist to this basic paradigm in *Roberte, ce soir,* since it is not the prized damsel or marriageable virgin who is subject to "theft" by a stranger/god, but rather the master's own wife. What Octave puts into circulation is not just a prized possession, or even a priceless one, but an *inalienable* possession: something that by its very nature can belong to no one else. Or as he himself puts it later on in the trilogy, "the wife, prostituted by the husband, is nonetheless still the wife: the husband's inexchangeable good, the priceless good who shows her worth when the wife surrenders to a lover chosen by her husband" (F304, my translation).

The tension between prestige and loss is even more complicated than it at first appears. It is qualified by a delicate balance between the claims of the host and the claims of the husband, between the faithfulness of the hostess and the fidelity of the mistress of the home, each of which appears to be mutually exclusive. How can the master make the transition to hospitality without simply losing his wife? In other words, how does hospitality avoid simply lapsing into adultery? And even more importantly, why does Octave need to force this limit? What is he trying to accomplish by trying to locate hospitality both within the marriage and in direct opposition to it? This apparent antinomy between the interests of the host and the master of the home seems all the more perplexing when we consider that the two terms are etymologically inseparable.

The Dissolution of Privative Personhood

In the introduction, we saw that the Indo-European root word for the host, *potis,* names the master of the home, the one who makes the law in the house or *casa.* But in his discussion of this etymology, Émile Benveniste makes clear that the mastery or power of the *potis* is thus nothing other than *ipseity itself,* the *chez soi* of identity in which the master gathers together and disposes of what is proper to him.[8] The archaic French term Klossowski uses to designate the master of the house, *maître de céans,* is closely tied to this genealogy, since *céans* is related not only to the house or *casa* where the master makes the law but to the *chez soi* as the "at-homeness" of ipseity as self-identity.

As we have seen, the notion of "personal identity" is grounded both historically and etymologically in a very precise understanding of personal property, which is intimately related to the domestic sphere and the sexual relation. In fact, many of the words in this linguistic family apply both to the "master" and to the "husband." This genealogy suggests that the master's ability to eminently personify not only his own identity, but that of the group, is upheld by his possession of and power over the human dependents who are defined as his property. In archaic practice, and in biblical tradition, we have seen that the host's offering of his "own" substance to his guest often takes the form of his ability to dispose of those female dependents who make up his personal property and who are equated with the host by virtue of their subordinate dependence. In the hospitality narratives of the Hebrew Bible, the host fulfills his duty toward the guest by offering up his mistress or unmarried daughters, as though this sacrifice of his chattel represented a surrender of some part of "himself."[9] However, such reasoning also implies that there is something heterogeneous about the host's identity as a master "equal to himself," since the personal identity he embodies is not self-identical or autonomous, but already a kind of plurality. What then is the property of the host? And who is the host, proper?

In his rich study of the concept of the "person," Marcel Mauss observes that in many clan-based societies, personhood inheres in the ownership of certain ritual objects that mark the bearer's responsibility for his whole clan. But for this very reason, personhood can also be acquired through inheritance, theft, or murder, which transfers to the usurping party the privative personhood of the last owner.[10] Although woman as "property" contributes to the master's "eminent personification" of personal identity, she also undermines the illusion of self-sufficiency and ipseity that the master is supposed to embody by drawing attention to its dependence upon an im-proper attachment or addition, which remains foreign even in being subordinated and internalized. The hostess attests to the presence of something improper within the host's personal property, a foreign presence internal to the host's "eminent personification" of identity.

Klossowski's work zeroes in on a paradox internal to the notion of personal identity the host embodies. Although the host as master is the one who personifies personal and group identity, his identity as host is nonetheless realized only through the *dispossession* and surrendering of his substance. When Octave exposes his own wife to theft, therefore, he is not only risking the loss of his *property,* but of his personhood as such. He wants to strain his proprietary claims to the breaking point, even to the point of breaking apart mastery itself, precisely because his status as master of the home stands in the way of his actualization as host. Although Klossowski's interpretation of hospitality is not necessarily unique in making a living woman the object of dispossession, it is nearly unique in proposing that the host's *wife* occupy this role—and more so for the particular stakes it attaches to this dispossession.

In most traditions, the "loss" incurred when the host's property is expropriated gets recovered in some way, making the dispossession he experiences merely immanent or temporary. Although the Hebrew Bible contains numerous examples of women being offered up to guests, it is significant that this offer is almost never acted upon. Typically the host is preserved from the complete loss of his personal property by some form of divine intervention, which either prevents the act from happening in the first place (as in the story of Lot) or valorizes it after the fact. The dispossession of identity is thus recovered dialectically and made the point of departure for a new actualization of identity. The same holds true in the logics of potlatch or sacred theft, where the symbolic prestige of the host grows in direct proportion to the loss of goods or human dependents.

In Klossowski's scenario, however, what the host desires is the *dispossession of identity itself,* and not the eventual dialectal recovery of mastery. His ultimate aim is to "become the guest in his own home," to savor the moment of expropriation at which he is dispossessed not only of his most defining property, but of the identity it guarantees. By soliciting a part of the hostess's nature that exceeds the master's proprietary hold over her, the guest points to a contradiction internal to the identity of the man who "possesses" her, a fissure or split within the principle of personal property the master embodies. When his wife is "surprised" by the guest in her quality as mistress of the house and actualized as *hostess,* the husband's determination as master (that is, as one who is "eminently equal" to himself and capable of symbolically personifying the household, according to Benveniste's definition) is rendered improper, alienated. In short, he is realized as host *precisely through* the loss of his identity as master. This is the defining logic of Klossowski's laws of hospitality, which in their aporia-like quality strive to maintain the paradox internal to hospitality as a simultaneous dispossession and realization of the host's identity. Although Octave admits, as mentioned earlier, that "one cannot at the same time take and not take, be there and not be there, enter a room when one is already in it," this is nonetheless precisely what he proposes to do, by forcing the impossible limit between the fidelity of the hostess and the fidelity of the wife, and between the curiosity of the host and the jealousy of the master.

If Octave's formulation of the "laws" favors the affect of "curiosity" over jealousy, it is not only because jealousy is a less-refined emotion. Rather, it is because jealousy is structurally tied to a particular notion of privative identity, in which the integrity of the person is made synonymous with his ability to jealously guard possessions to himself and thereby maintain the unity or coherence of the personal property of the self. This understanding of jealousy is directly related to the "curiosity" the host hopes to experience. Curiosity, as the "potentiality of the hospitable soul," is the emotion that corresponds to the erosion of privative personhood. This is why the host awaits the stranger not merely as a thief, but as a "liberator" he calls upon to free him of the privative constraints of personal identity.

But the notion of "jealousy" as a principle of privative identity also has a theological source. In the first commandment of the Decalogue, God's "jealousy" is invoked as the conditioning tenet of monotheism: "For I the Lord thy God am a jealous God, and thou shalt have no others before me" (Exodus 20:5). In chapter 1 we saw that within the logic of the Hebrew Bible, hospitality after the Decalogue is increasingly bound up in the problem of idolatry, or what the metaphor of Israel's "marriage" to God figures as the wife's adulterous "welcoming" of strangers in the place of her husband. But this antinomy between hospitality and monotheism suggests that what the hostess betrays is not only a bond of allegiance, but a principle of unity: God's jealousy is the index of his sublime singularity, the Oneness on which the doctrine of monotheism is based.

But this betrayal has important implications not just for God, but for the human subject whose personhood is modeled on this integral oneness. The Decalogue upholds the sanctity of individual personhood by giving it jealous dominion over the "things" it possesses, including the wife, which are coextensive with their possessor and thus off limits to the covetous neighbor or stranger. In his 1970 essay "Protase et apodose," Klossowski describes the importance of the wife's betrayal through a gloss of the tenth commandment of the Decalogue, "Thou shalt not covet thy neighbor's goods":

> The interdiction affirms a subject possessed of a person, who is here identified as an inalienable object. But to the extent that this object acts, it negatively reveals itself to have the quality of a subject, insofar as it consented to the possession of the first possessor. It then loses this subjective quality once again by substituting someone else for the first possessing subject. In this way, the interdiction institutes a moral agency of the object *[un moi de l'objet]*, which only possesses this intrinsic quality to the extent that it is legitimately possessed, and that, according to the interdiction, expropriates itself of that moral quality by expropriating its legitimate proprietor, in favor of a fortuitous and illegitimate possessor.[11]

In the logic of monogamous marriage the husband "possesses" his wife in an exclusive, inalienable way. However, her susceptibility to appropriation by an illegitimate possessor proves that he can never possess her completely. She is part of the husband's "property" only to the extent that she is im-proper to it, since the wife-as-object possesses a "moral agency" that gives her the "negative quality of a subject." But what is curious about this citation is that Klossowski references the commandment concerning the "neighbor's goods," and not the more obvious choice, the commandment against adultery. Perhaps this is because the first implies an essential link between the "thing" and its proprietor, while the second implies the independent agency of a subject who is linked to her spouse in a legal or "accidental" way, to use Klossowski's term. A subject (i.e., the "mistress of the home") can commit adultery, but an "object" (i.e., the "inactual essence" of the hostess as a hospitable offering) can do much more: it can actually *expropriate* its possessor. Whereas Israel's adultery destroys her marriage but doesn't contaminate or dissolve the "oneness" of her divine husband, Roberte's hospitality actually splinters her husband's oneness, since as a possessed "thing" she is implicated in his subjectivity.

This is why the tension between betrayal and fidelity is so important to Octave's formulation of the laws. For as he says, "If the essence of the hostess lay in infidelity, the outcome of the game would be a foregone conclusion and the host the loser before it starts." It is not *simple* infidelity he wants to experience (or what we might call adultery), but rather the fidelity of the hostess *within* the infidelity of the mistress of the home. Or as he puts it, "to possess the faithless one *qua* hostess faithfully fulfilling her duties, that is what [the host] is after." If Roberte is given to the guest simply as the mistress of the house, and not as hostess, the act of hospitality is compromised at the outset. If Octave and Roberte break through the privative constraints of the master and mistress of the home, and yet fail to find hospitality on the other side, this transgression will have been for naught—the wife would be no more than an adulteress, and the husband would experience nothing more than the wounded narcissism of the cuckold. The jealousy of the master of the house would preclude his curiosity, preventing the inactual essence of the host from manifesting itself. And as a result, the expropriation the host seeks would be impossible. For only the hostess can "let the stranger in," by admitting the guest into the intimacy of the exclusive marriage and thereby allowing *estrangement* to rupture the master's self-identity.

In privileging this dissolution of identity over the principle of coherence it betrays, Klossowski also revalues the meaning of the hostess's "idolatry," making it the basis of a new ethics. Roberte's hospitality dissolves monotheist integrity, giving rise to a divinity that is multiple, fragmented, and fortuitous. Her betrayal facilitates the "essential actualization" of the hospitality event, since it allows her to "idolatrously" surrender herself to the divinity of a chance stranger, and thereby actualize him as a guest.

Within the context of the trilogy, Roberte's disbelief and betrayal of this jealous "oneness" is important on a number of different levels. She is an atheist of Protestant origin who finds her husband's incessant attempts to offer a theological account of her soul thoroughly absurd. One of the holdovers from her Protestant upbringing is her refusal to accept the doctrine of divine mediation so central to Octave's scholastic Catholicism. But her "disbelief" is not restricted to her lack of religious faith, which is little more than a foil. More fundamentally, her "disbelief" is a function of woman's inherent infidelity or inadequation to the divine image, and the unanchoring of femininity with regard to the signifier. Women, Roberte suggests, are "natural-born atheists" (125). Their "atheism" indexes an inherently unbelieving nature, incapable of being equated with or "made in the image of" the divine person. But paradoxically, it is Roberte's "atheism" that makes her susceptible to the angelic intervention of the guest, the "illegitimate and fortuitous possessor" who "actualizes" the hostess through a substantial appropriation.

Hospitality after the Death of God

Klossowski develops the implications of Roberte's "atheism" in two different ways: first through a dense argument derived from scholastic theology, in which Octave "proves" Roberte's susceptibility to corporal expropriation, and second through an implicit allusion to the philosophy of Friedrich Nietzsche, and its critique of the Judeo-Christian origins of privative personhood.

In the extended theological dialogue that makes up the body of *Roberte, ce soir,* Octave suggests that the rupturing of the "privative" designations of the master and mistress of the home is possible only through the loss of the "incommunicability of souls," the theological principle according to which an individual's being remains attributable only to itself, and which constitutes identity as such (32). According to this principle, the incommunicability of the person can be suspended only in death, which separates body and soul and facilitates the soul's reassociation with another discrete body. But in Roberte's case, Octave theorizes that "disbelief has suspended her incommunicable character" (34, translation modified). As a result, the integrity of her person can no longer be guaranteed.

The language of "accidental" and "substantial" unions is drawn from the work of Thomas Aquinas, who derives a theological proof for the soul's essential unity with the body from the doctrine of incarnation.[12] According to Aquinas, the soul is able to unite substantially to the body, and retain its being even after the body's dissolution, because the integrity of body and soul is upheld by God.

Taking this Aquinian reasoning as his point of departure, Octave
uses a syllogistic composite of scholastic reasoning to demonstrate
that the terms of the theological argument for discrete personhood
actually provide justification for the dissolution of the person, in
those cases where the subject in question does not adhere to—and
therefore *cohere* through—a belief in the transcendental unity of
the divine person. When Roberte declares that "a woman's body
is her soul," her statement both references Aquinas's argument
and suggests how it might be overturned. Her "disbelief" means
her soul and her body are only accidentally united, making her
susceptible to corporal expropriation at the hands of another. In
other words, the dissolution of the soul effects the dissolution of
the body.

But this theological argument concerning privative personhood
is further qualified by Klossowski's understanding of Nietzsche's
"death of God" and his philosophy of the Eternal Return. In chapter 2, we saw that Nietzsche figures nihilism as the "uncanniest of
all guests," insofar as it embodies the nihilism internal to Christian
individualism as its logical limit.[13] For Nietzsche, Christianity is
the dominant expression of European nihilism. But he also envisions its abolition through the "ultimate nihilism," the logic of
the Eternal Return. As the ultimate nihilism, the Eternal Return
is also, presumably, the most uncanny of all guests: uncanny first
of all to Christian nihilism itself, whose cult of monotheism and
the positive principle of identity that depends upon it precludes any
sense of the other—or for that matter of the self—as an unknown.
In Nietzsche's wake, the hospitality relation once again becomes
the focus of an attempt to maintain an aporetic relation to the unknown in other than compensatory, salvational modes: an attempt
that paradoxically aligns itself with the concerns of ancient, "divine" hospitality.

Like Klossowski's chance stranger, whose seizure of the master's
personal property is both illegitimate and fortuitous, the Eternal
Return as the "uncanniest of guests" dissolves its host in a way that
is both destructive and liberating. If the monotheist God reifies not
only subjective boundaries, but also the unknown itself, then the
death of God allows the unknown to manifest itself in other forms.
But although Nietzsche sees the "murder" of God as essential to
this possibility, he also warns that, even "after" God, we run the
risk of preserving or instituting principles that will not transvalue

nihilistic Christian values, but simply create new and equally insidious ones. For the transvaluation of all values to be complete, he
argues, we must overcome not only the monotheist understanding
of God, but also the positive idea of personal identity that depends
upon it. This argument helps to explain why Klossowski makes
his protagonist a Christian theologian. Isn't all of Western culture
"Christian" in this regard—that is, in subscribing to an ontic view
of personhood?

In the postscript to *The Laws of Hospitality*, Klossowski develops the implications of Nietzsche's death of God within the theological argument for discrete personhood by demonstrating that
the formal identity of the "I" or self is necessarily submitted to a
divine order, a single God that conditions its possibility:

> Any identity rests solely upon the knowledge of a thinker outside of
> ourselves—if we grant that there is an inside and an outside—who
> agrees from the outside to think us as such. If it is God on the in-
> side as well as on the outside, in the sense of absolute coherence,
> then our identity is pure grace; if it is the ambient world, where
> everything begins and ends with designation, then our identity is
> merely a grammatical joke. (F337, my translation)

Although we tend to think of personhood as an innate, ontic property, Nietzsche and Klossowski both emphasize its often unacknowledged grounding in Christian theology. For example, Paul
famously reconceives personhood as a universal attribute by identifying it with baptism in Christ: "There is neither Jew nor Greek,
neither slave nor free, neither male nor female; for you are all one
person *[εἰς]* in Christ Jesus" (Galatians 3:28–29). But although this
verse seems to posit the inalienability of personhood, it actually
makes it contingent upon playing host to the oneness of Christ's
person, bestows a proper personhood by dwelling in one's heart.

This is no doubt what Nietzsche has in mind when he has
Zarathustra declare that human beings are merely wearing the
"mask" of the monotheist God, which gives the illusion of a coherent, privative self. In his study of the concept of the "person," Marcel Mauss notes the Roman notion of the person—the
persona—was derived from the idea of the mask, and specifically
the wax image of the dead ancestor. The legal concept of the "person" designated the one who possessed this mask, whether legiti-
mately or not. Although Roman law gradually came to associate

the concept of the *persona* with the "true nature" of the individual, its original identification with the mask also gave rise to another conception of the *persona,* as a simulated, artificial, or even duplicitous "mask" of the self.[14] Despite the best efforts of the church fathers, the survival of this genealogy continued to hint at the uncomfortable proximity between ontological personhood and its repudiated siblings, the simulacrum or theatrical *personnage.*

In his 1957 essay "Nietzsche, Polytheism and Parody," Klossowski argues that if God is the only possible guarantor of the identity of the "I" and of its substantial base, bodily integrity, then the death of God dissolves the "grammatical fiction" of the self, opening the way for a new understanding of subjectivity: as divided, multiple, dissolute, and irresponsible.[15] When the monotheist "mask" of God is stripped away, the artificial integrity of the self gives way to the multiplicity of the ego. In this sense, Klossowski makes clear that the declaration "God is dead" is not so much a call to atheism as the liberation of a "polytheism" that would abolish the privative constraints of the self. Paradoxically, the death of the monotheistic God also results for Nietzsche in a liberation of the divine: in *Thus Spoke Zarathustra* he writes: "Is not precisely this godliness, that there are gods but no God?"[16] When God dies, the ego becomes divine: but *as dissolved,* as conditioned not by the integrity of the one God, but by the disintegration of Dionysus, god of dismemberment and disindividuation.

Klossowski adapts Nietzsche's discovery to the logic of hospitality, in which the dissolution of the self is celebrated as a divine act. After the death of the eternal witness, who alone was capable of guaranteeing the identity of the self, divinity resides in a new kind of "witness": the guest who takes it upon himself to "liberate" the master from his privative identity. As a "liberator" from individuation, the guest partakes of the particular divinity of Dionysus, the sacred guest who very literally dispossesses or even dismembers his host.[17]

But while Klossowski's conception of hospitality is indebted to Nietzsche, it does not simply duplicate or enact his work, but rather develops this thought in a particular direction. To Nietzsche's discovery of the liberating potential of the Dionysian guest, he adds an insistence on the privileged role of the feminine in effecting this dissolution.

Welcoming the Unknown "in the Feminine"

As a Catholic who does not acknowledge either the "death of God" or the dissolution of identity that results from it, Octave can only experience this dissociation secondarily, through its effect on Roberte. Octave feels that he is too constrained by his identity, while Roberte is too little bound by hers. The dissociation from the divine foundations of what Klossowski calls the "grammatical fiction" of the "I" is more pronounced in her case, intensified by the already unanchored relation between femininity and the signifier. In their ambivalent relation to legal rights, women have always challenged the ontic view of personhood with the evidence of its nonuniversality. Even as Roman law began to identify the *persona* with the "true nature" of the individual, it continued to withhold personhood from those who did not own property, most notably women and slaves.[18] This history reminds us that the "mask" of unified personhood has always fit some subjects much better than others.

In Klossowski's trilogy, the marginal position accorded to femininity by traditional understandings of the subject appears as a singular force. It recalls the function of religion, in the sense in which Emmanuel Lévinas understands the term: "the possible surplus in a society of equals."[19] But at the same time, the feminine embodies an alterity that has no transcendent dimension, but is firmly materialist. If the feminine approximates the divine in its "excessive" quality, it is paradoxically because of its ambivalent relationship to the positive principle of personal identity that the monotheist God imparts. We see its importance in what Klossowski calls the *moi de l'objet,* the paradoxical agency the object—in this case the hostess—assumes within the subject who "possesses" it. By drawing attention to the relationship between the master's "eminent personification" of personal identity and his jealous identification with his possessions, the hostess insists on the heteronomous underpinnings of the "personal property" of the self.

Against the positive idea of personal identity, whose privative quality is guaranteed by the monotheist understanding of God as a unified oneness, Klossowski's vision of hospitality affirms the division and multiplicity internal to the subject in the form of a multiple cogito, a "polytheist" subjectivity that would abolish the privative constraints of the self. In the postscript to *The Laws of*

Hospitality, he develops this notion through the idea of a divided subject, or what Gilles Deleuze and Félix Guattari call the *cogito à deux:*[20] a cogito for whom the act of thought does not guarantee its being as a consistent subject, but rather calls it into question by suggesting that others may be "thinking in me." As Klossowski writes in the postscript to the *Laws,*

> The Word *[le verbe]* establishes the duration of the thinking subject through the fiction of the personal pronoun, as the source or home *[foyer]* of judgment, in order that thought as such always returns to one point among others. But does it always return to it? At each word I have to wonder whether it is I who am thinking or whether others are thinking in me or for me, or thinking me, or even thinking before I have really thought myself what they are thinking. . . . whether thought is a property, an appropriation, or even the expropriation of thought. (F337, my translation)

The possibility that "others" might be thinking *in* me challenges the notion that there is a thinker outside of me—"the Word," or God—who is conditioning my ego as an integral unity. If God is for Descartes the guarantor of the cogito, then the death of God— his failure to support the fiction of the personal pronoun as the source or "home" of judgment—results in the "home" of thought being susceptible to occupation by strangers: most notably the hostess. As the *moi de l'objet* or "Thing," the hostess is the one who thinks in the host insofar as he is *not-all,* revealing the uncanny dispossession of the home of judgment by a foreign object.

But for Klossowski, the implications of this experience of dispossession or "expropriation" are not at all negative, since the role of the hostess suggests how the identity of the post-Nietzschean host might be understood as other than a principle of self-adequation. It models an ethical position that is not limited to the female sex, but that consists in an "excessive" relation to the signifier of personal identity. Although Nietzsche associates Dionysus with a dissolution of the ego that is affirmatively revalued as "divine," and that opposes itself to the transcendental redemption of the self embodied by Christ, he also asserts that "after" God, mankind must assume an authentically "feminine" attitude in welcoming Dionysus. He associates it with the figure of Ariadne, as the one who welcomes the transfiguring advent of the divine guest.[21] Klossowski hints at something similar in the preface to his trilogy, when he writes that "for ten years now I have lived, or *believe* I have lived, under the sign of Roberte" (F7). To live under the sign of the hostess is, as Octave puts it in the last line of his "laws," to "become the guest" in one's own home: to become this foreign Thing, this spot of alterity or estrangement within the *chez soi* of identity.

The Fantasy of the Unique Sign

Roberte as hostess substitutes a "passive" corporal communication for the active synthesis of the Christian *logos*, effecting the dissolution of identity rather than its realization. But for Klossowski, this is not the only consequence of the hospitality relation. As a sign of relation, the hostess also imposes a "coherence" upon the host, and not merely a dissolution: in the postscript to *The Laws of Hospitality*, Klossowski describes Roberte as a "unique sign," a "coherent thought" (F337). Moreover, he relates the "coherence" of the unique sign to its function as a universal "value," able to stand in for everything that happens in the world: "As a sign, this name alone was worth [*ce nom valait à lui seul*] a gesture, a situation, a word and all of this at once, not haphazardly but integrally" (F335).

As the medium through which the essences of host and guest are "actualized," does Roberte simply render them equivalent, as variables in an equation of constant value? Are the "laws of hospitality" just the expression of a fantasy in which woman "completes" what is missing in a relation between men, offering the same promise of wholeness or continuity that the theological account of Christ's unique mediation provides in the Christian context, while at the same time disavowing this function? Michèle Montrelay suggests a strong parallel between the two operations when she observes that the host and the guest, because they both participate in the "actualization" of the hostess, are "heterogeneous entities who are made equivalent with one another when each of them becomes a 'value' of substance."[22] Montrelay equates the "coherence" imposed by the laws of hospitality with primary narcissism,[23] which she sees in Octave's characterization of the host's relationship to the guest as a "relationship of one with oneself" that amounts to what she calls a "fusion" of the host with the stranger. She observes that narcissism "has for its essence expropriation—which is produced 'like' the jouissance of a woman."[24]

In psychoanalytic terms, the "expropriation" of the subject is the mark of the fantasy, which both effects the evacuation or "fading" of the subject and at the same time produces a residual jouissance. The subject in its expropriation experiences this jouissance as an attribute of the Other of the fantasy: in this case the hostess, who bestows a kind of coherence in the very act of dissolving the host's integral character.

In the postscript to *The Laws of Hospitality*, Klossowski describes how the hallucinatory "coherence" of the unique sign has the effect of closing an "immobile circle," which not only dissolves his "memory" and "intelligible appearance" as a subject, but also opposes itself to the act of writing:

> Not writing, but remaining within a circuit that was closing in upon itself so incessantly that at points there was nothing but an immobile circle, it seemed to me that thought was being annulled in the sign by which it designated itself.
>
> How could I go on living? Consenting to develop ideas, describe scenes, or put words in the characters' mouths, referring to the world or to my life. . . . These were still nothing more than meditations destined to give me an intelligible appearance on the outside, an appearance furnished by memory and requisite for the discourse that was going on inside me as I wrote. As soon as I stopped writing, memory disappeared, and the immobile circuit formed again. (F333, my translation)

The "immobile circuit" and the coherence it imposes are recognizable in psychoanalytic terms as the logic of fantasy. Marie-Hélène Brousse notes that one of the most distinguishing features of fantasy is its "inertia," which Freud identifies in the silence that surrounds the fantasy, the difficulty the analysand experiences in trying to talk about or free-associate on it, its permanence, and its resistance to treatment.[25] Freud understands the fantasy as a kind of parenthesis, a suspended moment removed from the quotidian chains of signification that shape the subject's conscious existence.[26] If it is "inert," it is because the fantasy not only marks the suspension or removal of the subject's psychic life from quotidian existence, but also stages the subject's resistance to or disavowal of castration, and the "splitting" of the subject it effects.

In his linguistic transposition of the terms of Freud's analysis in "A Child Is Being Beaten," Jacques Lacan suggests how this reading of fantasy might be related to the logic of the "unique sign" and its opposition to quotidian signs.[27] As summarized by Brousse,

> [The subject's] identification with the primary signifier causes it to disappear: only a hole remains, insofar as a signifier—even a proper name—cannot conceive itself except in relation to another signifier, and thus cannot constitute a stable being for the subject who finds himself deported down the signifying chain. By causing a signifier to disappear, primary repression makes the subject into this hole in the signifying chain. As the interval between two signifiers, the subject seeks to represent himself, to stop up this hole. But what emerges is a being of a different register than the signifier with which the signifier articulates the non-being of the barred subject. When the subject fails to find his place in the signifying ensemble (A), since the element that would represent him once and for all is missing, the subject calls on the fantasy to regulate his position, veiling this lack in the Other *[Autre]* with the introduction of a heterogeneous element. The formula "a child is being beaten" comes to occupy the place delimited by the subject variable. Note that the subject does not appear in the formula: he merely sustains or enunciates it, but is not present in the enunciation, from which he has effectively disappeared.[28]

Like Klossowski's fantasy of the "unique sign," the fundamental fantasy is represented topologically in Lacan's schema as the closing of a circle: in this case, the symbolic order (A, in Lacan's notation) that is fantasmatically rendered complete by the subject's refusal to assume the signifier that represents him to that symbolic order. The fantasy effects a "fading" of the subject, since the subject's withdrawal from the signifier that represents it is what allows the circle to close.

The result is the production of a certain jouissance, which derives from the disavowal of the phallic signifier and the castration it imposes in favor of the imaginary completion of the symbolic Other of language: not as an endless and open chain of signifiers, but as a "coherent" whole. In the preface to *The Laws of Hospitality*, Klossowski describes his trilogy of novels as a "vain meditation upon a proper name," an attempt to describe a life lived under a "unique sign," Roberte. In the postscript, he further specifies that the name "Roberte" designates not a historical person, but an "intensity": "One name—Roberte—was an already specific designation of an original intensity" (F334). The "unique sign" as "original intensity" would thus be legible as the originary jouissance lost to the signifier, or what Lacan terms the *objet a*.

As this brief example shows, the "laws" certainly seem to invite psychoanalytic speculation. But is this relation really reducible to narcissism? Or even to "fantasy" in the strictly psychoanalytic sense of the term? Klossowski himself explores this possibility very fully, but in such a way as to underscore a fundamental difference between the "coherence" his practice bestows on the host and the coherence or imaginary plenitude imparted by the fantasy.

The "fantasy of the unique sign" is related to the fundamental fantasy described by Lacan in that it involves a critique of the reductive nature of the signifier. It thus shares with the unconscious fantasy a "perverse" dimension, so called because it consists in a disavowal of the signifier in favor of the reality of the jouissance or "intensity" it excludes from the register of quotidian signs. But in this case, the fantasy has to do not with the denial of castration, but rather with the affirmation of the subjective dissolution that the "coherence of the unique sign" effects. Accordingly, it is not the subject's "splitting" or division that is eliminated, but rather the privative identity he is supposed to embody. The "fantasy of the unique sign" is thus a fantasy of a very particular sort, which stages the experience of the signifier's inadequation to the subject in affirmative fashion. If Roberte functions as a fantasy, it is not because she, as a woman, would "complete" the relation between two men, but because she is the "unique sign" whose incommunicability and untranslatability resists the order of quotidian signs to which the subject is usually consigned.

The Intensity of the Unique Sign

In his essay "Protase et apodose," Klossowski distinguishes between the "unique sign," which he characterizes as a self-sufficient sign "isolated from any explicit context, and good for everything that happens in the world," and the world of "quotidian signs."[29] The "unique sign" differs from "everyday" signs or signifiers in that its meaning is not contingent upon its placement in a signifying field. Its value is not—as in a structuralist linguistics—determined in relation to other signifiers. Instead, the unique sign expresses the

"incommunicable coherence" of a thought (or "fantasy") that, at
its moment of greatest intensity, "designates itself" with a sign:

> I came to oppose this unique sign to the signs of the quotidian
> code through which we express ourselves. And I became aware of
> how limited this code was when it came to expressing something
> that doesn't always return. If what returns at any given moment
> never returns in exactly the same way, how can we justify the use
> of the same signs? As I reflected on this variation between the quo-
> tidian code of common sense and what it expresses, an inadequa-
> tion that was getting larger and larger, it seemed to me that it was
> all a matter of variations, drops or increases in intensity—in such
> a way that there where the quotidian code forced us to express
> ourselves with the sign marking the greatest intensity, "I" (or the
> grammatical fiction of the personal pronoun), it happened more
> than once that we remained perfectly absent from it. That in fact,
> beneath our usage of the signs of the quotidian code, each of us
> necessarily has in mind some sort of "unique sign" whose coher-
> ence we coincide with by the virtue of the specific intensity this
> unique sign ensures. But herein lies the dilemma: namely, that to
> remain within the coherence of a unique sign is to renounce liv-
> ing in the world constituted by the incoherence that reigns there
> thanks to the code of quotidian signs. To accept the constraint
> that thought exercises through the coherence of a unique sign is
> thus to accept madness. But to renounce this unique sign in order
> to live in the world is nonetheless to be subjected to the perpetual
> constraint of the unique sign, to the extent that this sign spies on
> us: in other words, to madness. The ruse of the unique sign is that
> this possible madness is effective as long as we believe we are be-
> traying the coherence in which it encloses us: a ruse for which we
> have to find an equivalent.[30]

The stakes of this passage can best be appreciated if it is read as
a send-up of psychoanalysis, and in particular its account of the
signifier's inadequation to the subject. Klossowski's theory of signs
can be read as a caricature of Lacan in his most structuralist moment, a model it both emulates and overturns. According to a
certain stock interpretation of Lacan's discourse, the "intensity"
of the thought/fantasy is something that cannot be reduced to or
conveyed by a signifier, by the signs of the everyday code. It is the

excess of signification, a surplus of jouissance that has taken refuge in a symptom, the "unique sign."

From the standpoint of analytic treatment, this "unique sign," if allowed to persist, will have one of two consequences: either the subject confronted with this "intensity" will go mad (i.e., he will be subjected to a psychotic delirium, haunted by the hallucinatory insistence of the sign), or he will repress this unbearable intensity, refuse to acknowledge it, in which case it will continue to oppress him by "spying" on him as a symptom—in other words, he will go mad. The only "cure" would be somehow to translate this "intensity" into the register of everyday signs, even if something were lost in the process: such is, after all, the metaphoric reality of the subject's relation to language.

Klossowski's response to the unique sign, however, is something else entirely. Our task should be to find not a substitute for the "ruse of the unique sign," but rather a means of *expressing* the irreducible intensity of the thought/fantasy without designating it. Thus Klossowski seeks to elaborate in language precisely what psychoanalysis-as-semiotics holds to be at odds with language, "intensity" or jouissance.

Against Universal Prostitution

But whether or not it serves to ensure some kind of narcissistic plenitude on the part of the subject, this "perverse" substitution of a libidinized intensity for the register of quotidian signs clearly merits some critical analysis. Most immediately, it invites association with one of Klossowski's obvious literary predecessors, the Marquis de Sade, whose work not only upholds the truth of jouissance against signifying regimes, but also stages a "dissolution" of identity as it is morally conditioned by exposing it as a religious or legal fiction. Is Klossowski's work simply perverse? That is, perverse in the strict sense of a transgressive relation to the law?

To answer this question, we would first have to consider why Klossowski chooses to stage the "dissolution" of privative identity—and the failure of the grammatical fiction of the "I" to guarantee the integrity of the person—through the host's "offering" of his wife to chance strangers. This strategy deserves some scrutiny, since Klossowski's work not only employs the thematics so ubiquitous in libertine literature, but also mounts a "demonstration" whose basic structure is strikingly similar to that of the perverse scenario: a woman's true nature is revealed through her complete surrender to erotic enjoyment, a truth so compelling that it overwhelms her moral will to resist it.

But although the perverse quality of *The Laws of Hospitality* both draws upon and invites association with the writings of Sade, it also differs from this heritage in important ways. Klossowski's Sadeian heritage is most obvious in his attempt to take down and show to be groundless the principles on which our legal or moral identity is based. At the beginning of chapter 3, I argued that Klossowski's work proceeds toward the demonstration of a thesis about the status of the signifier or law: namely, that the death of God means that the law of identity is unfounded, a "pure grammatical joke." Klossowski himself suggests a possible parallel between Sade's thesis and his own when he observes that "the logic of libertinage pure and simple is, from a conceptual point of view, a response to the abolition of the principle of identity, or of the permanent signification of the subject and of the object-subject: and thus the reign of the arbitrary."[31] The argument of Sade's demonstration is that the law cannot hold up against the real of jouissance, for example the destructive impulse within nature. In the human being, the jouissance of nature is upheld by the logic of the organism, whose "will to jouissance" overturns all human laws and reveals them to be without foundation. The result is the reign of the "arbitrary," in the form of chance or opportunistic enjoyment, on the one hand, and destruction or entropic anarchy on the other.

Klossowski's point, however, is subtly different. The apparent genre of the "laws"—perverse fantasy or erotica—is introduced as a foil for a more complex operation. For although Klossowski's fiction, like Sade's, deconstructs the concept of privative identity in its relation to the law, it does not abolish the law altogether. The "laws of hospitality" are, after all, laws. Hence the "dissolution" of the privative constraints of marriage through hospitality does not involve a mere transgression of the law. Instead, it grows out of and insists upon a contradiction internal to the law, a contradiction which is then affirmed as the basis for an ethics of hospitality. As Klossowski's characterization of the "unique sign" makes clear, it is not just that "intensity" or jouissance abolishes the legal or arbitrary nature of the sign, but rather that it invests it in a particular way.

Klossowski addresses the possible parallels between the "laws of hospitality" and Sade's transgressive sexuality in "Protase et apodose," where he argues that their conflation results from the gradual replacement of the monogamous logic of adultery by the logic of libertinage. While granting that it is completely unavoidable, and even necessary, Klossowski makes clear that this replacement or translation is also wholly inadequate. For although the logic of libertinage is one possible response to the abolition of the principle of identity, it remains within an economy of transgression that is entirely dependent upon the very order of quotidian codes it seeks to deconstruct:

> The enunciation of libertinage, whether moral or poetic in form, arises out of the inversion of the monogamous logic of adultery. As a content of experience, libertinage as a redemption or form of revolt is always a function of the code of quotidian signs. . . . Hence the inversion of the monogamous logic of adultery (or transgression) is expressed rationally by the postulate of universal prostitution, which as Sade illustrated is based on the abolition of the property of the self. But here we remain within the same conceptual field: in the name of the principle of identity, or property, the same interdiction applies both to adultery and to universal prostitution; and since both are enunciations of a single interdiction, this interdiction itself is precisely what guarantees the intelligible expression of the contents of experience called adultery or prostitution.[32]

If the abolition of identity as the personal property of the self results for Sade in the postulate of universal prostitution, it is because the law is no longer able to uphold the privative delimitation of subjects, who are now surrendered up to a generalized sexual economy in which an unlimited and undifferentiated "enjoyment" supplants the privative quality of ownership or of moral interdiction.

But as Klossowski suggests, this operation is still subservient to the principle of identity, or property, since the transgression of personal property derives its meaning from the very principle it pretends to abolish. In Sade's discourse, the symptom of this dependence is that economy remains in place even after the supposed abolition or deconstruction of the law. Although his argument exposes the unfoundedness of the signifier or law, it simultaneously pretends that there can be exchange—even "free" exchange—without the symbolic, as if in dismantling the moral agency of the law it has somehow eradicated the structure of the signifier. But the operativity of exchange is the very mark of the symbolic, which constitutes the possibility of exchange as such. In other words, what Sade calls the *droit de jouir de tous*—the complete interchangeability of all objects of sexual enjoyment—is still a kind of exchange, an equation in which a single variable or position represents a plurality of subjects "equally," and thus to the exclusion of their difference.

For Klossowski, on the other hand, the fact that the property of the self is unfounded and lacks substantial integrity results neither in its abolition nor in its transgressive inversion. The "dissolution" of the principle of identity or personal property is not just a disavowal of that law. The first indication of this difference is that the contestation of the law of monogamous property does not result in the postulate of universal prostitution or generalized adulteration, but rather in the animation—and affirmation—of the contradiction on which it is based. The second is that the "laws of hospitality"—unlike the practices of the libertine—do not define themselves in relation to the code of quotidian signs, either by reference, inversion, or transgression. But more than this, they are not even legible within that code. Within the system of quotidian signs, the practice or custom of hospitality is legible only as libertinage:

> What then can be said of the content of the experiences formulated in *The Laws of Hospitality*—in other words, Octave's behavior with regard to Roberte? Octave pretends to be instituting or reinstituting a custom. But even if it may have existed as such at other latitudes, it is unrecognizable in our occidental societies, except perhaps in the libertine milieu—and therefore never in the sense intended by Octave.[33]

The contradiction internal to the laws is precisely what renders them illegible within the system of "quotidian signs." As what eludes or gives the lie to the law of the signifier, therefore, this contradiction is itself the "real" that Klossowski opposes to the reign of quotidian signifiers. Whereas Sade upholds the real of organic jouissance against the signifier, Klossowski opposes to it the "coherence" or "intensity" of the unique sign. In the practice of hospitality, the irreducible or inscrutable quality of the law is privileged over the universalizing, deproprietary, and even organic or quasi-biological pretensions of libertinage.

Klossowski's critique of the law of personal identity is also a critique of economy, which is more subtle than Sade's in that it has to do with the resistance of the "sign" itself to translation, prostitution, or compromise. The unique sign is neither transcendent *logos* nor semiotic signifier, but an inscrutable "letter" whose coherence resists translation, in much the same way that the particular ethics of the "laws of hospitality" resist translation into quotidian signs. The correspondence between them is dramatized comically in the third novel in Klossowski's trilogy, *Le Souffleur* (The Prompter).

Why the Home Is Not a Hotel

Le Souffleur finds its protagonist, Théodore K., the author of *The Laws of Hospitality,* engaged in a polemic with the French government, which has decreed that all wives must be declared to the state and appraised for income-tax purposes. In the guise of payment of the couple's financial obligations to the state, each wife must report for a prescribed length of service to the Hôtel de Longchamp, a kind of Sadeian institution in which the "charms" of women are appraised as commodities to be sold on the open market. But when he confides his troubles to his psychoanalyst, one Doctor Ygdrasil, Théodore finds his opposition to the state practice pathologized as a symptom. The analyst finds the hotel economy to be the natural extension—or even the idealized embodiment—of Théodore's own "laws of hospitality."

In *Le Souffleur,* Théodore is repeatedly subjected to demands that he translate the "unique sign," Roberte, and its equivalent, the laws of hospitality, into codes of substitution and exchange. First, he is asked to translate his wife's bodily charms into money by the state apparatus of the Hôtel de Longchamp. But his own analyst intensifies the stakes of this first demand with a second, which is articulated within the framework of the "treatment." Although an intimate acquaintance of Théodore and his wife, the analyst dares to ask the question: "Who is Roberte?" (F195).[34] He is only capable of understanding Théodore's "unique sign" as a symptomatic signifier, to be surrendered in the course of analysis in exchange for an "everyday" interpretation or diagnosis.

As the novel unfolds, it becomes clear that the analyst's "cure" is more perverse than the "symptom" it tries to address. Klossowski not only reveals the semiotic logic of Ygdrasil's vulgar psychoanalysis to be antithetical to hospitality, but also stages its complicity with the Sadeian fantasy of perversion.

In a second encounter between Théodore and Ygdrasil near the end of the novel, the two demands for translation coalesce in the analyst's insistence that Théodore "cure" himself by surrendering his laws of hospitality in favor of a universal law of exchange: "You are absolutely determined to give without getting anything in return, and never to receive! But you cannot live without submitting to the universal law of exchange!" (F302). Ygdrasil upholds the practices of the Hôtel de Longchamp by offering a translation of the laws that is in strict adherence with Sade's principle of universal prostitution, a reciprocal logic of even exchange:

> The practice of hospitality such as you conceive it could never be unilateral. Like every hospitality, this one—and this one in particular—requires absolute reciprocity in order to be viable. But this is the step you are not willing to take: the free exchange of women by men and men by women. Such is the corollary of your laws of hospitality, the sole universal legitimation of the adulteration of the wife by the husband. Without it all of this remains a pure phantasm, in which monogamous morality is infinitely transgressed only to reestablish itself all the better, in which the sacrament of marriage is verified merely through sacrilege, the vestiges of a theology whose miasmas are poisoning you. . . . (F303)

Ygdrasil's interpretation of the "laws" brings to bear several kinds of economy: signifying, financial, legislative, and sexual. Most obviously, the analyst's discourse follows the logic of Sade's reasoning almost to the letter. But it also has affinities with numerous "economic" interpretations of the hospitality act, including Immanuel Kant's understanding of cosmopolitan hospitality as a state-run economy whose transactions are calculated in terms of discrete legal identities. What all of these views of hospitality share is a rejection of the notion that property could be personal, capable of resisting inscription in a logic of universal exchange. In its Kantian insistence on "universal legitimation," Ygdrasil's interpretation of Théodore's laws of hospitality suggests that in order to become an ethics, the laws must be susceptible to universalization. Otherwise they remain no more than a "fantasy," and by implication a pathology: not only a symptom or disorder, but a "pathological object" in the Kantian sense of what must be excluded from consideration in the formulation of moral maxims.

Although Roberte may function as a "pathological object" for

Théodore, he insists that in clinging to her singularity he is not just being pathological or neurotic. Rather, he is attempting to mount a systematic critique of the logics of "equal" sexual exchange on which the systems of his two most celebrated predecessors are based: Sade's universal *droit de jouir de tous,* and Kant's "even exchange" of sexual parts as constitutive of marriage. From his analyst's perspective, these responses to the sexual relation appear to be more "healthy," because each has "surrendered" or put into circulation the personal property that might otherwise become a pathological basis for ethical action. But although each of these logics finds in the negation of personal property an affirmation of autonomous freedom, each also reduces difference to an economy. Paradoxically, the absolute erasure of ownership or property turns out to be the supreme achievement of economy, the ultimate institution.

Conversely, Théodore's—and Klossowski's—formulations of hospitality challenge the apparent reversibility of an "equal" relation to the other with evidence of the fundamental inequality inherent in the sexual relation. In the logic of sexual difference, "equality" is a reduction of difference to one standard, an economic model of the sexes in which the signifier represents both sexes "equally," and thus inadequately. As a mark of the inadequation to the signifier that characterizes the position of woman, the "unique sign" is the embodiment of her irreducibility to all signifiers of exchange.

Of course, the antagonism between Théodore's and Ygdrasil's different views of exchange has implications that extend well beyond the nuances of wife-giving. In fact, the differend at the heart of their argument touches directly upon the stakes of modern hospitality and the ambiguity internal to its treatment of the stranger or guest. Ygdrasil is the voice of a certain vision of hospitality, one that has dominated European consciousness since the Enlightenment. In his advocation of a hospitality of unrestricted exchange, Ygdrasil aims at an "erasure of borders" (F305), an erasure that applies both to the problematic of sexual difference and to the relationship between the host and the guest; in each domain, it involves a neutralization of the irreversibility inherent in these relations and its replacement by economies of jouissance or of money. Predicated as it is upon the elimination of privative ownership, Ygdrasil's "erasure of borders" recalls Kant's vision of cosmopolitan hospitality, whose core tenet is the right to common possession of the surface of the earth, over and against the claims of privative ownership of territory.[35] (Interestingly, the name Ygdrasil refers to the hospitable "world tree" of Norse mythology, which cradles the entire world in its branches. It upholds a vision of hospitality that is both universal and cosmopolitan, insofar as the whole world is both contained in and united by the holistic hospitality the eternal tree provides.)

Théodore's dispute with Ygdrasil hinges upon their different understandings of the complicated relationship between *hospitality* and *hotel,* words and institutions that share a common root, but which historically have developed in different—and even mutually exclusive—directions. Traditionally, "hospitality" involves an interpersonal relationship that is not mediated either by money, law, or even the recognition imparted by proper names. Typically it involves the guest's penetration into the intimacy of the host's home, which may even be threatening or uncanny in character.

Conversely, the "hotel" receives the stranger in a mode that already de-emphasizes and even neutralizes his strangeness; it formalizes the host/guest relationship through the impersonal mediation of money, legal identification, and rules of conduct, thereby eliminating or choosing to overlook the guest's fundamental unknowability. But although its economic underpinnings run counter to the underlying tenets of the hospitality tradition, the "hotel" is in another sense really the modern culmination of the history of hospitality. One indication of this is that "hotel" also names the state or institutional incarnation of hospitality: in French, *hôtel* designates not only the economically motivated inn or resort, but any kind of building that houses a state institution—*Hôtel de Ville, Hôtel Dieu, Hôtel de la Police,* etc.

Théodore's objection to Ygdrasil's hotel-like vision of hospitality—which is secular, state-based, "equal," and fully legislated—also helps to explain the importance of the "divine" or "sacred" to Klossowski's understanding of hospitality. The "laws of hospitality" framed in Octave's guest bedroom (and Théodore's rearticulation of them in *Le Souffleur*) attribute a sacred quality to both the guest and the hostess, a divinity that is excluded or overlooked by Ygdrasil and his philosophical ballasts, Sade and Kant. While Sade's critique of the moral basis of "religion" as a legal construct dismisses divinity along with the institution that pretends to embody it, Klossowski's articulation of hospitality affirms a "divinity" irreducible to the prescriptive regime of morality. Although he is decidedly post-Nietzschean in his rejection of "religion" as a legitimate basis for relation, he nonetheless does not dispense with the irreducible excess to which it attests—the "possible inequality in a society of equals," to use Lévinas's expression. But as a "possible inequality"—to the law, to others, and even to oneself—"divinity" for Klossowski is no longer the special province of the gods, but inheres in the "dissolved" multiplicity of each participant in the hospitality relation. It is this irreducible multiplicity that Théodore seeks to uphold in clinging to his anachronistic view of hospitality, which cleaves to the "letter of the law"—its inherent irreducibility—over and above its symbolic or unifying pretensions.

For Ygdrasil, the problem is that Théodore does not want to cross the necessary step: he refuses to counter his wife's infidelity with his own, to be as untrue to her as he wishes that she be to him. But for Théodore, Roberte's infidelity is not reducible to adultery or prostitution: to say that identity is *dissolved* is not to say that it is altogether indifferent. For him the custom of hospitality does not consist in an uprooting of the law, but rather in an appeal to the contradiction it contains. In response to Doctor Ygdrasil's reduction of the laws of hospitality to Longchamp's practice of universal prostitution, Théodore insists: "I am in no way arguing for the free exchange of wives, nor pleading in favor of the universal prostitution that you would like to lead me to. I am not trading a random mistress to my friends in exchange for theirs, I am loaning them my wife" (F302).

Whereas Kant and Sade base their proposals for cosmopolitan hospitality and universal prostitution on the partial or complete elimination of privative ownership, Klossowski affirms the contradiction internal to it. Earlier I noted that the laws of hospitality introduce a contradiction into the logic of monogamous property, according to which what belongs to me "once and for all" cannot at the same time belong to someone else. The corollary is that Roberte's value inheres in being unsellable, wholly resistant to exchange: "the wife, prostituted by the husband, is nonetheless still the wife: the husband's inexchangeable good, the priceless good who shows her worth when the wife surrenders to a lover chosen by her husband" (F304). Roberte "shows her worth" when in surrendering herself she reveals to her husband something unknown or inaccessible to him, simultaneously exceeding and confirming the proprietary quality of the marriage relation. Such a possibility is completely lacking from the generalized adulteration or universal prostitution proposed by Ygdrasil, in which "value" or "worth" is a by-product of exchangeability.

In "Protase et apodose," Klossowski further contrasts the two practices by drawing a distinction between what he calls "internal" and "external" polygamy. The laws of hospitality concern "internal polygamy": the "adultery" that is inevitably internal to marriage, to the extent that one is always married to more than one person—or, more precisely, insofar as the person one is married to is never singular.[36] Understood in this way, "adultery" is not just the opposite, subversion, or violation of marriage, but its internal truth. This is why it is so important that Roberte and Théodore are married, joined in a unifying, exclusive relation in which personal property is determined as inalienable. In the preface to *The Laws of Hospitality,* Klossowski even makes this "internal adultery" the cornerstone of a creatively reconceived "nuclear family." After ten years spent "living under the sign of Roberte," he writes that he was able to "deduce from the sacrament of marriage the chain reaction produced by the wedding ring" (F9). In other words, by splitting what cannot by all accounts be separated—an inalienable bond—he was able to experience and affirm the singular force it contains.

Hospitality and Literary Form, or the Trilogy as Anti-Trinity

This logic has important implications for the literary treatment of hospitality, as well. Earlier I noted that Klossowski's response to the "ruse of the unique sign" is to seek for it not a translation, but rather an "equivalent." Where then should this "equivalent" be sought? Klossowski locates it within *The Laws of Hospitality* itself. The "unique sign" gives rise to a "custom" (the laws of hospitality as a practice) that introduces an aberration into the heart of the everyday world of signs. When they are transposed into the everyday code, it turns out that it is impossible to offer an intelligible articulation of the laws of hospitality:

> The signs of the quotidian code translate *The Laws of Hospitality* as follows: the adulteration of the wife by her husband. In the code of quotidian signs, this means that the husband incites his wife to commit adultery. But in truth, *The Laws of Hospitality* has to do

with something else altogether: the host offers his wife (the hostess) to their guests. Octave wants to discover Roberte's true identity through contact with a stranger, an unknown, because he believes that in his marital bond he only has access to the apparent, and therefore fallacious, identity of his spouse. Fundamentally, he apprehends in Roberte a plurality of natures, which can only be revealed through the intermediary of chance guests.[37]

Translated, the laws of hospitality are a practice of prostitution; *expressed* in the paradoxical logic of hospitality, they are the offering of a gift, the alienation of an inalienable good such that, in this alienation, it becomes inalienable once again. To attempt to translate this intensity into everyday codes is to lose the essential, namely the difference intrinsic to the way in which it returns.

In "Protase et apodose," Klossowski suggests that *The Laws of Hospitality,* as a series of novels, is to be considered as an equivalent for the unique sign, for two reasons. On the one hand, the unique sign gives rise to a "custom" (the laws of hospitality as a practice) that introduces an aberration into the heart of the everyday world of signs. On the other, because it is a literary equivalent, it eludes madness. Literature proposes a different kind of "cure" than psychoanalysis, one that stages the irresolvable contradiction internal to the "unique sign."

Deleuze suggests how the logic of expropriation or exchange might be distinguished from that of the unique sign when he differentiates between a "false" and a "true" relation to repetition. The first is the one that psychoanalysis identifies as an illness, the repetition-compulsion that makes us sick; but it is also institutionalized repetition, the implementation of regulated laws of exchange. "True" repetition, in contrast, affirms the *difference* intrinsic to the way in which the inexchangeable ("Roberte") returns as nonidentical to itself:

> exchange implies only resemblance, even if the resemblance is extreme. Exactness is its criterion, along with the equivalence of exchanged products. This is the false repetition which causes our illness. True repetition, on the other hand, appears as a singular behavior that we display in relation to that which cannot be exchanged, replaced, or substituted—like a poem that is repeated on the condition that no word may be changed. It is no longer a matter of an equivalence between similar things, it is not even a matter of

an identity of the Same. True repetition addresses something singular, unchangeable, and different, without "identity." Instead of exchanging the similar and identifying the Same, *it authenticates the different*.[38]

This expanded or "true" repetition describes not only the return of the "unique sign," but the structure of the *Laws* itself. In the postscript, Klossowski writes that the trilogy was constructed as three "variations on the same theme," whose "obscurity" and "clarity" alike are due to "what these variations were able to retain of the state of a thought that in no way wished to lend itself to their point of departure" (F334). But to the extent that they cohere—in their obscurity *or* in their clarity—the coherence of the three novels does not correspond to their consistency or repeatability. In fact, each "variation" is characterized by its failure to apprehend fully its theme, which in remaining the "same" in each novel is nonetheless impossibly nonidentical not only to its different variants, but even to itself. In different ways, each novel stages the difference internal to the way in which the "theme" of the unique sign manifests itself.

The Revocation is made up entirely of journal entries, which both follow the "confessional" style of Augustine and at the same time overturn it, insisting upon the tension or conflict between Roberte's and Octave's different views of hospitality rather than producing a unified single interpretation. *Roberte, ce soir* is composed in the genre of a theological dialogue, but in which different positions are conceived not as dialectical moments in a single discourse, but rather divided among different speakers as a kind of theatrical script. Finally, *Le Souffleur* effects the ultimate realization of the difference within the unique sign, with Roberte literally splitting into two "simulacra." Each of the three novels plays upon the dual meaning of *répétition* in French, which translates both as "repetition" and as "rehearsal." As the trilogy unfolds, Roberte is "repeated" and "rehearsed" in many different ways. In *Le Souffleur*, she even "plays" herself, performing the part of Roberte in her husband's production of *Roberte, ce soir*. But importantly, she is never adequate to her own self-representation; the other actors keep finding her inappropriate to her own role, which prevents the piece from ever being performed in quite the same way from one "repetition" to the next.

The resistance of the "unique sign" to translation or institution-alized repetition corresponds to Roberte's resistance to economies of exchange. The name "Roberte," like the practice of hospitality, introduces an illegible contradiction into the register of everyday signs. "Roberte" is, among other things, a feminization of the name for the French dictionary, *Le Robert*—in other words, where one goes to seek equivalences. But in this feminine version, the "unique sign" is one that cannot be exchanged—and, perhaps more impor-tantly, one whose value is not dependent upon exchange. In the postscript to the *Laws,* Klossowski specifies that "sufficient unto itself, the sign had nothing of the content of thesaurusized emo-tions" (F334). The unique sign is neither transcendent *logos* nor se-miotic signifier, but an inscrutable "letter" whose coherence resists translation. It is thus innately literary, to the extent that the literary form both doubles and extends the tension within the unique sign. Just as Roberte functions as a kind of anti-dictionary and anti-Christ, the trilogy of novels functions as an anti-confessional, an anti-trinity.

5. Welcoming Dionysus, or the Subject as *Corps Morcelé*

Nietzsche zeroes in on the guiltiest secret of modern metaphysics: that despite its declared secularism, it has not managed to separate itself from onto-theology when it comes to the concept of identity. Descartes finds the logical support for the *cogito* in the existence of God, the "thinker outside of me" in whose gaze I come into being as "myself."[1] However, this recognition of the Other at the source of human identity tends to fall under erasure in the philosophical tradition that emerges out of his work, which canonizes the "I think, therefore I am" at the expense of the heteronomous account of subjectivity that is so central to Descartes' thought.

Nietzsche's account of God as the metaphysical guarantor of being diagnoses the narcissistic logic Freud identified in the fantasy of seduction, where the ego comes into being by identifying with the image where it is constituted as an object for the Other. But while his myth of the death of God questions the consistent self that the monotheist God sustains, the aim of Nietzsche's analysis is not to debunk the existence of an Other outside of us, but to develop Descartes' insight in a new direction by revealing the degree to which the Other is absolutely integral to the subject. The "liberation" implied in the death of God is not simply a liberation of the subject from an external constraint, but a liberation *of the Other* from the image or "mask" that contained it and held it at bay. Nietzsche finds its traces in the violent impulses that take hold of the organism, fragmenting its natural wholeness as well as its transcendental unity, and that he identifies with the advent of Dionysus. In the process, he demonstrates not only that the autonomous personhood of the "self" or ego is a fiction, but that the unified body image it supports functions to repress another body, a body that is the true site of the subject.

If Nietzsche preferred the title of "psychologist" to "philosopher,"[2] it is no doubt because his critique of metaphysics is rooted in a profound engagement with the body and the contradictory and fragmenting "impulses" that animate it. His singular interpretation of the Dionysus myth anticipates Sigmund Freud's discovery of the drives, and especially of that avatar of the drives that Jacques Lacan calls the "jouissance of the Other." In his early study of the god, *The Birth of Tragedy,* Nietzsche approaches under the aegis of myth what he later pursues by following what he calls "the thread of the body," investigating the "impulses" that take possession of his being and dissolve his self-consciousness.[3] What his quest reveals is that to "welcome Dionysus" is to play host to the fragmented body of the drives, which dwells within "us" like a foreign agent, undermining the integrity of the self or ego. But Nietzsche also shares with Freud and Lacan an unswerving devotion to the ethics of living from the site of this fragmented body, without the support of narcissism and the unified image of the self it upholds.

The Body of Seduction, or the Invention of the Self

In his early work with hysteria, Freud discovers in the logic of conversion the contours of an erotic body whose erogenous zones bear the traces of the subject's encounter with the death drive. Jacques Lacan, in designating the erogenous zones as "letters of the body," emphasizes that the object of psychoanalysis is not the material body, the living organism, but rather something that *overwrites* this organism, substituting the logic of the fantasy for the neurophysiological functioning of the living being. For the human who speaks, being is exiled in the signifier. The erotic body is therefore born of the loss of the organism, through the encounter with the unbound drive energy—or jouissance—introduced by language. It overwrites the sexual organism in much the same way that a virus overwrites a computer disk, causing its neurophysiological systems to malfunction or operate according to another logic. The erotic body does not therefore "exist" in any conventional sense, since it can be located only in speech, in the signifying chain that bears the traces of the subject's encounter with the death drive.

Willy Apollon defines the letter as "the inscription of the pri-mordial division that inaugurates the body as detached from the organism." It articulates as a fragmented body, or *corps morcelé,* "that part of the organism whose jouissance must make way for the signifier of the Other."[4] The letter is thus the site of castration, marking "the indefinitely failed inscription of a jouissance lost in advance because the fact of language renders it impossible."[5] It signs the loss of natural or animal jouissance, the full instinctive poten-tial of the living being. But the letter also marks the fact that there are no organs on the human body to localize and limit jouissance, as there are organs of sexuality in the living organism. As such, it signals the return of another, excessive jouissance, incompati-ble with the satisfaction of the living being. The "polymorphous perversion" Freud identifies in the child is the direct result of the disorganization of the sexual field by eroticism, which unleashes the drives as unbound energies dissociated from any natural aim, that search in vain for an object capable of satisfying them.

But when Lacan designates the erogenous zones as "letters," he draws our attention not only to the inscription or cutting by which the body leaves its traces on the organism, but to the primacy of the structure of the address in human subjectivity. Apollon evokes its importance in a very suggestive formulation: the letters of the body are the erogenous zones where we address to our partner the effects of jouissance on the body; sex is the "post office," the site where these letters are exchanged.[6]

In the address, we use speech to *evoke* for the partner or the human community something that cannot be verified by a third party: the ravages of the death drive on the organism. Apollon ar-gues that "speech" in the human being marks the failure of "com-munication," the language of the natural world defined by the integral transmission of information: for example, the hormonal signals indicating that an animal is ready to mate. In contrast, the human need to "address" the letters of the body to the partner, is a direct consequence of their failure to be "communicated" or understood. Speech presupposes the structure of the address, the absence of the Other that language introduces into the human uni-verse. According to Apollon,

> the living being has to get its bearings in relation to this Other who
> is absent, but whose obscure presence nonetheless haunts it, and

also in relation to this excessive energy. As a result, it begins to see and hear things that are not perceptible as such. From this point onward, vision and hearing . . . no longer have anything to do with the visual and auditory perception of animals. A fantasmatic universe surges forth to articulate these sights and sounds, which are no longer able to be pinned down through recourse to perceptive reality, and that a scientific approach, in its demand for objectivity, would qualify as hallucinatory. Speech attempts to evoke for the group or fellow human being in the group these effects of the Other in the living being. . . . If man speaks, it is no doubt because a jouissance, which is the effect of the absence of this Other who now haunts his living universe, unleashes in him these things he has heard and that he needs to see, and that he looks to the other, his companion, to validate for him.[7]

As the site where the letters of the body are "addressed" to the partner, human sexuality is closely tied to the structure of myth, which defines what Apollon calls the "conditions of credibility" for the address by allowing the human subject to evoke for the community a real that cannot be verified empirically. As Freud once put it, "the drives are our myths." According to Apollon, "this is because they respond to an Other of whom we have no idea. . . . The drives respond to this absence of the Other by attempting to solve the handicap and the radical cut that the Other introduces into the living being."[8]

But who or what is this Other? As the "absolute pole of the address," writes Marie-Claire Boons-Grafé, "the Other is not a real interlocutor: it is essentially the Symbolic place required by the speech of the subject, where the subject both *is,* and at the same time *is not,* in so far as he is constituted by lack in the Other."[9] In the notion of the Other, we have to distinguish between the Other as such—that is, the field of the Other that Freud discovers by means of the unconscious—and the imaginary Other or Other of seduction. The first is the gap or emptiness at the center of human subjectivity, the source of the jouissance that overwhelms human life. The second is the Other of the subject's own fantasy, to which myth lends credibility by providing the representations that give consistency to the Other within a particular civilization. The two are nonetheless intimately related, since the imaginary Other gives a face to the Absent Other of the address, and thereby allows the subject to repress its absence: by fearing its judgments, appealing to it for help, relinquishing his fate to it, or making it the embodiment of justice or goodwill.

This logic is at the heart of what Freud called the fantasy of seduction,[10] which constructs an Other who would lend provisional consistency to the fragmented body by serving as the "addressee" of the letter. It gives a face to the empty center of the address by positioning the subject as the object of an Other, in whose gaze he might find the representation of himself.[11] Lucie Cantin describes seduction as the solution of neurosis to the mental representations that mark the body with the effects of anxiety and jouissance, offering the neurotic support against solitude.[12] She cites as an example Freud's story of a child who he once heard calling out of a dark room to his aunt, asking her to speak to him because he was afraid of the dark. When the aunt asked what good speaking would do, since he couldn't even see her, the child replied: "if anyone speaks, it gets light."[13] In the same way, says Cantin, the neurotic appeals to the Other to mask the void of the absence with "visibility." Seduction works to hide the fact that eroticism is founded on death, and that the human being is without recourse to any Other in its encounter with the effects of jouissance. It allows the neurotic to conceive of castration not as a structural necessity of the speaking being, but as the work of an Other who has it in his power to provide or withhold the object that would anchor the drives.

Lacan identifies the structural underpinnings of seduction in the mirror stage, where the ego comes into being as an object for the Other.[14] The child identifies himself with the object the mother smiles at in the mirror. In his specular image, the child finds an imaginary object with which it can identify in order to build an Ideal Ego. The mother's glance introduces visibility, offering an object to replace the void (like the aunt's words in Freud's example). An Other is put in the place of the Absence, producing the ego as the imaginary object of the Other's desire and building a unified image of the body. Seduction allows the child to repress the fragmented body of eroticism by identifying not with the real of the drives, the *corps morcelé* to which he is reduced by the loss of the organism, but with the *unified body image* presented by the mirror.

According to Cantin, this repression of the body by the body image is in turn upheld by the ego ideals supported by the paternal signifier or Name-of-the-Father *[Nom-du-père],*[15] which gives symbolic consistency to the Other by articulating being to the reference points of culture and civilization. On the one hand, culture offers the identificatory norms, ideals, and models that support the building of the ego and the production of the social scene. On the other, civilization gives consistency to the Other through the concept of God, which supports seduction as the Other of last recourse. Especially in the Western civilizations marked by Christianity, God is the Other who supports the structure of seduction by giving the subject an image of himself with which he can identify. At the same time, God is often presented as the source or guarantor of the narcissistic ego ideals supporting this body image on the social scene. With these representations, the fields of culture and civilization organize the forgetting of the Other's absence at the same time that they support the emergence of the body image.

Seduction obscures the truth that the subject's consistency has no "reality," since it resides solely in the image and is sustained by nothing more than a signifier. In this way, it is intimately tied to the complaint against the father that plays such an important role in neurosis, and that Freud identifies as the foundation of monotheist experience. The neurotic child, like the believer, chooses not to acknowledge the absence of any Other who could come to his aid. Instead, he compensates for the father's failure to provide the protection that would support him in his confrontation with the drives by constructing an imaginary Other capable of undoing the disorganizing effects of the drives, of restoring "life after death." In "The Question of a Weltanschauung," Freud argues that God is essentially a reconstructed ideal father, an "idealized super-man"[16] to whom men appeal for protection against the uncertainty of life when their real fathers fail to fulfill this function in childhood.

But as Freud wryly observes, "It seems not to be the case that there is a Power in the universe which watches over the well-being of individuals with parental care and brings all their affairs to a happy ending."[17] The goal of the analytic experience is to oblige the analysand to confront this truth by leading him to the point where the Other of seduction falls away, confronting him with castration. Fundamentally, castration is the experience of the absence of the Other of the address, which leaves the subject utterly alone and without any recourse in dealing with the effects of the death drive on the body.[18]

However, the aim of Freud's technique is not to "get rid" of the Other by exposing it as a fiction or figment of the subject's imagination. Instead, the transference works to *liberate* the field of the Other by upholding the "Other scene" of the unconscious against the narcissistic values that would seek to repress it. In other words, it is the consistency of the imaginary Other (mother, father, God . . .) that must be challenged, not the *field of the Other* that insists in the hallucinations and symptoms that disrupt the ego's equilibrium.

So what does Nietzsche have to tell us about this experience, and why does he link it to the murder of God? He is certainly not the first thinker in history to denounce the monotheist God as an "illusion," or bemoan the constraining "mask" it imposes on the human subject. But the singularity of his undertaking becomes clear when it is compared to the thinker who might be considered his most important predecessor in this project, the Marquis de Sade. A full century before Nietzsche, Sade outlined in meticulous detail the subordination of the erotic body to the moral principles ascribed to God the father, which impose teleological aims on the drives in an attempt to limit—and so deny—their polymorphous character. And like Nietzsche, Sade anticipated Freud's criticisms of the way civilization attempts to solve the absence of the Other by introducing the palliative "fiction" of an Other of last recourse. All three thinkers are united in their intolerance for the lack of moral courage implied in the neurotic's depressive symptoms, his avoidance of responsibility in the face of jouissance. But Nietzsche is much closer to Freud than to Sade in two ways. First, he confronts much more squarely than Sade the loss of the narcissistic ideal of identity that must necessarily accompany the recognition of the Other's absence. And second, he does not repudiate the exile in the signifier that defines human life, but affirms the *corps morcelé* it produces as the sole site of subjective experience.

Sade is undoubtedly one of the greatest critics of the neurotic fantasy of seduction, taking aim at the law the neurotic uses to hold at bay the jouissance he refuses to face. However, his perspicacity wanes when it comes to the castrating effects introduced into human life by the field of the Other, whose effects he attempts to sidestep. Ultimately, Sade is less interested in debunking the imaginary fiction of the unified Self than in denying the dominion of the Other over the subject: an Other that is not a fiction or symbolic construction, but an irrefutable fact of human life. In the last chapter, I elaborated Pierre Klossowski's argument that the logic of libertinage remains subservient to the principle of identity. Now we will see that this is because it clings to the value of the Self and refuses the *corps morcelé* that is the source of the subject's division. For while Sade deconstructs the dependence of symbolic identity on the moral principles of an illusory and impotent God, he never really touches the value of personal identity itself: the unified Self not only survives the dissipation of the "divine chimera," but emerges stronger than ever, healed of the losses imposed by the Other's law.

But for this reason, Sade allows us to appreciate the singularity of Nietzsche's endeavor. In calling for a "transvaluation of all values," including and most importantly the value of personal identity itself, Nietzsche realizes the critique of transcendental consciousness that is promised, but not really delivered, by Sade, completing his critique of symbolic identity without falling into the same traps. His work reveals that Sade's displacement of the laws of God by the "natural law" of jouissance is less a *transvaluation* of personal identity than a *revaluation,* one that regrounds the Self in a new support without touching the values it sustains. If we are to dismantle once and for all the value of personal identity, Nietzsche implies, it is not enough to murder God: we must also take aim at the myth of the "natural" body in which it takes refuge.

The Organism against the Body: Sade's Disavowal of Castration

In *La philosophie dans le boudoir* (1795), Sade indicts the way civilization gives consistency to the Other and attempts to limit the drives through the myth of God, which he dismisses as an "imaginary" idea without foundation. His dramatic treatise, in the form of seven dialogues, stages the perverse education of a young girl, Eugénie, under the tutelage of the libertine Dolmancé. In a series of detailed, rational arguments—interspersed with more intimate lessons in the pleasures of the flesh and the imagination—he seeks to liberate her from the moral beliefs and prejudices instilled by a devout mother. But more profoundly, Sade wants to prove to his readers the utter groundlessness of any law that would presume to limit jouissance. His aim is to show that religion, and the patriarchal laws that find support in its morality, know *nothing* about the body.[19]

His argument focuses on the Christian ideology that holds the body to be an inviolable temple, dedicated to God and faithful to his image.[20] By appealing to the authority of the biblical laws demarcating the proper and improper aims for the sexual drives, religious discourse subordinates the body to symbolic principles. In particular, the ideology that presents maternity as the only legitimate sexual destiny for girls allows them to be held prisoner by society, which uses this ideology to reproduce not only new citizens, but its own values and principles. In these ways, religion and the social practices it supports give us a false sense of the body, as directed toward teleological aims (57).

But Sade knows better. He details a series of profound insights concerning the erotic body, which he implicitly acknowledges as something irreducible to the natural organism.[21] He demonstrates for his audience the "polymorphous perversion" of the human, the capacity to invent new objects for the drives that have been cut loose from their sexual moorings. These new objects range from varieties of sexual experience—homosexuality, oral and anal sex, and coprophagy, just to name a few—to the erotically charged acts of blasphemy, murder, theft, and torture.

But for Sade, unlike Freud, the transition from a natural to an erotic state is unequivocally favorable for man. The body is to be found not in the loss of natural instincts, but in their exploration and multiplication: with respect to the animal organism, the human body is a *more,* and not a *less.* Or, more accurately, Sade really sees two bodies "beyond" the organism: first a body delimited by religion, that has lost its organs to the law; and second an immanent body of unbounded potential, that has gained additional possibilities of jouissance. The first body is a lie, a myth. How then has it managed to conceal the truth of the second, and to gain acceptance among men?

We find the answer in Sade's denunciation of those who "stupidly take social institutions for the divine laws of nature" (107). Why do men attribute authority to social institutions, investing them with false "divinity"? Sade shows us that neurotic culture—or what he calls the culture of "the imbeciles" (107)—invented it as protection against pain, suffering, and destruction. The neurotic is afraid of the violence at the heart of nature. But more than that, he is afraid of the limitless potential of the body, afraid of the unanchored drives that call the aims of human life into question. He doesn't want to know anything about what eroticism implies.

So he calls upon God to protect his being from the violent break-in of jouissance, to give him an image of himself that would hold eroticism at bay. Sade's analysis zeroes in on Christian discourse as something that both grows out of and supports the neurotic fantasy of seduction, by upholding the belief in an Other to whom the subject can appeal for help in his encounter with death. This is the Other whose absence the libertine master will very brutally demonstrate for his victim, by forcing the limit of a pain she must suffer without any recourse to the imaginary Other of her prayers. When her "sacred" body is violated by the libertine in his ruthless pursuit of jouissance, no Other will respond to her cries for help. Thus God is proved to be an "idea without prototype," of "imaginary origin" (200).

But strikingly, it is not only the imaginary Other who disappears with the illusion of God, but the castrating effects Sade attributes to God and his law in the form of the limitations imposed on the body's potential. If the father who imposes the law of castration is "imaginary," a "myth," then isn't Sade really saying that castration is merely a symptom of cowardice and fear—a myth we promote to protect ourselves against jouissance? He repudiates God and his law as not only heterogeneous with the natural world, but impotent by virtue of that heterogeneity. While he quite rightly observes that God is an "idea without prototype," one that doesn't belong to the real of nature, Sade reductively concludes that this idea is a "mere" fiction, an illusion: "Can an idea without prototype be anything other than a chimera?" (200).

With this reasoning, Sade goes in a very different direction than Freud and Lacan. His critique of symbolic law conceives of castration not as a structural effect of language, but as the work of a patriarchal morality that imposes it to deprive men of their "right" to jouissance. In unmasking the imaginary Other of the address as a groundless fiction, Sade seeks to disprove the structural necessity of castration at the same time. His irrefutable demonstration of the unfoundedness of the idea of God, and the religious laws it supports, works to occlude the field of the Other as such, the traumatic loss of the organism's natural aims that incited men to elaborate this imaginary solution in the first place.

What is the source of the polymorphous perversion that defines human sexuality if not the Other? How did the drives become unanchored from their natural aims? Does the eroticism that displaces sexuality in the human simply imply more possibilities for enjoyment, more orifices available for penetration? Or does it inevitably entail a subtraction as well, the loss of the organism's natural capacities and aims as a result of jouissance? On these points, Sade's reasoning is less precise.

In fact, he seems to identify the erotic field only to retreat from its most profound implications. Most notably, Sade's insight about the unnatural status of the body is absorbed into a somewhat paradoxical attempt to re-naturalize the body, and thereby restore its lost integrity. First, he attempts to reinscribe the polymorphous perversion that results from the fantasy into the natural world. We see this strategy in Dolmancé's lengthy argument about why the anus is the most "natural" orifice for sexual penetration: it is perfectly round like the penis, and thus offers a snug fit, while the vagina is oval in shape and thus affords only an approximate pleasure (144). From a biological standpoint, of course, there is nothing logical or "natural" about inserting a penis into an anus. Nonetheless, Sade's reasoning attempts to demonstrate that nature is the source of these drives, and not the fantasy provoked by the surging forth of the Other. He wants to reintegrate perversion as a manifestation of nature, and thus disavow precisely what introduces it into human life: the absent Other, and the castration it implies. In the process, he conceals the extent to which human eroticism is constituted by a loss of natural aims.

Second, Sade makes Nature the source of a "higher" law than those of the patriarchy, a "law beyond all laws" whose authority is grounded in the real and not on the signifier. Whereas the laws of society attempt to delimit the human sphere from the natural world (the prohibition of incest being paradigmatic), the laws of nature are not "laws" at all, but the complete set of all possibilities. Nature has only one law: she "tells us to enjoy ourselves" (129), to give free rein to jouissance in its many forms. To censor or fail to act on any impulse that comes to mind, even murder, is thus an act of human vanity, a second-guessing of Nature's designs: "it is our pride that attempts to erect murder as a crime" (108). If Nature gives us to think any action, it must express her will: if it can be imagined, therefore, it *must* be done. We could never outrage Nature by our acts, since even destruction and murder only "vary forms" (108), returning to Nature the raw elements that fuel her creative process.

What is most remarkable about Sade's demonstrations is that they literally eliminate death by reinscribing it into life. Instead of God the symbolic father guaranteeing eternal life in the signifier, it is Nature who promises to eliminate death by perpetually "varying forms," reabsorbing death into an infinite cycle of life—not the symbolic life of the signifier, but *real* life. Sade disavows castration and death in a single move. He upholds the organism against the body, occluding the castrated body of eroticism with a new-and-improved organism that is eternally "alive" thanks to the regenerative forces of nature.

But in the process, Sade also retreats from the most radical implications of his insight that the father's law, or God, is of "imaginary origin," an "idea without prototype" (200). In his own discourse, "Nature" assumes the position of the imaginary Other of seduction, who is called upon to lend consistency to the *corps morcelé* and protect the subject against the knowledge of his own castration.

Ultimately, Sade is most interested in effacing the symbolic Other, the lacking Other of language, and not the imaginary Other. In his notorious critique of the French revolution in the Fifth Dialogue—"Frenchmen, yet another effort if you want to be republicans . . ."—Sade provokes his compatriots with the observation that although they've beheaded the King, they have not yet decapitated the deeper law on which his authority was based. Yet in the brilliant attack on patriarchal morality that follows, Sade never really delivers on his promise to go further. Although he unmasks the symbolic order as an unfounded fiction, he does not dispense with sovereignty or order altogether. Instead, he installs a new head in the place of the decapitated one. "Nature," made manifest in the jouissance of the organ, now occupies the thrones vacated by the King and the Pope. For the pupils Sade hopes to cure of their allegiance to God, the "head" of the body is no longer Christ, or the immortal soul modeled on his image, but the erect penis. The inexhaustible jouissance of the organ—marked in his texts by the almost infinite erections and orgasms the characters achieve—bears witness to an uncastrated Nature that takes the place formerly occupied by the law, morality, and religion. It is as though the libertine seeks to undo the castration Nature suffers at the hands of the law, restoring to Nature the penis she has lost by getting off "for" her. The disavowal of castration consists in erecting the jouissance of the organ against the signifier, covering over the inroads it has made by making the *corps morcelé* whole again.

Nature thus displaces the symbolic order. But glaring inconsistencies appear in Sade's argument, particularly in frequent appeals to the oxymoronic notion of "natural rights." His character Dolmancé maintains that all men are "equal by right" (221), and that every individual has a "proprietary right over jouissance" (223); Eugénie is told she is the "sole owner" of her body, and that she alone has the right to decide who enjoys it (84). But are there really "rights" in Nature? Why should these limits be observed by anyone but ourselves? The notion of "rights" necessarily implies an Other who would guarantee that justice, those rights. Now it is Nature who plays this role, assuming the same position as God in the religious discourse Sade so adeptly dissects. Has Sade then become the dupe of seduction in his turn?

Despite his pointed critique of the religious appeal to something "beyond" the body that would guarantee its coherence, Sade invests Nature—and indeed the organism itself—with traits that have nothing to do with organic life. The real stakes of his argument appear in the relationship between the organism and the metaphysical integrity of the "self," which are not as incompatible as they might appear. Both, it turns out, work to conceal the castration that befalls the body when it is obliged to pass through the signifier of the Other.

Throughout his treatise, Sade reasons that men are no more capable of "outraging" nature than are plants and animals, since we are the products of Nature and thus an expression of her possibilities and impulses. But at important junctures in his argument, he recoils from this logic and attempts to draw a clear distinction between animals and mankind. He maintains that while animals and plants can be disposed of as property, the category of men—or what he calls "individuals who resemble us" (221)—cannot be owned, since we are "masters of ourselves"(123–24). But if Nature is a force that indifferently "varies forms" without any regard for their particularity, then how does Sade justify the specific sovereignty of man?

He does so by appealing to a coherent body image that "contains" the self, demarcating an inviolable limit beyond which the Other has no "right" to penetrate. But where does this body image come from? When the moral discourse of religion maintained that

God would protect the body from violation, Sade demonstrated that this alleged limit was easily breached at the whim of Nature. And Sade could hardly attribute to Nature any benevolent or protective motives in turn, since her apathy regarding the fate of all living beings is her defining characteristic. Strangely enough, it is the *organism itself* that for Sade guarantees the sovereignty of the self, providing the contours or limits by which the self recognizes its own image, and constituting the body image. In this respect the exemption of "individuals who resemble us" from the generalized destruction of Nature is very telling, since it appeals to "resemblance," or the image, as something sovereign. According to the laws of narcissism, is not the "individual who resembles us" our own body image, the ideal that reflects the ego back to itself as a consistent whole?

Sade wants to preserve the self without the signifier on which it is founded. For the narcissistic ego he describes cannot be recognized—much less respected—by others without being supported by the Name-of-the-father, which articulates the ego to the social scene as a unified individual. Once he identifies the Name-of-the-father as the sole foundation for the ego's body image—and an illegitimate and groundless foundation at that—it seems that Sade now wants to designate selfhood as an organic attribute, and so protect it from its fragile grounding in the symbolic. In this way, he obscures the truth of the lettered body as a *corps morcelé,* whose consistency can only come from without in the form of an image supported by the other.

Nietzsche Psychoanalyst: From the Body of Seduction to the *Corps Morcelé*

Like Sade, Nietzsche targets the imaginary consistency God provides. Nietzsche's critique of Christianity, and of the grounding of identity in the transcendental unity of God, unmasks the imaginary schemes through which culture attempts to occlude the fundamental loss of being wrought by the signifier. But he also goes much further than Sade by questioning the imaginary foundations not only of the religious law that imposes limits on the body, but of the "natural" body itself.

Nietzsche analyzes the metaphysical tradition in much the same way that Freud analyzes the individual ego, examining how it seeks narcissistic consolidation as a defense against the truth of the living being's complete solitude and lack of recourse—or castration—in the face of the death drive. His attack on the Judeo-Christian concept of God exposes the ontotheological guarantee of personal identity and its corollary, corporal integrity. Nietzsche targets the ego's unacknowledged dependence on an Other in whose gaze the integral body image or "self" comes into being, as a defense against the reality of the *corps morcelé*.

What Nietzsche reveals is that we appeal to God to lend consistency to the *corps morcelé* by giving us an image of ourselves: the self as a transcendental category, whose coherence is modeled on the integrity of the monotheist God. But his profoundly psychoanalytic insight is that the *corps morcelé* is all that remains either of the self *or of its corporal support* after the falling away of the fantasy of seduction, through the event that he calls the "death of God."

On the way to this demonstration, Nietzsche develops a theory of the body as defined by a fundamental split, between what he calls the "Ego" or "Body" *[das Ich, der Leib]* and the "Self" *[das Selbst]*.[22]

The Ego "speaks most honestly of its being . . . it speaks of the body, and insists upon the body, even when it fables and fabricates and flutters with broken wings" (60). It shows the body to be the site of warring impulses, "a multiplicity with one sense" (61), a "contradiction and confusion" (60). In contrast, the Self is "the Ego's ruler," the agency *"behind* [our] thoughts and feelings." The Self is teleological in its aims; it "aspires to heaven," longing for a "higher" meaning. It laughs contemptuously at the Ego's leapings as a "by-way to [its] goal," saying: "I am the Ego's leading-string and I prompt its conceptions" (62).

But it would be inaccurate to say that Nietzsche simply equates the Ego with the body, and the Self with the soul or consciousness. In fact, the Self and the Ego are really two different aspects of the body that evoke vividly Lacan's distinction between the body image and the *corps morcelé*.

Zarathustra says of the Self, "he lives in your body, he is your body" (62). But although the Self unifies and lends coherence to the body, it is but an "image," an artificial construct imposed on the subject from the "outside":

What are we ourselves? Are we not also nothing but an image? A something within us, modifications of ourselves that have become conscious?

>Our Self of which we are conscious: is it not an image as well,
>something outside of us, something external, on the outside? We
>never touch anything but an image, and not ourselves, not our Self.
>
>Are we not strangers to ourselves and also as close to ourselves
>as our neighbour?[23]

The Self/image works to disavow the "contradiction and confusion" of the drives, the forces that make us "strangers to ourselves." It buries the Ego under an image and calls this image "myself." But the Ego and its drives continue to assert themselves despite the Self's efforts to silence them; it teaches us "no longer to bury the head in the sand of heavenly things" (60), but to embrace the body in its "contradiction." Zarathustra says to the Self, "You say 'I' and you are proud of this word. But greater than this—although you will not believe it—is your body and its great intelligence, which does not say 'I' but performs 'I'" (62). The Self is the "I" projected onto the social scene as a "me," a coherent *body image*. Conversely, the Ego is a site of an enunciation that contradicts the Self's proprietary claims, "performing 'I'" without ever pretending to be "me" or "myself."

This analysis gives rise to one of the dominant motifs of Nietzsche's work: the Self as "mask." Zarathustra speaks of the "men of the present," the residents of the "Land of Culture," as having masks for faces:

>Painted with fifty blotches on face and limbs: thus you sat there to
>my astonishment, you men of the present!
>
>And with fifty mirrors around you, flattering and repeating your
>opalescence!
>
>Truly, you could wear no better masks than your own faces, you
>men of the present! Who could—*recognize* you!
>
>Written over with the signs of the past and these signs over-
>daubed with new signs: thus you have hidden yourselves well from
>all interpreters of signs! . . .
>
>He who tore away from you your veils and wraps and paint and
>gestures would have just enough left over to frighten the birds.
>
>Truly, I am myself the frightened bird who once saw you naked
>and without paint; and I flew away when the skeleton made ad-
>vances to me. (142–43, emphasis in original)

The Self is an artificial mask that imposes a recognizable face on what is fundamentally incoherent, and that sustains this illusion by means of the mirror image. But behind the mask—and beyond the tain of the mirror—is a truth that inspires terror not only in the observer, but in the mask-wearers themselves, who reject it so thoroughly that they dare not become conscious of it.

Where then does this mask come from? How is it created, how maintained? Zarathustra says to man: "you have put on the mask of a god" (146). This lapidary formulation condenses an extremely subtle critique of the history of metaphysics and its covert invention of the myth of discrete personhood. As we saw in the last chapter, the Roman notion of the person—the *persona*—was derived from the idea of the mask, and specifically the wax image of the dead ancestor. Nietzsche suggests that the "dead ancestor" whose mask we wear is God himself, the implied guarantor of the Self's transcendence. In this sense he follows Descartes in his insight that God is the "thinker outside of me" who alone guarantees my existence. But he takes this premise to its logical conclusion, by testing it against the *death of God* that his Zarathustra reveals. The death of God means that there is no longer any divine guarantee for the integrity of the person: the mask of the *persona* is stripped away. "Identity" is revealed to reside solely in the signifier, and not in being. Its status is that of a pure symbolic fiction, a "grammatical joke."[24] The metaphysical argument for the existence of the *cogito* is thus nothing more than a fragile house of cards founded on a faulty postulate, without any grounding in the real.

In this respect, Nietzsche's argument is not unlike Sade's. It demonstrates the vanity of the subject's narcissistic appeal to God or his laws to define the body and protect it from harm, revealing "God" to be nothing more than a fictional construction—or what Zarathustra calls a "poet's image" (150)—and not the Other of the address.

But in almost direct opposition to Sade, Nietzsche demonstrates that it is not the laws instituted in the name of God that imposed limits on the body and deprived men of their "natural rights," but rather quite the opposite: God lends an illusory consistency to a fragmented body that, in the absence of such an illusion, cannot even invoke a "self." Importantly, Nietzsche's realization that identity is a "grammatical joke," a mask, does not lead to a quest to restore identity or "reclaim" the Self from the ravages of a castration imposed from without. Rather, he clarifies that God is not simply a product of our imagination, but a phantom constructed "out of our own ashes": that is, out of—and as a solution to—the mortifying effects of the drives on the body:

> Once Zarathustra too cast his deluded fancy beyond mankind, like all afterworldsmen. Then the world seemed to me the work of a suffering and tormented God. . . .
>
> Thus I too once cast my deluded fancy beyond mankind, like all afterworldsmen. Beyond mankind in reality?
>
> Ah, brothers, this God which I created was human work and human madness, like all gods!
>
> He was human, and only a poor piece of man and Ego: this phantom came to me from my own fire and ashes, that is the truth! It did not come to me from the "beyond"! (58–59)

The death of God means that there is a void in the place of the Other of the address. But because of this, *we* are voids too. Once the mask is peeled away, we must face the void in Being, the "ashes" to which we are reduced by the drives. Now that God is "dead" (that is, absent), there is no longer any guarantee either for my narcissistic personality *or* for the integrity of the body. The "I" is subject to the disintegration of the "Self" with the surging forth of the drives in the *corps morcelé*.

Burying God means burying the Self, because they are one and the same. Whence Nietzsche's famous claim that "we have not yet gotten rid of God because we still believe in grammar."[25] As long as there is predication, and as long as the possessive pronoun continues to assert its dominion over the body, then "God" can never be far away, since he or one of his avatars is inevitably implied as the guarantor of that property, whether acknowledged or not.

Zarathustra's exposure of his afterworld as an illusion must, therefore, lead him to a different conclusion than Sade's. Announcing one of Nietzsche's signature motifs, he declares that he must live as a "convalescent," assuming the incomplete and fragmented body underlying the Self rather than trying to restore the plenitude of "good health," the body's illusory wholeness.[26] He resolves no longer to "believe in phantoms," but to "carry his *own* ashes to the mountains":

> What happened, my brothers? I, the sufferer, overcame myself, I carried my own ashes to the mountains, I made for myself a brighter flame. And behold! the phantom *fled* from me!

> Now to me, the convalescent, it would be suffering and torment
> to believe in such phantoms: it would be suffering to me now and
> humiliation. Thus I speak to the afterworldsmen. (58–59)

"After" God, man must emerge from his own ashes—but not as
the phoenix, rising unscathed from an only apparent destruction.
Nietzsche argues that we must make a "brighter flame," the better
to set fire to the Self and its values: "A very popular error: having
the courage of one's convictions. Rather it is a matter of having the
courage to *attack* one's convictions!!!"[27]

I read Nietzsche's work as evoking the subject's passage through
the experience of castration, as the only possible access to the ethics that would allow the subject to come into being as a subject of
desire, without the support of narcissism. Nietzsche invents a new
myth to account for this experience, and to explain how this loss of
being can be affirmed in its inevitability. In the process, he outlines
another destiny for myth: not giving consistency to the Other, but
providing an aesthetic space for the confrontation of the absence of
the Other and the jouissance it introduces into human life.

Importantly, Nietzsche does not seek to eradicate the *field of
the Other* in unmasking the monotheist "phantom." The fact that
there is no Other to whom the subject can appeal for help or redemption does not change the fact that he is faced with an Other
of whom he has no idea, an Other to whom the drives respond.
Nietzsche is profoundly aware that the human being cannot simply
get rid of the Other, and thereby recover the full possibilities of the
organic body by reinstating a fully jouissant being.

Georges Bataille once remarked that Jean-Paul Sartre wanted "a
world completed, but without God."[28] But although popular mis-
conceptions of his "death of God" would suggest otherwise, such
a criticism could not be applied to Nietzsche. His philosophy does
not seek a "completed world," in the form either of a secular humanism or of a contestation of the Other's sovereignty over us. The
"death of God" does not portend the death of the *Other* outside of
us—the end of the Other's heteronomous dominion over the Self—
but rather the dismantling of the image that gives it coherence. This
is why Nietzsche sees as its logical consequence a resurgent "polytheism," in which the manifestation of the Other is no longer limited to a single, unifying image. In *Zarathustra,* Nietzsche writes:
"Is not precisely this godliness, that there are gods but no God?"

(201). After the death of God, "godliness" names the reign of the real, its resurgence from beneath the imaginary face that gave it a false consistency.

This project explains Nietzsche's lifelong fascination with the Greek god Dionysus: the figure for the ancients of the jouissance of the Other. As the god of dismemberment—his own as well as his celebrants'—Dionysus is associated with the expropriation and dissolution of identity. His advent portends the disintegration of the Self's coherence, and its supplanting by a "contradiction and confusion," the multiplicity of the drives.[29] More than any other divinity, Dionysus lends credence to Lacan's comment that "the gods belong to the field of the real."[30] It is significant, therefore, that Nietzsche does not dismiss divinity—or the "real" the gods embody—in exposing the *monotheist* God as illusory. He envisions another possibility for the gods: to animate the field of the real, and thereby undercut the imaginary consistency that the monotheist God upholds in the Christian West.

"Have I been understood?—*Dionysus vs. the Crucified*."[31] Thus concludes the final aphorism of *Ecce Homo*. As a figure of divine dismemberment, Dionysus "is opposed to the Pauline invention of the Saviour on the cross, and thus to the obsession with a redeeming death, a redeeming of self."[32] Christ and Dionysus represent two different relations to death, but also to the body: one in which the body image is resurrected whole, secured and guaranteed by the Other of the address, and one in which the body is realized as a *corps morcelé,* as the "forgetting" of the narcissistic ideology of the self. But Dionysus is also the *god of the mask,* associated with the simulation of the theatrical persona. If the unified Self is wearing the "mask" of the monotheist God, whose oneness bestows discrete and integral personhood on the man "made in his image," then Dionysus insists on the detachable quality of this mask, its merely contingent relation to being. He underscores the truth that the faces or guises of the Other are merely "masking over" a senseless incoherence. When God "dies"—when the mask falls away— the body is subject to disintegration at the hands of Dionysus, god of dismemberment and dis-individuation.

In Nietzsche's Dionysus, the question of the Other is almost mathematically reduced to the essential: namely, the awareness that the jouissance of the Other carves out a fragmented body, "dissolving" me and making me live from this place of dissolution.

The declaration "God is dead" is not a call to atheism, therefore, but the recognition of a *polytheism of the real* that abolishes the monotheist imaginary, the inviolable Self.

The death of God means the death of the body. But which body? Clearly, the body image "dies" with the falling away of the fantasy of seduction that supports it. But what is less obvious, and absolutely essential to Nietzsche's argument, is that the *organism itself* cannot survive the death of God. Whereas Sade wants to restore the smooth functioning of an organism "healed" of its castration, Nietzsche is deeply suspicious of the pseudo-biologism implied in such a solution. His attack on "God" doesn't stop at the fantasies it spawns, but develops an implicit critique of any "scientific" or rational conception of consciousness that takes refuge in the organism.

The Bio-logic of Consciousness

Beyond deconstructing the metaphysical notion of transcendental identity, Nietzsche is really zeroing in on the organic individual it both supports and is supported by. The astonishing conclusion of his critique of consciousness is that *the self propagates itself by means of the organism.* In this argument I am guided by Pierre Klossowski, whose *Nietzsche and the Vicious Circle* is to my knowledge the only work to have seized upon this extraordinary dimension of Nietzsche's thought.

In *The Gay Science,* Nietzsche notes that the reasoning consciousness allies itself with the instinct of self-preservation, and thus with the preservation of the organic individual. Speaking of the "teachers of the purpose of existence," whose sole task is "to do what is good for the preservation of the human race," he writes:

> It is obvious that these tragedians promote the interests of the *species,* even if they believe that they promote the interest of God or work as God's emissaries. They promote the life of the species *by promoting faith in life*. "Life is worth living," every one of them shouts; "there is something to life, there is something behind life, beneath it: beware!"
>
> From time to time this instinct, which is at work in the highest and the basest men alike—the instinct for the preservation of the species—erupts as reason and as passion of the spirit. Then it is surrounded by a resplendent retinue of reasons and tries with all

the force at its command to make us forget that at bottom it is instinct, drive, folly, lack of reasons. Life *shall* be loved, *because*—!
Man *shall* advance himself and his neighbor, *because*—! . . .³³

Nietzsche reveals an unsuspected link between God and the con-
servation of the species: both have a teleological structure, both
are about "life after death." As Klossowski puts it, the convergence
of consciousness and the instinct of preservation gives rise to the
"fallacious notion of a stable, eternal consciousness, immutable
and consequently free and responsible."³⁴

But even more strikingly, Nietzsche implies that the teleological impulse is nothing other than a craving for *natural aims:* that
is, for an aim that would neutralize the drives that call human
life into question—causing it to "open onto an abyss"³⁵—and re-
ground them as instincts. In this respect, "consciousness" is to be
situated at the level of the pleasure principle, which attempts to
recover the homeostasis that was lost to the death drive along with
the organism's instincts and natural aims.

Nietzsche shows us that the transcendental self and the organism are one and the same, and that both work to occlude the body
in the properly Freudian sense: the *corps morcelé* carved out of
the organism by the death drive. The organism not only suppresses
evidence of the body, but controls consciousness by censoring any
thoughts that would challenge its coherence. Klossowski expresses
Nietzsche's findings in the following terms:

> *I* am sick in a body that does not belong to me. *My* suffering is
> only an interpretation of the struggle between certain functions or
> impulses that have been subjugated by the organism, and are now
> rivals: those which depend on me and those which escape my con-
> trol. Conversely, the physical agent of my self *[le suppôt physique
> de moi-même]* seems to reject any thoughts I have that no longer
> ensure its own cohesion, thoughts that proceed from a state that is
> *foreign* or *contrary* to that required by the physical agent, which is
> nonetheless identical to myself.³⁶

The organism is the henchman *[suppôt]* of the self, upholding
its dominion over the body by ruthlessly censoring any drive or
thought that points to the "Other scene" of the body.

Paradoxically, the greatest threat to conscious identity is thus
"physical dissolution," the erosion of the corporal support of the
self. In Klossowski's words,

the ages of the body are simply the *impulsive movements* that form and deform it, and finally tend to abandon it. But just as these impulses are resources for the body, they are also threats to its cohesion. The purely functional cohesion of the body, in the service of the self's identity, is in this sense irreversible. The *ages* of the self are those of the body's cohesion, which means that the more this self begins to age in and with the body, and the more it aspires to cohesion, the more it also seeks to return to its starting point—and thus to *recapitulate* itself. The dread of physical dissolution requires a retrospective vision of its own cohesion. Thus, because the *self,* as a product of the body, attributes this body to itself as its *own,* and is *unable* to create another, the self too has its own *irreversible* history.[37]

This reasoning suggests that the "mask of a god" that humans wear is not just the body image or "self," but the organism that functions as the "physical support" of this self. Nietzsche reveals that "identity" cannot survive without a body to support it. Perhaps this argument also explains the paradoxical corporeality of Christianity: God resurrects the body, because without it there's no "soul." But when God dies—when the fantasy of seduction falls away—the self loses its corporal support; the teleological organism loses its goal, succumbing to the "multiplicity and confusion" of the fragmented being. The jouissance that accompanies the advent of the Other erodes not only the "identity" fictitiously instituted by the signifier, but the physical integrity of the organism.

The Ethics of the *Corps Morcelé*

Klossowski suggests that Nietzsche is "no longer concerned with the body as a *property of the self,* but with the body as the locus of impulses, the locus of their confrontation." To find it, he "followed what he called, in several places, *the guiding thread of the body.* By examining the alterations in his own valetudinary states, he sought to follow this Ariadne's thread through the labyrinth of the impulses."[38]

What would it mean to take Ariadne as a guide? To head into the heart of the labyrinth and kill the monster? Yes, but with an important revision. Here it is not the conquering hero, the Self, who confidently marches forth to slay the irrational beast, but the reverse. When the thread of the dismembered erotic body is laid out, it spells the demise of the monstrous amalgam of God and ego, the end of the Self. In *Beyond Good and Evil,* Nietzsche suggests that "after" God, "man must assume an authentically 'feminine' attitude in welcoming Dionysus."[39] He models it on Ariadne, as the one who welcomes the transfiguring—or even *disfiguring*—advent of the god.[40]

In Klossowski's trilogy, we saw how the marginal position accorded to femininity by traditional understandings of the subject appears as a single force within the hospitality relation and suggests how the identity of the post-Nietzschean host might be understood as other than a principle of self-adequation. Although Roberte is an "atheist," she shares with the incredulous Sarah an apperception of an Other in and beyond language that motivates the subject's division. Her "atheism" paradoxically allows her to welcome the Other in its fragmenting alterity, by rejecting the imaginary coherence that the monotheist God would seek to impose not only on the field of the Other as such, but also on her. Precisely because she is not "made in the image of God," that is, the hostess is able to receive the guest in its multiplicity, to "let the stranger in."

But Nietzsche's Ariadne anticipates the historical legacy of the hysteric, who invents psychoanalysis by guiding Freud to the errant jouissance inscribed in the somatic body. Her example suggests that to "follow the thread of the body" is to follow the traces left on the organism by the advent of Dionysus, or the jouissance of the Other. Ariadne's love for Dionysus recalls the "love for savoir" that guides the transference, the love for the signifiers of the Other that makes it possible for the subject to embrace the erosion of the narcissistic ego to which they lead.

The next chapter will further explore these questions through an analysis of Jacques Lacan's writings on femininity. Lacan follows Freud in noting that the illusion of the "unified body image" is less stable in women than in men. But he sees this instability as an advantage rather than a handicap, in that it allows her to access more readily than man a "jouissance beyond the phallus," a jouissance that is experienced not merely as a menace to the subject, but as the source of a pleasure linked to the experience of the lack or inconsistency of the Other. In Lacan's work, the ethical import of femininity inheres in the specific *savoir*—or knowledge—it accesses: a knowledge about the unfoundedness of the signifier and the unified body image it sustains. He calls it a "gay *sçavoir*," highlighting the importance of the *ça*—the "Thing" or *es* of Freud's theory of the unconscious—in its elaboration. But not incidentally, its name is also a reference to Nietzsche's *Gay Science,* the text in which he announces the death of God, and that Klossowski translated into French as *Le gai savoir.* For both Nietzsche and Lacan— albeit in different ways—the gay savoir is the knowledge that results from a relation to the signifier—and to identity—that is no longer sustained by a transcendental guarantee. But for Lacan, as for Klossowski, it is also intimately related to the specific jouissance experienced by a woman, as the one whose relation to the signifier is "not-all" inscribed within the phallic function.

6. The Other Jouissance, a Gay *Sçavoir*: Feminine Hospitality and the Ethics of Psychoanalysis

Jacques Lacan describes the unconscious as the home in which the subject lives, a home that is not so much the possession of an owner as the dispossession of any possibility of ownership. The remark appears within his discussion of Freud's enigmatic statement concerning the ethics of the unconscious, *Wo es war, soll Ich werden:*

> I won't say that it was Freud who introduced the subject into the world—the subject as distinct from the psychic function, which is a myth, a confused nebulous—because it was Descartes who did that. But I will say that Freud addresses himself to the subject to say this, which is new: Here, in the domain of the dream, you are at home *[chez toi]*. *Wo es war, soll Ich werden.*[1]

In defining the subject's relation to the unconscious as one of co-habitation under the same roof, Lacan reverses the well-known phenomenological interpretation of the *chez soi,* as the "at-homeness" of identity, the principle of autonomy.[2] Freud's formula, translated in the Standard Edition as "there where id was, there ego shall be," had traditionally been interpreted by the proponents of ego psychology to mean that the ego must come to dominate or subsume the id, to bring it within its parameters. But Lacan understands Freud's remark very differently. Instead of implying the colonization of the id by the ego, it points to the necessary *expropriation* of the ego *by the id:* there where "it" was—the id, the Thing—the subject shall come into being *as a subject of the unconscious,* and not as a self-possessed ego.[3]

If the subject is at home in the dream, it is first of all because it cannot be at home in the ego and the homeostatic ideal it upholds. But Lacan makes clear that the unconscious is not simply an uncanny guest in the domain of the ego, an unwelcome force of exile and estrangement. This is because the dispossession it effects does not only dislodge the ego, but creates a dwelling space for the subject: a space defined not by the proprietary dominion of the *chez soi,* but by a singular hospitality. If the subject is "at home" in the dream, it is because it is only from the vantage point of this "home" that the subject can play host to something else, something the ego cannot entertain.

This is because, says Lacan, the interrogation of its desire causes the subject to run up against something "that it feels within like a stranger,"[4] something foreign or strange that challenges the consistency of the ego, and whose insistence is behind the analysand's demand for analysis. In "The Mirror Stage," Lacan identifies one avatar of this "stranger" in the *corps morcelé,* the fragmented body of the drives that is the legacy of the subject's encounter with the Other.[5] We are "hosts" to the erotic body, which dwells within "us" (the organism, the self) like a virus, overwriting the natural logic of the living being and undermining the integrity of the Self. The question is, how will the subject respond to this dispossession? Will it play host to the body, or will it choose instead to identify with something outside of or beyond its experience, the heterogeneous image of consistency that it wears like a mask in order to repress the body? Like Nietzsche, Freud locates the ethics of the unconscious in the particular mode in which the subject receives this stranger. His *Wo es war* implies the transition from a mode of hospitality dominated by the master/host, who shores up the *chez soi* by identifying with the imaginary principle of identity the ego embodies, to an ethics of hospitality dominated by the stranger, who forces the *chez soi* to open on to the Other.

As its etymological connotation of "dwelling" suggests, ethics traditionally seeks to describe man there where he is at home, in his place, possessed of an essential autonomy. This ethics of "dwelling at home" is the ideal expressed by what Freud calls the pleasure principle, the homeostatic mechanism that seeks to maintain organic and affective equilibrium by binding or draining off the unbound energy of the drives.[6] Lacan evokes it in a commentary of Aristotle, whose ethics aims at a lowering of tension, an affective equilibrium or stasis: "what else is the famous lowering of tension with which Freud links pleasure, other than the ethics of Aristotle?"[7] Lacan suggests that Aristotle, like Freud, places a certain "pleasure principle" at the heart of his formulation of ethics. But he nonetheless differentiates between the two by noting that in Aristotle, "what cannot fail to strike us right away is that his pleasure principle is an inertia principle,"[8] one that posits pleasure as something fixed and unmoving: "Aristotle's thought on the subject of pleasure embodies the idea that pleasure has something irrefutable about it, and that it is situated at the guiding pole of human fulfillment."[9] In other words, Aristotle suggests that pleasure—and more specifically the equilibrium it sustains—is the rightful home of man, there where he is in his place.

Conversely, what Freud makes central to his ethics is not the pleasure principle as regulatory mechanism, but its "beyond." With his famous declaration that "the aim of all life is death,"[10] Freud suggests that the death drive, and not pleasure, is the guiding pole of human life, its ultimate "fulfillment." His theorization of the death drive challenges the Aristotelian ideal of affective equilibrium or "inertia" with evidence of a destabilizing force internal to human life, that Freud first identifies in a compulsion to repeat whose energy underscores the pleasure principle.[11] This repetition interferes with the logic of the organic instincts, which Freud characterizes as the fundamentally conservative expressions of an "inertia inherent in organic life" whose aim is "to restore an earlier state of things."[12] The introduction of this extra-organic drive energy means that this inertia is forever lost to the human subject, whose neurophysiological functioning is irrevocably compromised by the unbound energy the death drive introduces into the living being. The corollary is that for Freud, pleasure is neither instinctual nor native to man but the expression of a fundamentally nostalgic quest for a lost state of equilibrium, which becomes the goal or "guiding pole" of human life (and ethics) precisely because it is no longer available to the human being. He views the pleasure principle as an attempt to mediate between an always already-lost instinctual homeostasis and the unbound energy of the death drive, by attempting to bind some of the drive energy to a "partial object" modeled on an instinctual aim.[13]

Lacan takes this thesis further, characterizing the pleasure principle as a corrective or compensatory mechanism that is directly overdetermined by the death drive.[14] In translating Freud's *Totestrieb* with the concept of jouissance, Lacan underscores the continuum between pleasure and the death drive. If pleasure is an attempt to bind the excess energy of the drive to a provisional aim, jouissance is what insists in and beyond pleasure, an excess that fails to be anchored. The corollary is that the pleasure principle inevitably fails in its quest to hold the death drive at bay. This is because its route to its goal can only follow the paths etched by the drive, and thus aggravate the very wounding of the subject's being that it attempts to compensate for or assuage.[15]

In recentering the ethics of psychoanalysis on the subject's response to the jouissance at work in the body, Lacan highlights the "real" dimension of ethics as dwelling, as opposed to its imaginary dimension as "at home-ness" or autonomy. He defines the *real* of jouissance—and not the ego or the pleasure principle that maintains its equilibrium—as "that which is always in the same place":[16] it remains, insists, and repeats, dwelling uncannily within the subject in a way that forever disrupts the equilibrium that Aristotle's ethics, as a "lowering of tension," would take as its ultimate aim. But precisely because the real is always in the same place, it sets the subject adrift.

The Hysteric, Hostess to the Drives

If the hysteric occupies a privileged place in the discourse of analysis, it is in part because the vagaries of the "wandering womb" attest so powerfully to this drift. Freud first encounters the dispossession that characterizes the subject of the unconscious in the hysterical symptom, whose recurrence bears witness to another, less-familiar aspect of *ethos*—its derivation from the Greek verb meaning "to repeat."[17] Her experience suggests that ethics concerns not the possibility of dwelling at home in equilibrium or inertia, but the subject's position with regard to what returns, what cannot be bound. For both Freud and Lacan, therefore, woman is not only the inventor and privileged subject of psychoanalysis, but the model for the ethics of psychoanalysis and the stakes of its specific savoir.

In this respect, both thinkers are very close to Nietzsche, for whom the experience of femininity not only bears witness to the decentering of the ego by the drives, but also points forward, to something new. While Nietzsche appeals to Ariadne for help in following the "thread of the body" through the labyrinth of the impulses, Freud uses hysterical discourse to guide him to the unconscious and its particular savoir. And just as Nietzsche sees in Ariadne's love for Dionysus an affirmation of the fragmented body of the drives, a body whose inadequation to the ideal of unified selfhood allows it to "welcome the future" in its immanence,[18] Lacan sees in the uniquely feminine mode of encountering jouissance the possibility of an ethics of subjectivity—and a new social link—beyond the pleasure principle and the ego it sustains.

What her experience tells us, says Lacan, is that

> affect befalls a body whose essence it is said is to dwell in language—
> I am borrowing plumage which sells better than my own—affect,
> I repeat, befalls it on account of its not finding dwelling-room, at
> least not to its taste. This we call moroseness, or equally, moodi-
> ness. Is this a sin, a grain of madness, or a true touch of the real?[19]

Lacan stresses again and again—here by allusion to Heidegger[20]—that the human subject dwells in language. But from a psychoanalytic perspective, the implications of this statement are twofold. On the one hand, the body dwells in language because it can no longer dwell in the organism, since language has evicted it from its natural abode. But on the other, language is itself unable to house the subject adequately or fully. It dwells in language in such a way that not all of it finds dwelling room, not all of it manages to be spoken. In his return to Freud, Lacan emphasizes that the subject's exile from being manifests itself as a failure to say, an inability to put into words what is happening in the subject's body. The corollary is that the excess of jouissance manifests itself as something that exceeds speech, that cannot be spoken. And so in its search for dwelling room it takes up residence in the body, for example in the somatic symptom through which this wandering affect expresses what does not manage to be wholly spoken.

What then is the role of the analyst with respect to this dispossession, the suffering of the symptom that sets the subject adrift? In the *Ethics* seminar, Lacan notes that one guise under which the analyst appears to the analysand is as "something that welcomes the supplicant, something that gives it a place of refuge."[21] The analyst entertains the hysteric's discourse, giving it a place to dwell. But how? One possible interpretation of Lacan's statement is that analysis allows the patient to say what has been left unsaid, to anchor this drift with words. Certainly the very notion of the "talking cure" suggests that speech can relieve suffering, a possibility whose full potential becomes clear when Freud discovers in the logic of the dream work under transference a means of treating the real with the signifier, and thereby dissipating some of the errant drive energy at work in the patient's body. In "welcoming" the hysteric, then, is the analyst helping her to find in speech the dwelling-room that eludes her in her suffering?

This formulation tells only part of the story. Although the analyst "welcomes" the subject, it is not in order to resecure its home—to restore the homeostasis that would allow the ego to dwell in comfort—but to welcome something within the subject that calls this home into question. Lacan suggests that the function of the analyst's discourse is not to welcome the ego (or its narrative or complaint), but to "give ex-sistence to the unconscious,"[22] whose signifiers surface in the slips or breaks within the ego's discourse. The analyst uses the savoir of the unconscious—the signifiers furnished by the dream—to question the ego's discourse and challenge its version of events. To "give ex-sistence" to the unconscious is thus to give dwelling room to the *subject* at the expense of the ego, since the constitution of the signifying chain allows the subject of the unconscious to emerge by contesting and dislodging the ego narrative that sought to repress it. To the extent that the "talking cure" allows for a partial binding or delimitation of the real from which the patient suffers, this binding takes place at the level of the unconscious, and not at the level of the patient's own speech. Moreover, although the signifiers of the dream "treat" the real, they do not allow it to be mastered or neutralized. In fact, they ultimately work to unleash the real held in abeyance by repression, by soliciting or provoking a crisis or symptom that brings to the fore an irresolvable psychic conflict.[23] The constitution of the signifying chain leads up to a hole, a real for which there is no signifier.[24]

Jacques Derrida aptly describes Freud's technique as "hospitable to the death instinct."[25] This is because the analyst is interested not in welcoming the supplicant, but in welcoming or soliciting whatever is making her suffer. His desire to know concerns that *es* that eludes speech, a real that insists in and beyond the signifier. Lacan takes Freud's fundamental insight further, by making the clinic of the death drive—and the errant jouissance that results from it—the center of his clinic, and not speech in its binding function. While Lacan follows Freud in his hypothesis that the real must be treated through the signifier, he also posits that this treatment is limited to the first phase of the analysis and cannot lead to its logical conclusion. In this respect Lacan is not so much departing from Freud as developing something implicit in his technique that is often overlooked by subsequent practitioners: his emphasis on the clinic of the symptom as a distinct phase of the analysis that cannot be assimilated to the construction of the unconscious as signifying chain. The clinic of the symptom involves a direct interrogation of the jouissance inscribed in the letters of the body, which intervenes there where the signifier fails.[26]

But Lacan's remark that the real "does not find dwelling-room" in language has implications that extend beyond the technical question of the signifier's efficacy in the logic of the transference. The fact the real cannot be spoken or contained in language points to an inescapable fact of human life: the experience of the inadequacy of language, its failure to fully name—and therefore limit—jouissance. In underscoring that language cannot give dwelling-room to the real, Lacan takes Freud's clinic farther by suggesting that the analyst's role is not to push for the articulation—and thus dissipation—of the real from which the subject is suffering, but to sustain the "not-all," supporting the truth that not all of the real can be wholly spoken. This emphasis appears most clearly in Lacan's treatment of femininity.

In Lacan's work, the ethical import of femininity is tied to the specific *savoir*—or knowledge—it accesses: a knowledge about a structural defect in the signifier, its failure to fully limit jouissance. He calls it a "gay *sçavoir*," a gay science.[27] By rewriting *savoir*—inserting the *ça*—Lacan insists on its elaboration in the unconscious: *ça* is the French translation of Freud's *es*, or "id"—that part of the real that eludes the signifier. The gay *sçavoir* is an ethics in which the "it" uncannily internal to the subject dispossesses the ego of the illusion of its self-adequation, allowing the savoir of the subject of the unconscious to emerge. But not incidentally, its name also alludes to Nietzsche's *Gay Science,* the text in which he announces the death of God and that Pierre Klossowski translated into French as *Le gai savoir.* For both Nietzsche and Lacan—albeit in different ways—the gay savoir is the knowledge that results from a relation to the signifier—and to identity—that is no longer sustained by a transcendental guarantee: the savoir of the "not-all." But for Lacan, as for Klossowski, it is also intimately related to the specific jouissance experienced by woman, whose relation to the signifier that would support the "mask" of unified personhood is particularly unanchored.[28] Lacan calls it the "Other jouissance," and links it both to the savoir of the unconscious and to the pleasure of the analyst.

If it is a *gay* savoir, and not a morose one, it is because the subject, in experiencing the limits of the phallic signifier, also experiences something beyond it: beyond the pleasure principle, certainly, but also beyond the phallic function and the particular version of pleasure it sustains. If it is gendered feminine, it is because feminine jouissance arises from a *savoir* inaccessible to the subject placed within the phallic function—a *savoir* of the "it":

> the question is to know, in whatever it is that constitutes feminine jouissance inasmuch as it is not all concerned with the man—and I would even say that feminine jouissance as such is not concerned with him at all—the question is to know what her knowledge is all about *[la question est de savoir ce qu'il en est de son savoir].*
>
> If the unconscious has taught us anything, it is firstly this, that *somewhere, in the Other, it knows [ça sait].*[29]

In positing this "somewhere," Lacan suggests how femininity might model another way of dwelling, another approach to ethics.

A Feminine Encore

In the opening lecture of his 1972–73 seminar on femininity, *Encore,* Lacan describes the seminar as a "supplement" or "leftover" of the earlier seminar on *The Ethics of Psychoanalysis,* something whose avoidance stalled its publication:

> It happened that I did not publish *The Ethics of Psychoanalysis.* . . . Over time, I learned that I could say a little bit more about the subject. And then too, I realized that what was guiding my steps was something of the order of an avoidance, a not wanting to know

anything about it *[un je n'en veux rien savoir]*. No doubt this is what explains the fact that after all this time, I am still here: *encore*.[30]

In its relation to ethics, femininity finds itself on the side of this "encore," this "something more" that remains, endures, and insists in and beyond what has been said of the ethics of psychoanalysis.

In the introduction to the *Ethics* seminar, Lacan admits that analysis has by and large failed women where the question of their desire is concerned, a failure already implicit in Freud's famous query, *Was will das Weib?* Far from improving on Freud's impasse, Lacan suggests, the development of psychoanalysis has even aggravated it: "analytical experience has if anything stifled, silenced, and evaded those areas of the problem of sexuality which relate to the point of view of feminine demand."[31] Psychoanalysis has contented itself with bemoaning "woman's" failure to articulate her desire, rather than drawing upon her experience to consider whether the notion of desire might itself be insufficient where the ethics of femininity is concerned, inadequate to account for the "strangeness" she encounters within and the particular exile it imposes upon her. But despite these forceful remarks, the *Ethics* never really takes up the question of femininity as a subject position. Although the seminar devotes considerable attention to the traditional identification of the feminine with *das Ding*—the interdicted object or Thing as embodiment of a deadly jouissance—it does not address the particularity of woman's own experience as a subject confronted with the excess of jouissance.

However, the opening lines of *Encore* suggest the specificity of the feminine position has come to assume an increasing importance for Lacan in his return to this "something more" of ethics. In *Television,* an interview broadcast while the *Encore* seminar was taking place, Lacan reconsiders the question of ethics through a direct interrogation of the Other of the sexual relation, woman, and the particular negation under which she falls:

> We'll go on, then, starting off from the Other, the radical Other, evoked by the nonrelation embodied by sex—for anyone who can perceive that One occurs, perhaps, only through the experience of the (a)sexed.
>
> For us the Other is as entitled as the One to generate a subject out of an axiom. Hence, here is what the experiment suggests: first,

that women cannot escape the kind of negation that Aristotle discards for the reason that it would apply to the universal; namely, they are the not-all,   . As if by protecting the universal from its negation, Aristotle didn't simply render it futile: the *dictus de omni et nullo* guarantees no ex-sistence, as he himself demonstrates, when attributing this ex-sistence to the particular, but without—in the strong sense of the term—accounting for it, that is to say, giving a full account: the unconscious.[32]

In suggesting that "the Other is as entitled as the One to generate a subject out of an axiom," Lacan posits another basis for subjectivity than identification with the whole, the One: the unified body image, the ego, and the "artificial" groups it founds.[33] In her negation, woman represents the possibility of an ethics that would be based on something other than the universal, that would acknowledge that a full account of the subject's truth can be sought only in the unconscious.

In a lecture from *Encore* entitled "God and the Jouissance of The Woman," Lacan specifies that

> When any speaking being whatever lines up under the banner of women, it is by being constituted as *not all* that they are placed within the phallic function. It is this that defines the . . . the what? The woman precisely, except that The woman can only be written with The crossed through. There is no such thing as The woman, where the definite article designates the universal. There is no such thing as The woman since . . . of her essence she is *not all*.[34]

But if woman[35] is "not all," it is also because she embodies a "something more," a jouissance beyond the phallus that arises precisely from this negation: "if she is excluded by the nature of things, it is precisely because in being *not all,* she has, in relation to what the phallic function designates of jouissance, a supplementary jouissance."[36]

As an unanchored, errant jouissance, feminine jouissance presents itself in two distinct but interrelated ways, each of which finds expression in the multiple resonances of the word *encore:* yet, still, more, again. It is an *encore* in the sense of a return, repetition or repeat performance, what returns precisely because it fails to be anchored. It may be traumatic or even incapacitating, repetitively staging itself within the subject's body through the somatic symptom, a straying jouissance she cannot defend against or account for. But for Lacan, a woman's inability to speak of it is due not to her own limitations, but to the limits of the phallic signifier. In testifying to what remains—unnegated and uncancelled—after the law or prohibition makes its cut, her jouissance gives rise to a savoir about a defect in the signifier, its failure to limit jouissance. It is this savoir that Lacan professes to have been avoiding in the *je n'en veux rien savoir,* the "not wanting to know anything about it" that was guiding his steps in his formulation of the ethics of psychoanalysis. His avoidance indexes the fact that there is still more to be said concerning the remainder, the leftover, what the signifier fails to anchor: not only the excess jouissance from which she suffers, but a *supplemental* jouissance inaccessible to the subject lined up under the banner of the phallic function.

Lacan elaborates the thesis that woman is "not all under the phallic function" in several distinct ways, each of which draws upon a different understanding of her "jouissance beyond the phallus." First, he suggests that woman is confronted with a jouissance that cannot be localized in a genital organ or limited through sexuality. Lacan understands orgasm, or what he calls "phallic jouissance," as an attempt to limit the drive by localizing jouissance in the genital zone, provisionally anchoring it to a sexual aim. In arguing that this limit is less effective for women than for men, Lacan both draws upon Freud's theses concerning early female sexuality and contests their underlying assumptions. Freud notes that "women tolerate masturbation worse than men, they more frequently fight against it, and . . . are unable to make use of it in circumstances in which a man would seize upon it as a way of escape without any hesitation."[37] He hypothesizes that during the Oedipal phase, in which the father is supposed to take the mother's place as the little girl's love-object, the change in erogenous zone from the clitoris to the vagina causes her to abandon the masturbatory activity that enabled her to center the drives around an organ. He further proposes that the little girl's lack of a penis is experienced as a wound to her narcissism, impeding the formation of a unified body image.[38] The result is that she is less able to repress the fragmented body of the drives, or *corps morcelé,* by "escaping" into the imaginary unity of the body image or its "natural" counterpart, the sexual organism.

But while Lacan follows Freud in observing the different relationship between anatomy and body image in girls and boys, he distances himself from Freud's thesis that femininity is structured by the quest to recover or find a substitute for the missing phallus. Working from the assumption that all women suffer from penis envy, Freud identifies three possible outcomes of the Oedipal phase for a girl, none of which is particularly encouraging: the abandonment of sexuality through dissatisfaction with the inferiority of her organ (which leads to hysteria); identification with the phallic ideal and refusal to abandon masculinity (which leads to a virility complex); or a resigned acceptance of the limitations of her situation and redemption through the socially validated project of maternity (the circuitous path to "normal" femininity).[39] Freud understands maternity as the resolution of the little girl's quest to find an alternative for the missing penis, in the form of an object that would anchor the drive.[40] Maternity is thus a fundamentally phallic project, albeit a "successful" one. In interpreting the girl's eventual motherhood as the culmination of a quest for an object that would satisfy desire, Freud does not identify an alternative to the phallic function that structures masculine sexuality, but rather inscribes the girl within it by mapping the form of her quest onto that of the little boy. In asking *what* the girl wants, Freud gets entangled in the fundamentally phallic problematic of the object, rather than considering how the lack of any object to anchor the drive might be understood not as a mark of incompleteness or as the basis for a lifelong inferiority complex, but as a challenge to the object economy on which the Oedipal solution is based.

In contrast, Lacan's declaration that woman is "not-all under the phallic function" challenges the universality of the Oedipal complex by suggesting that the feminine subject is confronted not with the lack in drive—the prohibition or impossibility of the object that would satisfy desire—but with an excess that is not anchored by any object. His second thesis is that woman is not wholly inscribed within the phallic logic of the signifier and the complex relation to the object it both proffers and maintains at a safe distance. For the man who stands "under the banner of the phallic function," says Lacan, the absence of the sexual relation is experienced when he approaches a woman, since "what he approaches is the cause of his desire that I have designated as object a."[41] Conversely, he notes

that "on the side of ~~The~~ woman, something other than the object a
is at stake in what comes to make up for [suppléer] the sexual relation that does not exist."42

If femininity constitutes a challenge to the ethics of psychoanalysis, it is because in being "beyond the phallus," her jouissance
is therefore also beyond the scope of the ethics of psychoanalysis
as delineated by Lacan in *The Ethics of Psychoanalysis*: the duty
not to give up on one's desire, *ne pas céder sur son désir*. If the
phallus is the signifier of desire or lack, the corollary is that any
woman who is "not all" under the phallic function is necessarily
confronted with an excess against which the phallus offers no support. Juliet Flower MacCannell argues that the ethics of femininity
must be understood as an attempt to manage this excess without
recourse to the defense against errant jouissance that the phallus
provides: "Wounded by femininity, she bears the brunt not . . . of
embodying the lack in Drive, but its excess."43

As such, it also calls into question one of the key developments
of the *Ethics* seminar, concerning the signifier's role in limiting jouissance by maintaining a barrier between the subject and *das Ding*,
the Thing that represents the ultimate fulfillment of the (death)
drive and thus the annihilation of the subject's desire. Declaring
that "distance between the subject and *das Ding* is the condition
of speech,"44 Lacan underscores the role of the signifier not only
in the logic of the transference (Freud's technique of "treating the
real with the signifier"), but in such fundamental articulations of
the symbolic as the incest prohibition and the commandments of
the Hebrew Decalogue. Noting that the commandments are "nothing other than the very laws of speech," Lacan suggests that the
essence of speech is prohibition, the "no!" that paradoxically sustains desire by prohibiting its fulfillment. But more fundamentally,
the characterization of the signifier as what erects a barrier against
das Ding derives from the logic of the Oedipus complex, where
the paternal signifier holds the maternal Thing at bay through the
incest prohibition that debars her as a possible object of the child's
desire. While the prohibition consigns the mother to the status of a
"lost" or impossible object, it also proposes metaphorical objects
of desire that promise to "restore" the lost object, thereby giving
rise to the phallic economy of the object a. In this respect, the function of the signifier is closely linked to the pleasure principle: both
maintain distance from *das Ding* while promising "little" jouis-

sances that would compensate for it. As Lacan puts it, "the pleasure principle governs the search for the object and imposes the detours which maintain the distance in relation to its end."[45] What we call "pleasure" is merely a detour away from the ultimate "fulfillment," the Thing that cannot be born and that, when the subject gets too close, is experienced as the most unbearable pain.

In this logic, woman appears either as a possible embodiment of *das Ding* for a man (and therefore as what is held at bay by the signifier) or as a "pleasurable" substitute object, and not as a subject confronting the excess of jouissance without the full support of the signifier.[46] If woman is "not all under the phallic function," it is because her experience causes her to mistrust the signifier and to suspect its complicity in the phallic function that makes woman into man's symptom—an object alternately sought after and feared as an avatar of castration—while at the same time providing no support for her in her own quest to manage jouissance. When he indicts the "not wanting to know anything about it" that limited the scope of the *Ethics* seminar, Lacan suggests that he—and psychoanalysis more generally—never really stepped outside the problematic of the object to think about the ethical stakes of femininity: not as reliant upon the phallic function that would both procure the object and hold it at bay, but as an indictment of the limits of the phallic function—and more specifically the phallic signifier—in its inability to limit jouissance.

Although femininity has occupied a place of prestige in psychoanalysis ever since Anna O's invention of the talking cure, Freud consistently saw the feminine subject as ethically deficient, citing her lack of investment in matters of morality or justice as proof of an inadequately installed superego.[47] But his indictment of the ethical limitations of women upheld a traditional view of ethics predicated upon an ideal of life in the signifier: an ideal that is by no means irrelevant for the feminine subject, but inadequate to address her particular experience of jouissance and the savoir to which it leads. When Freud does note the friction between woman and the signifier or law, it tends to be blamed on her as a moral failing. Lacan, on the other hand, begins to see in the feminine contestation of the signifier or law a special *savoir* concerning what Willy Apollon has termed the *Infondé,* the unfoundedness of the signifier, which woman experiences all the more radically in being "not all" under the phallic function.[48] Danielle Bergeron notes that for

Lacan, femininity is qualified by "its failure in relation to the rules defined by the phallus as the representative of lack: to be a woman is not only to be situated within the phallic as subject of language, but also to be one who cannot trust language or bring herself to make phallic laws the sole foundation of the meaning of her life."[49] Without renouncing the phallic signifier altogether, the ethics of the feminine subject must be founded upon something other than the limit it represents.

Finally, Lacan shows that there is in femininity the potential for a "jouissance beyond the phallus," what he calls the "Other jouissance," that consists in an experience of the lack in the signifier: not as an object of contestation or complaint, but as the source of a specific savoir. In Lacan's reformulation of the ethics of psychoanalysis, the pleasure of this Other jouissance, and of the *savoir* it accesses, is also the pleasure of the analyst: one that, following the experience of the feminine, guides the way to a life lived without the full support of the signifier. But in his attempt to formulate this Other jouissance, Lacan also develops a more nuanced understanding of the signifier: not just as an avatar of the pleasure principle in its binding function (and thus more or less equivalent to the narcissistic or phallic object), but as the object of a "deciphering" without meaning or symbolic equivalences. The gay *sçavoir* gives rise to a pleasure based not on the apprehension or capture of meaning, but on the enjoyment of a tangential encounter with it: "not understanding, not a diving at meaning, but a flying over it as low as possible without the meaning summing up this virtue, thus enjoying the deciphering. . . ."[50]

It is the pleasure that appears in the inscrutable laughter of the saint, the figure who, perhaps more than any other, embodies for Lacan the most radical potential of feminine jouissance. In *Encore,* he locates its traces in the ecstatic writings of Saint Teresa, where we find the contours of what Lucie Cantin has brilliantly analyzed as a feminine "ethics of the impossible."[51] But the experience of the saint finds its echoes not only in the jouissance of woman, but in the ethics of the psychoanalyst: "There is no better way of placing him objectively than in relation to what was in the past called: being a saint."[52] In his relation to ethics, he echoes the errant wandering of the feminine subject of jouissance: "The saint doesn't really see himself as righteous, which doesn't mean that he has no ethics. The only problem for others is that you can't see where it leads him."[53] But in his wandering, the analyst—like the hysteric who first sets him to his task—puts the subject on the path to a new savoir, the savoir of the unconscious. In a formula that I will return to at the end of this chapter, Lacan proposes that the analyst, *qua* saint, "acts as trash . . . so as to embody what the structure entails, namely allowing the subject, the subject of the unconscious, to take him as the cause of the subject's own desire."[54] The analyst's ethics is closely linked to the ethics of femininity, since both get their bearings in relation to the "not-all," the refuse of the phallic signifier and the cultural values it sustains.

Lacan suggests how an appreciation of feminine jouissance might afford the analyst a new approach to the elusive truth of the unconscious: "truth is already woman insofar as it's *not-all,* unable, in any case, to be wholly-spoken."[55] In its resistance to being wholly spoken, the "something more" of feminine jouissance is there motivating the performance of the *Television* interview from the very beginning, from the first words: "I always speak the truth. Not the whole truth, because there's no way, to say it all. Saying it all is literally impossible: words fail. Yet it's through this very impossibility that the truth holds onto the real."[56]

In saying that not all of the truth can be spoken, Lacan opposes the "real" quality of truth to the imaginary dimension of signification, meaning; for some meaning to be conveyed, a certain loss of truth is required. By symbolizing this loss, the phallus serves as the guarantor of the cultural articulation of meaning. For a man, it also serves to link his jouissance to his cultural role, as the one who is responsible for the procreation of the speaking being. Phallic jouissance is in this sense a "meaningful" pleasure, as Lacan's play upon the word "jouissance" suggests: "who doesn't get the meaning *(sens)* along with the pleasure *(joui)?*"[57] However, this meaningful pleasure does not account for the whole of jouissance; Lacan adds, "the saints alone stay mum; fat chance of getting anything out of them."[58] When he qualifies the saint as "the refuse of jouissance,"[59] this characterization must be understood in two ways: the Other jouissance is what the saint refuses to put into words, but not out of sheer obstinacy; for it is also what the signifier, by its very nature, refuses. The Other jouissance is thus at the same time the refuse of phallic jouissance, the "beyond meaning" refused by the phallic signifier.

If the phallus is what gives meaning to jouissance, by articulating it to the symbolic order—that is, the terms of coexistence within a given society—then a woman's relation to jouissance presents itself as something outside of meaning.[60] Feminine jouissance is not bound to the reproduction or procreation of the speaking being; in fact, it has no necessary relation even to sex (most concretely, a woman does not have to reach orgasm to become pregnant, but a man has to have an orgasm to impregnate a woman).[61] This "Other" jouissance has no use, utility, or purpose: in other words, no signifying "value," in the economic sense the term necessarily acquires under the phallic function. Instead, feminine jouissance is qualified by its ungrounded relation to the signifier.

Lacan's meditations on femininity lead to a reformulation of the ethics of psychoanalysis. To the ethics of lack articulated in the *Ethics* seminar—the duty "not to give up on one's desire"—he adds what he calls "the duty to be well-spoken" [*l'éthique du bien-dire*], "to find one's way in dealing with the unconscious, with the structure."[62] The duty to be well-spoken *about the truth* hinges upon the possibility of being well-spoken about the feminine experience of jouissance, so as to access the *savoir* it contains: a *savoir* about the defamatory, devaluing effects of the phallic signifier.

In *Encore,* Lacan draws attention to a homonymy in French between the *dit femme*—what is called woman—and what is *diffâme,* defamed: "The most famous things that have been handed down in history about women have been strictly speaking the most defamatory that could be said of them."[63] The susceptibility of woman to "defaming" is one of the things that marks the specificity of her jouissance as one that is "beyond the phallus," precisely insofar as this defamation—this failure to "speak well" of her—indexes the signifier's failure to name "all" of her.

Devaluation, Doubt, and the Feminine Object

If "not all" of woman's subjective truth can be brought under the aegis of the signifier, then how can the particularity of her relation to jouissance—and the ethics to which it gives rise—be well-spoken: that is—at least in part—*spoken well of,* without defamation?

What is certain is that where this jouissance is concerned, the ethics of being well-spoken will not involve finding an equivalent for it, making a translation, or forcing words on its silence. This is why Lacan tends to define the Other jouissance in a negative mode, through its opposition to capitalism, on the one hand, and *caritas*—the Christian virtue of charity—on the other.

> A saint's business, to put it clearly, is not *caritas*. Rather, he acts as trash *[déchet]*, his business being *trashitas [il décharite]*.[64]
>
> The more saints, the more laughter; that's my principle, to wit, the way out of capitalist discourse.[65]

If Lacan focuses his critique on this particular pair, an odd couple by almost any account, it is because capitalism and charity represent what are perhaps the two most potent examples, in Western culture, of signifying reduction. Lacan even suggests that the starting point of capitalism was "getting rid of sex";[66] in other words, it involves a reduction of all parties to one signifier that represents them "equally," and therefore inadequately. But in so doing, it paradoxically establishes an illusory "oneness": one market, one currency, one standard of value—so many avatars of the phallus, the unary signifier. From the vantage point of capital, "supply and demand" become two complementary halves of one holistic economy, in which excess is already reinscribed within the whole. (It is worth recalling that the French *jouissance* derives from the language of economics, denoting the "surplus value"—usufruct—of what is "enjoyed" without being owned.[67]) In such an economy, woman can never be anything more than a commodity, an object of exchange, reduced to embodying those imaginary *objets a* that promise plenitude or enjoyment to the subject who can append them to himself.

But what does this economy have to do with *caritas,* the "selfless" Christian virtue par excellence? The transcendental complement of capital, as a reduction of disparate entities to a common measure of exchange, is the inclusive, conversional nature of the Christian *logos:* the Word through which all Christians are rendered equal as "values" of the one Christ. But while Christian charity aspires to make One out of a vast multitude, anything that cannot be incorporated into this unity necessarily becomes a bad object, an unholy remainder, "debased" or "defamed" in a moral sense because of its inadequation to the signifier; in Lacan's neologism, *diffâme* also reads "de-souled."

In *The City of God,* Saint Augustine celebrates *caritas* as the cornerstone of a community of grace in which many are bound together in "one heart." But as we have seen,[68] the precondition of its wholeness is the exclusion of what Augustine calls "private will" or personal interest:

> . . . the children of grace . . . form a community where there is no love of a will that is personal and, as we may say, private, but a love that rejoices in a good that is at once shared by all and unchanging—a love that makes "one heart" out of many, a love that is the whole-hearted and harmonious obedience of mutual affection.[69]

In Augustine's "private will," we see the real dimension of the *objet a,* that remainder, supplement, or excess refused by the signifier. And here, as in the logic of capitalism, the first step is getting rid of sex: sexual difference is replaced by a desexualized "affection." Any notion of alterity is necessarily excised from the community of grace, where all members renounce private will in order to "make 'one heart' out of many." Even more generally, there is an exclusion of all impulses or desires precluding identification with this "one," including disbelief and doubt. But the saint, in "acting as trash," reminds us that the One can absorb the Other only at the expense of some remainder or excess, whose expulsion and denigration is the condition of possibility of the Whole.

In a departure from the logics of capitalism and *caritas,* the feminine subject is obliged to acknowledge her fundamental inadequation to the One. Although from a man's point of view she may appear as the (phallic) object whose appendage would make him "whole," her own vantage point does not allow her to espouse the same fantasy. This inadequation suggests how the Other jouissance opposes itself to *eros,* the "we two make one" of Love conceived as an imaginary plenitude—including, and even especially, Christian love. For as the excess of man, the one not made in the image of God, woman is the symptom of Christian love's inclusive Oneness.

In characterizing the "ethics of being well-spoken" as a Gay Science, a gay *sçavoir,* Lacan opposes it to all such "meaningful" economies. Its name alludes most obviously to Nietzsche's *Gay Science,* with its critique of Christianity and its reductive relation to the foreign, the other, the unknown. But it alludes also to the work Nietzsche credited with inspiring it, Stendhal's 1822 treatise *Love (De l'amour),* which focuses on the asymmetry of the male and female experiences of "crystallization," or the onset of love.

For man it offers the promise of an imaginary plenitude, while for woman it centers around the experience of *doubt:* a risking of her being rather than an imaginary completion of it.

Crystallized love, says Stendhal, proceeds according to three general steps. But the process happens differently for men and women. In its masculine form, crystallization parallels the imaginary process whereby woman as "object" or commodified "property" becomes appended to man as that which would fill his lack: a process that is not without parallels to the Christian, all-inclusive love named by *caritas,* insofar as it promises to make the subject "whole." For the male subject, the three moments of crystallization are defined by the degree of assurance each offers the lover of his success with regard to his beloved. In the first crystallization,

> It is a pleasure to endow with a thousand perfections a woman whose love you are sure of, and to count your blessings with infinite satisfaction. In this end you overrate wildly, and fancy her some exquisite property, something fallen from Heaven, unknown as yet, but certain to be yours.[70]

What makes her "exquisite" is the promise of her eventual possession, her complementary appendage to the lover. The beloved object has every perfection, she is *exactly what he needs;* the process of crystallization works to garnish the beloved with charms precisely so that the lover might experience satisfaction from them. This first stage is thus summed up in the idea that "of all the women on earth, she alone could give me such pleasures" (47). The pleasures the beloved promises to produce for him, furthermore, have less to do with who she is than with what he wants; her charming qualities are the inverse projection of his lack.

The second stage in the process of crystallization—doubt—is precipitated by a sign from the beloved that seems to say: "you believe yourself to be further advanced than you really are." In the face of the beloved's coldness or apparent indifference, her lover "begins to be less sure of the good fortune he was anticipating, and subjects his grounds for hope to a critical examination." But this doubt is in turn dissipated by a new crystallization, "which deposits diamond layers of proof that 'she loves me'" (47). On what is this new certainty based? Interestingly, the anxiety caused by the idea that *he needs her* ("she alone could give me such pleasures") is displaced by the assurance that he can *satisfy* her—and, by implication, himself: "Each new beauty gives you the full and complete fulfillment of a desire. . . . she seems to be your property, because you alone can make her happy" (59–60). These two fundamentally different steps are collapsed in a logic whose fundamental ungroundedness is both highlighted and occluded by the necessity of each to the other. The possibility of satisfaction is dependent, in male crystallization, upon the affirmative answer to the double question: *Can I please her? Does she love me?* (55). He solves the dilemma of doubt through recourse to a phallic logic of jouissance, when he succeeds at making love with her and thereby gains "proof" of his success.

The confirmation man seeks in crystallization is the assurance of his own plenitude, guaranteed by the appendage of the delightful qualities he adorns the beloved with in order to enjoy the use of them. These "extensions" or "supplements" have a decidedly phallic character, inasmuch as they promise to fill in or complete a lack. From the vantage point of male crystallization, woman is thus a highly phallicized object who promises to realize or achieve male identity by adding her pleasure to his.

Stendhal notes that a woman cannot experience love in the same way as a man. Love for her means putting her subjective integrity at stake: her reputation, her social standing, but also her imaginary integrity—the illusion of consistency that is as impossible for her experience of crystallization as it is essential to his. The asymmetry between their modes of crystallization inheres in their disparate relations to the experience of doubt, since hers cannot be dispelled even with the second fateful crystallization. Stendhal observes that experience inevitably makes a mature woman mistrust the illusion of love; but for that very reason, her crystallization is especially potent, since it is based on a risking of her being. The instability of her symbolic status and her susceptibility to commodification are key to her experience of love, since she is someone who is subject to defaming, to devaluation, and who must therefore risk herself without any guarantee that her wager will be successful:

> Now a sensitive person has acquired some self-knowledge by twenty-eight; she knows that any happiness she can expect from life will come to her through love; hence a terrible struggle develops between love and mistrust. . . .
> The dissimilarity between the way love is born for the two sexes

corresponds with a difference in the nature of hope for man and woman. One is attacking, the other defending; one asks, the other refuses; one is bold, the other shy.

The man wonders: "Shall I be able to please her? Will she love me?"

And the woman thinks: "Perhaps he's only joking when he says he loves me. Is he reliable? Does he really know himself how long his love will last?"....

For a man, hope depends simply on the actions of the woman he loves, and nothing is easier to interpret than these. For a woman, hope must be based on moral considerations which are extremely difficult to assess. Most men seek a proof of love which they consider dispels all doubt; women are not lucky enough to be able to find a like proof. It is one of life's misfortunes that what brings certainty and happiness to one lover brings danger and almost humiliation to the other. (55)

This dissymmetry highlights the fact that although we find the feminine by following the traces of the *objet a* (the phallicized object endowed with "a thousand perfections"), we ultimately also find that it is irreducible to this object in its imaginary quality. She must occupy this position as an agent, as a subject of desire and not just its object. The experience of doubt, and the mistrust of the signifier it sustains, is essential for the feminine subject not only as the index of her defamation, but also as a guide. For it is from this "defamed" or "de-souled" position—from the risk she assumes every time she encounters the signifier—that woman will come into being as a subject of desire.

"The object raised to the dignity of the Thing"

Lacan's gay *sçavoir* privileges the real of the sexual relation over its imaginary dimension, attending to what these economies exclude or overwrite. The gay *sçavoir* as an ethics is one that will be elaborated from the perspective of the real object, and not of the signifier. In her "excess," her irreducibility to the One, woman animates another dimension of the object: not the phallic *objet a,* but what Lacan designates in the *Ethics* seminar as "the object raised to the dignity of the Thing."[71]

But here, too, there is a potential ambiguity: Lacan's "Thing" also alludes to the original Thing, *das Ding:* the mother. The mother, too, is "beyond" the economy of the signifier, insofar as she is the one Thing or object that is not put into circulation. For the male subject she is at once the ultimate object or aim of desire and at the same time what is forbidden to it, withheld from the traffic in goods only to become The Good, sublimely untouchable. She appears to be the one exception to castration who proves the rule, the unbarred Other who enjoys fully. But this supreme or ultimate enjoyment is precisely the death drive, what the phallus holds at bay by preventing the subject from confronting it head-on; as Lacan notes in the *Ethics* seminar, "the distance between the subject and *das Ding* is precisely the condition of speech."[72]

Thus although her incompatibility with the logics of capitalism and *caritas* proves that woman cannot function merely as phallicized goods, a commodity for consumption, neither is it enough simply to remove her from economies of signification altogether. For such a position is not only untenable in its own right—since her jouissance, too, must distinguish itself from the Death Drive—but also fails to provide a real alternative to the traffic in goods. In fact, the mother as Supreme Good actually underwrites that economy precisely by being withheld from it. In her essay "Love Outside the Limits of the Law," Juliet Flower MacCannell notes: "Lacan fully conceded that, for those who take up a masculine position, phallic jouissance is directed to those body parts (designated as *objets a*) which seem to the subject to be the residue or remains of what would have been the supreme, but forbidden, Good: the jouissance of the Mother."[73]

Whereas the One upheld by the logics of capitalism and *caritas* is a phallic One, a signifier that pretends to have no remainder, this One is sustained through a disavowal of castration, a complete refusal of the signifier. Whence Lacan's observation that "man cannot reach Woman except by running aground on a field of perversion."[74] The "polymorphous perversion" of male sexuality disavows the not-all to which she inevitably points in one of two ways: by making woman the phallic object who would complete Man, or by upholding Woman as the unbarred Other whose existence would permit the disavowal of the universality of castration.

Both possibilities are ultimately inadequate where woman is concerned. MacCannell observes that "femininity's position vis-à-vis the Other jouissance . . . works the distance between object and other;"[75] neither pole is alone sufficient to express the complexities of her subjective position in relation to jouissance. This necessary oscillation highlights both the particularity of her Other jouissance and its difference from what Lacan calls the "jouissance of the Other," the positing of an unbarred Other of complete jouissance that is upheld and sustained by the subject's disavowal of castration.

In qualifying the specificity of her position as that of the "object raised to the dignity of the Thing," Lacan suggests that woman must balance between two positions: neither submitting fully to the neutralizing reduction of the phallic signifier, nor allowing herself to be exempted or expulsed from it entirely. Here it is important to remember that Lacan specifies that woman is "not all" inscribed within the phallic function, and not that she is "not at all" inscribed. Woman necessarily retains some link to the signifier, however problematic it may be. The doubt that anchors her experience of jouissance is different than disavowal, since it identifies the failure of the signifier to guarantee or speak all of the truth, without renouncing it altogether.

"Raised to the dignity of the Thing," the object no longer lends itself to this perversion. It finds its dignity *in* its defamation, rather than in being made completely off-limits, fantasmatically inaccessible. Grazed by the signifier without being fully inscribed within it, the feminine positions itself in this "between," a space Lacan calls "poetry": the place where "meaning" is waylaid by the creation of a space inaccessible to the signifier. "To make love, as the expression indicates, is poetry. But there is a world between poetry and the act. The act of love is the polymorphous perversion of the male, in the case of the speaking being."[76] To act on signs—to "read" or translate them as favorable to oneself—is something entirely different than to make poetry out of them on the condition of their not being clearly interpretable, to acknowledge the way in which they resist inscription within a signifying chain.

In this respect it is significant that Lacan's *gay savoir* has as its first and perhaps most important source the Provençal troubadours, the poets of courtly love, who used the term to describe their poetry. What then does this poetry bespeak? It inaugurates a mode in which the signifier skirts around the object, sketching out a space in which it can manifest itself: not as a representation, but *as* a void. It allows for the emergence of what MacCannell calls the "vacancy of the feminine Thing," the "void created at the center of the flow of terms."[77]

The songs of the troubadours create a space defined by its inaccessibility and exaltation, but also by its highly original staging of the defaming and domination borne by the Thing, as "that which in the real suffers from the signifier."[78] If their example is still compelling today, it is in part because the poetry of courtly love eschews the "solution" to this defaming that we find so frequently vaunted today, the drive toward increased "equality" between the sexes that, while it certainly has its virtues in the purely legislative domain, risks lapsing into perversion where the sexual relation is concerned. This is because the discourse of legal equality is itself profoundly invested in what Lacan critiques under the aegis of "capitalist discourse," a commodity market predicated upon the reduction of all parties to one signifier that represents them "equally," and therefore inadequately. If, as Renata Salecl argues, "woman is a symptom of the rights of man,"[79] then her legal status can never protect her from the defamation and devaluation of her being that the signifier of legal rights imposes as the cost of her obtaining personhood. The originality of the troubadours' contribution is that their poetry neither disavows the truth of this defamation, nor seeks to rectify it by somehow leveling the playing field. Instead, it responds to it by carving out a space internal to this defamatory inequality, dignifying woman there where she is defamed.

As Stendhal observes, the paradox of women's place in courtly love is that "they were but a step from the horrors of the Middle Ages and of feudalism, where force reigned supreme, yet the weaker sex were less oppressed then than they are *legally* today."[80] If the example of courtly love is key for Lacan, it is not because it departs entirely from the defaming traffic in goods that defines the sexual relation under the sign of the phallus, but because it is situated at its very heart. Lacan notes that the position of woman in feudal society is profoundly shaped by precisely those economies of exchange that leave no place for femininity as a subjective position:

> Strictly speaking, she is what is indicated by the elementary structures of kinship: that is, nothing more than a correlative of the functions of social exchange, the support of a certain number of

goods and of signs of power. She is essentially identified with a social function that leaves no place for her person or her liberty, except by reference to religious rights.[81]

Courtly love thus serves to highlight the actual property dimension
of woman as commodity. But it also does so in such a way as to establish the implication of feudal society in what Stendhal's text formalizes as the phallic logic of male crystallization, whose key moment is the idea "she seems to be your property," in which woman
finds herself appended to man as the object that would complete
his self-image.

At the same time, courtly love rises up here, in the midst of
this terribly reductive economy, as proof of something else. Like
Stendhal's analysis of crystallization, its logic insists upon the commodification of woman precisely in order to reveal that woman is
not reducible to this position, but rather animates its excess or remainder. For although woman is reduced to being nothing more
than an object of exchange, the flip side of this objectification is her
uncanny status as that "Thing" that feudal society is unable to account for, what has no place in its economy. And, precisely because
this economy leaves no place for her as a person, her displacement
and dispossession point to another place, something off the map or
outside of the market, voicing what this economy must overwrite
or exclude in order to function. Her position makes it possible to
undermine the imaginary wholeness of the feudal economy by considering it from the vantage of its own blind spot. Thus although
the poetry of courtly love comes to the Lady by following the traces
of the object, it also insists upon her inadequation to it: whence the
lady's legendary inaccessibility, the index not only of her sublimity
and interdiction, but of her occupying this position as a subject,
possessed of a particular agency that both inheres in and resists her
status as a possession or object of commerce.

Lacan evokes it in his mention of Dante's Beatrice:

> A gaze, that of Beatrice—that is to say, three times nothing, a flut-
> tering of the eyelids and the exquisite trash that results from it—
> and there emerges that Other whom we can identify only through
> her jouissance: her whom he, Dante, cannot satisfy, because from
> her, he can have only this look, only this object, but of whom he
> tells us that God fulfills her utterly; it is precisely by receiving the
> assurance of that from her own mouth that he arouses us.[82]

The object, the gaze, is all he gets of the beloved. And between this object (a) and her jouissance, there is strictly speaking no relation: "he gets an idea of beatitude, an idea which is forceful enough for him to feel himself exiled from it."[83] The "thingliness" of Beatrice resides in her inadequation to the object. The feminine Thing opposes itself to the traffic in feminine goods, and thus to woman's determination as an object of phallic jouissance, by giving voice to the excessive, supplementary quality of the object vis-à-vis this economy. Beatrice's gaze does not apprehend her there where she enjoys, but only marks the dissymmetry between her jouissance and the object of desire. Her jouissance marks her as the Other unattainable by means of the phallus, the Other whose gaze never responds to the subject's own, but rather points beyond it: thereby illustrating Lacan's theorem concerning the gaze as *objet a,* that "you never look at me there where I see you."[84]

Property and Expropriation

The paradox of her position is that although there is no place for her as a person, her function is elaborated within a discourse that concerns and upholds the status of the person. In *Encore,* Lacan suggests that courtly love is "rooted in the discourse of fealty, of fidelity to the person."[85] The person this discourse names and sustains, however, is not the de-personalized, dis-placed woman, but the man whose personhood she upholds in being appended to it as a proprietary attachment. Lacan writes that "for the man, whose lady was entirely, in the most servile sense of the term, his subject, courtly love is the only way to pull off elegantly the absence of sexual relation."[86] She is a subject in this discourse only to the extent that she is *subjected* to man, the object of his power and law.

This subjection contains an important clue to the position of woman in this discourse, since, according to Lacan, "the 'person' always has to do with the master's discourse."[87] The discourse of mastery, and the personhood it upholds, necessarily has a despotic component, one that is not without parallels to the defaming effects of the signifier. For the master is also a master *signifier,* the representative or embodiment of the possibility of total adequation to the signifier of personal identity. As we saw in the introduction, the ancient root meaning "master," *pot-,* originally denotes the one who "eminently personifies" personal identity. The master signifier and mastery as a despotic subjection are actually closely linked, since this self-adequation corresponds to and is reinforced by a power over others, a reduction of a plurality of essences to one signifier. The Greek *despótes,* and its Latin equivalents *potis* (master, potentate) and *dominus* (master, lord), represent the extension of domestic authority into the field of social and symbolic power, an extension facilitated by a very particular interpretation of the sexual relation.

In this semantic genealogy, as we have seen, self-mastery and personal identity extend into social and symbolic authority through the possession and subordination of dependents bereft of symbolic status, above all the household dependents who are defined as the property of the master of the home. These possessions are at once heterogeneous with the master—subjected to him—and at the same time constitutive of his subjectivity, his eminent personification of identity, his total self-adequation. The master's identity as a subject is defined by his possession of woman as chattel. But at the same time, his failure to possess her absolutely also undermines his identity, his status as a master "equal to himself," by insisting on the heterogeneity of the appendage that makes him "whole." Although the woman as "property" contributes to the master's "eminent personification" of personal identity, she also undermines the illusion of self-sufficiency and of adequation to the signifier that the master is supposed to embody by drawing attention to its dependence on an im-proper attachment or addition, which remains foreign even in being subordinated and internalized, thereby assuming an agency all its own.

In testifying, through her subjection, to the power and brutality of the master and the historical conditions that made it possible, the woman underscores the defaming and subjecting nature of the master signifier and its proprietary relation to those objects (a) that it puts into circulation without managing to take possession of them altogether. If the "integral" quality of mastery consists in its appearance of adequation to the (phallic, impersonal) signifier of personal identity, then woman's resistance to and critique of mastery inheres precisely in her lack of personhood, her exclusion from any notion of legal rights or symbolic status. Her position highlights the fact that any subject who takes it upon himself to incarnate the master signifier always has an excess or residue—"something extra"—that does not allow itself to be inscribed within the symbolic function.

She animates that dimension of the *objet a* as something lost to or torn from the subject, something whose inaccessibility leads to the disintegration of the master's "own" integrity. Commenting on the phallic rules governing the sexual relation for a man, Renata Salecl writes:

> Lacan points out that it is because of this anxiety that men created the myth of Eve being made out of Adam's rib. This myth allows a man to think that if just a rib was taken from him, then he is essentially not missing anything, that is, there is no lost object and woman is, therefore, just an object made from man. Although this myth tries to assure men of their wholeness, it nonetheless does not alleviate their anxiety. Anxiety often arises precisely when a man encounters a woman who becomes an object of his desire.[88]

Recall that in Stendhal's treatment of crystallization, woman's "property" status is confirmed for a man by an affirmative answer to the double question "can I please her, does she love me?" His ability to satisfy her—to "possess" her sexually—is what makes her seem like property. The discourse of mastery that sustains such an operation is thus deeply invested in the imaginary of the sexual relation, which supposes a meaningful whole of jouissance: One enjoy-meant. When the assurance sought in crystallization is withheld, however, this illusion crumbles.

When Lacan notes that Dante is "exiled" from the beatitude of which Beatrice alone gives him the idea, this implies that in being deprived of her, Dante is exiled not only from the jouissance that she alone accesses, but from *himself.* Through her jouissance, woman insists on the im-propriety at the heart of the proprietary relation that conceives her as a possession or object, since it prevents her from being appended to man as an imaginary complement. Although her inaccessibility is certainly key, she is not inaccessible in the same way the mother is. Rather, her inaccessibility results from the fact that she cannot be wholly satisfied by the phallus. If she provokes this feeling of exile in him, it is because the glimpse of her jouissance "beyond the phallus" points to the possible inadequacy of a phallic solution and the imaginary consistency it guarantees: not only for her, but for a man too. And, within the psychoanalytic domain, to the inadequacy of ego psychology. Lacan's critique of ego psychology implies that psychoanalysis must distinguish itself from the psychotherapeutic aim of helping the subject to be more "self-possessed." If woman is a privileged guide in Lacan's quest for the ethics of psychoanalysis, it is because in suffering the possession and dispossession of the master signifier, she nevertheless does not—and indeed cannot—strive to be self-possessed. Her experience highlights the fact that subjectivity is always a *subjection*, a receiving of the signifier that leaves the subject fundamentally split, divided.

The Uncanny Jouissance of the *Nebenmensch*

Courtly love, in bringing this uncanny, extimate dimension of subjectivity to the fore, also suggests how the inaccessible jouissance of the Lady might model an alternative ethics, one that emphasizes the dispossession of the subject over its imaginary wholeness. Through her inaccessibility, she attests to the insurmountable barrier surrounding the very Thing that man most desires, the supreme object. But in so doing, she also animates the function of the *cause* of desire: the cause that, fallen from the chain of signifiers, engenders sublimation by "depriving the subject of something real":

> In this poetic field the feminine object is emptied of all real substance. That is what made it easy for a metaphysical poet such as Dante, for example, to choose a person whom we definitely know existed—namely, little Beatrice whom he fell for when she was nine years old, and who stayed at the center of his poetry from the *Vita Nuova* to *The Divine Comedy*—and to make her the equivalent of philosophy or indeed, in the end, of the science of the sacred. That also enabled him to appeal to her in terms that are all the more sensual because the person in question is close to allegory. It is only when the person involved is transformed into a symbolic function that one is able to speak of her in the crudest terms.
>
> Here we see functioning in the pure state the authority of that place the instinct aims for in sublimation. That is to say, that what man demands, what he cannot help but demand, is to be deprived of something real. And one of you, in explaining to me what I am trying to show in *das Ding,* referred to it neatly as the vacuole.[89]

In contrast with the imaginary endowment of the beloved that defines the logic of crystallization, the Lady's exalted status emphasizes the subject's *privation* over his completion or plenitude.

Stendhal offers a hilariously literal example of this "extraction of the real" in his recounting of a medieval story about a poet who had offended his lady:

> after he had been in despair for two years she deigned at last to reply to his numerous appeals, and conveyed to him that he should pull out one of his fingernails and send it to her by fifty lovelorn faithful knights, whereupon she might perhaps forgive him. The poet hastened to undergo this painful operation. Fifty knights wearing their ladies' favours took the fingernail and presented it with all possible solemnity to the offended fair one. It was as imposing a ceremony as that of a prince of blood entering one of his royal cities. The lover in the garb of repentance followed his fingernail at a distance. The lady, having seen the exceedingly long ceremony to its conclusion, condescended to forgive him and he was reinstated to all the delights of his former happiness. The story goes on to relate that they spent many long and happy years together. Undoubtedly these two years of unhappiness proved that the passion was true, and they would have engendered it if it had not existed so strongly in the first place.[90]

The story is not simply one of "playing hard to get," but an expression of the way in which the Lady's *doubt* comes to dominate the scenario, sending her lover wandering and forcing him to surrender some bit of the real. Her doubt, and not his word, is highlighted as the basis of a new ethical standard: the doubt with which, as Stendhal tells us, a sensitive woman cannot fail to be plagued when she encounters the advances of phallic desire and the word through which it makes its case. In making her man suffer trials for her to prove his love, she both combats the imaginary lures of a love too quickly made reassuring ("she seems to be your property"), and at the same time makes him suffer for the inadequacy of his word, suffer the inadequacy of the signifier in being deprived of something real.

In offering a glimpse of her "jouissance beyond the phallus" the Lady points to an ethics of the real, an ethics that turns her lover into a "knight errant" in more senses than one. She is the real Thing that stays in one place, but that sets the subject adrift in a quest for *savoir*. The importance of her example where psychoanalysis is concerned is that it suggests how the wandering and drifting that qualifies hysteria—and feminine experience in general—might be transferred or adapted to the experience of man, or of any subject who assumes a masculine position, through the analytic act: not as a pathology or symptom, but as an ethics of living without the full support of the signifier.

One of the most remarkable aspects of courtly love, the inversion whereby man becomes the servant of the woman who is legally his subordinate, thus finds its discursive parallel in the subversion of the discourse of the master by the *ça:* that abjected cause that, in eluding the grasp of the signifier, forces the subject into a position of desire. In noting that the lovelorn poet's two unhappy years deprived of his lady would have engendered his passion if it had not already existed, Stendhal insists upon the importance of the barrier surrounding the Lady, the Thing, to her function as the cause of his desire. In this operation, the discourse of mastery succumbs to the dominion of the *ça,* the Thing—the Lady in her guise as *la Domnei,* "she who dominates":

> The object involved, the feminine object, is introduced oddly enough through the door of privation or of inaccessibility. Whatever the social position of he who functions in this register—some of them were in fact servants, *sirvens,* at their place of birth—the inaccessibility of the object is posited as a point of departure.
>
> It is impossible to serenade the Lady, in her poetic position, without the presupposition of a barrier that surrounds and isolates her.
>
> Furthermore, that object or *Domnei,* as she is called—she is also frequently referred to with the masculine term, *Mi Dom* or my Lord—this Lady is presented with depersonalized characteristics, to such a degree that writers have noted that all of the poets seem to be addressing the same person.[91]

The Lady as *Domnei* is both like and unlike the Christian *dominus,* Christ as Lord and master. While the Christian *dominus* is the image in which man is made (as whole), the Lady attests to the "vacuole" at the center of this image, the blind spot. Against the "eminent personhood" of the master, the Lady as Thing is characterized by her extreme depersonalization. She is "lord" insofar as she mobilizes a part of the lover's desire that undermines his integrity as a subject, occasioning the loss of something real. Although she is represented with a masculinized term of power *(Mi Dom)* displaced into a uniquely feminine field, the Lady embodies another kind of dominion altogether, one that is importantly not predicated on her obtaining "equal" status, "becoming the man." Instead, her "lordliness" is linked to her inaccessibility—and even her abjection and defamation.

When he specifies that "for us the Other is as entitled as the One to generate a subject out of an axiom,"[92] Lacan suggests that woman, in assuming the place of the cause of desire, founds a subject in a way that runs directly counter to the "whole-hearted" Oneness that bestows personhood within the logic of *caritas*. The lady's "mastery" or domination undermines the notion that we might live as neighbors, *semblables,* or equals within One holistic economy, by revealing the apparent integrity of the person to be the illusion of the phallic signifier. The Lady's animation of the Thing makes her into another kind of "neighbor," an uncanny one:

> ... at a certain point in his poems, the extraordinary Guillaume de Poitiers calls the object of his aspirations *Bon vezi,* which means "Good neighbor." As a result of which, historians have abandoned themselves to all kinds of conjectures and have been unable to come up with anything better than the name of a Lady who, it is known, played an important role in his personal history, a forward woman apparently, whose estates were close to Guillaume's.
>
> What is for us much more important than the reference to the neighbor, who is supposedly the Lady whom Guillaume de Poitiers occasionally played naughty games with, is the relationship between the expression just referred to and the one Freud uses in connection with the first establishment of the Thing, with its psychological genesis, namely, the *Nebenmensch.* And he designated thereby the very place that from the point of view of the development of Christianity, was to be occupied by the apotheosis of the neighbor.[93]

In relation to the lover who considers her from an infinitely distant proximity, the Lady as "neighbor" is an adjoining property that cannot be annexed, but that persists and insists behind an insurmountable barrier. They dwell next to one another not as self-sufficient and equal neighbors in one community, one love, but as uncanny cohabitants of an intersubjective space in which the Other functions as the cause of the subject's "own" desire. Woman's failure to be identified with the One—her failure to be a "good neighbor," in the Augustinian sense—is precisely what facilitates her function as the *Bon vezi* or *Nebenmensch* of the courtly love scenario.

The Ethics of the Host-*es*

By attesting, through her Other jouissance, to the fact that "somewhere, in the Other, it knows," woman models how the subject must dwell in the unconscious in order to access its *savoir*. In assuming her Other jouissance there where "it" is, assuming subjectivity precisely *as* a Thing, she serves as a guide for the ethics of psychoanalysis as articulated by Freud in his *Wo es war, soll Ich werden*. Following her example, we might restate Freud's formula as follows: there where the Thing was, the subject of the unconscious shall come into being as the subject of an Other jouissance, a gay *sçavoir*.

Although Lacan draws on the Freudian practice wherein the analyst plays host to the discourse—and the *savoir*—that are the hysteric's, he also pushes this relationship one step further. The analyst must be not merely the "bee to the honey" that the hysteric produces,[94] but must himself assume a feminine position in relation to the *savoir* that she embodies. He must himself become a host-*es*, one whose discourse allows the truth of the unconscious to emerge: not as its master or as one who knows, but as one who allows the *savoir* of the Other to come into being, "there where the Thing was."

In Lacan's remarks about the saint who "acts as trash," and who thereby allows the subject of the unconscious to "take him as the cause of the subject's own desire," he emphasizes that "it is through the abjection of this cause that the subject in question has a chance to be aware of his position."[95] In other words, it is only insofar as this cause is abjected, debased, and defamed that the subject can come to some awareness of his position within the structure of discourse. The analysand is like the knight working for the Lady, the knight errant whose *savoir* must be sought in relation to this abjected cause for which he wanders and labors.

Psychoanalysis thus shares with courtly love its status as a discourse in which the Thing points the way. It is a gay *sçavoir* only to the extent that it allows the *savoir* of the Thing to emerge: a knowledge concerning the way in which the real suffers from the signifier, and the subject from the real that sets it adrift. Central to the poetry of courtly love, as a *gay savoir,* is the understanding that the knowledge belongs to the Thing, the Lady, and not to the poet who sings her praises, always on the condition of leaving intact the barrier that surrounds her. Similarly, in analysis, the *savoir* is on the side of the subject, and not the analyst. Although the analyst is the subject "supposed to know," his role is in fact to allow the subject's "own" *savoir* to emerge.

But Lacan suggests that although this *savoir* emerges out of the relation between analysand and analyst, its importance is not limited to the analytic act. In fact, it is called upon to serve as the foundation of a new social bond. Willy Apollon has suggested that human cultures define and justify themselves by the ways in which they manage feminine jouissance, what is inherently "beyond" culture.[96] If psychoanalysis has something to offer to that cultural project, it is that it proposes to manage this jouissance not by containing or neutralizing it, but by allowing its *savoir* to emerge—a *savoir* concerning the possibility of a social bond based on other than phallic ties. Since, as Lacan suggests, the unconscious "is witnessed clearly only in the discourse of the hysteric," her discourse alone is capable of serving as the foundation for the *savoir* of psychoanalysis, as a *savoir* constitutive of a social tie: "what's to be found everywhere is just grafted onto it: yes, even, astonishing as it may seem, in the discourse of the analyst, where what is made of it is culture. . . . What I call the analytic discourse is the social bond determined by the practice of an analysis."[97] The culture that analytic discourse proposes would be a culture on the model of courtly love, a culture of poetry devoted to the deciphering of signs, a "flying low over meaning" that allows this space to open and endure.

To the extent that the gay *sçavoir* represents a "knowledge" about this supplementary jouissance, it is a knowledge that is not reducible to comprehension, to the inscription of this excess within the imaginary register of meaning. As a gay *sçavoir,* the ethics of being well-spoken calls for a speaking that would not attempt simply to apprehend its object through the signifier, or to displace it altogether, but would rather open a space in which this Thing might present itself in its irreducibility: a space of poetry. The social bond that analytic discourse proffers will borrow from the poetry of courtly love in its articulation of a gay *sçavoir* based on a deciphering, one that allows the Thing, the "it," to speak itself; a *savoir* in which the analyst will play host to the *es* of the subject's desire, receiving it in the manner of the Lady who sends her knight wandering, erring on the side of truth.

Feminine jouissance is a *savoir* of the "it," the *savoir* of the one who is inhabited by, or plays host to, the *es:* the *host-es.* In each of the narratives we have examined, the hostess's function both illuminates and gives new resonance to the subjective logic delineated in Lacan's reading of Freud's *Wo es war, soll Ich werden.* As a "thing" uncannily internal to the host, she is that "stranger within" whose irreducibility to the identity of the host defines hospitality as something other than a confirmation of the ego's mastery. I take Freud's formulation as the foundation for my own thesis concerning the subjective status of the host in the ethics of hospitality: namely, that the importance of the hostess consists in the dispossession of the host-"I" (the master eminently equal to himself) by the host-*es,* the Thing irreducible to the identity of the host that opens onto the Other.

We have seen this Thingly agency of woman, the "object raised to the dignity of the Thing," in the story of Sarah, which also bears witness to the *savoir* of a certain jouissance. Like the Lady of the courtly love relation, Sarah comes into being as the subject of an other jouissance by working the distance between the object and the Thing, between the exigencies of the phallus and the errant pleasures of poetry. From the point of view of the "official," mythic story—which has only one subject, her husband Abraham—she is an object, chattel, a commodity. But in another way, she reveals herself to have what Klossowski calls the "negative quality of a subject," insofar as she assumes a Thingly agency irreducible to the subject or the signifier that represents it. The hospitalities of Sarah and Roberte contest the phallic logic in which woman functions as an imaginary extension or supplement to the male host/master by revealing the *"moi de l'objet,"* the paradoxical "selfhood" or agency of the object or thing within the subject who "possesses" it. The result is that the host is "deprived of something real," deprived of his personhood in surrendering that part of "himself" the wife represents.

She is that part of the host that is not named by the covenant, the excess of the signifier who animates the function of the *objet a* or Thing in both its imaginary and real dimensions: that spot of pseudo-consistency that appears to fill in or make up for the splitting

of the subject, at the same time that it serves as a persistent reminder of that split. As an object or possession, the wife as "property"
completes the identity of the patriarch. But as a "Thing" possessed
of a singular agency within the patriarch who both possesses and
is possessed *by* her, the wife animates the excess of the patriarch,
that part of him that had to be repressed to allow for his inscription
in the covenant. In this case, the possibility of his own doubt—a
possibility foreclosed by his status as a keeper of the covenant.

Sarah's famous laughter, and the doubt to which it bears witness, are not without a certain pleasure. As in the case of the Lady
of courtly love, both the doubt and the pleasure inhere in Sarah's
"thingliness," which allows her to access an experience from which
her husband, as a subject of the signifier, is debarred. But as the
"excess" of her husband's covenantal identity, the embodiment of
that part of him that is unequal to the signifier, Sarah's laughter
insists upon an inadequation to God's word and a disbelieving relation to the promise it sustains. If Eve is the one who incites Adam to
forget that he cannot have knowledge, and who urges him to prove
his mastery by taking on God himself, then Sarah is the one who
redeems this "wicked emancipation" by opposing to it another kind
of knowledge. The *savoir* that Sarah transmits is one that concerns
the ungroundedness of the signifier, the misrecognition that presides over the transmission of the divine word: in other words, the
impossibility of "all" of the truth being transmitted.

But at the same time, this inadequation allows for another jouissance. The relation between doubting laughter and her "shall I have
pleasure . . . ?" is not inconsequential, since her enjoyment consists not only in the untimely "pleasure" she is promised—sexual
pleasure or the pleasure of maternity—but in the negative mode in
which this possibility is considered: the laughter that mistrusts the
signifier, that deforms the word, that insists on its inadequation
to the promise. Sarah's doubt leaves behind a residue, a remainder that—even after the promise has been fulfilled—persists in and
beyond the meaning of the sacred narrative as a kind of laughing
commentary upon it. I am referring to Isaac himself, the child of
the promise, whose name means "he laughs." His name is a poetic
remainder of Sarah's jouissance, one that exceeds the transcendent
meaning of the text. Isaac sustains the excess of Sarah's laughter,
the lingering doubt that hovers over the promise fulfilled.

Notes

Introduction

1. All etymological roots are taken from Émile Benveniste's analysis of the Indo-European origins of the concept of hospitality. "L'hospitalité," in *Le vocabulaire des institutions indo-européennes,* vol. 1 (Paris: Éditions de Minuit, 1969), 87–101. Subsequent citations from the same text will be given as page numbers in parentheses; all translations are my own.

2. For a discussion of the relation between mastery and ipseity in Benveniste, see Jacques Derrida with Anne Dufourmantelle, *De l'hospitalité* (Paris: Calmann-Lévy, 1997), 53.

3. For an in-depth study of the institution of potlatch, see Marcel Mauss's work *The Gift: The Form and Reason for Exchange in Archaic Societies,* trans. W. D. Halls (New York: Norton, 1990). Parts of Mauss's thesis will be commented on in more detail below.

4. Gilles Deleuze, *Logic of Sense,* trans. Mark Lester with Charles Stivale (New York: Columbia University Press, 1990), 254; translation modified.

5. Michel Foucault, "Theatrum Philosophicum," in *Language, Counter-Memory, Practice,* ed. Donald F. Bouchard (Ithaca: Cornell University Press, 1977), 167.

6. Jacques Derrida, *Aporias,* trans. Thomas Dutoit (Stanford: Stanford University Press, 1993), 8–17.

7. See in particular Heidegger's "Letter on Humanism" (1947), "Building, Dwelling, Thinking" (1951), and ". . . Poetically Man Dwells . . ." (1951).

8. Martin Heidegger, "Letter on Humanism," in *Basic Writings,* ed. David Farrell Krell (New York: Harper and Row, 1977), 232.

9. Aristotle, *De parte animalium* (I, 5, 645A 17). Cited by Heidegger, "Letter on Humanism," 233.

10. Derrida made this argument in his seminar at U.C. Irvine entitled "Hospitality and Hostility," April 3, 1996.

11. Emmanuel Lévinas, *Totality and Infinity: An Essay on Exteriority,* trans. Alphonso Lingis (Pittsburgh: Duquesne University Press, 1969), 27. Subsequent citations from the same text will be given as page numbers in parentheses.

12. Benveniste, "L'hospitalité," 91.

13. Both examples were suggested to me by Jacques Derrida in his lecture "Hospitality and Hostility."

14. Heidegger, "Letter on Humanism," 218.

15. As much as I appreciate Lévinas's argument, I do not entirely endorse the well-worn philosophical reading of Odysseus as a figure of ipseity, or of return to the same. I believe that the ambivalence internal to Odysseus's status as host already complicates this interpretation, pointing to the possibility of a dissimulating, disappearing, or duplicitous self unequal to its initial designation. In my view, Odysseus's status as host is qualified not only by his difference from and triumph over the "false" pretendants to his home, but by the distinction between two versions of Odysseus himself: the "true" suitor or figure of dialectical recovery, on the one hand, and on the other the disguised, covert figure who is himself a dissimulating guest, an impish trickster who roams the world unrecognized, who lies to the gods and delights at his wife's rusing nature, and who—in the famous encounter with Polyphemos—names himself "No one." Although I do not have space to pursue a more complete interpretation of *The Odyssey* here, I will argue in subsequent chapters that this fundamental division within the identity of the host is an essential feature of the hospitality act, which undercuts the dialectical recovery of identity traditionally ascribed to Odysseus.

16. Emmanuel Lévinas, "The Trace of the Other," in Mark C. Taylor, ed., *Deconstruction in Context* (Chicago: University of Chicago Press, 1986), 348; translation modified. For the unabridged original essay, see Lévinas, "La trace de l'autre," in *En découvrant l'existence avec Husserl et Heidegger* (Paris: Vrin, 1994), 190–91.

17. This heritage will be explored in detail in chapter 1, "Israel, Divine Hostess."

18. Derrida, *De l'hospitalité,* 29.

19. I am reminded of Jacques Derrida's argument that a gift is never truly generous or disinterested because of the reward that inevitably accompanies it: a return gift, gratitude, increased "credit" with the recipient, or even the self-satisfaction that attends the gesture of generosity.

Derrida, *Given Time: 1. Counterfeit Money,* trans. Peggy Kamuf (Chicago: University of Chicago Press, 1992), 13.

20. Georges Bataille coins this term to describe the total destruction, squandering, or exhaustion of goods in the potlatch (which may include the destruction, burial, or submersion of precious goods, the immolation of homes or of persons, or ritual sacrifice), which he understands as an anti-economy of pure loss. See Bataille, "The Gift of Rivalry: 'Potlatch,'" in *The Accursed Share,* trans. Robert Hurley (New York: Zone Books, 1991), 63–77.

21. Foucault, "Theatrum Philosophicum," 168.

22. Derrida, *De l'hospitalité,* 13–17.

23. Jacques Lacan, *The Four Fundamental Concepts of Psycho-Analysis,* ed. Jacques-Alain Miller, trans. Alan Sheridan (New York: W. W. Norton and Company, 1978), 44. Freud's statement appears at the end of one of the *New Introductory Lectures on Psychoanalysis,* "The Dissection of the Psychical Personality," in *The Standard Edition of the Complete Psychological Works of Sigmund Freud,* ed. and trans. James Strachey et al. (London: The Hogarth Press, 1952, 1974), 22:80.

24. Lacan, *The Four Fundamental Concepts,* 44–45.

25. This argument will be explored in detail in chapters 5 and 6.

26. Jacques Lacan, *The Seminar of Jacques Lacan Book VII: The Ethics of Psychoanalysis 1959–60,* ed. Jacques-Alain Miller, trans. Dennis Porter (New York: W. W. Norton and Company, 1992), 7.

27. Jacques Lacan, "The Mirror Stage as Formative of the *I* Function as Revealed in Psychoanalytic Experience," in *Écrits,* trans. Bruce Fink (New York: W. W. Norton and Company, 2002), 3–9.

28. Lévinas, *Totality and Infinity,* 155.

29. The formulation is Catherine Chalier's, from her essay "Ethics and the Feminine," in *Re-Reading Lévinas,* ed. Robert Bernasconi and Simon Critchley (Bloomington: Indiana University Press, 1991), 119. For Lévinas's argument, see the fourth chapter of *Difficile Liberté* (Paris: Albin Michel, 1963 and 1976).

30. Chalier, "Ethics and the Feminine," 126.

31. Emmanuel Lévinas, "Judaism and the Feminine Element," in *Judaism* 18, no. 1 (1969): 33; originally appeared in Lévinas, *Difficile liberté,* 55–66.

32. Chalier, "Ethics and the Feminine," 122.

33. The same could be said of Deleuze and Guattari's "becoming woman," understood as a step on the way to "becoming invisible," eroding the contours of the responsible self (*A Thousand Plateaus,* trans. Brian Massumi [Minneapolis: University of Minnesota Press, 1987]). Although their account is important to my own thinking about femininity

(and informs my reading of "becoming woman" in the work of Friedrich Nietzsche), I do not think it is adequate to account for the role that women play in the cultural practice of hospitality or for the specific psychological stakes of femininity.

34. In many ancient narratives, even when a woman appears to offer hospitality independently (like the Hebrew matriarch Rebecca or Odysseus's wife Penelope), she generally extends this offer in the name or in the interest of a male relative, the master of the home for whom she acts as a representative or emissary. In the cultures of the Mediterranean, the hostess is rarely understood as having the ability to offer hospitality "on her own," either legally or culturally, until relatively late in the Roman empire, when a new word is finally coined to designate the "hostess" as distinct from the host. The importance of these restrictions, which are structural as much as historical, will be discussed in detail in subsequent chapters.

35. Benveniste, "L'hospitalité," 91.

36. Marcel Mauss, "A category of the human mind: the notion of person; the notion of self," trans. W. D. Halls, in *The Category of the Person,* ed. Michael Carrithers et al. (Cambridge: Cambridge University Press, 1985), 8. Subsequent citations from the same text will be given as page numbers in parentheses.

37. Antoine Destutt de Tracy, *Traité de la volonté* (Paris: 1826), 17; my emphases.

38. "If it is possible that the idea of individuality and personality should exist in the manner we have said, in a being conceived to be endowed with sensibility without will, at least it is impossible it should produce there the idea of property such as we have it. For our idea of property is privative and exclusive: it imports the idea that the thing possessed appertains to a sensible being, and appertains to none but him, to the exclusion of all others. Now it cannot be that it exists thus in the head of a being which knows nothing but itself, which does not know that any other beings besides itself exist. If then we should suppose that this being knows its *self* with sufficient accuracy to distinguish it from its modes, and to regard its different modifications as attributes of this *self,* as things which this *self* possesses, this being would still not have completely our idea of *property.* For this it is necessary to have the idea of *personality* very completely, and such as we have just seen that we form it when we are susceptible of *passion* and of *action.* It is then proved that this idea of property is an effect, a production of our willing faculty. . . . If it be certain that the idea of property can arise only in a being endowed with will, it is equally certain that in such a being it arises necessarily and inevitably in all its plenitude; for as soon as this individual knows accurately itself, or its moral person, and its capacity to enjoy and to suffer, and to act

necessarily, it sees clearly also that this self is the exclusive proprietor of the body which it animates, of the organs which it moves, of all their passions and their actions; for all this finishes and commences with this self, exists but by it, is not moved but by its acts, and no other moral person can employ the same instruments nor be affected in the same manner by their effects. The idea of property and of exclusive property arises then necessarily in a sensible being from this alone, that it is susceptible of passion and action; and it rises in such a being because nature has endowed it with an inevitable and inalienable property, that of its individuality." Antoine Destutt de Tracy, *A Treatise on Political Economy*, ed. Thomas Jefferson (New York: Augustus M. Kelley Publishers, 1970), 46–47.

39. In particular, Rousseau's *Discourse on Inequality*.

40. De Tracy, *A Treatise on Political Economy*, 36.

41. Karl Marx and Friedrich Engels, *The German Ideology*, ed. C. J. Arthur (New York: International Publishers, 1995), 100.

42. Benveniste explains that *hostia*—which later becomes the name for the Christian "host" or eucharist—is a close derivative of *hostis* in its compensatory connotation, designating "the victim who serves to compensate the anger of the gods"("L'hospitalité," 93).

43. René Descartes, *Oeuvres philosophiques*, Tome II, ed. Ferdinand Alquié (Paris: Garnier Frères, 1967), 430–54.

44. Jean-François Lyotard, *The Hyphen: Between Judaism and Christianity*, trans. Pascale-Anne Brault and Michael Naas (Amherst: Humanity Books/Prometheus Books, 1999), 1–2; translation modified.

45. According to Lévi-Strauss, "Elementary structures of kinship are . . . those systems which prescribe marriage with a certain type of relative, or, alternatively, those which, while defining all members of the society as relatives, divide them into two categories, viz., possible spouses and prohibited spouses." *The Elementary Structures of Kinship*, trans. James Harle Bell and John Richard von Sturmer (Boston: Beacon Press, 1969), xxiii. In contrast, "complex structures" are those that define the circle of relatives, but leave the selection of spouses up to other mechanisms. But Lévi-Strauss cautions that the distinction is not a strict one, since there is always some choice in an elementary structure, just as there is always some limitation of choice in a complex structure. In stressing the mechanisms of "elementary" structures, Lévi-Strauss wants to show that they are not so much rendered obsolete by "complex" structures as obfuscated by an ideology of autonomy and free choice that is belied by the persistence of the gift logic, even in its most modern, apparently disinterested manifestations. On this point, see in particular pp. 58–65.

46. Claude Lévi-Strauss, *Structural Anthropology*, trans. Claire Jacobson and Brooke Schoepf (New York: Basic Books, 1963), 60.

47. Lévi-Strauss, *Elementary Structures*, 115.

48. Mauss, *The Gift,* 20. Subsequent citations from the same text will be given as page numbers in parentheses.

49. Sigmund Freud, "Psychoanalytic Notes Upon an Autobiographical Account of a Case of Paranoia (Dementia Paranoides)," in *The Standard Edition,* 12:9–82.

50. Willy Apollon, Danielle Bergeron, and Lucie Cantin, "The Treatment of Psychosis," trans. Tracy McNulty, in Stephen Friedlander and Kareen Malone, eds., *The Subject of Lacan: A Lacanian Reader for Psychologists* (Albany: State University of New York Press, 2000), 209–27.

51. Lacan, *The Ethics of Psychoanalysis,* chaps. 4–6.

52. Lévi-Strauss, *Elementary Structures,* 51.

53. Ibid., 65.

54. Lacan, *The Ethics of Psychoanalysis,* 70.

55. This logic will be explored more fully in chapter 6.

56. Though the incest prohibition is experienced as a limitation of the subject's desire, it actually works to support the subject by holding at bay the Thing that would "satisfy" desire only at the cost of effacing it. This is why Lacan will say of the law that "the distance between the subject and *das Ding* is the condition of speech" (*The Ethics of Psychoanalysis,* 69).

57. Shakespeare's late romance *The Winter's Tale* offers one of the most compelling dramatizations of this problem. It stages the punishment of a virtuous hostess by her jealous husband as a result of his fantasmatic imputation of crime, which hinges upon the question of sexual difference—specifically, the heterogeneity or difference that woman introduces into a reversible relation between men. The bond of "mutual affection" uniting King Leontes and his guest Polixenes is first splintered when Leontes interprets his wife Hermione's warm hospitality toward their guest as adulterous desire, thereby introducing rivalry and uncanny difference into what seemed to be a perfectly equal, reversible relation between host and guest. In her rich analysis of monotheism and idolatry in Shakespeare's play, Julia Reinhard Lupton reads Leontes's jealous imputation of adultery to his wife as structured by Yahweh's demand for monotheistic allegiance: "I the Lord thy God am a jealous God." See the chapter devoted to *The Winter's Tale* in Lupton's *Afterlives of the Saints: Hagiography and Secular Literature* (Stanford: Stanford University Press, 1996). Her reading has important implications for this study, since it suggests how "feminine" hospitality can be construed as a violation of God's jealousy and the privative personhood it guarantees. This possibility will be explored in detail in subsequent chapters.

58. The legends of both figures will be considered in chapter 1 as representing one pole of the extremely charged attitude toward the hostess in the Hebrew Bible.

59. Cf. 1 Corinthians 11:7: "For a man indeed ought not to cover his

head, forasmuch as he is the image and glory of God: but the woman is the glory of the man. For the man is not of the woman, but the woman of the man." (NRSV)

60. This possibility is richly exploited by Milton's *Paradise Lost*, which casts Eve's seduction by Satan as an overturning of the Pauline metaphor. See *Paradise Lost*, IV:299–953.

61. See in particular *The Ethics of Psychoanalysis*, chaps. 4–6 and 8. The relation of the "extime" to femininity will be developed in detail in the final chapter of this book, which is devoted to Lacan's late essays on feminine sexuality and ethics.

62. Sigmund Freud, *Civilization and Its Discontents*, in *The Standard Edition*, 21:57–146; see in particular chapter 5. In his commentary of this chapter, Lacan notes that for Freud the *Nebenmensch* designated what from a Christian perspective could only be understood as "the apotheosis of the neighbor," understood as the support for the imaginary unity of the ego. *The Ethics of Psychoanalysis*, 152.

63. Lacan, *The Ethics of Psychoanalysis*, 66–70.

1. Israel, Divine Hostess

1. Emmanuel Lévinas, *Totality and Infinity: An Essay on Exteriority*, trans. Alphonso Lingis (Pittsburgh: Duquesne University Press, 1969), 64.

2. Martin Buber, *Moses* (New York: Harper and Row, 1958), 126.

3. In his commentary of Genesis 12:8–9, which describes how Abraham "moved on" from his father's country, Robert Alter notes that "the Hebrew vocabulary in this sequence is meticulous in reflecting the procedures of nomadic life"; Abraham doesn't just leave the land of his fathers, he "pulls up his tent stakes"; moreover, "the verb for 'journey' in verse 9 also derives from another term for the pulling up of tent stakes, and the progressive form in which it is cast is a precise indication of movement through successive encampments." Robert Alter, *Genesis: Translation and Commentary* (New York: W. W. Norton and Company, 1996), 51n.

4. In the families of the patriarchs, the failure of natural sexuality is practically synonymous with divine election: the barrenness of Sarah, Rebekah, and Rachel, redeemed through God's promise, marks the supplanting of natural reproduction by the procreative potential of the divine signifier.

5. Although Abraham seems to address one man alone as "Lord," his address is secular and does not necessarily imply the identification of a single actor behind the plurality of persons. According to Rashi, "The Hebrew for 'my lord' is *Adonai* (literally, 'my lords,' plural). Abraham addressed himself to the chief among them, though he called them all 'my lords.' To their chief he said, 'Do not go away from your servant,'

meaning that if he would remain the others would also stay with him. According to this translation, the meaning of the word *Adonai* is secular here." Rashi, *Commentaries on the Pentateuch,* ed. and trans. Chaim Pearl (New York: W. W. Norton and Company, 1970), 45.

6. Jean-François Lyotard, *Un trait d'union* (Quebec: Le Griffon d'argile, 1994), 18. Translated as *The Hyphen: Between Judaism and Christianity,* trans. Pascale-Anne Brault and Michael Naas (Amherst: Humanity Books/Prometheus Books, 1999), 8.

7. Robert Alter, *The Art of Biblical Narrative* (New York: Basic Books, 1981), 30.

8. Ibid., 31.

9. Ibid., 32.

10. Sharon Pace Jeansonne offers a similar reading of the episode, suggesting that Sarah's laughter is, if not the projection or externalization of her husband's doubt, then at least a narrative underscoring of its magnitude. She offers a further insight into the logic of the episode by noting the extent to which Abraham himself contributes to Sarah's state of unknowing. According to Jeansonne, "It is most striking that although God reveals to Abraham that Sarah will have a child, Abraham refuses to believe it. . . . The narrator casts doubt on Abraham's willingness to accept God's messages by describing his response from his own perspective. Abraham has a direct revelation wherein he hears of Sarah's name change and is told twice of her role as ancestress. Nonetheless, Abraham falls to the ground in order to laugh to himself and expressly question his ability and that of the aged Sarah to have a child. Although he does not repeat his doubts aloud to God, he dares to propose an alternative, asking God to allow Ishmael to be the inheritor of the covenant. God refuses and adds specific information to the revelation that a son will be born to Sarah. . . . When this revelation is completed, Abraham circumcizes the men of his household, as he is commanded, but at this point the narrator introduces an important gap. Abraham does not inform Sarah of God's promise that they will have a child. Indeed, the narrator closes the gap in the next scene when it will become clear that Sarah first learns of the promise only when she overhears another conversation between God's messengers and Abraham. Esther Fuchs argues that because the revelation of the change of Sarai's name was given to Abraham instead of to Sarah herself, Sarah is shown to be in a subordinate position. However, the narrator uses the revelation to Abraham to develop a crucial aspect of the story. The narrator underscores Abraham's questioning and doubting by revealing his questioning of God about the wisdom of God's plan. By withholding this information from Sarah, Abraham's continuing doubt is underscored, whereas Sarah cannot be expected to anticipate God's words about her

upcoming role." Sharon Pace Jeansonne, *The Women of Genesis* (Minneapolis: Fortress Press, 1990), 21–22.

11. Jeansonne offers support for this interpretation when she notes that Abraham is made to answer for Sarah's laughter, which both suggests that her action is a reflection upon him and at the same time distances it from him, since the doubting laughter is attributed to a dependent for whom Abraham is responsible rather than to his own belief or lack thereof. She writes: "God continues to address Abraham concerning Sarah and demands that he account for Sarah's laughter. Sarah dramatically interrupts, making her presence known and feebly attempting to protect Abraham. Sarah, who has not been addressed by God, claims that she did not laugh. The narrator does not judge Sarah harshly for this deception, but relates, from the omniscient viewpoint, that she acted 'because she was afraid' (18:15)" (Ibid., 24). By assuming responsibility for her laughter, Sarah deflects attention away from Abraham's doubts.

12. The scriptural support for Augustine's interpretation is Paul's famous interpretation of Isaac's birth as figuring the Christians' unique status as "children of the free woman," released from enslavement to the law: "Tell me, you who desire to be under law, do you not hear the law? For it is written that Abraham had two sons, one by a slave and one by a free woman. But the son of the slave was born according to the flesh, the son of the free woman through promise. Now this is an allegory: these women are two covenants. One is from Mount Sinai in Arabia; she corresponds to the present Jerusalem, for she is in slavery with her children. But the Jerusalem above is free, and she is our mother. For it is written, 'Rejoice, O barren one that dost not bear; break forth and shout, thou who art not in travail; for the desolate hath more children than she who hath a husband.' Now we, brethren, like Isaac, are children of promise. But as at that time he who was born according to the flesh persecuted him who was born according to the Spirit, so it is now. But what does the scripture say? 'Cast out the slave and her son; for the son of the slave shall not inherit with the son of the free woman.' So, brethren, we are not children of the slave, but of the free woman." (Galatians 4:21–31).

13. Augustine, *City of God*, trans. Henry Bettenson (London: Penguin Books, 1972, 1984), 15:3, 599.

14. Lambros Kamperidis, "Philoxenia and Hospitality," in *Parabola* 15, no. 4 (1990): 5.

15. Ibid., 7.

16. This principle is the cornerstone of apostolic hospitality, as expressed in Jesus's words to his disciples: "Whoever welcomes this child in my name welcomes me, and whoever welcomes me welcomes the one who sent me; for the least among all of you is the greatest" (Luke 9:48; see also Matthew 18:5, Mark 9:37, and John 13:20).

17. Robert Alter notes that this echo is especially strong in the Hebrew text. In Genesis 17:17 (. . . and he laughed), the verb of laughter, yitshaq, is identical to the Hebrew form of Isaac's name; the same verb appears in a slightly modified form, tsahaq, in 18:15 (I did not laugh . . . Yes, you did laugh), foregrounding the laughter in Isaac's name. Alter, Genesis: Translation and Commentary, 75n, 79n.

18. Many commentators read Sarah's laughter as a simple expression of delight, citing as support her remarks following the birth of Isaac: "God has brought laughter for me; everyone who hears will laugh with me" (Genesis 21:6). However, this view is at odds with God's response in 18:15, and inconsistent with other uses of the same verb in Genesis. In Genesis 19, the same verb is used when Lot, urging his family to leave Sodom, "seemed to be joking to his sons-in-law" (19:14); Robert Alter observes that "the verb, though in a different conjugation, is the same as the one used for Sarah's and Abraham's 'laughter.' It is, of course, a wry echo—the laughter of disbelief of those about to be divinely blessed, the false perception of mocking laughter by those about to be destroyed. The common denominator in the antithetical usages is *skepticism about divine intentions*, for good and for evil" (*Genesis: Translation and Commentary*, 87n; my emphases).

19. Lyotard, Un trait d'union, 17; idem, The Hyphen, 10.

20. See The Interpreter's Bible in Twelve Volumes: Introduction, Exegesis, Exposition for Each Book of the Bible (New York: Abingdon Press, 1952), 1: 629–30, as well as The Book of J, trans. David Rosenberg, interpreted by Harold Bloom (New York: Grove Weidenfeld, 1990), 87.

21. See John H. Otwell, And Sarah Laughed: The Status of Woman in the Old Testament (Philadelphia: Westminster Press, 1977), 67–87.

22. Émile Benveniste, "L'hospitalité," in Le vocabulaire des institutions indo-européennes, vol. 1 (Paris: Éditions de Minuit, 1969), 88.

23. See in particular Lacan, The Seminar of Jacques Lacan Book VII: The Ethics of Psychoanalysis 1959–60, ed. Jacques-Alain Miller, trans. Dennis Porter (New York: W. W. Norton and Company, 1992), chaps. 4–5.

24. Ibid., see chapter 8.

25. Erich Auerbach, "Odysseus' Scar," in Mimesis, trans. William R. Trask (Princeton: Princeton University Press, 1968), 12.

26. Otwell, And Sarah Laughed.

27. The Interpreter's Bible, 1:632. Calum Carmichael offers a different interpretation of the same event, according to which the incestuous act of Lot's daughters is retribution for his attempt to preserve his own safety by treating his daughters as harlots to be abused by other men. He writes: "Given the consistent pattern in the Genesis material of deeds meeting with exact retribution, this interpretation of Lot's seduction would fit

into it. The episode would therefore stand as a sequel to the preceding material about it. [. . .] Ordinarily, men of the depraved mob mentality of Sodom can be expected to respond with alacrity to the offer of two women. These men, however, are different in that they only respond sexually to men. When we turn to the initiative of Lot's daughters in seducing their father we observe that their desire was the natural one of seeking sexual relations with other men, but their situation was such that they ended up having unnatural union with their father, a deed that ordinarily would be wholly repugnant. The homosexual lust of the Sodomites led to Lot's decision to exploit his daughters, who are passive in this situation. The affliction of blindness, however, prevents the Sodomites from gratifying their homosexuality. Their lust being rendered inactive is, in a way, made to fit the girls' passivity. By contrast, Lot's daughters initiate the action with their father. Moreover, they complete it because having made him drunk he becomes an instrument to be used by them. Drunkenness and blindness are often viewed as interrelated. Here there is a link between one and the other in that it is blindness that prevents unnatural sexual activity taking place in one situation and drunkenness that enables it to happen in another." *Women, Law, and the Genesis Traditions* (Edinburgh: Edinburgh University Press, 1979), 55–56. While I do not dispute Carmichael's interpretation, I think it is important to consider that the text of the Genesis passage never directly indicts Lot's behavior or marks it as requiring retribution, but rather allows the father's activity in the first instance—an activity that the Deuteronomist, according to Carmichael, finds perverse and abhorrent (54)—to be manifested externally through its inverted reflection in the perverse activity of the two daughters. Through the inverted symmetry of the two passages, then, the daughters are made to "embody"—in this case quite literally—an aspect of their father's personality that is inconsistent with his status as one of YHWH's chosen.

28. *The Interpreter's Bible,* 1:632.

29. Augustine, *City of God,* 15:16, 623.

30. Franz Rosenzweig, *The Star of Redemption,* trans. William W. Hallo (Notre Dame: University of Notre Dame Press, 1985), 300.

31. "Stranger," *New Strong's Exhaustive Concordance of the Bible* (Nashville: Thomas Nelson Publishers, 1990); see also Kenneth Reinhard, "Freud, My Neighbor," *American Imago* 54, no. 2 (Summer 1997): 171.

32. "Stranger."

33. Chapter XVIII, folio 127a of Tractate Shabbath, Mo'ed II, *The Babylonian Talmud,* trans. and ed. Rabbi Dr. I Epstein (London: The Soncino Press, 1938), 632. Emphases and brackets in the original.

34. In numerous biblical passages, stranger worship is intimately related to adulterous prostitution, as an infidelity to the symbolic rights of

the husband: "The LORD said to Moses, 'Soon you will lie down with your ancestors. Then this people will begin to prostitute themselves to the foreign gods *[zhn 'hry 'lhy nkr-h'rs]* in their midst, the gods of the land into which they are going; they will forsake me, breaking my covenant that I have made with them'" (Deuteronomy 31:16). The verb *znh* and related abstract nouns describe illicit sexual activity by a woman. But when followed by the preposition *'hry, znh* also designates the worship of gods other than YHWH. What the root implies is that in each case, "the offender has transferred the exclusive rights of the one in authority . . . to a second, competing party"—in the first case the husband or father is forsaken for a lover, in the second YHWH is abandoned for a foreign god. Julie Galambush, *Jerusalem in the Book of Ezekiel: The City as Yahweh's Wife* (Atlanta: Scholar's Press, 1992), 27–31.

35. Gilles Deleuze and Félix Guattari, "1227: Treatise on Nomadology—The War Machine," in *A Thousand Plateaus,* trans. Brian Massumi (Minneapolis: University of Minnesota Press, 1987), 351–423.

36. Ibid., xii, 369–73, 380–81.

37. Sharon Pace Jeansonne suggests that the language of the Abraham hospitality narrative can even be read as anticipating the difficult conditions of the exile in and exodus from Egypt: "Abraham speaks to Sarah in impassioned, abbreviated speech: 'Hurry! Three measures of choice flour! Knead and make cakes!' (18:6). By employing language that foreshadows the hasty flight of the Israelites from Egypt, the narrator suggests that another dramatic development in the history of the Israelite people is at hand." *The Women of Genesis,* 22.

38. Jacques Derrida with Anne Dufourmantelle, *De l'hospitalité* (Paris: Calmann-Lévy, 1997), 29.

39. This passage resonates with an earlier one from the eighth-century prophet Isaiah, who also compares the destruction wrought by receiving strangers to the annihilation of Sodom and Gomorrah (Isaiah 1:7–9).

40. Galambush, *Jerusalem in the Book of Ezekiel,* 95.

41. Julie Galambush suggests that this analogy, although it is richly exploited by Ezekiel, is not unique to him: "Mishnah describes women's sexual organs in architectural terms: within the woman are 'a chamber, an ante-chamber, and an upper room: blood in the chamber is unclean; if it is found in the ante-chamber, . . . it is deemed unclean, since it is presumed to be from the fountain' (*The Mishnah,* ed. H. Danby [Oxford: Oxford University Press, 1933] *Nid.* 2:5). Curiously, the Mishnaic tractate on purity and impurity is named 'Oholoth,' "tents.'" *Jerusalem in the Book of Israel,* 111.

42. Like Oholibah, Sarah is both a tent-dweller who offers hospitality and a hospitable tent. The three references to Sarah in the hospitality episode all occur in relation to the *ohel,* in a way that identifies the tent with

her person: Abraham goes "into the tent unto Sarah" to announce the arrival of their guests, and before the angels unveil the miracle of Isaac's birth they ask Abraham "Where is Sarah thy wife?" to which he answers, "Behold, in the tent." Sarah in turn "heard it [the blessing] in the tent door" (Genesis 18:6–10). The *ohel* seems to function as a symbol both of her barrenness and of her miraculous conception, the tent that is able to receive only by the grace of God.

43. Iconographically, this revisionist interpretation is often literalized in the replacement of Abraham's nomadic and permeable tent with a very solid—or even fortress-like—dwelling, replete with heavy doors and small, high windows. If Sarah is represented at all, she is often pictured looking out of a tiny window rather than standing in the doorway, a revision that both insists upon the inviolable sanctity of her hidden body and exempts her from participation in the hospitable offering. Louis Réau, *Iconographie de l'art chrétien,* Tome II, Volume I: *Ancien Testament* (Paris: Presses Universitaires de France, 1956), 131–32.

44. Anita Diamant, *The New Jewish Wedding* (New York: Simon and Schuster, 1985), 91.

2. Cosmopolitan Hospitality and Secular Ethics

1. Jacques Derrida with Anne Dufourmantelle, *De l'hospitalité* (Paris: Calmann-Lévy, 1997), 29.

2. See the second half of chapter 1.

3. Immanuel Kant, "To Perpetual Peace: A Philosophical Sketch," in *Perpetual Peace and Other Essays,* trans. Ted Humphrey (Indianapolis: Hackett, 1983), 118. Subsequent citations from the same text will be given as page numbers in parentheses. For clarification I have also included certain expressions from the German text, collected in Kant's *Schriften zur Anthropologie, Geschichtsphilosophie, Politik une Pädagogik I,* Werkausgabe Band XI (Frankfurt: Suhrkamp Verlag, 1977), 195–251.

4. Émile Benveniste, "L'hospitalité," in *Le vocabulaire des institutions indo-européennes,* vol. 1 (Paris: Éditions de Minuit, 1969), 92–93.

5. Ibid., 95.

6. René Schérer, *Zeus Hospitalier: Éloge de l'hospitalité* (Paris: Armand Colin, 1993), 53.

7. And as the implication of Christianity in global colonization demonstrates, the Christian doctrine of "brotherly love" does not provide an adequate moral basis for cosmopolitan community, especially when it lends itself so easily to un-Christian abuses. This connection will be explored more fully in the second part of this chapter (see "European Nihilism: From Kant to Nietzsche").

8. In his amusing biographical study, E. A. Wasianski, the philosopher's former disciple and secretary, suggests that Kant's own relation to

hospitality was marked by an aversion to intimate contacts. Although he was a regular at "host's tables" all his life, he began to entertain only in his late years, and then with considerable reluctance. See "The Last Days of Immanuel Kant," in *Kant Intime,* ed. and trans. Jean Mistler (Paris: Grasset, 1985), 63.

9. Schérer, *Zeus Hospitalier,* 43–44.

10. Kant, "Idea for a Universal History with a Cosmopolitan Intent," fourth thesis, in *Perpetual Peace and Other Essays,* 31–32 (emphases in original).

11. Schérer, *Zeus Hospitalier,* 48.

12. See in particular Proudhon, *What Is Property?* trans. Benjamin R. Tucker (London: The Bellamy Library, undated).

13. Schérer, *Zeus Hospitalier,* 53.

14. See "Property and Personhood" in my introduction.

15. Jean-François Lyotard, *Un trait d'union* (Québec: Le Griffon d'argile, 1994), 11; translated as *The Hyphen: Between Judaism and Christianity,* trans. Pascale-Anne Brault and Michael Naas (Amherst: Humanity Books/Prometheus Books, 1999), 6. Subsequent citations from the same text will be given as page numbers in parentheses, preceded by an "F" for the French edition and an "E" for the English translation.

16. Juliet Flower MacCannell, *The Regime of the Brother* (London: Routledge, 1991), 31. Subsequent citations from the same text will be given as page numbers in parentheses.

17. Freud, "Thoughts for the Times on War and Death," in *The Standard Edition of the Complete Psychological Works of Sigmund Freud,* ed. and trans. James Strachey et al. (London: The Hogarth Press, 1952, 1974), 14:273–300.

18. Mladen Dolar, "Théorie du discours fasciste," in *Analytica* 33 (1983): 41–54 (my translation, from Dolar's French), 43.

19. Ibid., 43 (my translation).

20. Emmanuel Lévinas, *Totality and Infinity: An Essay on Exteriority,* trans. Alphonso Lingis (Pittsburgh: Duquesne University Press, 1969), 64.

21. See Sigmund Freud, *Civilization and Its Discontents,* in *The Standard Edition,* 21:57–146.

22. For an in-depth treatment of this fascinating and complicated history, see l'Abbé de Vertot's seventeenth-century study, *The History of the Knights Hospitallers of St. John of Jerusalem* (New York: AMS Press, 1981), as well as Ernle Bradford's *Shield and the Sword: The Knights of St. John, Jerusalem, Rhodes and Malta* (New York: E. P. Dutton and Co., Inc., 1973).

23. Friedrich Nietzsche, *The Antichrist,* trans. R. J. Hollingdale (New York: Penguin, 1968), 10, 121.

24. Gilles Deleuze, *Nietzsche and Philosophy*, trans. Hugh Tomlinson (New York: Columbia University Press, 1983), 93.

25. Lyotard, *Un trait d'union*, 7–15; idem, *The Hyphen*, 3–9.

26. Pierre Klossowski, "Nietzsche, le polythéisme et la parodie," in *Un si funeste désir* (Paris: Gallimard, 1963), 220. This interpretation will be developed more fully in chapter 4.

27. Deleuze, *Nietzsche and Philosophy*, 88.

28. Friedrich Nietzsche, *The Will to Power*, ed. Walter Kaufmann (New York: Vintage Books, 1968), 7. The fragment in question opens the first paragraph of Book I, "On European Nihilism."

29. Friedrich Nietzsche, *Thus Spoke Zarathustra*, trans. R. J. Hollingdale (London: Penguin Classics, 1969), 87.

30. Of Derrida's works, see in particular *Aporias*, trans. Thomas Dutoit (Stanford: Stanford University Press, 1993); *On the Name*, ed. Thomas Dutoit , trans. David Wood, John P. Leavey, Jr., and Ian McLeod (Stanford: Stanford University Press, 1995); and *Adieu: À Emmanuel Lévinas* (Paris: Galilée, 1997).

31. Gilles Deleuze, *Logic of Sense*, trans. Mark Lester with Charles Stivale (New York: Columbia University Press, 1990), 281.

3. Under the Sign of the Hostess

1. My understanding of perversion as a logic of "demonstration" is borrowed from Willy Apollon, who in a series of recent articles and seminars has argued that the logic of perversion—as one of the three subjective structures for psychoanalysis—consists in the methodical demonstration of what he calls *l'Infondé*, the fact that the signifier is not founded in the real and therefore cannot serve as a legitimate guarantor of law. Although this specific formulation was developed in Apollon's annual training seminar in Quebec, under the auspices of the École freudienne de Québec, he makes a similar argument in his analysis of the writings of the Marquis de Sade, "Psychanalyse et literature: Passe et impasse," in *L'Universel, perspectives psychanalytiques* (Quebec: Gifric, 1997), 243–65.

2. See the chapter "Why Is Woman a Symptom of Rights?" in Salecl, *The Spoils of Freedom* (London: Routledge, 1994), 112–33.

3. Klossowski, *"Roberte Ce Soir" and "The Revocation of the Edict of Nantes,"* trans. Austryn Wainhouse (London: Marion Boyars, 1989), 141. Subsequent citations from the same text will be given as page numbers in parentheses. Where appropriate, I have also provided page references to the original French text, *Les lois de l'hospitalité* (Paris: Gallimard, 1965). Where both the English and French texts are cited, their respective page numbers are prefaced with "E" or "F."

4. That is, the identification of the Whore of Babylon in Revelation with the Roman Catholic Church.

5. "The disjunction is always a disjunction; the 'either-or' never ceases to be an 'either-or.' Rather than signifying that a certain number of predicates are excluded from a thing in virtue of the identity of the corresponding concept, the disjunction now signifies that each thing is opened up to the infinity of predicates through which it passes, on the condition that it lose its identity as concept and as self." Gilles Deleuze, "Klossowski or Bodies-Language," in *Logic of Sense,* trans. Mark Lester with Charles Stivale (New York: Columbia University Press, 1990), 296.

6. Michel Foucault, "The Prose of Acteon," in Pierre Klossowski, *The Baphomet,* trans. Sophie Hawkes (Hygiene, Colorado: Eridanos Press, 1988), xxx.

7. The structural features of Roberte's narrative—the stranger/woman who violates the sanctity of the tabernacle or house of God, but who is herself also a hostess who receives strangers—are almost identical to those of Ezekiel 23, as analyzed in my reading of Israel-as-hostess in chapter 1.

8. The French *renverser* connotes a more radical subversion than the mere "knocking over" of a physical object, implying the overturning, upsetting, or subversion of one thing by another.

9. In a very suggestive reading of the preface to Klossowski's translation of Johann-Georg Hamann's *Biblical Meditations* (Klossowski, *Les méditations bibliques de Hamann* [Paris: Éditions de Minuit, 1948]), Jeffrey Mehlman suggests that the motif of "sisterhood" in *The Laws of Hospitality* is in part an allusion to Hamann's troubled relationship to hospitality. As a young man Hamann enjoyed the generous hospitality of the Berens family of Riga, which he then alienated by declaring his intention to marry the sister of the Berens family, causing himself to be expelled from the house. Not incidentally, the mediator in the dispute was the Berens's Koenigsberg associate Immanuel Kant, upon whom the surly and ill-mannered Hamann unleashed all "the fury of the parasite expelled" when the former became the object of the mature Hamann's radical Lutheran attacks against Enlightenment thought. In this episode, as well as in a similar one that occurred some years later, hospitality between men is interrupted by a "sisterly" presence, which proves disastrous to the repressed homosociality of the relationship between benefactor and protégé. Mehlman observes that "Klossowski's laws of hospitality, which entail a yielding of the woman of the house to the exemplary guest, read like an exacerbated fulfillment of the fantasy informing the scandal joining (asunder) Hamann and Berens." Mehlman, "Literature and Hospitality: Klossowski's Hamann," *Studies in Romanticism* 22, no. 2 (Summer 1983): 34, 337.

10. Nietzsche's letter of January 14, 1880, to Malwyda von Meysen-

bug, cited by Klossowski in *Nietzsche et le cercle vicieux* (Paris: Mercure de France, 1969), 43.

11. Ronald Hayman, *Nietzsche: A Critical Life* (London: Weidenfeld and Nicolson, 1980), 193.

12. Ibid.

13. Ibid., 244.

14. Ibid., 245.

15. In a disputed late text, Nietzsche writes that he was the unwilling object of his sister's precocious sexual games. *My Sister and I*, trans. Oscar Levy (Los Angeles: Amok Books, 1990), 6ff. Although there is no independent evidence that an incestuous relationship was ever consummated between Nietzsche and his sister, both of them described their devotion to one another as a passion greater than the love between two siblings. Walter Kaufmann writes of Nietzsche's relationship with Elisabeth: "It is conceivable that his passionate love of her as a boy had something to do with his later remark: 'To Byron's Manfred I must be profoundly related: I found all these abysses in myself—at thirteen, I was ripe for this work' (*Ecce Homo* II:4)." Walter Kaufmann, *Nietzsche: Philosopher, Psychologist, Antichrist* (Princeton: Princeton University Press, 1974), 42. Hayman's biography stops short of attributing to Nietzsche any inappropriate feelings for his sister, suggesting that it was Elisabeth who was infatuated with her brother—and who turned down numerous marriage proposals as a result—without ever implying that her feelings were reciprocated. Hayman, *Nietzsche*, 52, 180.

16. Letter of May 1884. Hayman, *Nietzsche*, 273.

17. Letter of November 1882. Ibid., 254.

18. Letter of September 1882. Ibid., 251.

19. Ronald Hayman notes that the Wagners in particular objected to Nietzsche's friendship with Rée (191), and gives the following account of his friends' reactions to the publication of *Menschliches, Allzumenschliches*: "For Rée, who said that he threw himself on it like a beast of prey, it was the 'book of books'; for [Erwin] Rohde it was full of unpleasant surprises. 'Is it possible to divest oneself so completely of one's soul and substitute another? Suddenly to become Rée instead of Nietzsche?' [Franz] Overbeck was surprised at Nietzsche's *volte-face*, and for Cosima [Wagner], who claimed to have read little of the book, it represented the culmination of a process she had long been trying to resist. 'Finally Israel intervened in the form of a Dr. Rée, very sleek, very cool, at the same time as being wrapped up in Nietzsche and dominated by him, though actually outwitting him—the relationship between Judaea and Germany in miniature.'" Ibid., 204.

20. Letter of June 1878. Ibid., 204.

21. The relationship between health and sanity is obviously a very problematic one where the reception of Nietzsche's work is concerned, and is not confined to the repudiation of Judaism as an unhealthy influence; many of Nietzsche's readers have historically sought to diminish the impact of his work by speculating that some of his key works—including *Zarathustra* and *The Gay Science*—were the works of a madman, already influenced by the insanity that would later claim him altogether. To a lesser degree, the same calculation is at work in the Roberte–von A. relationship as well. At the scene of their first encounter, when von A. reveals his secret mission to her, Roberte tries to diminish the importance of his strange story by pretending he is hallucinating and telling him to go "sleepy-bye" (198), a technique she learned from her moralistic supervisor Louise. Although Roberte will eventually overcome her initial reaction, it points to one of the limitations of "nursing" as a way of relating to the other, since it rejects the contamination implicit in a hospitable reception of the foreign in favor of a reductive insistence upon "health."

22. Interestingly, both kinds of "degeneracy" are also suggested by the Latin homonym of Malwyda's name, *mal vita,* meaning "sick life."

23. Kaufmann, *Nietzsche,* 26.

24. Ibid., 39. See also the selections from Nietzsche's works and letters on the theme of the "Good European" compiled in David Farrell Krell and Donald L. Bates, *The Good European: Nietzsche's Work Sites in Word and Image* (Chicago: University of Chicago Press, 1997).

25. Note that this was precisely Nietzsche's criticism of his sister Elisabeth: that she opposed a moralizing resistance to his ideas, and one that ultimately sheltered anti-Semitism. Although Roberte's is a good, liberal, Western morality that is friendly to the cause of Jewish children, it is nonetheless still susceptible at this point to making incorrect judgments based on superficial information.

26. Roman "hospitality" is now itself called into question, on two levels: first for the inhospitable treatment of free thinkers by the papacy, and second for Rome's "entertaining" of Nazism: its occupying troops, most obviously, but ultimately also its ideology and its hostile attitude toward the stranger. In the first case Rome is accused of not being hospitable *enough* (to free thinking), in the second of entertaining something interested and economic under the guise of charity. This relationship suggests something duplicitous about the hospitality itself, insofar as Rome—the capital not only of the Catholic Church but also of fascist Italy—has "welcomed" fascism into its bosom, revealing itself to be hospitable to a political program whose tenets contradict the articles of the Christian faith. In other words, it has offered its own ethics—and with it the stranger it pretends to nurture—for sale.

27. "All these simulacra-figures pivot in place: rakes become inquisi-

tors, seminarians become Nazi officers, the confused persecutors of Theodore Lacase find themselves in a friendly semicircle around the bed of K. These sudden twists only come about by means of the play of 'alternators' of experience. These alternators are, in Klossowski's novels, the sole peripeties but in the literal sense of the word: that which ensures the detour and return. Thus: the test-provocation (the stone of truth which is at the same time the temptation of the worst: the fresco of the *Vocation*, or the sacrilegious task assigned by von A.); the specious inquisition (censors who present themselves as former rakes, like Malagrida or the psychiatrist with dubious intentions); the two-sided conspiracy (the 'resistance' network which executes Dr. Rodin). But most of all the two great configurations which cause appearance to alternate are hospitality and the theatre: two structures which stand face to face with each other in reverse symmetry" (Foucault, "The Prose of Acteon," xxx). I will return to the significance of the relationship between hospitality and theater in Klossowski's trilogy in the next chapter (see "The Fantasy of the Unique Sign"), which concerns the novel *Le Souffleur*.

28. Roberte's "transvaluation" of charity will thus turn upon the difference between two kinds of "collaboration": Nazi collaboration within the church (wherein the Christ-like gesture of "turning the other cheek" begins to meld with the collaborative stance of "looking the other way"), and the "neutral" Roberte's collaboration with opposing sides. Both types of collaboration happen under the cover of "charity": in one case cynically (the priest who profits from war victims), in the other out of adherence to a principle of hospitality that suspends all laws, subverting symbolic determinations. The first collaboration, which is political in nature, happens under the sign of identity, whether national, religious, or personal. We see it in Roberte's account of the atmosphere at the cocktail parties held in "neutral diplomatic circles" in Rome during the last air raids: "A good many people, not only Italians and Germans but also of Balkan origin and naturally some stray Englishmen and Frenchmen too, would try to crash our [the Red Cross and other neutral forces] get-togethers, eager to draw a smoke screen over the undefinable functions they had exercized under the regime of oppression, and would angle for odd jobs, anything that would look well on their record in case the Anglo-American police subsequently got on their trail" (194–95). The second kind of "collaboration," on the contrary, effects or results from the dissolution of identity.

29. The term is again Foucault's, from his eloquent articulation of the aporias internal to the identity of the host: "The host (a word which in French—*hôte*—already whirls about its interior axis, meaning both the thing and its complement, host and guest), the host offers what he possesses, for he can only possess what he proposes—which is there before his eyes and is for everyone." "The Prose of Acteon," xxxi.

30. Mehlman, "Literature and Hospitality," 340. Of Hamann's predilection for Judaism, Klossowski writes: "The very choice of this most refractory and most opinionated of all races—but at the same time one of the most mistreated and despised among the peoples of Antiquity, as well as the most humble, before it incarnated itself in one of its sons—this mad choice constitutes the scandal of reason and of science, of the philosophers and the Jews." *Les méditations bibliques de Hamann* (Paris: Éditions de Minuit, 1948), 18. My translation.

31. Mehlman, "Literature and Hospitality," 340.

32. Ibid., 345.

33. Along with Georges Bataille and the other members of the Collège de Sociologie, Klossowski was one of the earliest critics in France of the Nazi appropriation of Nietzsche's philosophy. In 1937 the journal *Acéphale*, published by Bataille, Klossowski, and Georges Ambrosino, produced a special issue entitled "Réparation à Nietzsche," which denounced Elisabeth Förster-Nietzsche's warm reception of Hitler at the Nietzsche-Archiv and outlined the group's counter-interpretation of Nietzsche's work, which would later be elaborated by Klossowski in a number of articles (most notably, "Nietzsche, le polythéisme et la parodie" [in *Un si funeste désir* (Paris: Gallimard, 1963)] and "Circulus vitiosus" [in *Nietzsche aujourd'hui?* 2 vols. (Paris: Union Générale d'Éditions, 10/18, 1973), 2:91–121]) and in the book-length study *Nietzsche and the Vicious Circle* (trans. Daniel W. Smith [Chicago: University of Chicago Press, 1997]). This interpretation will be discussed in more detail in chapter 4.

34. This opposition suggests another possible interpretation of Roberte's "overturning" of the host. In disclosing the Jewish letters within the Christian tabernacle, she also inverts the hospitality relationship according to which the Christian interpretation of the Bible has traditionally structured itself. Rather than the Old Testament "hosting" the New Testament, disclosing the revelatory "spirit" of Christ, here it is the Christian tabernacle that "hosts" the Jewish letter, which thereby overturns the Christian meaning imposed upon it. Instead of the Old Testament "hosting" Christ, Christ the Host is displaced by an inscrutable guest.

35. In other words, the future site of the Nazi War Crimes Tribunal—a detail that further complicates the already undecidable relationship between Nazism and Catholicism in the novel.

36. "Of the Apostates" is also the name of the chapter in *Thus Spoke Zarathustra* in which Nietzsche introduces the notion of a diffuse polytheism as the logical consequence of the death of the one God: "Is not precisely this godliness, that there are gods but no God?" *Thus Spoke Zarathustra*, trans. R. J. Hollingdale (London: Penguin Books, 1969), 201.

37. For a succinct treatment of the place of different iconographic models in the development of trinitarian art, see Louis Réau, *Iconographie de l'art chrétien,* Tome II, Volume I (Paris: Presses Universitaires de France, 1956), 14–28.

38. The sexual and theological importance of "jealousy" to Klossowski's vision of hospitality will be developed in chapter 4.

39. Deleuze, *Logic of Sense,* 282.

40. See Bernard Dupriez, *A Dictionary of Literary Devices,* trans. Albert W. Halsall (Toronto: Toronto University Press, 1991), 424–25.

41. *Institutio Oratoria* I.v.36. *Institution Oratoire,* Tome I, trans. Jean Cousin (Paris: Belles Lettres, 1975), 96; cited by Octave in his first entry from *The Revocation of the Edict of Nantes,* 97.

42. This logic will be developed more fully in chapter 4, which deals with Octave's articulation of the "laws of hospitality" in *Roberte Ce Soir.*

43. Deleuze, *Logic of Sense,* 290; translation modified.

44. Klossowski's manipulation of the Augustinian doctrine of "affection" is discussed in the following chapter.

45. Augustine, *The City of God,* trans. Marcus Dods, D.D. (New York: The Modern Library, 1950), 1:19, 23.

46. See Book X of Augustine's *Confessions,* trans. W. Watts (Cambridge: Harvard University Press, 1912), 1988.

47. This argument will be developed in the first part of chapter 4.

48. This offense or impropriety—and the solecism-like form in which it manifests itself—is evident in the way that Roberte describes herself and conceives of her mission in Rome; earlier we saw how Roberte adapts the language of the gospel to justify her complicity with opposing sides, appropriating Christ's words on the cross and modeling them to her own ends.

49. Augustine, *City of God,* 1:16, 47.

50. In his preface to the tract, Bentley Layton writes: "In Gnostic myth the role of afterthought—also known as "life" *(Zoe),* the female instructing principle, and the holy spirit—is to assist both Adam and all humankind, in order to recollect the power stolen by Ialdabaoth and now dispersed in the Gnostic race. She is immanent in all Gnostics who have the holy spirit." *The Gnostic Scriptures,* trans. Bentley Layton (New York: Doubleday, 1987), 77.

51. "The Thunder—Perfect Intellect," 14:9–14; *The Gnostic Scriptures,* 80.

52. For a historical account of the ascendancy and influence of the Valentinian school, and of Valentinus's rivalry with Tertullian, see Kurt Rudolph, *Gnosis: The Nature and History of Gnosticism* (San Francisco: Harper, 1987), 317–23. Tertullian's *Against the Valentinians* offers his own rendition of the theological conflict between the two representatives of the early Church, as well as a rather disparaging synopsis of the

"heresies" of Valentinian Gnosticism (Rev. Alexander Roberts, D.D., and James Donaldson, LL.D., eds., *The Anti-Nicene Fathers, Volume III: Latin Christianity, Its Founder Tertullian* [Grand Rapids: Eerdman's, 1978], 503–20).

4. Hospitality after the Death of God

1. Pierre Klossowski, *"Roberte Ce Soir" and "The Revocation of the Edict of Nantes,"* trans. Austryn Wainhouse (London: Marion Boyars, 1989), 11; idem, *Les lois de l'hospitalité* (Paris: Gallimard, 1965), 109. All citations from the English translation will hereafter be designated as page numbers preceded with an "E," while page numbers from the French text will be preceded with "F."

2. Augustine, *City of God,* trans. Marcus Dods, D.D. (New York: The Modern Library, 1950), 481.

3. Lambros Kamperidis, "Philoxenia and Hospitality," in *Parabola* 15, no. 4 (1990): 5.

4. The Christian notion of "eucharistic hospitality" derives from the Latin *hostia,* which names the "offering that compensates the anger of the gods" the sacrificial victim who "buys back" man's salvation and the possibility of an essential relation with God. Émile Benveniste, "L'hospitalité," in *Le vocabulaire des institutions indo-européennes,* vol. 1 (Paris: Éditions de Minuit, 1969), 93.

5. In *The Revocation,* we saw that Roberte is presented as a kind of Christ figure, who under the guise of "charity" ministers to "them who know not what they do, the 'guilty' and the 'innocent' alike." Her hospitality allows her to tend indiscriminately to opposing parties, making no distinction between friend and enemy. However, what emerges out of this "generous" gesture is not a unified community, as in the Christian model, but rather a fissure within the identity of the hostess herself: her "collaboration," or complicity with two opposed positions.

6. Claude Lévi-Strauss, *The Elementary Structures of Kinship,* trans. James Harle Bell and John Richard von Sturmer (Boston: Beacon Press, 1969).

7. For this argument I am grateful to Peter Canning, who both pointed me to Lévi-Strauss's analysis of exogamy and "theft" and suggested its connection to Klossowski's understanding of the guest.

8. Benveniste, "L'hospitalité," 88.

9. See chapter 1.

10. Marcel Mauss, "A category of the human mind: the notion of person; the notion of self," trans. W. D. Halls in *The Category of the Person,* ed. Michael Carrithers et al. (Cambridge: Cambridge University Press, 1985), 8.

11. Pierre Klossowski, "Protase et apodose," *L'Arc* 43 (1970): 13. My translation.

12. Thomas Aquinas, *Basic Writings of Saint Thomas Aquinas,* Volume I, ed. Anton C. Pegis (New York: Random House, 1945). See in particular his summary and rebuttal of Aristotle's argument in Book III, chapter 5 of *De Anima* that the intellectual principle is not united to the body as its form. In Aquinas's words, Aristotle's thesis is that ". . . whatever exists in a thing by reason of its nature exists in it always. But to be united to matter belongs to the form by reason of its nature, because form is the act of matter, not by any accidental quality, but by its own essence; or otherwise matter and form would not make a thing substantially one, but only accidentally one. Therefore, a form cannot be without its own proper matter. But the intellectual principle, since it is incorruptible, as was shown above, remains separate from the body, after the dissolution of the body. Therefore the intellectual principle is not united to the body as its form" (696).

The union of intellect and body is for Aristotle "accidental," made possible by the fact that man, as an intelligible species, has a "double subject, namely, the possible intellect and the phantasms which are in the corporeal organs" (697). The intellectual principle is capable of uniting itself to these corporeal phantasms, but it is not substantially united to them by its nature. Aquinas's response to this thesis is that the intellectual soul is the very form of the body: "The soul communicates that being in which it subsists to the corporeal matter, out of which and the intellectual soul there results one being; so that the being of the whole composite is also the being of the soul. This is not the case with other non-subsistent forms. For this reason the human soul retains its own being after the dissolution of the body; whereas it is not so with other forms" (699).

13. Friedrich Nietzsche, *The Will to Power,* ed. Walter Kaufmann (New York: Vintage Books, 1968), 7.

14. Mauss, "A category of the human mind," 17.

15. Klossowski, *Un si funeste désir* (Paris: Gallimard, 1963), 220. For a rich analysis of this dimension of Klossowski's thought, see Gilles Deleuze's extraordinary essay "Klossowski or Bodies-Language," in *Logic of Sense,* trans. Mark Lester with Charles Stivale (New York: Columbia University Press, 1990), 280–301.

16. Friedrich Nietzsche, *Thus Spoke Zarathustra,* trans. R. J. Hollingdale (London: Penguin Classics, 1969), 201.

17. Klossowski, "Don Juan selon Kierkegaard," in *Acéphale* 3–4 (1937): 28.

18. Mauss, "A category of the human mind," 17.

19. Emmanuel Lévinas, *Totality and Infinity: An Essay on Exteriority,* trans. Alphonso Lingis (Pittsburgh: Duquesne University Press, 1969), 64.

20. Gilles Deleuze and Félix Guattari, *Anti-Oedipus: Capitalism and Schizophrenia,* trans. Robert Hurley, Mark Seem, and Helen R. Lane

(Minneapolis: University of Minnesota Press, 1983). See in particular Chapter 4, part IV, "The First Positive Task of Schizoanalysis," which is based in part on Klossowski.

21. Friedrich Nietzsche, *Beyond Good and Evil*, trans. Walter Kaufmann (New York: Vintage, 1966), 236.

22. Michèle Montrelay, "*Les lois de l'hospitalité* en tant que lois du narcissisme," in *L'Arc* 43 (1970): 65.

23. Ibid., 64.

24. Ibid., 63.

25. Marie-Hélène Brousse, "La formule du fantasme? $\mathcal{S} \Diamond$ a." In Gerard Miller, ed., *Lacan* (Paris: Éditions Bordas, 1987), 108.

26. See in particular Sigmund Freud, "A Child Is Being Beaten," in *The Standard Edition of the Complete Psychological Works of Sigmund Freud*, ed. and trans. James Strachey et al. (London: The Hogarth Press, 1952, 1974), 17:175–204.

27. Jacques Lacan, *Écrits* (Paris: Seuil, 1966), 829–50.

28. Brousse, "La formule du fantasme," 114–15. My translation.

29. Klossowski, "Protase et apodose," 10.

30. Ibid., 10–11.

31. Ibid., 14.

32. Ibid.

33. Ibid.

34. All citations from *Le Souffleur* are taken from the French text of *Les lois de l'hospitalité*; I have provided my own translations of them here.

35. Immanuel Kant, "To Perpetual Peace: A Philosophical Sketch," in *Perpetual Peace and Other Essays*, trans. Ted Humphrey (Indianapolis: Hackett, 1983), 118.

36. Klossowski, "Protase et apodose," 15.

37. Ibid., 12.

38. Deleuze, "Klossowski or Bodies-Language," 287–88.

5. Welcoming Dionysus, or the Subject as *Corps Morcelé*

1. René Descartes, *Oeuvres philosophiques*, Tome II, ed. Ferdinand Alquié (Paris: Garnier Frères, 1967), 430–54.

2. See in particular *Beyond Good and Evil*, trans. Walter Kaufmann (New York: Vintage Books, 1966), and *The Will to Power*, ed. Walter Kaufmann (New York: Vintage Books, 1968).

3. For a remarkable reading of Nietzsche's exploration of his own "valetudinary states" as the realization of his thought concerning the death of God and the experience of the eternal return, see Pierre Klossowski's *Nietzsche and the Vicious Circle*, trans. Daniel W. Smith (Chicago: University of Chicago Press, 1997).

4. Willy Apollon, "Psychanalyse et littérature: Passe et impasse," in *L'Universel, perspectives psychanalytiques* (Quebec: Gifric, 1997), 247. My translation. Lacan's first published use of the term *corps morcelé* occurs in "The Mirror Stage as Formative of the *I* Function as Revealed in Psychoanalytic Experience," where it designates the fragmented body of the drives as opposed to the unified specular image. Jacques Lacan, *Écrits*, trans. Bruce Fink (New York: W. W. Norton and Company, 2002), 3–9.

5. Apollon, *L'universel, perspectives psychanalytiques*, 247. My translation.

6. Apollon made this comment in the context of his Annual Training Seminar in Lacanian Psychoanalysis in Quebec City, Canada, Summer 1996.

7. Apollon, "Psychoanalysis and the Freudian Rupture." Unpublished address to the Society for Psychological Anthropology, October 1999.

8. Ibid.

9. Marie-Claire Boons-Grafé, "Other/other," in *Feminism and Psychoanalysis: A Critical Dictionary*, ed. Elizabeth Wright (Oxford: Blackwell, 1992), 298.

10. See in particular Sigmund Freud, "A Child Is Being Beaten," in *The Standard Edition of the Complete Psychological Works of Sigmund Freud*, ed. and trans. James Strachey et al. (London: The Hogarth Press, 1955), 17:179–204.

11. See Willy Apollon, *Notes sur la rupture freudienne sur la question de la sexualité, II: Masculinité/Féminité* (Quebec: École freudienne de Québec, 2000), 42.

12. Cantin made this argument during a course at Gifric's Annual Training Seminar in Lacanian Psychoanalysis, Quebec City, Canada, Summer 2001.

13. Sigmund Freud, *Three Essays on the Theory of Sexuality*, in *The Standard Edition*, 7: 224n.

14. Lacan, "The Mirror Stage," 3–9.

15. In French, Lacan plays on the homonym between "the father's name" and "the father's no"; the paternal signifier is the "no" that functions to limit jouissance. On the importance of the *nom-du-père* for the emergence of the subject, see Lacan, *The Seminar of Jacques Lacan Book III: The Psychoses*, ed. Jacques-Alain Miller, trans. Dennis Porter (New York: W. W. Norton and Company, 1992).

16. Freud, "The Question of a Weltanschauung," in *The Standard Edition*, vol. 22, 162.

17. Ibid., 167.

18. Apollon, "Psychoanalysis and the Freudian Rupture."

19. My analysis of Sade is informed by Lacan's reading in *The Seminar*

of Jacques Lacan Book VII: The Ethics of Psychoanalysis 1959–60, ed. Jacques-Alain Miller, trans. Dennis Porter (New York: W. W. Norton and Company, 1992), 71–84 and 191–204, as well as Willy Apollon's "Psychanalyse et littérature," 243–65.

20. Marquis D.A.F. de Sade, *La philosophie dans le boudoir* (Paris: Gallimard Folio, 1976), 68–73. Subsequent citations from the same text will be given as page numbers in parentheses; all translations are my own.

21. Significantly, Sade's argument is elaborated through a discussion of female sexuality, where the split between reproductive sexuality and eroticism is especially apparent. Dolmancé demonstrates to Eugénie that human jouissance is not limited to the organs of reproduction by distinguishing between the uterus, as the site of female sexuality and reproduction, and the potentially limitless erogenous zones that can be colonized by eroticism (56). In this way, he debunks all attempts to define feminine sexuality solely within the culturally sanctioned confines of maternity. Second, he shows that the body's real potential for jouissance can be glimpsed only in the *imagination,* the true source of all pleasure (101). This is especially true for girls, in whom the experience of jouissance has no relation whatsoever to natural sexuality; Dolmancé marvels that the young Eugénie "gets off *in her head* without anyone even touching her" [*elle décharge* de tête *sans qu'on la touche*] (177).

22. Nietzsche, *Thus Spoke Zarathustra,* trans. R. J. Hollingdale (London: Penguin Classics, 1969). See in particular the aphorisms entitled "Of the Afterworldsmen" and "Of the Despisers of the Body," 58–63. Subsequent citations from the same text will be given as page numbers in parentheses.

23. Cited by Pierre Klossowski in *Nietzsche and the Vicious Circle,* 36.

24. The expression is Pierre Klossowski's, from the postface to *Les lois de l'hospitalité* (Paris: Gallimard, 1965), 337. For Nietzsche's analysis of the relation between grammar and God, see the first part of *Beyond Good and Evil,* the fifth book of *The Gay Science,* trans. Walter Kaufmann (New York: Vintage Books, 1974), and chapters 3–6 of *"Twilight of the Idols" and "The Anti-Christ,"* trans. R. J. Hollingdale (London: Penguin Classics, 1990).

25. Nietzsche, *"Twilight of the Idols" and "The Anti-Christ,"* 48.

26. Nietzsche's oft-repeated contempt for "the healthy" no doubt relates to the etymological link between health and "wholeness" or "completion" (as in the Old English *hale,* "whole").

27. Cited by Walter Kaufmann, *Nietzsche: Philosopher, Psychologist, Antichrist* (Princeton: Princeton University Press, 1974), 19.

28. Georges Bataille, *L'expérience intérieure* (Paris: Gallimard, 1943/1954).

29. In his comprehensive study of Dionysus, Walter Otto suggests that

the clamor associated with the advent of the god challenges the every-day world of consciousness with a "truth that brings on madness": "The world man knows, the world in which he has settled himself so securely and snugly—that world is no more. The turbulence which accompanied the arrival of Dionysus has swept it away. Everything has been trans-formed. But it has not been transformed into a charming fairy story or into an ingenuous child's paradise. The primeval world has stepped into the foreground, the depths of reality have been opened, the elemental forms of everything that is creative, everything that is destructive, have arisen, bringing with them infinite rapture and infinite terror. The inno-cent picture of a well-ordered routine world has been shattered by their coming, and they bring with them no illusions or fantasies but truth—a truth that brings on madness." *Dionysus, Myth and Cult*, trans. Rob-ert B. Palmer (Bloomington: Indiana University Press, 1965), 95.

30. "Freud addresses the subject in order to say to him the following, which is new—*Here, in the field of the dream, you are at home. Wo es war, soll Ich werden.* . . . It is not a question of the ego in this *soll Ich werden;* the fact is that throughout Freud's work—one must, of course, recognize its proper place—the *Ich* is the complete, total locus of the net-work of signifiers, that is to say, the subject, *where it was,* where it has always been, the dream. The ancients recognized all kinds of things in dreams, including, on occasion, messages from the gods—and why not? The ancients made something of these messages from the gods. And, anyway—perhaps you will glimpse this in what I shall say later—who knows, the gods may still speak through dreams. Personally, I don't mind either way. What concerns us is the tissue that envelops these messages, the network in which, on occasion, something makes itself heard, but it is a long time since men lent their ears to them in their original state—it is well known that the ears are made not to hear with. But the subject is there to rediscover *where it was*—I anticipate—the real. I will justify what I have just said in a little while, but those who have been listening to me for some time know that I use, quite intentionally, the formula—*The gods belong to the field of the real.*" Lacan, *The Four Fundamental Concepts of Psycho-Analysis,* ed. Jacques-Alain Miller, trans. Alan Sheridan (New York: W. W. Norton and Company, 1978), 45. For a fuller commentary of this citation, see the beginning of chapter 6.

31. Nietzsche, *"On the Genealogy of Morals" and "Ecce Homo,"* trans. Walter Kaufmann (New York: Vintage Books, 1989), 335.

32. Paul Valadier, "Dionysus versus the Crucified," in David Allison, ed. *The New Nietzsche* (Cambridge: MIT Press, 1985), 250.

33. Nietzsche, *The Gay Science,* 74.

34. Pierre Klossowski, "Nietzsche, le polythéisme et la parodie," in *Un si funeste désir* (Paris: Gallimard, 1963), 197; my translation.

35. The expression is Willy Apollon's, from the title of his essay "La vie

humaine ouvre sur un abîme," *L'universel, perspectives psychanalytiques*, 17–25.

36. Klossowski, *Nietzsche and the Vicious Circle*, 28. Emphases in original.

37. Ibid., 29.

38. Ibid., 30.

39. Valadier, "Dionysus versus the Crucified," 249.

40. Nietzsche, *Beyond Good and Evil*, 236.

6. The Other Jouissance, a Gay *Sçavoir*

1. Lacan, *The Four Fundamental Concepts of Psycho-Analysis*, ed. Jacques-Alain Miller, trans. Alan Sheridan (New York: W. W. Norton and Company, 1978), 44. Freud's statement appears at the end of one of the *New Introductory Lectures on Psychoanalysis*, "The Dissection of the Psychical Personality," in *The Standard Edition of the Complete Psychological Works of Sigmund Freud*, ed. and trans. James Strachey et al. (London: The Hogarth Press, 1952, 1974), 22:80.

2. See my development on this point in the introduction.

3. Lacan, *The Four Fundamental Concepts*, 44–45.

4. Lacan, *The Seminar of Jacques Lacan Book VII: The Ethics of Psychoanalysis 1959–60*, ed. Jacques-Alain Miller, trans. Dennis Porter (New York: W. W. Norton and Company, 1992), 7.

5. Jacques Lacan, "The Mirror Stage as Formative of the *I* Function as Revealed in Psychoanalytic Experience," in *Écrits*, trans. Bruce Fink (New York: W. W. Norton and Company, 2002), 3–9.

6. Sigmund Freud, *Beyond the Pleasure Principle*, in *The Standard Edition*, 18:34–35.

7. Jacques Lacan, *Television*, trans. Denis Hollier, Rosalind Krauss, and Annette Michelson (New York: W. W. Norton and Company, 1990), 19.

8. Lacan, *The Ethics of Psychoanalysis*, 27.

9. Ibid., 13.

10. Freud, *Beyond the Pleasure Principle*, in *The Standard Edition*, 18:38.

11. Ibid., 20.

12. Ibid., 36.

13. For example, the erotic object that takes the form of a "sexual"—and therefore natural—aim, but which cannot be inscribed within the logic of the reproductive system.

14. This argument is elaborated most fully in the first three chapters of *The Ethics of Psychoanalysis*.

15. Consider the case of the Wolf Man, whose quest for sexual satisfaction is overdetermined by a fantasy that both motivates it and renders

it impossible. While the act of having intercourse *a tergo* with women bent over procures him some pleasure by reversing—and so repressing—his position in the unconscious fantasy (where the Wolf Man, identifying with his mother's position in the primal scene, both receives pleasure from and is castrated by his father), it is nonetheless completely overdetermined by that fantasy and unable to dodge its debilitating effects. The symptoms affecting the digestive/excremental tract belie the Wolf Man's true position in the fantasy, identifying the anal orifice as the erogenous zone colonized by the jouissance of the fantasy. Sigmund Freud, "From the History of an Infantile Neurosis" (1918), in *The Standard Edition,* 17:72–88.

16. Lacan, *The Ethics of Psychoanalysis,* 70.

17. Ibid., 10n.

18. Friedrich Nietzsche, *Beyond Good and Evil,* trans. Walter Kaufmann (New York: Vintage, 1966), 236.

19. Lacan, *Television,* 23.

20. See Heidegger's "Letter on Humanism," in *Basic Writings,* ed. David Farrell Krell (New York: Harper and Row, 1977), 189–242, as well as his reading of Hölderlin in ". . . Poetically Man Dwells," *Poetry, Language, Thought,* trans. Albert Hofstadter (New York: Harper and Row, 1971), 211–29.

21. Lacan, *The Ethics of Psychoanalysis,* 8.

22. Lacan, *Television,* 14.

23. Willy Apollon, Danielle Bergeron, and Lucie Cantin, pioneers in the psychoanalytic treatment of psychosis, have argued that the analyst must "welcome the crisis" as a means of gaining access to the subject of the unconscious, using the signifiers of the dream to provoke a destabilization of the delusion that structures the patient's psychic reality. See "The Treatment of Psychosis," in Stephen Friedlander and Kareen Malone, eds., *The Subject of Lacan: A Lacanian Reader for Psychologists* (Albany: State University of New York Press, 2000), 209–27.

24. Apollon, Bergeron, and Cantin express this logic with the notation [SSS... −1], which identifies the signifying chain (or symbolic Other) as structurally incomplete, defined by the absence of the signifier that would name the real. For a discussion of the link between this primordial lost signifier and the fundamental fantasy, see Marie-Hélène Brousse, "La formule du fantasme? $\$ \lozenge a$." In Gerard Miller, ed., *Lacan* (Paris: Éditions Bordas, 1987).

25. Jacques Derrida, *Politics of Friendship,* trans. George Collins (London: Verso, 1997), 113.

26. When the "Wolf Man" case reaches an impasse where the patient's dreams and associations are no longer moving the analysis forward, Freud turns his attention to the symptom of constipation, the writing on the body of the fantasy of the primal scene. When he manages to treat his

patient's symptom psychoanalytically, Freud writes with satisfaction that "his bowel began, like a hysterically affected organ, to 'join in the conversation,'" furnishing a response to the analyst's questions there where the signifiers of the dream were unable to (*The Standard Edition*, 17:76).

27. Lacan, *Television*, 22.

28. For my treatment of this problem in Klossowski's fiction, see chapter 4.

29. Jacques Lacan, *The Seminar of Jacques Lacan Book XX: Encore 1972–1973*, trans. Bruce Fink (New York: W. W. Norton and Company, 1998), 87–88, translation modified. *Le séminaire livre XX: Encore,* ed. Jacques-Alain Miller (Paris: Seuil, 1975), 81. Because I depart from Fink's translation on numerous occasions, subsequent citations from the same text will cite both editions, with the page numbers of the original French text preceded by an "F" and page numbers of the English translation preceded by an "E."

30. Ibid., F1/E9; translation modified.

31. Lacan, *The Ethics of Psychoanalysis,* 9.

32. Lacan, *Television,* 40.

33. In *Group Psychology and the Analysis of the Ego,* Freud designates as "artificial groups" those forms of group organization (the army, the church) that are predicated upon the ego and its projections, rather than the rule of speech as symbolic limit (i.e., castration) (*The Standard Edition,* 18:69–143).

34. Lacan, *Encore,* F68/E72–73; translation modified.

35. Importantly, Lacan's characterization of "woman" is not strictly or even necessarily related to the female sex; "masculine" and "feminine" are for Lacan positions taken up in relation to the signifier, and not biological determinations.

36. Lacan, *Encore,* F68/E73; translation modified.

37. Freud, "Some Psychological Consequences of the Anatomical Distinction Between the Sexes," in *The Standard Edition,* 19:255.

38. "After a woman has become aware of the wound to her narcissism, she develops, like a scar, a sense of inferiority." Ibid., 19:253.

39. Freud, "Female Sexuality," ibid., 19:229–30; idem, "Some Psychological Consequences of the Anatomical Distinction Between the Sexes," ibid., 19:252–53.

40. "By means . . . of the equation 'penis = child' she gives up her wish for a penis and puts in place of it a wish for a child." Ibid., 256.

41. Lacan, *Encore,* F67/E72.

42. Ibid., F59/E63; translation modified.

43. Juliet Flower MacCannell, "Facing Fascism: A Feminine Politics of Jouissance," in *Lacan, Politics, Aesthetics,* ed. Willy Apollon and Richard Feldstein (Albany: State University of New York Press, 1996), 87.

44. Lacan, *The Ethics of Psychoanalysis*, 69.

45. Ibid., 58.

46. In his early essays on femininity, Freud makes clear that woman encounters the death drive in the mother in a way that cannot be mitigated by the symbolic. The protection that the phallic function proffers is not relevant for her experience of the death drive, which is not encountered in the body of the other sex (as it is for man, in the form of feminine or maternal demand), but in her own body.

47. Sigmund Freud, "Femininity," in *The Standard Edition*, 22:134.

48. For Apollon's discussion of the *Infondé*, see "A Lasting Heresy, the Failure of Political Desire," in *Lacan, Politics, Aesthetics*, ed. Willy Apollon and Richard Feldstein (Albany: State University of New York Press, 1996), 35ff; he discusses its relation to femininity in "Féminité dites-vous?" in *Savoir* 2, nos. 1 and 2 (1995): 15–44.

49. Danielle Bergeron, "Femininity," in *Feminism and Psychoanalysis: A Critical Dictionary*, ed. Elizabeth Wright (Oxford: Blackwell, 1992), 93.

50. Lacan, *Television*, 22.

51. Lucie Cantin, "La féminité: D'une complicité à la perversion à une éthique de l'impossible," in *Savoir* 2, nos. 1 and 2 (1995): 47–90.

52. Lacan, *Television*, 15.

53. Ibid.

54. Ibid.

55. Ibid., 41.

56. Ibid., 3.

57. Ibid., 16.

58. Ibid.

59. Ibid.

60. Willy Apollon, "La Jouissance," unpublished manuscript.

61. For this distinction between masculine and feminine jouissance I am indebted to Willy Apollon, who made the observation during a training seminar sponsored by the GIFRIC (Groupe Interdisciplinaire Freudien de Recherches et d'Interventions Cliniques) in Quebec, Canada, in June 1996.

62. Lacan, *Television*, 22.

63. Lacan, *Encore*, F79/E85, translation modified.

64. Lacan, *Television*, 15.

65. Ibid., 16.

66. Ibid., 30.

67. *Jouir de* means to reap profit from something, whether or not it is owned; for example, a feudal lord or an aristocrat who profits from the crops harvested by the serfs or tenants who work the land in his domain would be said to "enjoy"—*jouir de*—the fruits of their labor.

68. See chapter 1.

69. Augustine, *The City of God,* trans. Marcus Dods, D.D. (New York: The Modern Library, 1950), 15:3; translation modified.

70. Stendhal, *Love,* trans. Gilbert and Suzanne Sale (London: Penguin, 1975), 45; translation modified. Subsequent citations from the same text will be given as page numbers in parentheses.

71. Lacan, *The Ethics of Psychoanalysis,* 112.

72. Ibid., 69.

73. Juliet Flower MacCannell, "Love Outside the Limits of the Law," in *New Formations,* no. 23 (Summer 1994): 32.

74. Lacan, *Television,* 38.

75. MacCannell, "Facing Fascism," 70.

76. Lacan, *Encore,* F68/E72; translation modified.

77. MacCannell, "Love Outside the Limits of the Law," 27.

78. Lacan, *The Ethics of Psychoanalysis,* 125.

79. See the chapter "Why Is Woman a Symptom of Rights?" in Salecl, *The Spoils of Freedom* (London: Routledge, 1994), 112–33.

80. Stendhal, *Love,* 166.

81. Lacan, *The Ethics of Psychoanalysis,* 147; translation modified.

82. Lacan, *Television,* 23.

83. Ibid., 23.

84. Lacan, *The Four Fundamental Concepts of Psycho-Analysis,* 103 (translation modified).

85. Lacan, *Encore,* F65/E69; translation modified.

86. Ibid.

87. Ibid.

88. Renata Salecl, "Love Anxieties" in *Reading Seminar XX: Lacan's Major Work on Love, Knowledge, and Feminine Sexuality,* ed. Suzanne Barnard and Bruce Fink (Albany: State University of New York Press, 2002), 94.

89. Lacan, *The Ethics of Psychoanalysis,* 149.

90. Stendhal, *Love,* 167.

91. Lacan, *The Ethics of Psychoanalysis,* 149; translation modified.

92. Lacan, *Television,* 40.

93. Lacan, *The Ethics of Psychoanalysis,* 151–52.

94. Lacan says that the genius of Freud's technique is that he "invents the work of the bee, who does not think, calculate, nor judge," but who merely gathers the hysteric's "honey"—her *savoir.* Lacan, *Television,* 19.

95. Ibid., 15.

96. Apollon, "Féminité dites-vous?" 20ff.

97. Lacan, *Television,* 14.

Index

Abraham: circumcision of, 7; as
ethical model, xix–xx; hospitality of, xlv, 1–3, 6–15, 18–19,
23, 29–30, 33, 141, 243n;
laughter of, 7–8, 10–12, 15;
and Lot, 15–17; as patriarch, 1,
3, 5, 7–9; as stranger, 25–26;
wandering of, 4–5, 24, 26. *See
also* Isaac; Sarah
Adam, 5, 9–11, 17, 228, 236
adultery: internal to marriage,
171; of Israel as metaphor
for idolatry, xlv, 3–4, 28–29,
148–50, 247n; of Jerusalem/
Oholibah in Book of Ezekiel,
37–39
affection: Augustinian doctrine
of, 13–14, 21–22, 126–27, 129,
133, 141, 218
Agamemnon, xii
Alter, Robert, 10–11
alterity, viii, xiv, xvii, xix; femininity as internal marking of,
xxvii; of God, xlv, 9, 15; of
guest, xlv, 8–10, 14–15, 243n;
neutralization of in Christianity,

xxi, 13–15, 83. *See also* femininity; Other; sexual difference
angels, 8, 14–15, 19, 23–24
annunciation, 12
antinomy: between hospitality and
monotheism, xlv, 2–3, 27–32,
42–44; between Jewish and
Christian conceptions of hospitality, 75–77; of obligations to
integrate foreigner and respect
his foreignness, xiv; between
the particular laws and the unconditional Law of hospitality,
35, 42, 46, 100
Apollon, Willy, 177–78, 213, 234,
251n
aporia: Derrida on, 84; of hospitality obligation, xiv, 78; of
simultaneous constitution and
dissolution of identity, xx, 137,
148
Aquinas, Thomas, 151–52, 259n
Ariadne, l–li, 156, 197–98, 204
Aristotle, 202–3, 209
Auerbach, Erich, 19
Augustine, xv, xxxv, 12–14, 21–23,

to Augustine, 125–27, 129–33,
141; allusions to biblical hospitality, 141–42, 147–49; on
betrayal, 143, 150; on charity,
99–103, 111; on Christian
hospitality, 104, 116–17, 143,
256n; on "Christ-like" role
of hostess, 142, 157; on "collaboration within resistance,"
103, 116, 122, 124, 255n; and
confessional genre, 128–31,
173–74; on conflict between
duties of hostess and duties
of wife, 136, 145, 147, 150;
on conflict between host and
husband, 145, 147, 150; on
conflict between ownership and
offering up, 137, 149, 164; on
conflict or contradiction within
hostess, 92–93, 102, 119–22,
124, 129, 137, 142; on death of
God, 87–88, 152–56, 163; on
dissolution or expropriation of
identity, 88–89, 143–44, 148,
150, 152, 154, 157, 162–65,
170; on fantasy, 94, 158–61;
gnosticism in, 132–33; on
"grammatical fiction" of the
I, 154–55, 162–63; on guest
as divine, 136–37, 142–43,
150–51, 154, 156, 169; on
hostess as agent of expropriation, 142, 150, 152, 154–57; on
incest, 105, 109, 113; on jealousy, 142, 148–50; on Judaism,
105–10, 113–15; "laws of hospitality" in, 88, 121, 135–41,
163–65, 167, 169, 171–72; on
libertinage, 93, 162–65, 182;
on marriage and monogamous
property, 134, 145, 163–65,
170–71; on offering of wife,
135, 142–45, 147, 149–50, 162,

170; on nazism, 99, 111, 114,
256n; on Nietzsche, 81–82,
106, 109–12, 151–56, 170,
195–97, 256n; *Nietzsche and
the Vicious Circle,* 195–97; on
"privative identity," 88–89,
148, 151; "Protase et apodose,"
149, 160–66, 171–72; on Protestantism, 91, 97–98, 100–104,
112–14, 150; on rape of Lucretia, 123–27, 130; *Revocation
of the Edict of Nantes, The,*
91–133, 134–36; *Roberte, ce
soir,* 91, 121–22, 132, 134–52,
173; on Sade, 162–70, 173; on
sexual relation, 88–91; on signs
and semiotics, 135, 160–66,
174; on sister, 102, 104–10,
112–16; on solecism, 119–25,
129–32, 135; *Le Souffleur,* 132,
166–71, 173; transvaluation of
values in, 110–12, 255n; wife
as inalienable property of the
husband, 145, 170; on woman's
relation to signifier and signs,
135, 174; on "unique sign,"
157–66, 168, 171–74
Knights of Malta, 77

Lacan, Jacques: on analytic practice, 205–6, 208, 213–16,
233–34; on courtly love, 223,
225–34; on *das Ding* (the
Thing), xl, xlii, xliv, li, lii,
212, 222, 224, 229–31, 233;
Encore, 207–9, 214, 216, 226;
on "ethics of being well-spoken," 216, 218, 234; *Ethics of
Psychoanalysis,* 204, 207–8,
212–13, 221–22; on fantasy,
158–61; on feminine jouissance,
206–7, 209, 226, 226–27,
233–36; on gay *sçavoir,* 206–7,

Tracy McNulty is assistant professor in the Department of Romance Studies at Cornell University.